KU-021-733

Ripley's Believe It or Not!®

2013

Executive VP Norm Deska
VP, Exhibits & Archives Edward Meyer

Publisher Anne Marshall

Editorial Director Rebecca Miles
Senior Researcher & Picture Manager James Proud
Researcher Lucas Stram
Assistant Editor Charlotte Howell
Additional Research Rosie Alexander
Text Geoff Tibballs
Additional Text James Proud
Editors Judy Barratt, Sally McFall
Factchecker Alex Bazlinton
Indexer Hilary Bird

Art Director Sam South
Design Dynamo Design
Reprographics Juice Creative

First published in Great Britain in 2012 by
Random House Books
Random House, 20 Vauxhall Bridge Road,
London SW1V 2SA

www.randomhouse.co.uk

Addresses for companies within The Random House Group Limited can be found at: www.randomhouse.co.uk/offices.htm

The Random House Group Limited Reg. No. 954009

ISBN 9781847946737
10 9 8 7 6 5 4 3 2 1

The Random House Group Limited supports The Forest Stewardship Council (FSC®), the leading international forest certification organisation. Our books carrying the FSC label are printed on FSC® certified paper. FSC is the only forest certification scheme endorsed by the leading environmental organisations, including Greenpeace. Our paper procurement policy can be found at www.randomhouse.co.uk/environment.

A CIP catalogue record for this book is available from the British Library

Printed in China

PUBLISHER'S NOTE
While every effort has been made to verify the accuracy of the entries in this book, the Publishers cannot be held responsible for any errors contained in the work. They would be glad to receive any information from readers.

WARNING
Some of the stunts and activities in this book are undertaken by experts and should not be attempted by anyone without adequate training and supervision.

Ripley's Believe It or Not!® 2013

DOWNLOAD THE WEIRD

a Jim Pattison Company

CONTENTS

Ripley's Believe It or Not!®

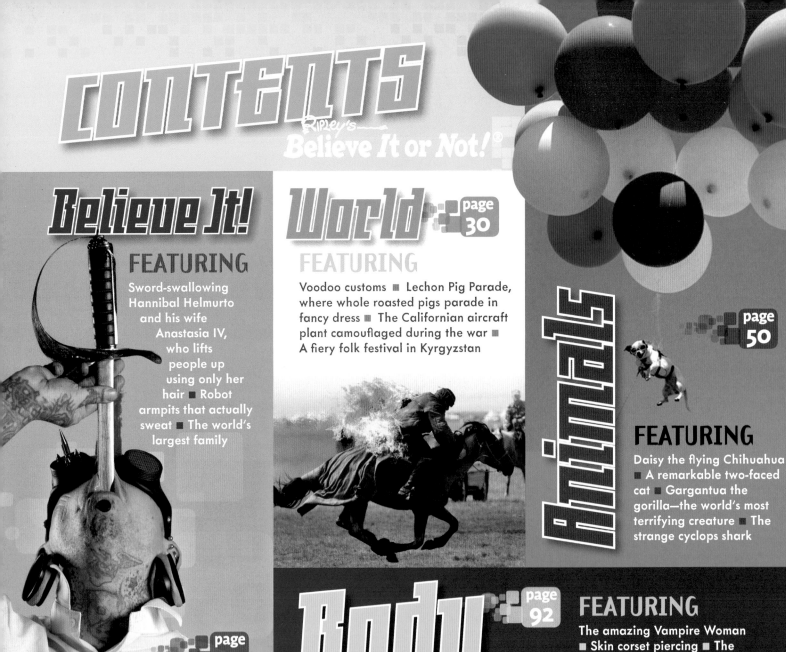

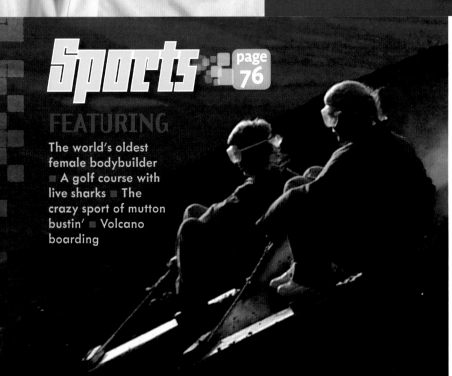

WARNING
ZOMBIES
AHEAD

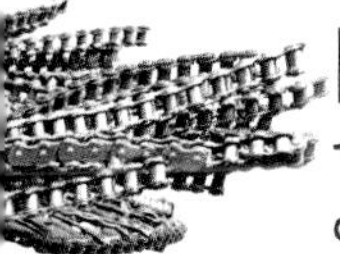

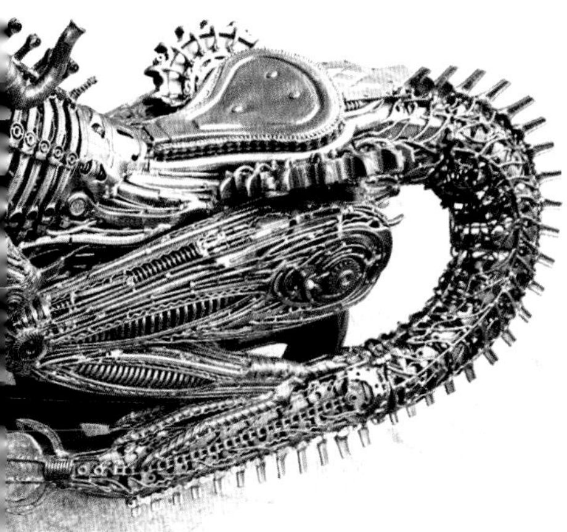

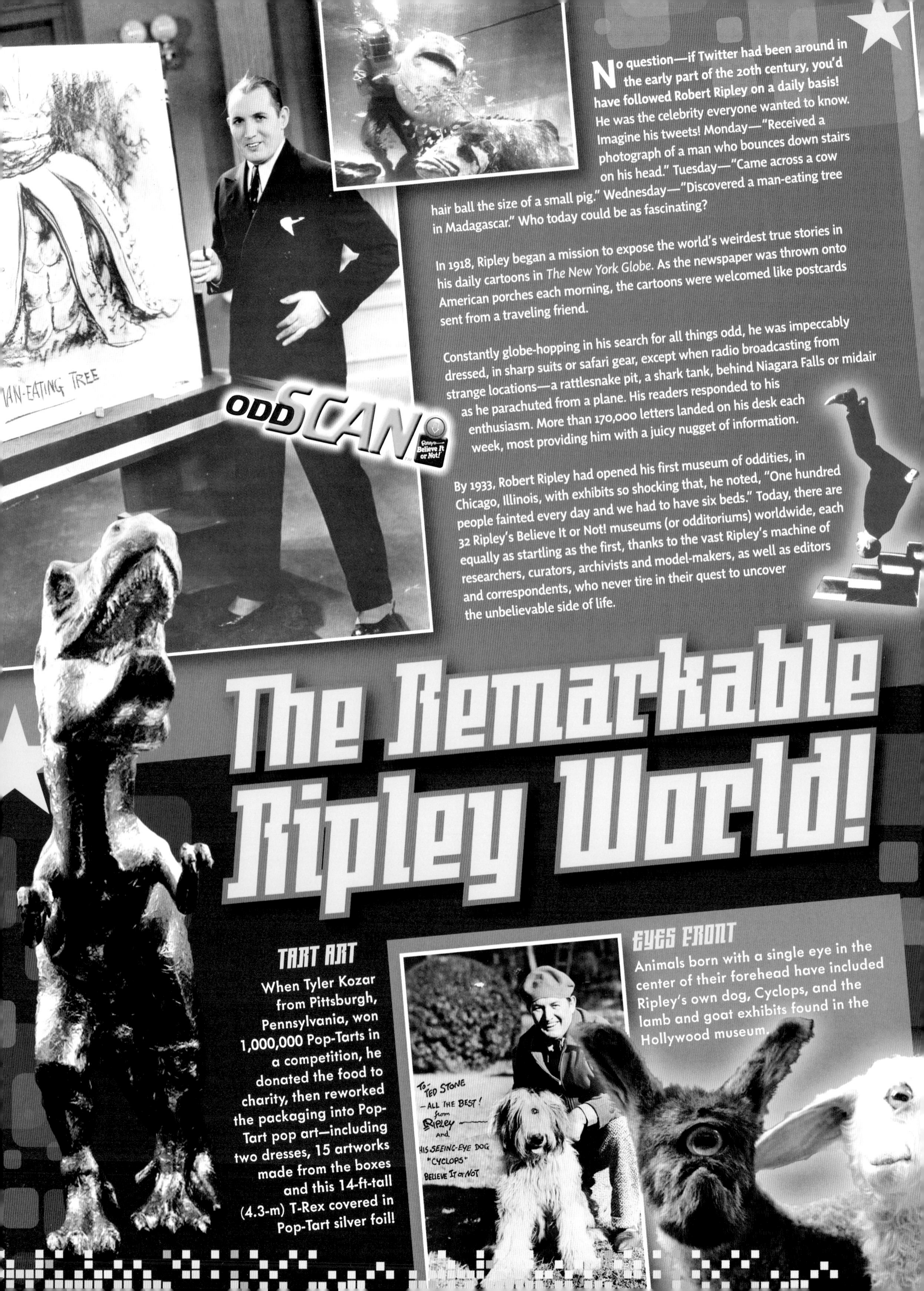
MAN-EATING TREE
ODD SCAN
Ripley's Believe It or Not!
To TED STONE
— ALL THE BEST!
from
Ripley
and
HIS SEEING-EYE DOG
"CYCLOPS"
BELIEVE IT or NOT

No question—if Twitter had been around in the early part of the 20th century, you'd have followed Robert Ripley on a daily basis! He was the celebrity everyone wanted to know. Imagine his tweets! Monday—"Received a photograph of a man who bounces down stairs on his head." Tuesday—"Came across a cow hair ball the size of a small pig." Wednesday—"Discovered a man-eating tree in Madagascar." Who today could be as fascinating?

In 1918, Ripley began a mission to expose the world's weirdest true stories in his daily cartoons in *The New York Globe*. As the newspaper was thrown onto American porches each morning, the cartoons were welcomed like postcards sent from a traveling friend.

Constantly globe-hopping in his search for all things odd, he was impeccably dressed, in sharp suits or safari gear, except when radio broadcasting from strange locations—a rattlesnake pit, a shark tank, behind Niagara Falls or midair as he parachuted from a plane. His readers responded to his enthusiasm. More than 170,000 letters landed on his desk each week, most providing him with a juicy nugget of information.

By 1933, Robert Ripley had opened his first museum of oddities, in Chicago, Illinois, with exhibits so shocking that, he noted, "One hundred people fainted every day and we had to have six beds." Today, there are 32 Ripley's Believe It or Not! museums (or odditoriums) worldwide, each equally as startling as the first, thanks to the vast Ripley's machine of researchers, curators, archivists and model-makers, as well as editors and correspondents, who never tire in their quest to uncover the unbelievable side of life.

The Remarkable Ripley World!

TART ART

When Tyler Kozar from Pittsburgh, Pennsylvania, won 1,000,000 Pop-Tarts in a competition, he donated the food to charity, then reworked the packaging into Pop-Tart pop art—including two dresses, 15 artworks made from the boxes and this 14-ft-tall (4.3-m) T-Rex covered in Pop-Tart silver foil!

EYES FRONT

Animals born with a single eye in the center of their forehead have included Ripley's own dog, Cyclops, and the lamb and goat exhibits found in the Hollywood museum.

WE'RE LOOKING GOOD!

This year, the Believe It or Not! museum in Hollywood had a magnificent makeover, and in Baltimore (*below*) had a magnificent makeover, and in Baltimore (*left*) a brand new museum has been built. Located in the city's Inner Harbor, the Baltimore museum's façade has a gigantic sea serpent wrapped around it.

Ripley's Believe It or Not!
HOLLYWOOD
Incredible

SWEET RIDE This motorcycle (*left*) by Christian Ramos is entirely made of candy. Spot it in the Ripley's Believe It or Not! museum in Hollywood.

ON THE CASE

ODD SCAN

Recently, one of our researchers stumbled upon a 1936 video that sheds more light on a story previously reported by Ripley's. At just three years of age, Leslie Bowles from the U.K. weighed a mighty 142 lb (64.5 kg)! The video provides a shocking insight into how human rarities were presented at that time.

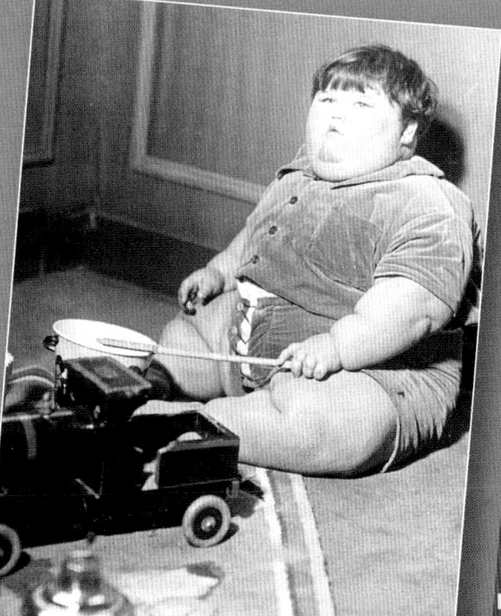

SPARKY CELEBRATION

In 2012, Ripley's celebrated the 75th anniversary of the first published drawing of Charles M. Schulz, creator of Charlie Brown and the famous "Peanuts" cartoons. When he was 15, Schulz submitted a drawing of his dog Sparky to Robert Ripley, and wrote how his dog would eat pins, razor blades and more. Ripley included the drawing in his Believe It or Not! cartoon on February 22, 1937. Later, Sparky became the inspiration for Schulz's Snoopy character!

LUCY VAN PELT

75 YEARS OLD
Owned by
FRANKLYN PEARCE
-Philadelphia
Drawn by "SPARKY"
A HUNTING DOG THAT EATS PINS, TACKS, SCREWS
St. A. RAMIREZ
TAMPA CHAMPION CIGAR SMOKER
AVERAGED 10 CIGARS

Ripley's Newsflash

Look what we've been up to!

STICKY SITUATION

Ripley's awarded Barry Chappell from Los Angeles a coveted certificate of recognition for his enormous ball of chewed gum. Built and carefully sculpted over six years, the175-lb (79.4-kg) gumball measured 62 in (157 cm) in circumference and was made from 95,200 pieces of gum!

Barry softened tiny chewed gumballs in a sauna, spraying them with water to make them less sticky.

RIPLEY'S UPDATE!

In Fall 2010, Ripley's supported this abandoned dog. His fur was so long and matted that he couldn't see or even walk (*below left*). We are delighted to report that Ripley, as he is now known, is happy and well with his adopted parents. Check out this recent photograph of him (*below right*).

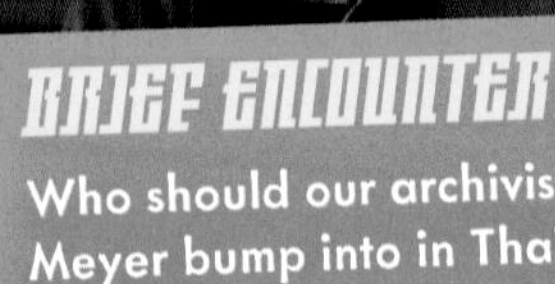

BRIEF ENCOUNTER

Who should our archivist Edward Meyer bump into in Thailand while walking along a beach? None other than Supatra Sasuphan—a girl featured in Ripley's Believe It or Not! *Strikingly True*. Supatra was born with Ambras Syndrome, a rare congenital disease that causes excessive hair growth. The encounter was quite by chance—Supatra lives in Bangkok but had escaped to the beach during severe flooding in the city. Edward was delighted to meet her and hear about her plans to become a teacher.

BOXING CLEVERLY

Ripley's art department made this life-size, lifelike replica of Bernard Hopkins. Known as "The Destroyer," the American champion boxer fortunately seemed happy with the result when we delivered the model to his home in Delaware for his birthday!

SHARP PRACTICE

On February 25, 2012, many of the world's estimated 200 sword-swallowing men and women showed up at various Ripley's Believe It or Not! odditoriums around the world to swallow their swords at exactly 2.25 p.m. local time for 12 seconds.

PRIME PRIMATE

The Florida-based Ripley's archivist trekked to Thailand to hunt down this giant gorilla made from recycled car parts. At 16 ft 4 in (5 m) in height, 6 ft (1.8 m) wide, and weighing several tons, the gorilla was tricky to ship back to Orlando, but, as this book goes to press, it's on its way!

TAKING PAINS

Lucky the Painproof Man won Ripley's Unbelievable Talents Contest, held at our museum in New York, by eating a glass lightbulb and lying on a bed of broken glass, before climbing on a staircase of sharpened swords!

HIGH ROAD

Ripley's pulled off the most amazing vehicle trade-in ever when it exchanged a Swarovski crystal-covered Mini Cooper for a knitted Ferrari sports car. Trouble was, the Mini was an exhibit within London's Believe It or Not! museum and needed to be removed—then the Ferrari had to be installed inside. The only way to make the swap was through the roof of the museum! A massive crane made the switch in the early hours of a Saturday morning. It was a procedure that closed some of London's busiest streets, but the Mini emerged unscathed and is now bound for the new Ripley's museum in Batimore, Maryland.

Look what we found this year!

SMALL WONDERS

The collection of 97 Willard Wigan miniature sculptures that Ripley's bought this year could fit inside a single matchbox, but in the opinion of the art world, it's a colossal selection. Willard carefully places his microscopic scenes in the eye of a needle, on a grain of sand or on the head of a pin. Read more about it on page 147.

JUNK GEMS

The models in this set of Star Wars characters, designed by Anchalee Saengtai from Thailand and assembled by Thai master welders, are made from recycled car parts. Spot them in our museums in Hollywood and Jeju Island, Korea.

EARNING A CRUST

In British artist Adam Sheldon's home there are piles of toast all over the floor! After drying out the toast so it doesn't go moldy, Adam scrapes it to create light areas, and uses a blowtorch to create darker patches. He's recreated, among others, the whole of Leonardo da Vinci's *Last Supper* and this cheeky portrait of Albert Einstein.

WHEN DUST SETTLES

American artist Heidi Hooper works with an unconventional medium—dryer lint! Ripley's has bought many of Heidi's artworks, including this radiant rooster.

Make sure you don't miss... The Science of Ripley's Believe It or Not!

This traveling show will be visiting 18 different science centers over the next six years, stopping in each location for three months.

GET IN TOUCH!

WRITE TO US

BION Research
Ripley Entertainment Inc.,
7576 Kingspointe Parkway, 188,
Orlando, Florida 32819, U.S.A.

Follow us on Facebook and Twitter@RipleyWorld

Contribute via our website **www.ripleybooks.com**

Or send an email to **bionresearch@ripleys.com**

Please include photos where possible

Download Ripley's new APP!

Ripley's Believe It or Not!®

Museums

Events

ODD SCAN™

Stories

News

Ripley ISword

ODD SCAN™

Download our NEW Ripley's Believe It or Not! APP and activate the ODD SCAN feature to unlock amazing additional content from within the pages of this book. Every time you see the ODD SCAN icon, scan the page with your phone and POW! incredible extra pictures and videos will appear!

cringe
LAUGH
learn more
WATCH
read
GASP
giggle

SCAN the page

VAMPIRE WOMAN VIDEO & PICS!!

…y videos › more pictures › full-length interviews › silly stories › galleries of art › wacky wonder…

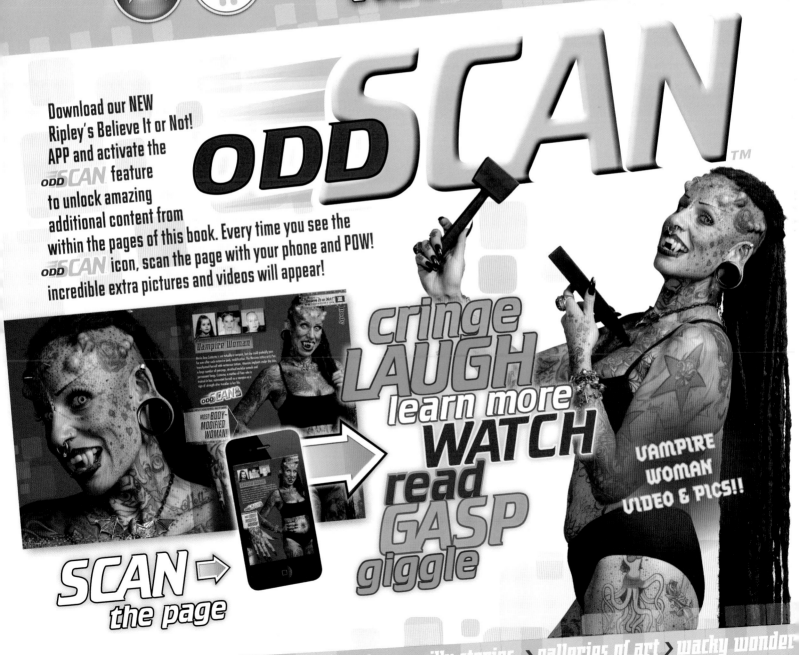

The Odd Couple
CRASH MAN
FULL HOUSE
SWEATY ROBOTS

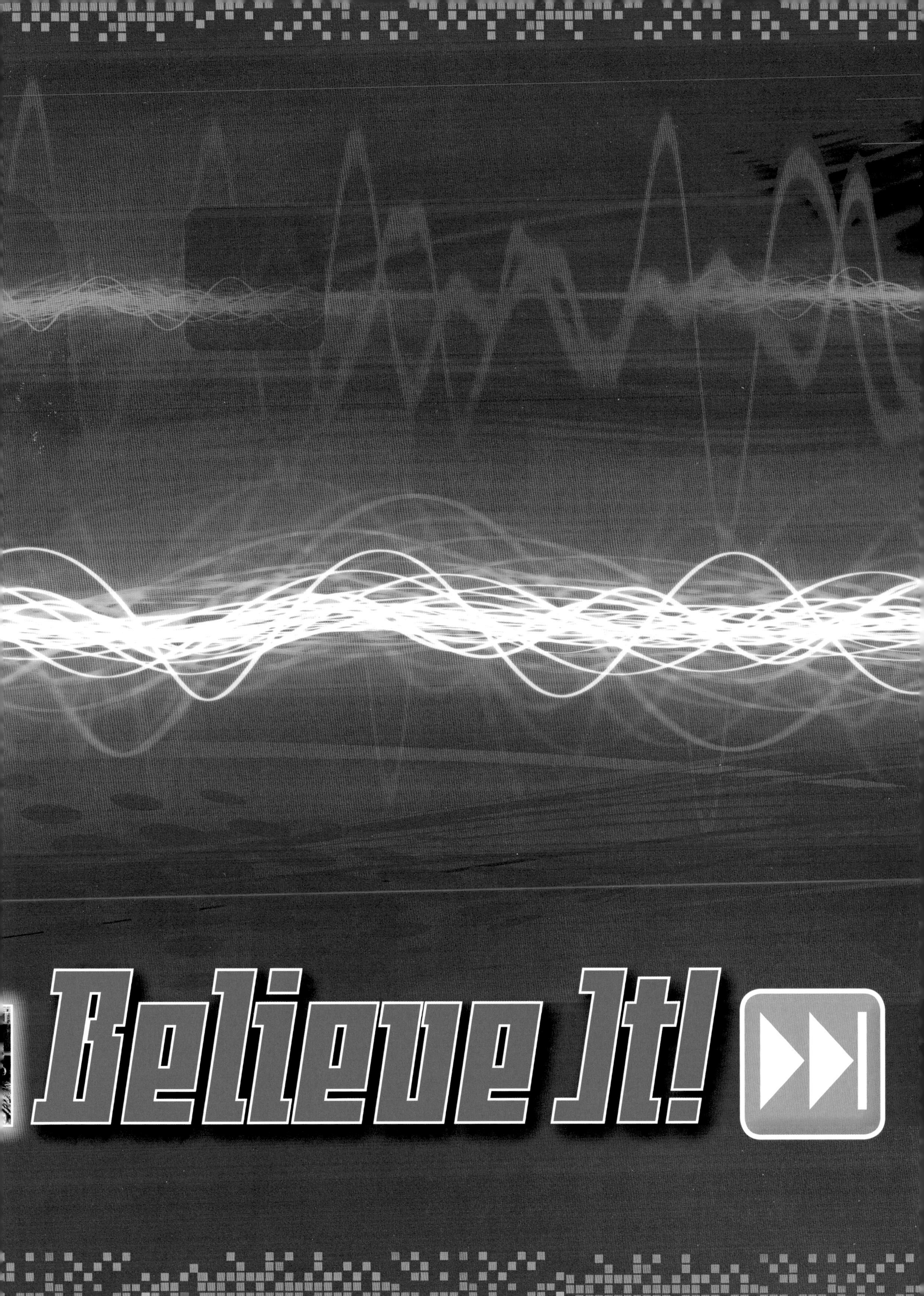
Believe It!

The 100-room mansion where the family all live

A giant communal bedroom

EY'S WEIRD RECORD • RIPLEY'S WEIRD RECORD

WORLD'S LARGEST FAMILY!

RIPLEY'S WEIRD RECORD • RIPLEY'S WEIRD RECORD

THERE ARE 181 MEMBERS OF ZIONA CHANA'S FAMILY (AND COUNTING)

HE ONCE MARRIED TEN WOMEN IN ONE YEAR

HE LIVES WITH THEM ALL IN A 100-ROOM MANSION

A ROTATION SYSTEM OPERATES SO THAT HIS WIVES TAKE TURNS SHARING HIS BED

HE HAS UP TO EIGHT WIVES WITH HIM ALL THE TIME TO WAIT ON HIS EVERY NEED

A TYPICAL DINNER REQUIRES COOKING 30 WHOLE CHICKENS, PEELING 132 LB (60 KG) OF POTATOES AND BOILING 220 LB (100 KG) OF RICE

Believe It!

FULL HOUSE

Ziona Chana, 67, is head of the world's largest family—consisting of 39 wives, 94 children, 33 grandchildren and 14 daughters-in-law. They all live in a rambling four-story house in a hill village in the Indian state of Mizoram, where Ziona is head of a religious sect that allows members to take as many wives as they want. While he has his own double bed, his wives sleep in giant communal dormitories, the youngest women sleeping closest to his bedroom. His oldest wife, Zathiangi, organizes the other wives to carry out the daily household chores so that the compound is run with military precision. The house even has its own school, as well as a vegetable garden big enough to feed the entire extended family.

MONSTER WOMBAT In 2011, paleontologists in Queensland, Australia, uncovered an almost complete skeleton of a diprotodon, a prehistoric wombat-like creature the size of an SUV car that was the world's biggest marsupial. The three-ton monster, which had large tusks but a tiny brain, became extinct about 35,000 years ago.

ROBOT MARATHON At the world's first robot marathon—raced around 423 laps of a track in Osaka, Japan, in February 2011—the winner completed the 26-mi (42-km) course in just over two days at an average speed of 0.48 mph (0.77 km/h). At the finish, the winning robot—16-in-tall (40-cm) Robovie-PC—waved its arms and bowed to the crowd.

MILLION-DOLLAR BOTTLE For the woman who wants to smell like a million dollars, DKNY created a million-dollar bottle of perfume. Their special bottle of Golden Delicious fragrance was carved from polished 14-carat yellow and white gold. Covered in 2,700 white diamonds and 183 yellow sapphires, it also has a flawless single diamond in the bottle cap.

STEEL CAGE April Pignatoro and Michael Curry married in Riverhead, New York State, on June 6, 2010, in a steel cage placed underwater in a shark tank.

NOT AGAIN! Two years after being ticketed for speeding in London, England, a man emigrated to Christchurch, New Zealand, and was again booked for speeding—by the same police officer who had stopped him in England! Like the disbelieving driver, Constable Andy Flitton had recently moved to New Zealand.

WEED WHEELS We could soon be driving cars or riding bicycles with tires made from weeds. A species of dandelion—*Taraxacum kok-saghyz* (TKS)—produces molecules of rubber in its sap, and scientists at Ohio State University are conducting crossbreeding experiments in the hope of increasing the rubber yield from the plant so that it can be used commercially.

Ripley's Research

Grennan envisages the synthetic sweat glands being installed on at least three different types of industrial robot—a bomb disposal robot, a surgeon robot and an industrial picker robot. On the bomb disposal robot, it would release the smell of human fear, which has been proven to enhance a person's cognitive performance. On the picker robot, the gland would release a chemical called androstadienone, which is found in male sweat, and, if dispersed on an assembly line, could improve the performance of nearby female workers. The surgery robot would release a mist of oxytocin, a chemical found in the human brain, which, when breathed in through the nose, causes people to become more trusting. So meeting the robot before surgery should increase the patient's trust in the operation.

SWEATY ROBOTS

U.K. designer Kevin Grennan has created robots with sweaty armpits. He has augmented three existing robots with "sweat glands" made from Japanese artificial sweat, a product used to test fabrics for sweat stains. In response to a chemical stimulus, each robot targets a specific form of human subconscious behavior—fear, focus and trust—to improve its effectiveness.

TREBLE CHANCE Believe it or not, Jennifer and Driss Allali from Eastbourne, England, have three children with the same birthday—Najla, Adam and Sami were all born on October 7, in 2005, 2007 and 2010 respectively.

BANK ERROR While renovating a former bank in Ghent, Belgium, as a base for his accounting firm, Ferhat Kaya opened an old safe that had been left behind by the previous owners and found bags of 20 and 50 euro bills, totaling around $380,000.

HUMAN COW Scientists in Argentina have created a cow that produces "human" milk. By incorporating two human genes into the cow before birth, scientists from the National Institute of Agribusiness Technology in Buenos Aires have developed an animal that will produce milk similar to that of humans.

SPACE LESSON People who spend long periods of time in space have to relearn to place objects down rather than letting go of them in midair.

MICROSCOPIC FROG A computer sciences professor at a university in Nanchang, China, has artificially bred a tiny species of frog that can be seen clearly only through a magnifying glass. Hu Gansheng's frogs are just 0.2 in (0.5 cm) long but can leap 4 in (10 cm)—20 times their body length.

DIAMOND PLANET Astronomers believe they have discovered a planet made entirely of diamonds orbiting a tiny spinning star 4,000 light-years away. The planet, which is about 37,000 mi (60,000 km) wide—over five times the diameter of Earth—is thought to be all that remains of a once-massive star in the Milky Way. Its high density indicates that it must be made of crystalline carbon—in other words, diamonds.

ARTIFICIAL BRAIN Scientists at the University of Pittsburgh, Pennsylvania, created a tiny artificial brain that demonstrated 12 seconds of short-term memory. The microbrain was derived from rat brain cells and grown in a petri dish.

BACON CLOCK California-based inventor Matty Sallin has devised an alarm clock that wakes you up with the smell of bacon. Wake n'Bacon turns on ten minutes before you are due to wake up and slowly sizzles frozen slices of bacon beneath two halogen lightbulbs. Its built-in fan then wafts the aroma of cooking bacon around the room to wake you up gently.

Snake Twist

For over 30 years, Liu Fei of Jiangxi Province, China, has been pulling 3-ft-long (0.9-m) snakes through his nose, sometimes even using two snakes simultaneously. His most unnerving moment came when he accidentally swallowed one of the snakes, but luckily for Liu it died in his stomach before it could cause any harm.

ROBOT SAFETY Robot-driven cars created by the software company Google have traveled more than 140,000 mi (224,000 km) on U.S. streets with only a single accident. The cars use artificial-intelligence software that can sense anything near the vehicle and mimic the decisions made by a human driver. Engineers say that robot drivers react faster than humans, have 360-degree perception and do not get distracted, sleepy or intoxicated.

SINGING MICE Japanese scientists have created mice that can sing. By tinkering with a mouse's DNA so that it randomly mutated, they have managed to develop more than 100 mice that can chirp like sparrows.

BUTTER BLUNDER

In May 2011, a visitor to Boijmans van Beuningen museum in Rotterdam, the Netherlands, accidentally trod in an artwork made of peanut butter. He absentmindedly wandered onto *Peanut Butter Platform*, a piece by Dutch artist Wim T. Schippers that was acquired by the museum in December 2010. It features 290 gal (1,100 l) of peanut butter—enough to fill more than 2,000 regular-sized jars.

Mouth Camera

TINY CAMERA U.S. catalog company Hammacher Schlemmer has introduced the world's smallest fully functional digital camera—which is no bigger than a human fingertip. The tiny camera measures just over 1 in (2.5 cm) in all dimensions and weighs only 0.5 oz (14 g).

BEACHED WHALE A dead 33-ft-long (10-m) whale was found in a field in Yorkshire, England—half a mile from the sea. It became stranded after being carried to shore by an exceptionally high tide while it was hunting.

SHARED HUSBAND Undecided whether to marry for love or proceed with an arranged marriage to a bride chosen by his family, Azhar Haidri found a solution by marrying both women in the space of 24 hours at Multan, Pakistan, in October 2010. Both brides—21-year-old Rumana Aslam, and his family's choice, 28-year-old Humaira Qasim—were happy to marry the same man.

FIRST-CLASS MALE Chester Arthur Reed, aged 95, of Riverside, California, retired from his job as a U.S. postal worker after 37 years with nearly two years of unused sick time.

TOILET TANTRUM A man who owns a toilet tissue roll that was once rejected by The Beatles has been offered $1,500 for a single sheet. The Liverpool, U.K., band refused to use the paper while recording at London's Abbey Road studios in the 1960s because it was too hard and shiny and had the name of record company EMI stamped on every sheet. The roll was bought at auction by Beatles fan Barry Thomas for $120 in 1980.

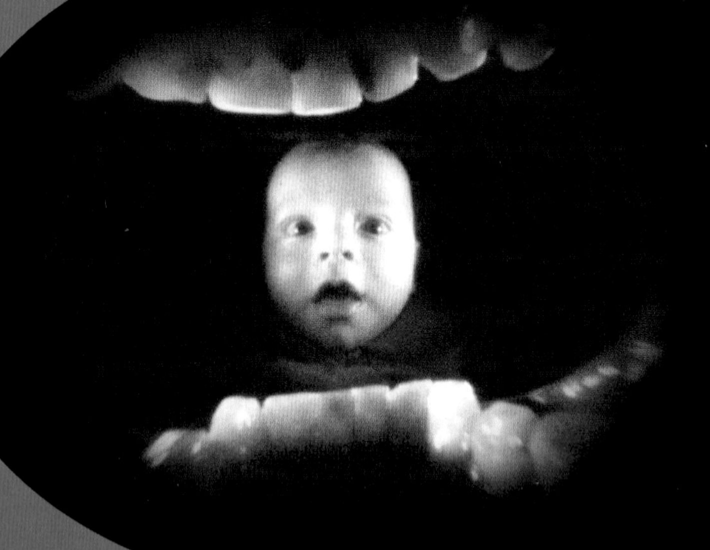

This photo of young Louis Quinnell was taken with a pinhole camera fitted in the back of his dad's mouth! Justin Quinnell from Bristol, England, positioned the film in his mouth so that his back teeth could keep it stationary, and then held his mouth wide open to take the pictures. He created the pinhole camera by placing tinfoil over a pinprick one-fifth of a millimeter wide on the cartridge, and used it to take unique mouth's-eye pictures of the world around him, including the Sydney Opera House in Australia and more everyday occurrences such as taking a bath. Sometimes he had to stand still with his mouth open in front of his subject for a minute to ensure that the film was properly exposed.

WASTE OF MONEY The U.S. Bureau of Printing and Engraving produced more than a billion $100 bills for release in 2011 that were rendered worthless when a machine improperly creased the bills during printing.

HARD TO SWALLOW Australian sword swallower Chayne Hultgren, who once swallowed 27 swords simultaneously, was arrested in 2011 while performing before a large crowd in a New York City square—for brandishing a sword in public.

ON TIME All three children born to Lowri Dearsley of Manchester, England, have arrived at precisely the same time, 7.43. Overcoming incredible odds, daughter Ella was born at 7.43 a.m. on October 10, 2005, another daughter, Evie, was born at 7.43 p.m. on December 26, 2007, and a son Harrison was born at 7.43 a.m. on January 20, 2011.

WHERE THE STREETS HAVE NO NAME About 100 street signs mysteriously disappeared from the town of Northborough, Massachusetts, in the first six months of 2011.

100-FT GEYSER When a car smashed into an L.A., California, fire hydrant in 2011, shearing off the top, the broken hydrant sprayed a fountain of water 100 ft (30 m) into the air, flooding streets and causing people to be evacuated from their homes.

INVISIBLE BEGGAR Fed up with being ignored by passersby, street beggar Nemanja Petrovic from Subotica, Serbia, tossed his cap and shoes down on the sidewalk with a handwritten card saying "Invisible Beggar" and abandoned his pitch. He returned to find his cap full of money—so now he puts down the card and a pair of shoes as a prop and goes to a nearby café while the donations pour in.

BANANA ATTACK A costumed gorilla mascot at a cell-phone store in Strongsville, Ohio, was attacked in July 2011—by a banana. The store manager reported that a boy dressed as a banana emerged from bushes and leaped at the man wearing the gorilla suit. The banana split before police arrived.

RED ROSES Xiao Wang, a groom in Qingzhen, China, spent a year's salary buying 99,999 red roses for his 2010 wedding to Xiao Liu—because in China the number nine is considered lucky. The flowers had to be flown in from the other side of the country and were delivered to the wedding in a fleet of 30 cars.

SPECIAL PEN Bangladeshi businessman Dr. Moosa Bin Shamsher has a 24-carat gold ballpoint pen, encrusted with 7,500 diamonds, which he uses to sign only business deals worth $10 million or greater.

RING REUNITED Joan Spiers was reunited with a diamond ring that she had flushed down the toilet two-and-a-half years earlier. Following the mishap—at a hotel near Gatwick in Surrey, England—she hired a waste firm to search 12,000 gal (54,500 l) of sewage for the ring, but to no avail. Then, by coincidence, an employee from the same firm stumbled across it 30 months later at a sewage works.

TUSKS SEIZED In January 2011, a court in St. Petersburg, Russia, confiscated 3 tons of mammoth tusks—64 full and 14 reconstructed—from a criminal gang that had been trying to smuggle them out of the country. The tusks came from Siberian mammoths and had survived for thousands of years because of the permafrost that covers most of the region.

DUTCH SHARE Dutch student Ruben Schalk found an early share of the Dutch East India Company in the archives of Hoorn, Netherlands. The company was disbanded more than 200 years ago, but the share is still worth over $750,000 to collectors.

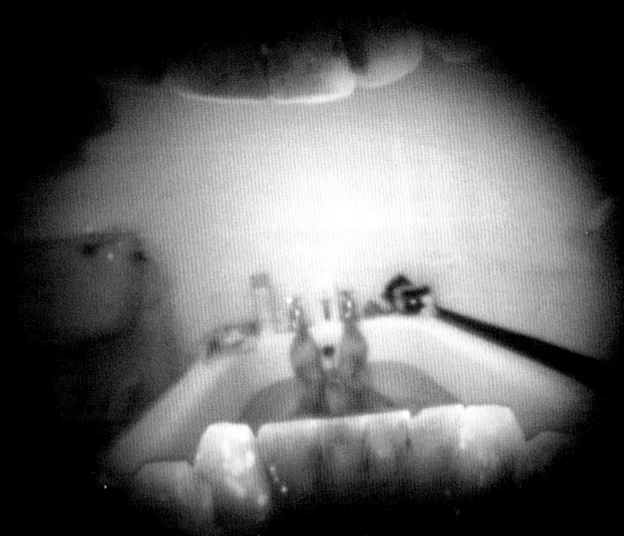

DEMOLITION DERBY Seventy-seven-year-old Marlies Schiller caused over $200,000 damage to five brand new cars in a showroom while she was trying to take one out for a test drive. She shot backward and forward across the Volkswagen garage in Apolda, Germany, smashing into everything in her path, her trail of destruction ending only when she crashed through a window and hit a car parked outside.

LONGEST INTERVIEW Australian radio presenter Richard Glover set a world record for the longest-ever radio or TV interview when he talked to journalist and author Peter FitzSimons for 24 hours in a Sydney studio.

TWINS PEAK Among the 34 employees on duty at the Bexley Park Pool, South Euclid, Ohio, in the summer of 2011 were four sets of twins (including two identical sets), meaning that nearly a quarter of the staff were twins.

RED TAPE Although he has been living in America for almost a century, 95-year-old Leeland Davidson of Centralia, Washington State, discovered in early 2011 that he wasn't officially an American because his parents did not fill out the proper paperwork.

BANK PARTY On June 2, 2011, June Gregg celebrated her 100th birthday with a party at the Huntington National Bank branch in Chillicothe, Ohio—where she still held the same savings account her father opened for her in 1913.

BANNED NAMES Among baby names that have been banned in New Zealand in recent years are Yeah Detroit, Keenan Got Lucy, Fish and Chips (given to twins) and Talula Does The Hula From Hawaii. Believe it or not, however, Number 16 Bus Shelter was permitted.

WET GUESTS Eva and Pavel Jaworzno got engaged and married underwater. Their August 2011 wedding ceremony took place in a flooded open-pit mine in southern Poland, diving with 275 guests, making it the world's largest underwater wedding.

JACKPOT JOY Four workers from the Bell Canada call center in Scarborough, Ontario, who were members of a syndicate that won a $50-million Lotto Max draw in January 2011, were also part of a group of Bell employees who won $1 million in 2007.

BOTTLE MESSAGE Paula Pierce's father folded a message into a bottle and put it in the ocean at Hampton Beach, New Hampshire. More than 50 years later, it turned up 2,000 mi (3,200 km) away on the Turks and Caicos Islands in the West Indies and was returned to Paula.

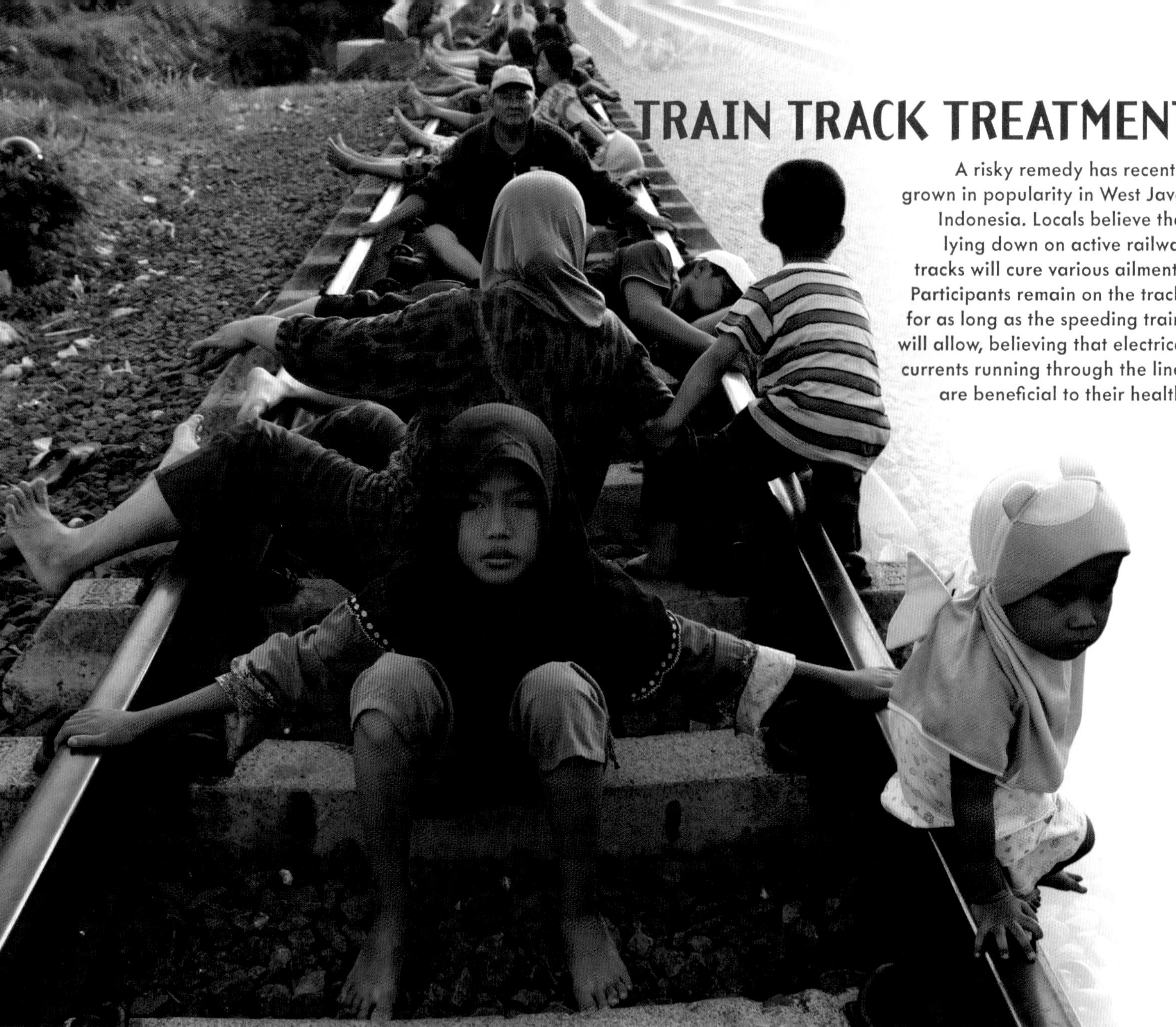

TRAIN TRACK TREATMENT

A risky remedy has recently grown in popularity in West Java, Indonesia. Locals believe that lying down on active railway tracks will cure various ailments. Participants remain on the tracks for as long as the speeding trains will allow, believing that electrical currents running through the lines are beneficial to their health.

WEDDING MACHINE In 2011, Marvin's Marvellous Mechanical Museum in Detroit, Michigan, bought a new vending machine that enables couples to get married for just $1. Devised by British company Concept Shed, the AutoWed has a robotic voice that takes couples through their vows, at the end of which they either press one button for "I do" or another for "Escape." At the end, they get a wedding receipt and two plastic rings.

SHOT ORNAMENT Called to a home in Kansas City, police officers shot an alligator twice in the head before realizing it was a garden ornament. It was only when the second shot bounced off the alligator that they realized it was made of concrete.

DIG THE BRIDE! To save money on wedding cars, groom Zhang Zongqiang, who works for a heavy machinery company, used a fleet of six mechanical diggers to transport himself, his bride Ye Yuzi and their guests to the marriage ceremony in Henan Province, China. The couple stood in the bucket of the lead digger, which was decorated with ribbons and balloons, and tossed sweets to well-wishers along the route.

DOUBLE DELIGHT Shop owner Ron Rea of Belle Vernon, Pennsylvania, sold himself a winning $1.8-million lottery ticket in November 2010—and as the seller of the ticket, he received an extra $10,000!

THE TRAIN TRANSPORTING IRON ORE FROM INLAND MAURITANIA TO THE COAST IS OFTEN 1.5 MI (2.4 KM) LONG.

STONES FAN In October 2010, police in Chennai, India, arrested a man for smuggling more than 2,000 diamonds and precious stones in his stomach.

CASH JIGSAW After a Taiwanese businessman had inadvertently dropped the equivalent of U.S. $6,000 of banknotes into a shredder, justice ministry worker Liu Hui-fen put them back together in just seven days. The 200 New Taiwan $1,000 bills were each ripped into about 20 pieces, but by locating the Chinese character *guo* (country) on each bill and then working outward, she managed to complete the cash jigsaw.

I DOOOOOOO Jason Jenkins of Stoke-on-Trent, England, proposed to his girlfriend Melissa Bowen by having her engagement ring delivered by an owl. Carrying a diamond ring in a pink velvet bag on its leg, Zulu the owl swooped from a perch and landed on Jason's arm.

METAL MARRIAGE

Elaine Davidson, who has nearly 7,000 body piercings, got married in June 2011 to Douglas Watson... who has none. At her wedding in Edinburgh, Scotland, only her face was visible—and that was painted with bright colors and covered in 192 piercings.

LATE DELIVERY A postcard from a soldier serving in the British Army in World War I was finally delivered in 2010—94 years late. The loving message from 19-year-old Alfred Arthur to his sister Ellen did not reach her address in Norwich, England, until long after both of them had died, but with the help of a genealogist it has been forwarded to members of the family.

MEMORABLE DATES Tyler Ashton Marx was born in Meridian, Idaho, at 11.11 a.m. on 1/11/11 (January 11, 2011). His older sister was born on September 9, 2009—09/09/09.

RICH PICKINGS Armed with a pair of tweezers, former jewelry setter Raffi Stepanian made $450 a week by searching the pavement cracks of New York City for dropped gems and gold. He found chips of diamonds and rubies, and bits of platinum and gold fragments stuck in the mud or in pieces of discarded gum.

HOLD TIGHT!

This brave lamb was snapped hitching a ride on the back of his owner's motorcycle in Havana, Cuba, in early 2011.

LUCKY BREAK

A three-year-old boy had an amazing escape when he fell from the eighth-floor window of an apartment building in Beijing, China, but became wedged behind an air conditioner protruding from a window on the floor below. Trapped between the conditioner and the wall, he was unable to fall any further and was rescued with nothing worse than a few scratches and bruises.

ASHES TOUR Deb Green from Vancouver, Canada, advertised on the classified ads website craigslist for volunteers to take a vial of her late parents' ashes around the world and to sprinkle them at major landmarks. As a result, their ashes are now sprinkled, among other places, in a fountain in Las Vegas, in a beer garden in Amsterdam and at the base of the Eiffel Tower in Paris. Deb said Alice and William Green could never afford to travel but had always wanted to visit far-flung countries.

MARRIED HERSELF On November 6, 2010, Chen Wei-yih, a 30-year-old office worker from Taipei, Taiwan, got married to herself. She arranged the ceremony that was held at a hotel and witnessed by 30 relatives and friends to show she was confident and happy with who she was.

BEGINNER'S LUCK Just minutes into his first attempt at metal detecting, three-year-old James Hyatt, of Billericay, England, struck gold—in the form of a 16th-century religious locket valued at nearly $4 million.

PREMATURE AGING To demonstrate their commitment to growing old together, Zhang Jin, 25, and his fiancée Yao Zenni, 26, of Nanjing, China, had pre-wedding photographs taken showing them as an elderly couple battling against the cold. The pair wore makeup and dyed their hair gray to make themselves look 50 years older.

MERCY MISSION World-War-II German fighter pilot Franz Stigler allowed a heavily damaged American B-17 bomber to escape during a 1943 mission—and 46 years later he became good friends with Charlie Brown, the bomber's pilot.

UNDER-QUALIFIED The Italian government funded a Libyan man to attend a training program in Rome so that he could learn how to be an underwater frogman, only to discover that he couldn't actually swim. It was later revealed that the candidate was the cousin of the official tasked with choosing participants for training programs and had liked the idea of a vacation in Rome.

LUCKY NUMBERS Twice in the space of a month in 2010, Israel's biweekly national lottery drew the same six winning numbers—13, 14, 26, 32, 33 and 36.

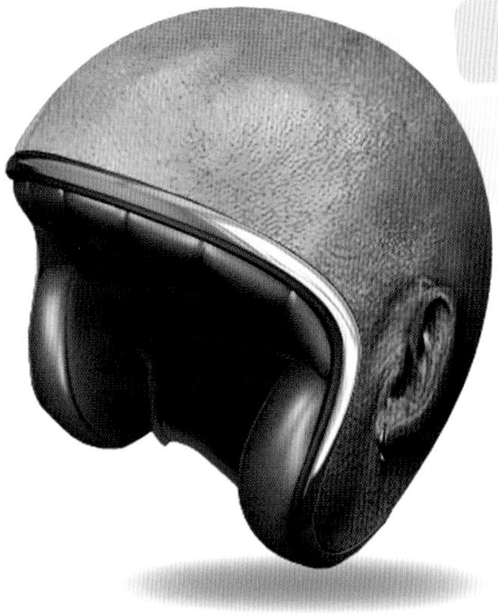

POETIC JUSTICE U.K. filmmaker Martin Cassini defended himself on a charge of speeding to overtake a truck by pleading his case to the court in Barnstaple, Devon, in rhyming couplets. Despite his testimony in verse, he was fined £175.

CLEVER FELLER In May 2010, a man lost in the wilderness of Northern Saskatchewan, Canada, signaled for help by chopping down electrical poles. He was rescued when the power company came out to investigate the downed lines.

THAT'S PROGRESS! It took three years for the first U.S. mint to produce its first million coins. Today, the Philadelphia, Pennsylvania, mint can stamp out a million coins in 30 minutes.

GRAVE VOWS In May 2011, two couples held their weddings in a Chinese cemetery, exchanging their vows among the gravestones. Wu Di and his bride Yang Xi and Wei Jian and his bride Liu Ling, all of whom work at the cemetery, chose the unusual venue as a declaration of their intention to be together until death. The wedding procession to Yong'an Cemetery in Tianjin consisted of 26 decorated cemetery carts.

PRODUCT PLACEMENT

A British advertising firm was accused of bad taste after placing a billboard promoting TV drama *The Walking Dead* on the wall of a funeral parlor in Consett, County Durham.

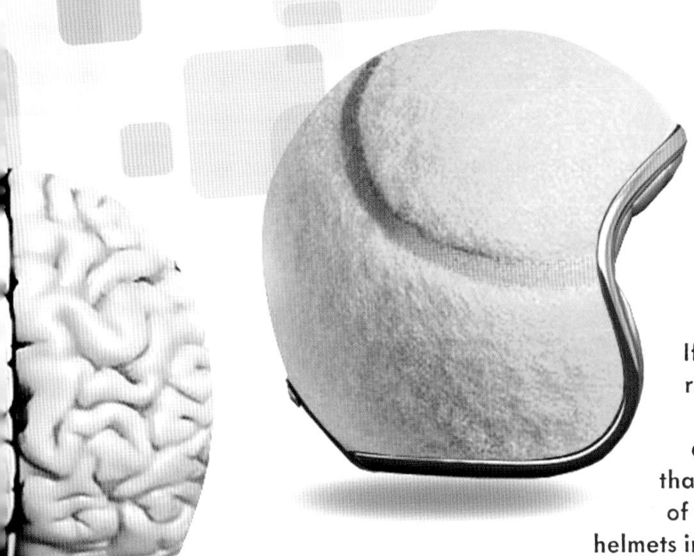

BIZARRE BIKERS

If you see a watermelon riding a bike, it's almost certainly the result of a Kazakhstan company that has designed a range of weird motorcycle crash helmets in such styles as a brain, a tennis ball, a cracked walnut and a watermelon.

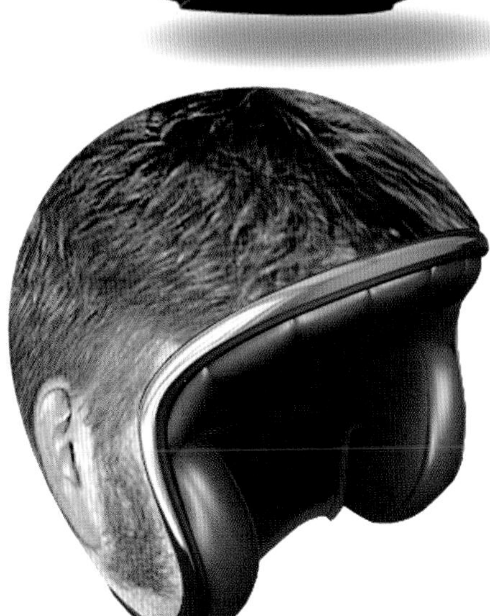

UNDERPANTS RUN On September 24, 2011, thousands of people stripped down to their underwear and ran through Salt Lake City in protest at what they considered the strict laws of Utah.

FLORIDA TATTOO A burglary suspect in Tampa, Florida, was arrested after his alleged victims recognized him from a distinctive facial tattoo on his left cheek—an outline of the state of Florida.

HOME LOVER A couple from Mestre, Italy, took legal action in a desperate attempt to force their 41-year-old son to leave home. The parents said their son had a well-paid job but refused to move out, preferring to have his clothes laundered and his meals cooked by his mother. Forty-eight percent of Italians between the ages of 18 and 39 still live at home.

WHEELCHAIR ROBBER Peter Lawrence, 71, robbed a San Diego, California, bank of more than $2,000 in 2010... while in a wheelchair.

TWO-TOED TRIBE Many of the Vadoma people, a reclusive tribe in western Zimbabwe, have only two toes on each foot.

FALSE FRECKLES Scottish prosthetic technology company Touch Bionics has introduced a highly realistic range of false limbs that feature freckles, hairs and even tattoos.

CUSHIONED FALL In January 2011, a woman survived falling 23 stories from a hotel rooftop in Buenos Aires, Argentina, after she landed on the roof of a taxi, which broke her fall.

FOOD TATTOOS Chef Lauren Wilton of Toronto, Canada, has decorated her body in food-related tattoos, including a whisk, a fork and spoon, two garlic heads, dandelion greens and a boar's head on a platter.

MARRIED ON THE RUN A couple from Houston, Texas, got married during the 2011 city marathon. David Upton and Molly Johnston started the race as boyfriend and girlfriend but crossed the finish line as husband and wife after pausing briefly at the 16-mi (26-km) mark to exchange their marriage vows in front of friends. The bride complemented her running cap with a small white veil.

FEATURED ARTISTS: HANNIBAL AND ANASTASIA ★ FEATURED ARTISTS: HANNIBAL AND ANASTASIA

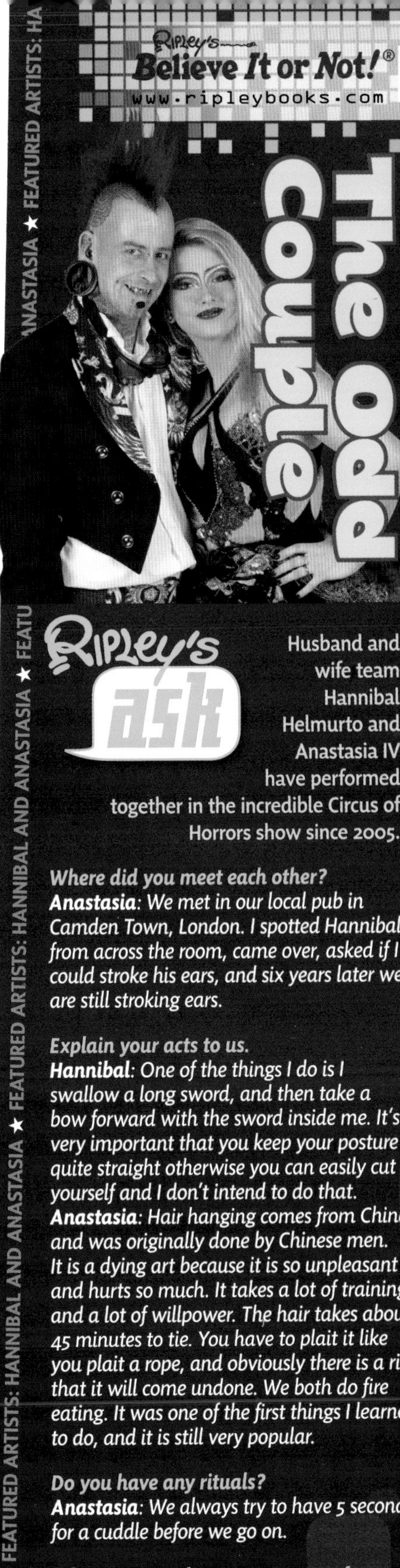

Ripley's ask

Husband and wife team Hannibal Helmurto and Anastasia IV have performed together in the incredible Circus of Horrors show since 2005.

Where did you meet each other?
Anastasia: *We met in our local pub in Camden Town, London. I spotted Hannibal from across the room, came over, asked if I could stroke his ears, and six years later we are still stroking ears.*

Explain your acts to us.
Hannibal: *One of the things I do is I swallow a long sword, and then take a bow forward with the sword inside me. It's very important that you keep your posture quite straight otherwise you can easily cut yourself and I don't intend to do that.*
Anastasia: *Hair hanging comes from China, and was originally done by Chinese men. It is a dying art because it is so unpleasant and hurts so much. It takes a lot of training and a lot of willpower. The hair takes about 45 minutes to tie. You have to plait it like you plait a rope, and obviously there is a risk that it will come undone. We both do fire eating. It was one of the first things I learned to do, and it is still very popular.*

Do you have any rituals?
Anastasia: *We always try to have 5 seconds for a cuddle before we go on.*

When you watch your partner perform, are you ever worried about the risks?
Anastasia: *We are always a bit worried, because the acts we do in the Circus of Horrors always contain a high element of danger. Everything we do has a calculated risk—we have to know our anatomy, and how far we can push each other so we are always looking out for each other. But when I decided to marry Hannibal, I married him the way he is and I wouldn't like to change him for the world.*

Turn the page

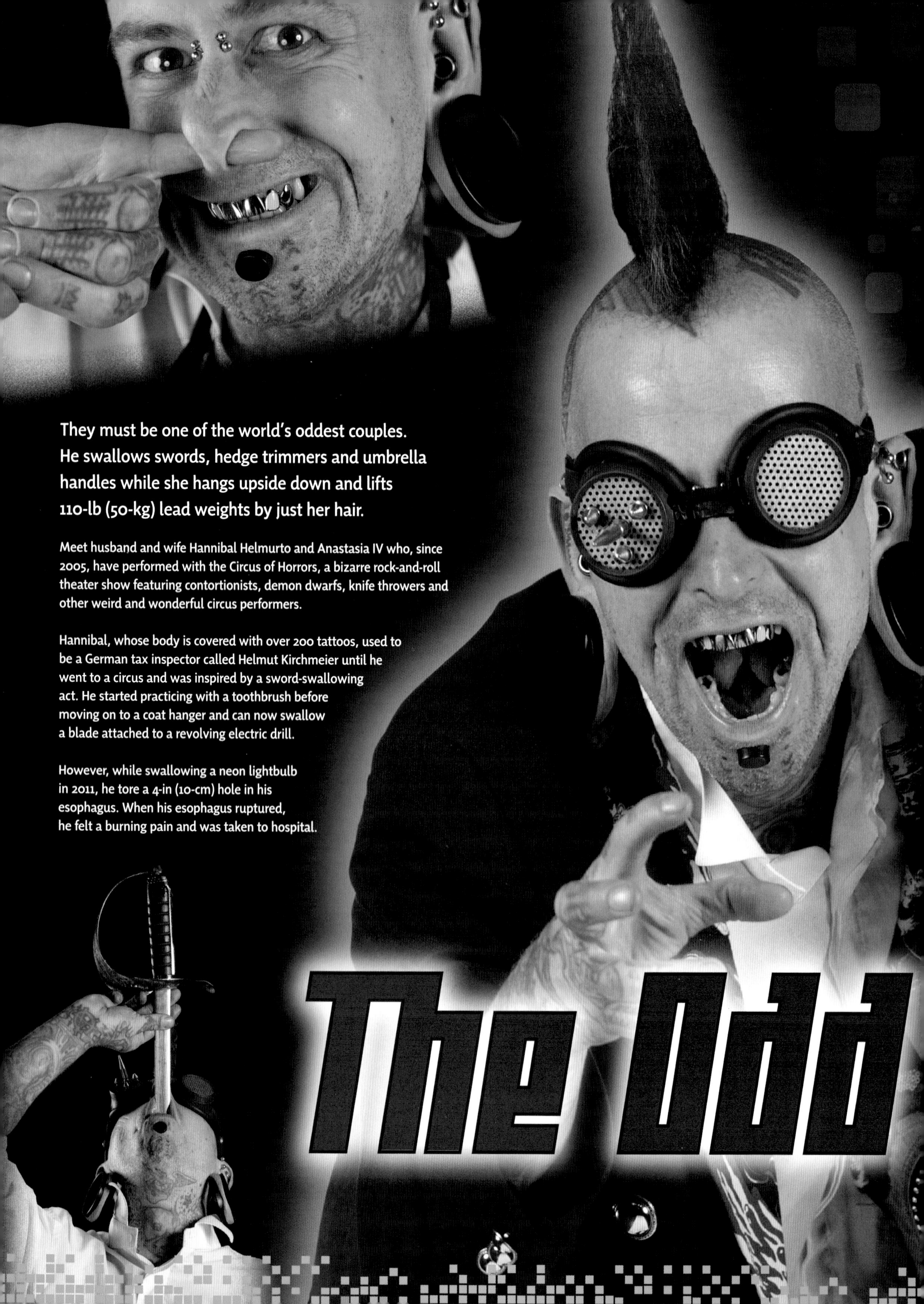

They must be one of the world's oddest couples. He swallows swords, hedge trimmers and umbrella handles while she hangs upside down and lifts 110-lb (50-kg) lead weights by just her hair.

Meet husband and wife Hannibal Helmurto and Anastasia IV who, since 2005, have performed with the Circus of Horrors, a bizarre rock-and-roll theater show featuring contortionists, demon dwarfs, knife throwers and other weird and wonderful circus performers.

Hannibal, whose body is covered with over 200 tattoos, used to be a German tax inspector called Helmut Kirchmeier until he went to a circus and was inspired by a sword-swallowing act. He started practicing with a toothbrush before moving on to a coat hanger and can now swallow a blade attached to a revolving electric drill.

However, while swallowing a neon lightbulb in 2011, he tore a 4-in (10-cm) hole in his esophagus. When his esophagus ruptured, he felt a burning pain and was taken to hospital.

The Odd

While there, he was unable to speak for two weeks and had to be fed through tubes for five weeks. However, he was able to start training again just 12 weeks after leaving hospital.

Polish-born Anastasia Sawicka studied science before running off to join the circus at 18. She used to walk on sword blades but, for the last two years, she has specialized in hair hanging. Suspended upside down from a rope, she can use her hair to lift a 120-lb (54-kg) woman off the ground. She has also pulled a minibus weighing 70 times her body weight... with her hair. She strengthens her hair before each performance by spraying it with water, which makes it less likely to break. Even so, when she first performed her hair-hanging routine she cried because the pain was so intense.

Brave Hound

Vernon Swart from Stellenbosch, South Africa, was horrified when he returned home to find his dog Bella running around with a large knife lodged firmly in her skull. The six-year-old Alsatian terrier crossbreed had suffered the injury as she chased burglars away from the property, but incredibly she did not appear to be in any pain, and later recovered. The veterinarian who eventually removed the knife said the dog had been only a fraction of an inch from death.

FATED TO MARRY Amy Singley and Steven Smith of Bushkill Township, Pennsylvania, were born at the same hospital on the same day in 1986—when their mothers shared a hospital room—and on June 12, 2010, the 24-year-olds married.

DANCING CARROTS To pave the way for proposing to his girlfriend, Pang Kun persuaded 48 of his friends to dress up as giant dancing carrots in a shopping mall at Qingdao, China. He spent $15,000 on carrot costumes and they rehearsed their dance routine for two days. The idea was to attract the attention of Zhao Xinyu because orange is her favorite color.

BIRTH PATTERN Emily Beard was born in 1997 in Portsmouth, England, at 12 minutes past 12 on the 12th day of the 12th month. Her father David had been born at 40 minutes past four on the fourth day of the fourth month, her mother Helen was born on the tenth day of the tenth month, her brother Harry arrived on the sixth day of the sixth month, and their grandmother Sylvia was born on the 11th of the 11th.

PARALLEL LIVES Graham Comrie, 45, and Graham Cormie, 47, who live just 10 mi (16 km) apart in Scotland, look almost identical, are both professional photographers and married to redheads, and have two daughters, and Lhasa Apso dogs as pets. Both men celebrated their silver wedding anniversaries in 2011. People confuse them for each other all the time, and they get messages from each other's friends on Facebook.

MISS MAPLE Using detective skills she had learned at a Junior District Attorney crime-fighting summer camp, 12-year-old Jessica Maple quickly solved a burglary at her late great-grandmother's house in Atlanta, Georgia—a crime that had baffled the police.

LIMPED AWAY One of South Africa's most wanted criminals—due to stand trial in relation to 35 armed bank robberies—escaped from police custody by simply walking out of a Pretoria courtroom door... on crutches.

MISSING RING Robert McDuffy, a firefighter from Wareham, Massachusetts, lost his wedding ring while fighting a house fire. However, luckily for Robert, the homeowner found the ring—11 years later—and returned it.

ACTING DOUBLE

Margaret Clark was an entertainer born with her twin attached by the head to her stomach. That was the backstory proclaimed at her performances at sideshows across the U.S.A., but Margaret did not have a conjoined twin, indeed Margaret did not actually exist. She was an act played by longtime sideshow operator Billy Logsdon, who ran "Side Show Beautiful" out of Indiana in the 1940s. The unfortunate baby twin was merely a rubber "gaff" taped to Billy's belly. His face was covered because he played another character in his shows, a hermaphrodite, also thought to be a hoax, and he did not want to be recognized. "Margaret" would appear alongside Billy's other classic sideshow acts including sword swallowers, small people, and "The Human Pincushion."

"CASHIER NUMBER FOUR, PLEASE" The voice of Terry Green is heard in the U.K. about 30 million times every month as his is the voice that directs customers at banks and post offices to the next available counter.

NO NAME Maximus Julius Pauson of Pasadena, California, wasn't given a name on his birth certificate and went without an official name for 19 years.

IRONIC CRASH On January 31, 2011, a driver accidentally crashed into the same Tampa, Florida, insurance office that provided her with car insurance.

LATEX MASKS Robbers who stole $60 million worth of jewelry in a 2009 raid in London, England, reportedly hired an unsuspecting makeup artist to disguise their faces with liquid latex masks. The artist, who thought the pair were appearing in a music video, also changed their hair color and skin tone during the $700, four-hour session.

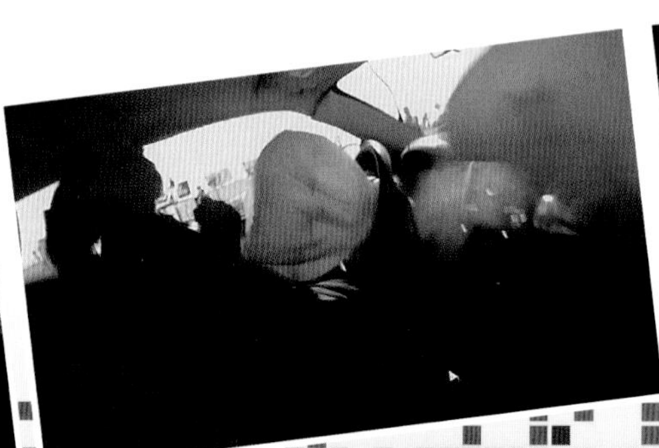

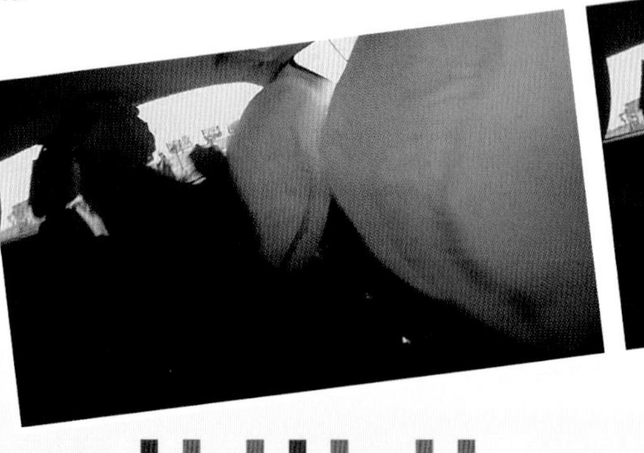

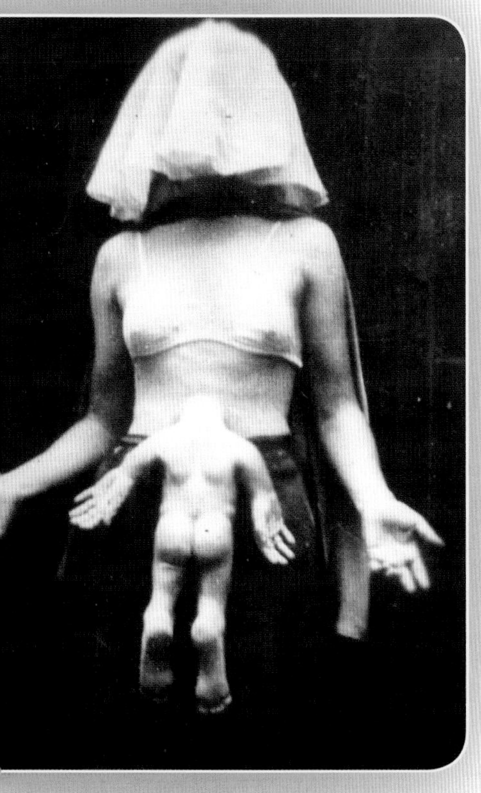

LUCKY FIND When Reg Barker of Suffolk, England, bought a box of old postcards at a garage sale, he was amazed to find one of them featured a picture of his mother. He paid $4 for the box stuffed with more than 200 postcards in 2009. When he looked through them, he saw one of crowds celebrating Victory in Europe Day on May 8, 1945. There, dancing with Canadian troops in London's Leicester Square, were his adoptive mother and aunt.

JOB SEARCH During 2008 and 2009, a homeless, jobless Californian economics graduate landed 50 jobs in 50 different U.S. states in 50 weeks. In his search for work around the country, former financial analyst Dan Seddiqui became—among other things—a lobster fisherman, a jazz-band conductor, a TV weatherman, a syrup processor and even a Las Vegas wedding planner! He said that his favorite job was as a bartender in Louisiana during the Mardi Gras festival.

WALL VAULTER The U.S. military's research arm has devised a robot the size of a shoebox that can jump over walls 25 ft (7.5 m) high. The Precision Urban Hopper is a four-wheeled, GPS-guided remote control car fitted with a piston leg that can propel it over obstacles up to 60 times its own size.

FACIAL RECOGNITION A Japanese company has invented a vending machine that uses facial recognition to recommend drinks to customers. The machine uses sensors to work out the age and gender of a customer and then suggests items based on that information, while also taking into account factors such as the time of day and the weather. When the first interactive drinks machine was introduced at a Tokyo train station, sales were three times that of its predecessor.

ODD SCAN

CRASH MAN

Rusty Haight is the human crash-test dummy. As director of the San Diego-based Collision Safety Institute, Rusty has experienced more than 950 violent vehicle crash tests at speeds of up to 54 mph (87 km/h), and taken 140 air bags to the face. A former police traffic officer, Rusty uses his unique car-wreck experience to research automobile safety and investigate and reconstruct collisions.

BIRD BRAINED

Sally Arnold from Kendal, England, returned home one day to find a perfect imprint of an owl on her window. The bird had flown into the window and left behind the eerie image—complete with eyes, beak and feathers—before flying off. The silhouette was made by the bird's powder down, a substance that protects its growing feathers.

GLADIATOR FIGHT In August 2011, undercover police officers in Rome, Italy, dressed up as gladiators—complete with togas and capes—to prevent the escalation of a turf war between Italian gladiator impersonators who prey on tourists outside the Colosseum and other city landmarks. When the officers impersonating gladiators came under attack from the regular gladiator impersonators, they were rescued by other undercover officers dressed as garbage collectors and tourists!

SAME JUDGE Mark Steven Phillips was arrested on January 27, 2011, in West Palm Beach, Florida, more than 31 years after fleeing from a criminal drug trial, and coincidentally faced the same judge that presided over his 1979 case.

SPEED CHASE Female police officers in Chengdu, China, patrol the city's Tianfu Square on rollerblades so that they can pursue criminals at speed—giving chase at speeds of up to 25 mph (40 km/h).

HIGH FIRE Germany's Paris Gun, a World War I artillery cannon, could bombard the French capital from 70 mi (112 km) away and could be fired so high that the rotation of the Earth affected its trajectory.

TALBOT SOCIETY The Talbot Society holds gatherings for people named Talbot. They drive to Port Talbot, South Wales, in their Talbot cars, stopping en route at hotels and inns called the Talbot.

CAVE WEDDING Jude Onions married Johnny Latimer where they met—in an underground cave. The potholers' nuptials took place 334 ft (102 m) deep in Ingleborough Cave, North Yorkshire, England.

PANTS CARGO A man was arrested at Miami International Airport as he tried to board a flight for Brazil—with seven exotic snakes and three tortoises stuffed down his pants.

THE FEET ON THE STATUE OF LIBERTY ARE 25 FT (7.6 M) LONG AND WOULD REQUIRE U.S. WOMEN'S SIZE 879 SHOES.

CLASS OF THEIR OWN A 2011–12 freshman class at Maine South High School, Park Ridge, Illinois, contained 16 sets of twins and three sets of triplets.

KILLED BY ROOSTER Jose Luis Ochoa died from a wound inflicted by a rooster during an illegal cockfight in Tulare County, California, on January 30, 2011. He was stabbed in the leg by a bird that had a knife attached to its leg.

BLUES BROTHER Bill Smith-Eccles (aka Jake Blues) of Derbyshire, England, is such a fan of the 1980 cult movie *The Blues Brothers* that he wears sunglasses all the time—even on his driver's license photo, making him the only person in the U.K. that has been allowed to do so.

OUT WITH A BANG Following his death in 2009, the ashes of Alfonse Kennedy Goss, a keen member of New Zealand's Wellington Cannon Society, were fired from a cannon over the city harbor.

ALIEN CLOUD

Is it an alien spaceship hovering in the sky about to land on Earth? No, it's a spectacular example of a lenticular cloud (*Altocumulus lenticularis*), a cloud that gets its name from its smooth, lenslike shape. When the wind on the sheltered side of mountains forms standing waves of air, and moisture in the air condenses at the top of those waves, it creates lenticular clouds. If the wind is constant, the clouds can remain stationary in the sky for long periods, leading to them sometimes being mistaken for flying saucers.

Leap of Faith

At the annual Goat Jump Festival in the village of Manganeses de la Polvorosa in northern Spain, a goat is thrown from the 50-ft-high (15-m) church bell tower and safely caught by villagers holding a large tarpaulin. The festival is based on a local legend about a priest who owned a special goat, whose milk helped him to administer to the poor. One day the hapless goat wandered into the church belfry and jumped off the ledge in fright when the bells rang for Sunday mass. The goat was luckily caught in a blanket and saved.

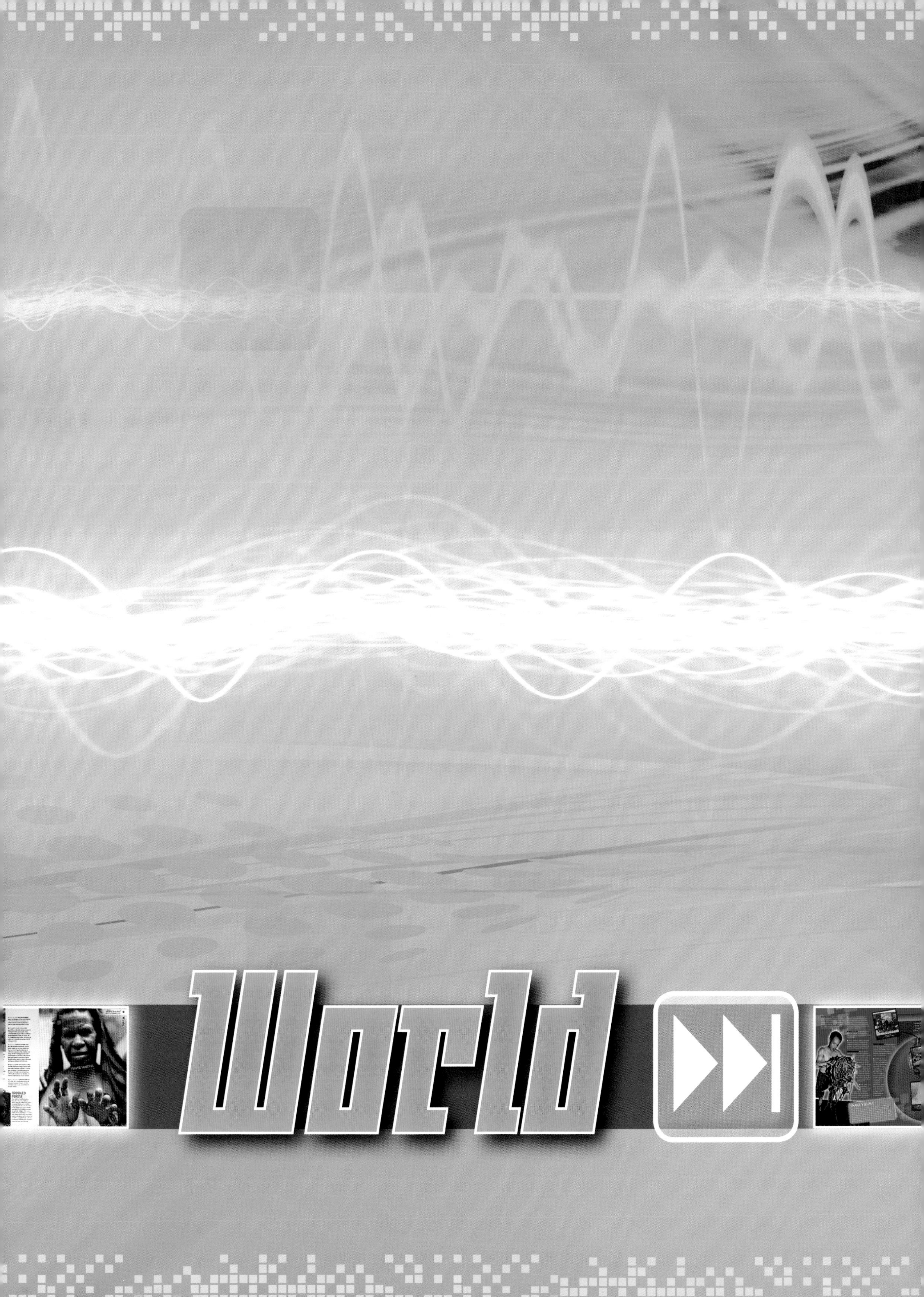
World

Clever Camouflage

After the catastrophic raid on Pearl Harbor on December 7, 1941, the Army Corps of Engineers raced to hide the Lockheed Burbank Aircraft Plant in California to protect it from a possible aircraft attack. This was no time for half measures—the Corps opted for deception on the grandest scale, covering every inch of the plant with camouflage netting to make it look like a rural subdivision from the air. Aircraft hangers, factory buildings, runways, planes, as well as the accommodation and everyday comings and goings of the 90,000 employees took cover beneath the netting. On top, to create a countryside illusion, neighborhood scenes were painted on canvas, fake houses and hundreds of imitation shrubs and trees were built, and rubber automobiles were strategically placed. The canopy was even strong enough to support people hired to ride bicycles randomly. To an enemy pilot, the scene would have seemed perfectly authentic. Below cover, the plant's vital wartime role carried on as normal.

Lockheed manufactured more than 19,000 planes during World War II, many of them "under the net."

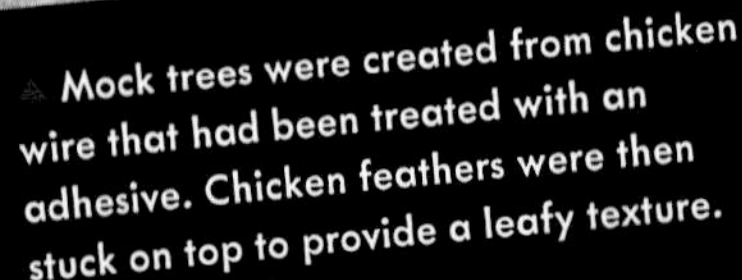

Mock trees were created from chicken wire that had been treated with an adhesive. Chicken feathers were then stuck on top to provide a leafy texture.

Life continued as normal beneath the huge canopy, with workers having space to park their cars and able to hold mass meetings.

HOLLYWOOD GETS INVOLVED

Disney Studios designed the camouflage used at Lockheed, and the detail and techniques used in Lockheed's camouflage bore many similarities to those in nearby Hollywood's film-set construction. Warner Studios were only a couple of miles away from Lockheed and were also disguised during World War II—but were made to look like the Lockheed plant—to deflect a possible hit away from the important airplane-production site!

The only buildings on view were those that looked like typical rural dwellings or farm buildings.

The peaceful, rolling countryside above the plant.

HIDDEN

In the Indian state of Meghalaya, ancient tree vines and roots are trained to stretch horizontally across rivers in order to create latticework structures that are solid enough to be used as bridges. Some of these living bridges are 100 ft (30 m) long and can support the weight of 50 people at the same time.

LIVING BRIDGE FACTS

- Conventional wooden bridges would quickly rot in the region, which is one of the wettest places on the planet, receiving around 590 in (1.5 m) of rainfall per year—about 30 times more than London, England.
- The Indian rubber tree—*Ficus elastica*—grows on riverbanks and supports its upward growth by sending out low-level vines, which grip onto boulders, other trees and soil. Some 500 years ago, villagers began guiding these roots out over rivers, hoping to create river crossings.
- The roots used in the bridges are about 6 in (15 cm) thick.
- It takes about 15 years for a tree bridge to be established, but they can then last for hundreds of years—and, unlike manmade structures, they grow stronger with age.
- The Umsiang Double-Decker Root Bridge in Nongriat is unique for being two root bridges—one stacked over the other.

BAD SINGING The Philippines House of Representatives passed a law in October 2010 making it a crime to sing the country's national anthem poorly. A guilty singer could get up to two years in jail.

PUMPKIN RACE Each year Ludwigsburg Castle in Germany stages a pumpkin festival, the highlight of which is a giant pumpkin boat race in the former royal palace's massive fountain. The pumpkins can weigh more than 200 lb (90 kg) before their tops are cut off and their flesh scooped out to turn them into paddleboats. The 2010 festival also featured a giant statue of a seahorse made out of pumpkins.

POPULATION CENTER Mongolia covers more than 600,000 sq mi (1.5 million sq km)—about four times the size of Germany—but nearly half its citizens live in one city, its capital Ulan Bator.

SEA OF CORN In November 2010, a grain silo collapsed in Norwalk, Ohio, spilling more than 100,000 bushels of corn and creating a "sea of corn" 12 ft (3.6 m) deep that knocked a nearby home from its foundation.

HYDRANT TOSS Sherrodsville, Ohio, has an annual fire-hydrant tossing contest. Participants hurl heavy 113-lb (51-kg) hydrants distances of over 20 ft (6 m). A women's competition uses lighter 40-lb (18-kg) hydrants.

GIANT TREE Since 1981, the Italian town of Gubbio has created an illumination in the shape of the "biggest Christmas tree in the world" on a mountainside above the town. In 2010, the spectacle boasted more than 800 lights, and used nearly 8 mi (13 km) of cables and thousands of plugs to create a tree that stretched over 2,600 ft (795 m) tall.

DRIFTWOOD MUSEUM Bandon, Oregon, has a museum dedicated solely to driftwood, displaying weird and natural shapes from gnarled root balls to whole tree trunks.

SUCKLING COW

A young Cambodian boy feeds himself daily by suckling directly from a cow. The boy had watched a calf nurse from its mother and instinctively did the same thing.

SMALL CEMETERY Ocracoke Island, North Carolina, is home to a cemetery owned by Britain that has only four graves. All four souls were washed ashore from a capsized British trawler in 1942.

CAVE SCHOOL Until 2011, a school in a remote mountain community in Guizhou Province, China, had all its classrooms and its playground in a cave. The 186 pupils at the Getu Village Cave Primary School took their lessons in a vast cave the size of an aircraft hangar, surrounded by bats and lizards. The acoustics helped the school to have the best choir in the area.

OLD-STYLE HOLIDAYS Hotel Morava in Tatranska Lomnica, Slovakia, hosts vacations in the style of the former Communist worker holidays—complete with strict 7 a.m. wake-up calls, compulsory morning exercises and even a re-enactment of a May Day rally.

SIGNPOST FOREST The Signpost Forest, near Watson Lake, Yukon, Canada, displays more than 65,000 city limits signs that have been collected from around the world. The collection was started in 1942 after a homesick G.I., Private Carl K. Lindley, accidentally drove a bulldozer into the original sign that pointed out the distances to various locations along the Alaska Highway. While carrying out repairs following the accident, Private Lindley added a sign pointing to his hometown of Danville, Illinois. Each year up to 4,000 new signs are added by tourists and visitors as they pass through Watson Lake, so that the Signpost Forest now occupies a couple of acres.

TOTEM POLE Over a three-month period, a 40-ft-tall (12.1-m) redwood tree at Confusion Hill, Piercy, California, was carved by chainsaw into a gigantic totem pole. The pole is the largest free-standing redwood chainsaw carving in the world.

HOBBIT HOTEL Fans of *Lord of the Rings* can stay in an underground hobbit hotel in Trout Creek, Montana. Steve Michaels has built the 1,000-sq-ft (93-sq-m) Hobbit House of Montana into a hill and designed it so that it looks just like Middle Earth from the outside, but has modern comforts such as HD Blu-Ray TV and WiFi access on the inside.

BEDROOM SINKHOLE A sinkhole 40 ft (12 m) deep and 2 ft 7 in (80 cm) in diameter suddenly appeared overnight beneath the bed of a woman's home in Guatemala City in July 2011. Guatemala City is prone to sinkholes because it is built on volcanic deposits and experiences abnormally high rainfall.

GIANT FUNGUS A enormous fungus found in China is 33 ft (10 m) long, 2 ft 7 in (80 cm) wide and 2¼ in (5.5 cm) thick—and it weighs half a ton. It was discovered living under a fallen tree and is estimated to hold 450 million spores.

Fiery Rider

Believe it or not, this rider from Kyrgyzstan set light to his back during a spectacular fiery stunt at the 2011 Lake Son-Kul folk festival in the north of the country.

HIGH RISK

Thousands of feet above the ground, at the top of a sheer drop, with no safety precautions and working on an area no wider than a dinner table, a worker takes his life in his hands to transport building materials for a wooden plank road on Shifou Mountain in China's Hunan Province.

THE WORLD'S MOST DANGEROUS JOBS

- **ICE ROAD-TRUCKERS** Driving hundreds of miles at a time, they power 50-ton trucks carrying vital supplies across frozen Arctic lakes, rivers and seas, knowing that any crack in the ice could be fatal.
- **SULFUR MINER** Workers in East Java, Indonesia, collect sulfur from the floor of the 660-ft-deep (200-m) acid crater lake of the Ijen Volcano. As well as the fear of volcanic eruption, they endure toxic gases and carry up to 220 lb (100 kg) of mined sulfur by hand for several miles down the mountain every day.
- **ALASKAN CRAB FISHERMEN** These men toil in the Bering Sea seven days a week, often in the dark and without breaks. With a death rate of more than 350 per 100,000 (mostly from drowning or hypothermia), the fatality rate is 50 times that of most workers. On average, one Alaskan crab fisherman dies every week.
- **CROCODILE WRESTLERS** At Thailand's Samphran Elephant Ground & Zoo, men put on a show by wrestling crocodiles for an hour, even putting their head between the jaws of some of the zoo's monster crocs.

STANDING STONES The French village of Carnac is home to more than 3,000 standing stones arranged in straight lines over 5,000 years ago by an ancient civilization.

LIGHTNING STRIKE A single lightning bolt at a military base in Hattiesburg, Mississippi, in June 2011 struck an entire troop of cadets, sending no fewer than 77 of them to hospital.

JUNK WINDMILL In 2002, the village of Masitala in Malawi had electricity for the first time when local resident, William Kamkwamba, built a windmill from junk and spare parts to generate power.

DUCT TAPE FESTIVAL Since 2004, the town of Avon, Ohio, has held an annual festival celebrating duct tape, complete with artistic exhibits made from the tape.

ON THE EDGE Groups of up to six people who enjoy living on the edge can pay $175 per person to walk hands-free for 30 minutes around a high, narrow ledge on the outside of the CN Tower in Toronto, Ontario—attached only by a cable. The ledge is just 5 ft (1.5 m) wide, has no guardrail and is 1,168 ft (356 m) above ground, but offers exhilarating views of the city and Lake Ontario.

TREE CHAPEL

An 800-year-old oak tree in the French village of Allouville-Bellefosse has two chapels in its hollow trunk. They were built in the late 1600s, along with an exterior spiral staircase, after lightning burned through the tree. Each year, on August 15, a religious pilgrimage is made to the Chapel Oak.

GREAT WALL Following in the footsteps of the country's ancient emperors, in January 2011 the wealthy residents of Aodi, Zhejiang Province, China, built a 23-ft-high (7-m) wall around their village for protection. They created the 28-in-thick (70-cm) wall from more than 70,000 adobe bricks. The only entrance to the village is via a huge iron gate.

HOPPING PROCESSION Echternach, Luxembourg, hosts an annual hopping procession. Up to 9,000 men, women and children—linked by a chain of handkerchiefs—hop through the streets in celebration of a local saint, St. Willibrord.

FOSSIL FIND In February 2011, miner Jay Wright was working 700 ft (210 m) underground at a coalmine in Webster County, Kentucky, when he discovered a 300-million-year-old shark jawbone.

FOUGHT TSUNAMI While most of the 3,500 people on the Japanese island of Oshima ran to the hills on hearing the March 2011 tsunami warning, 64-year-old Susumu Sugawara took his fishing boat out to sea and rode out a succession of 60-ft-high (18-m) waves. When the tsunami abated, his was the only boat from the island that had not been destroyed.

Pig Parade

At the Lechon (roasted) Pig Parade in La Loma, Philippines, shop proprietors dress up roasted pigs to advertise their businesses—in guises including a singer, a racing driver and even characters from the movie *Matrix Reloaded.*

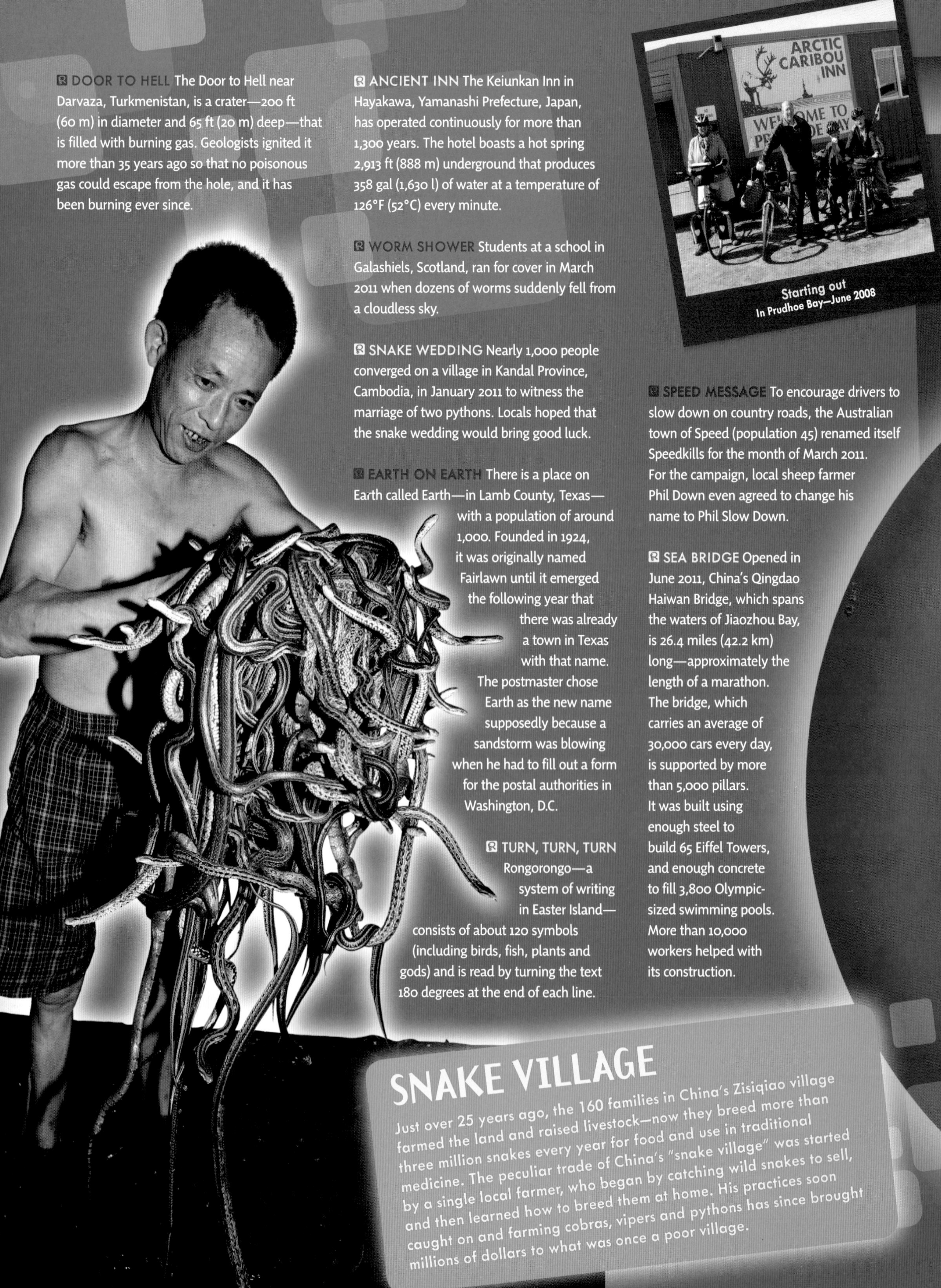

Starting out
In Prudhoe Bay—June 2008

DOOR TO HELL The Door to Hell near Darvaza, Turkmenistan, is a crater—200 ft (60 m) in diameter and 65 ft (20 m) deep—that is filled with burning gas. Geologists ignited it more than 35 years ago so that no poisonous gas could escape from the hole, and it has been burning ever since.

ANCIENT INN The Keiunkan Inn in Hayakawa, Yamanashi Prefecture, Japan, has operated continuously for more than 1,300 years. The hotel boasts a hot spring 2,913 ft (888 m) underground that produces 358 gal (1,630 l) of water at a temperature of 126°F (52°C) every minute.

WORM SHOWER Students at a school in Galashiels, Scotland, ran for cover in March 2011 when dozens of worms suddenly fell from a cloudless sky.

SNAKE WEDDING Nearly 1,000 people converged on a village in Kandal Province, Cambodia, in January 2011 to witness the marriage of two pythons. Locals hoped that the snake wedding would bring good luck.

EARTH ON EARTH There is a place on Earth called Earth—in Lamb County, Texas—with a population of around 1,000. Founded in 1924, it was originally named Fairlawn until it emerged the following year that there was already a town in Texas with that name. The postmaster chose Earth as the new name supposedly because a sandstorm was blowing when he had to fill out a form for the postal authorities in Washington, D.C.

TURN, TURN, TURN Rongorongo—a system of writing in Easter Island—consists of about 120 symbols (including birds, fish, plants and gods) and is read by turning the text 180 degrees at the end of each line.

SPEED MESSAGE To encourage drivers to slow down on country roads, the Australian town of Speed (population 45) renamed itself Speedkills for the month of March 2011. For the campaign, local sheep farmer Phil Down even agreed to change his name to Phil Slow Down.

SEA BRIDGE Opened in June 2011, China's Qingdao Haiwan Bridge, which spans the waters of Jiaozhou Bay, is 26.4 miles (42.2 km) long—approximately the length of a marathon. The bridge, which carries an average of 30,000 cars every day, is supported by more than 5,000 pillars. It was built using enough steel to build 65 Eiffel Towers, and enough concrete to fill 3,800 Olympic-sized swimming pools. More than 10,000 workers helped with its construction.

SNAKE VILLAGE

Just over 25 years ago, the 160 families in China's Zisiqiao village farmed the land and raised livestock—now they breed more than three million snakes every year for food and use in traditional medicine. The peculiar trade of China's "snake village" was started by a single local farmer, who began by catching wild snakes to sell, and then learned how to breed them at home. His practices soon caught on and farming cobras, vipers and pythons has since brought millions of dollars to what was once a poor village.

American Odyssey

For nearly three years from June 2008 to March 2011, John and Nancy Vogel and their twin sons Daryl and Davy of Boise, Idaho, cycled the entire length of the Pan-American Highway from Alaska to the tip of Tierra del Fuego, Argentina—a pedaling distance of 17,300 mi (27,850 km). The boys were just ten years old when they set off, making them the youngest people to cycle the length of the Americas.

Southern Bolivia
"Our planned route through Bolivia was thwarted when a major strike closed one of the cities we would need to pass through. We ended up taking a 400-mile detour up and over the Andes." (August 2010)

In the Colombian Andes
"The Andes took us by surprise with their long, steep climbs. This photo was taken near the top of our first major climb—it was 'only' a 6,000-ft (1,800-m) climb, which, later, would be considered easy. Our longest climb was a whopping 14,856 ft (4,528 m) from sea level to the top of the pass in just 225 mi (362 km)." (August, 2009)

Small town in South America
"Most of our time was spent either out on the open road or in small villages. Large cities were few and far between." (September 2010)

Endless roads
"In Argentina, I never thought we would reach the end of the road!" (November 2010)

Arriving at the end of the world
Ushuaia, Argentina. (March 2011)

Ripley's ask

Ripley's spoke to Nancy about her incredible journey.

What inspired you to start this trip with your family? *We wanted time together as a family before the kids grew up and flew the coop. As for the route, it could easily have been Asia or Africa or Europe—although there was a special draw to the longest road in the world.*

How many miles did you have to cycle each day? *Our overall average was a mere 17 miles per day. Although we did cycle 17 miles many days, there were many days when we cycled more and many days we took off completely. We aimed for around 30–50 miles on the days we cycled, but that varied tremendously due to hills, winds or availability of resources.*

What was the hardest stretch of your trip? *Northern Argentina. When we crossed into Argentina, our brains told us we were nearly done—our last country means nearly there, right? But Argentina is a HUGE country! We had been warned many times about the winds in Patagonia in southern Argentina, but nobody mentioned the headwinds in the north—and they were horrible! So, mentally we thought we should be nearly there and we had daily unexpected headwinds. That's a very tough combination to cope with!*

What was the most rewarding? *Arriving in Ushuaia at the end of the world. After spending three years cycling 17,300 miles through 15 countries, to pull up to that sign in Ushuaia announcing that we were at the end of the world was a moment I will never forget. We did it!*

RIPLEY'S WEIRD RECORD • RIPLEY'S WEIRD RECORD

YOUNGEST PEOPLE TO CYCLE THE LENGTH OF THE AMERICAS

RIPLEY'S WEIRD RECORD • RIPLEY'S WEIRD RECORD

CASTLE CLIMB

Ma Jei climbed the 70-ft-high (21-m) wall of Zhonghua Gate Castle, China—without a rope or safety equipment—just so that she could avoid paying the $3.75 admission fee. When other visitors tried to follow her example, two fell and broke their legs, and three others had to be rescued.

CARDBOARD BOATS The Cardboard Boat Museum in New Richmond, Ohio, displays some of the weird and wonderful craft that have competed in 20 years of the annual cardboard boat race on the Ohio River.

SOMALI SPLIT When Somalia's dictator, Siad Barre, was overthrown in 1991, the northwestern part of the country seceded and declared independence as Somaliland. They have a currency, a police force and democratic elections but are not recognized by any other country.

SIESTA TIME Spain's first National Siesta Championship took place in Madrid in 2010 to help revive the tradition of taking a short sleep after lunch. Competitors were monitored as they tried to doze for 20 minutes on sofas in the middle of a shopping mall. The highest points were awarded to people who managed to sleep for the full 20 minutes, but marks were also awarded for inventive sleeping positions, distinctive outfits and the loudest snore.

CHINA CENSUS China, the world's most populated country, employed six million people—more than the entire population of Denmark—simply to administer its 2010 population census.

FIRST SNOW In August 2011, a cold blast from the Antarctic brought snow to Auckland, New Zealand, for the first time in 35 years—snow was last seen there in the 1970s. The unusual weather created such excitement that people rushed to post pictures and videos online of the snow as it fell in the city.

UNDERWATER SUITE To celebrate its fifth anniversary, the Conrad Maldives Rangali Island Hotel converted its famous underwater restaurant into a honeymoon suite beneath the waves, complete with a double bed, complimentary champagne breakfast and uninterrupted views of exotic sea life.

FINGER OF FATE

This cloud in the shape of an arm and a hand was photographed pointing from the sky over Tenerife, Canary Islands, by a British couple on holiday there in October 2011.

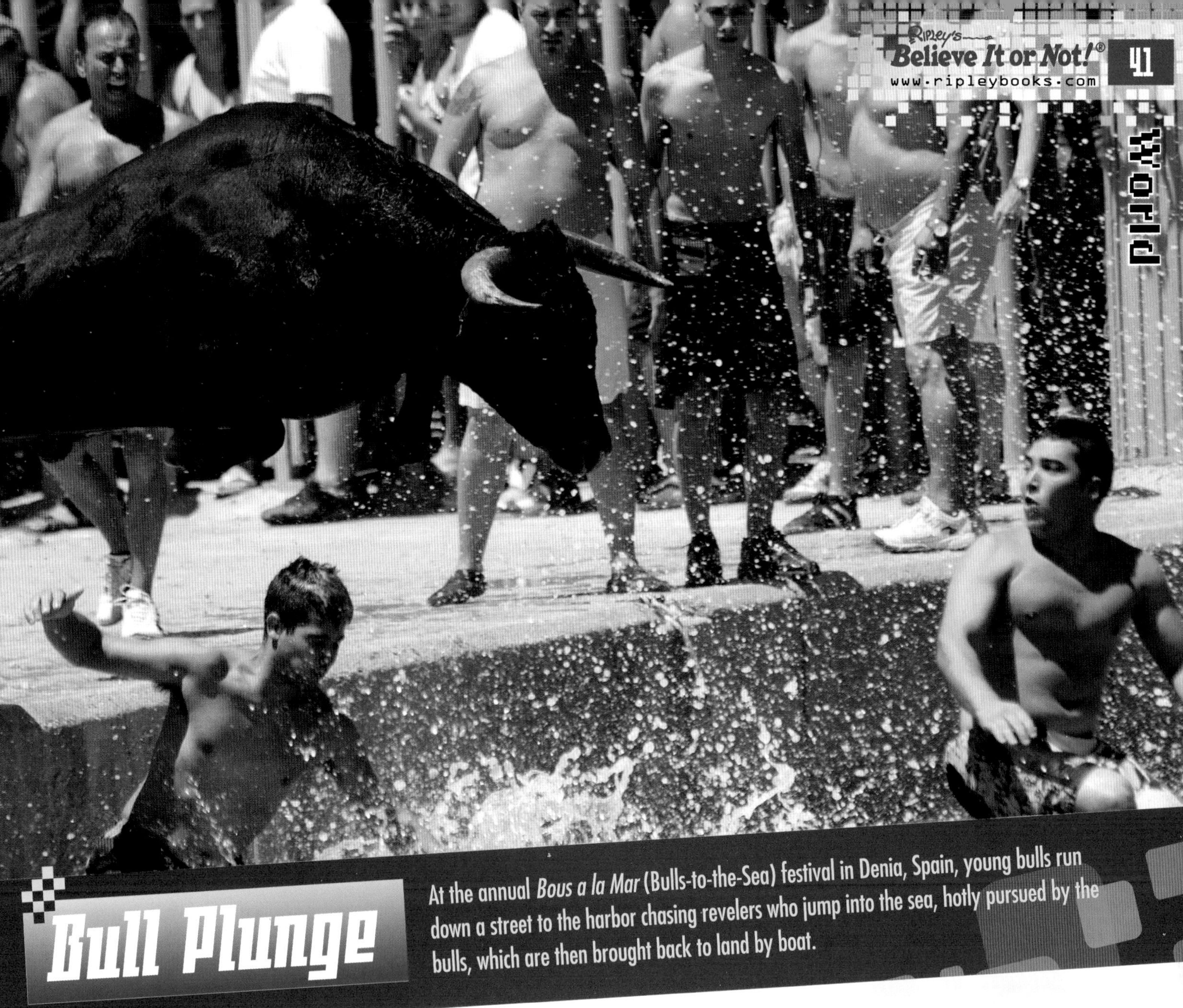

Bull Plunge

At the annual *Bous a la Mar* (Bulls-to-the-Sea) festival in Denia, Spain, young bulls run down a street to the harbor chasing revelers who jump into the sea, hotly pursued by the bulls, which are then brought back to land by boat.

SANTA PENTATHLON The 54th World Santa Claus Congress, held near Denmark's capital, Copenhagen, in 2011, featured a Santa pentathlon—a five-discipline event between two teams of Santas, one from Denmark and one from the rest of the world, including the U.S.A., Sweden, Russia and Germany. The fitness contest required the Santas to throw gifts, fire cannon balls, ride bumper cars, race over an obstacle course and compete in a horse-race game.

MYSTERY FIREBALL When Croatians spotted a mysterious ball of fire dart through the sky over Bjelovar in February 2011, many thought it was a comet or even an alien attack. Instead, it turned out to be nothing more than a patch of burning grass caught by the wind. Local farmer Marin Kiselic had decided that, with no time to mow his fields, it was cheaper to set them on fire.

TEARFUL BRIDES The Tujia people in Central China maintain an ancient tradition of "crying marriages." Brides begin daily crying a month before the wedding, with female friends eventually joining in so that they can weep together.

UNDERSEA VOLCANOES A chain of 12 huge, underwater volcanoes has been discovered in the icy waters of the Southern Ocean. The volcanoes—some of which are active—are dotted over an area the size of Britain and several are around 2 mi (3 km) high, making them nearly four times higher than the world's tallest building, Dubai's Burj Khalifa.

FAIRY ROCK A builder was forced to redesign a luxury housing estate in Perthshire, Scotland, around a rock because local people said fairies lived under it and would be upset if it were moved.

GLOWING LAKES Gippsland Lakes in Victoria, Australia, glow in the dark—owing to a combination of fires, floods and algae. The fires of 2006 were followed by severe floods, which washed ash and nitrogen-rich soil into the lakes. When temperatures warmed up in the summer, blue-green algae feeding on the high level of nutrients, appeared across great swathes of the water. When organisms were disturbed, they created a chemical reaction called bioluminescence, which emitted an eerie blue light, making the lake glow at night.

$10 MILLION TREE For Christmas 2010, the Emirates Palace Hotel in Abu Dhabi displayed a jewel-encrusted Christmas tree worth more than $10 million. The tree's branches were draped in bracelets, necklaces and watches containing diamonds, pearls, emeralds, sapphires and other precious stones.

ICELANDIC FESTIVAL The town of Gimli in Manitoba, Canada, holds an annual festival that celebrates all things Icelandic. Since 1890, the Icelandic Festival of Manitoba—or Islendingadagurinn—has been crowning a Fjallkona (maid of the mountain) and reenacting Viking warfare tactics.

NATIONAL PERFUME Lithuania has launched its own national perfume—a blend of sandalwood, cedar and musk designed to convey the Indo-European origins of the Lithuanian language as well as strength of character. Samples of the perfume were sent to Lithuanian embassies, hotels and airports and to the country's soldiers deployed in Afghanistan.

UNDERGROUND HOSPITAL Ukraine's Solotvyno salt mine has a subterranean hospital ward for convalescing asthmatics and people with other respiratory problems. Its salty air is said to have created a unique microclimate that helps people who suffer from breathing difficulties.

HIDDEN TUNNELS In May 2010, police searched the residence of a man in East Austin, Texas, and discovered he had dug a three-story network of tunnels beneath his home. The tunnels went as far as 35 ft (11 m) deep and in several places were big enough to allow an adult to stand up.

LONGEST REIGN The 76th Maharana of Udaipur, India, is part of the longest ruling dynasty in the world. His family has ruled there since AD 566—that's an unbroken run of nearly 1,450 years.

SACRED RATS

At the Karni Mata Temple in Deshnoke, India, rats are treated with such reverence it is deemed a great blessing to have a rat run across your feet, or to taste food or water that a rat has also tasted. The 20,000 (and rising) temple rodents are protected, regularly fed, and if anybody accidentally kills one, they are expected to buy a gold or silver rat to replace it.

CLOSED WINDOWS To ensure that the exterior of Buckingham Palace, the home of Queen Elizabeth II in London, England, maintains a unified appearance, none of the front windows are ever opened.

NO DOORS The homes in the village of Siala in Orissa, India, have no doors. Residents believe a goddess watches over their village and protects it from theft.

WRAP FANS The last Monday in January in the U.S.A. is Bubble Wrap Appreciation Day, when bubble wrap fans celebrate the packing material, which was originally designed in 1957 as insulated wallpaper, by popping plastic all over the country. The day, known as BWAD, was started in 2001 by two radio DJs in Bloomington, Indiana, to fill the news void between Martin Luther King Day and the Super Bowl.

WAR TOURS A Swiss travel agency offers vacations in the world's most dangerous war zones. Babel Travel's catalog has package tours for Iraq, Sudan and Somalia, as well as giving tourists the chance to spend Christmas in Afghanistan or enjoy a New Year's party in Iran. A 45-day vacation in Afghanistan costs more than $30,000—and that's without adding in the cost of travel insurance.

WHISTLING LANGUAGE The whistling language of Silbo Gomero has only four vowels and four consonants, and its speakers can easily converse while standing 2 mi (3 km) apart. It is used only by inhabitants of La Gomera in the Canary Islands and is communicated by whistling at different tones.

LOST COPY During its 40th anniversary of independence from Britain, the island nation of Fiji announced that it had lost its copy of the 1970 Independence Order, which granted the country self-rule.

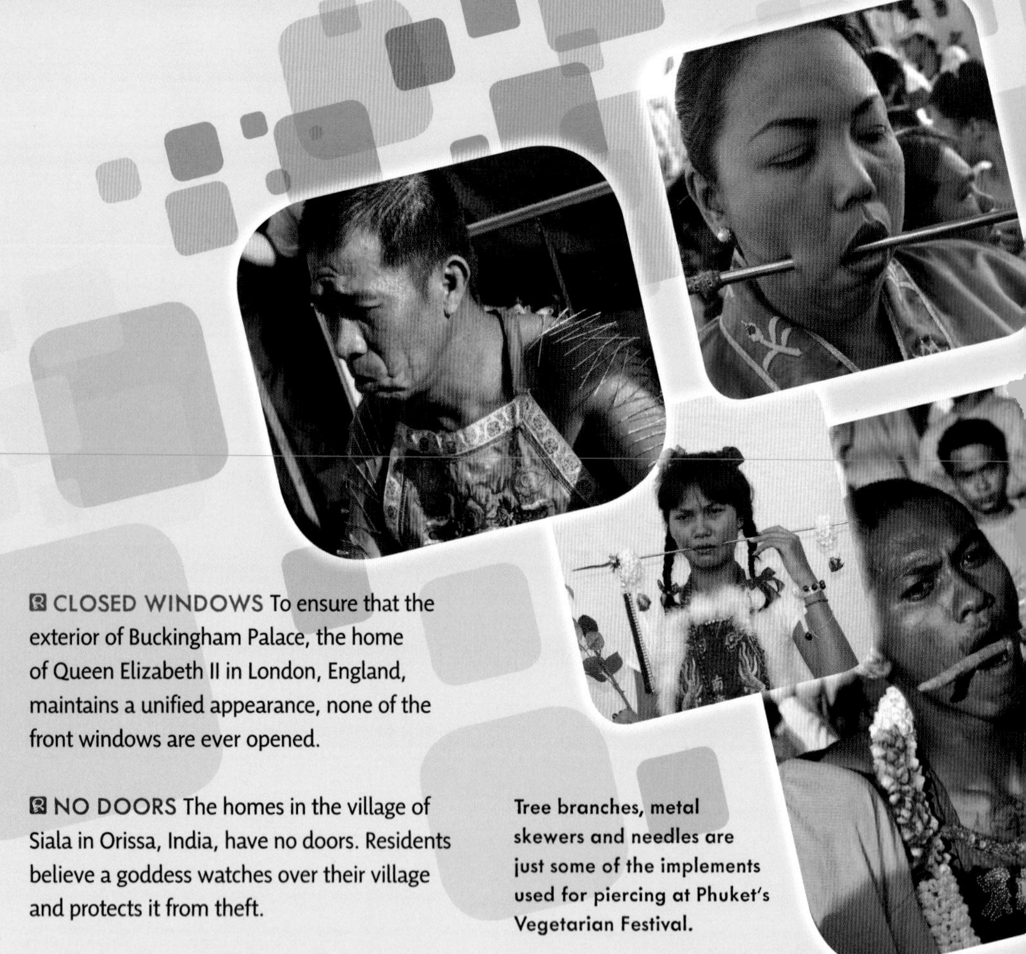

Tree branches, metal skewers and needles are just some of the implements used for piercing at Phuket's Vegetarian Festival.

CHAIN WHIPPING The Festival of Ashura is celebrated by some Shia Muslims with flagellation ceremonies where participants cut their own scalps with knives or whip their chests and backs with chains.

FREE FLAGS Flags that fly over the Canadian Parliament's Peace Tower are free to residents who request one—but there is a 27-year waiting list to receive one.

STATUES STOLEN The Dutch city of Nijmegen removed ten large bronze statues from the streets in November 2010 after four of them had been ripped from their foundations, probably stolen to be sold as scrap metal.

SILVER LADY The Silver Queen, a 19th-century hotel in Virginia City, Nevada, has a 15-ft-tall (4.6-m) painting of a lady in an evening gown adorned with 3,261 real silver coins. Her belt is made from 28 gold coins and her choker and bracelets are made from dimes.

TREE HOUSE Farmer Xiong Yuhu from Xingping, Hunan Province, China, has built a house—with a kitchen, bathroom, bedroom and lounge—at the top of a 50-ft-high (15-m) tree. Inspired by the Bird's Nest Olympic Stadium in Beijing, this luxury tree house is reached by a long wooden staircase. The structure is so solid that 18 adults have stood in the house together.

GETTING THE NEEDLE

At the Phuket Vegetarian Festival in Thailand, devotees self-mutilate by piercing their faces and bodies with dozens of needles. Ritual vegetarianism in Phuket dates back to the early 19th century and participants at the nine-day festival perform acts of body piercing to purge others of evil spirits and bring good luck to the community.

WICKED PLANTS

Around 70,000 people are poisoned annually by plants in the U.S.A. alone. Here are some of the chief suspects.

THE PLANT THAT ALMOST KILLED CLEOPATRA
Strychnine tree ***Nux vomica***
Before committing suicide with a poisonous asp, Egyptian ruler Cleopatra was intending to kill herself by ingesting parts of the strychnine tree. However, when she saw that the plant caused her servant to suffer terrible seizures, stiffness and convulsions, all while conscious, she chose the snake instead.

THE PLANT THAT KILLED LINCOLN'S MOTHER
White snakeroot ***Ageratina altissima***
Abraham Lincoln's mother, Nancy Hanks Lincoln, died of deadly milk sickness in 1818 after drinking milk from a cow that had been eating white snakeroot. Every part of the plant contains tremetol, a lethal liquor that causes tremors in livestock before killing them.

THE PLANT THAT CAN STRIKE YOU DUMB IN THE OFFICE
Dumb cane ***Dieffenbachia amoena***
A popular office and house plant because it is tolerant of shade, the plant's leaves contain a toxic sap which, if chewed, can cause drooling, swelling, and, in extreme cases, paralysis of the vocal cords.

THE PLANT THAT WAS USED TO EXECUTE SOCRATES
Hemlock ***Conium maculatum***
A highly poisonous member of the carrot family, hemlock contains a neurotoxin that results in death owing to lack of oxygen to the heart and brain. Eating just a few leaves can be fatal. The ancient Greek philosopher Socrates was sentenced to death in 399 BC by drinking a mixture containing hemlock.

THE FUNGUS THAT MAKES YOU CRY
Sweater mushroom ***Clitocybe dealbata***
Toxins in the sweater mushroom of Europe and North America make you sweat profusely, drool and cry uncontrollably. These symptoms are followed by blurred vision, vomiting, diarrhea and painful abdominal cramps.

THE PLANT THAT PARALYZES
Coyotillo ***Karwinskia humboldtiana***
A flowering shrub in the buckthorn family and native to Texas and Mexico, the berries of the coyotillo contain deadly neurotoxins that cause a slow but deadly paralysis in both livestock and children.

THE PLANT THAT HOUSES A LETHAL WEAPON
Castor oil plant ***Ricinus communis***
Although castor oil has been a medicine for centuries, its seeds contain ricin, a poison that has been used by the Soviet KGB to murder dissidents. It has also been considered for use in chemical warfare. Just one milligram is enough to kill an adult.

KILLER PLANT

A carnivorous pitcher plant at a garden nursery in Somerset, England, killed and ate a great tit—only the second documented case in the world of a pitcher plant eating a bird. The plant's inner wall secretes a nectarlike substance to attract insects, and the bird probably leaned in too far in pursuit of one and became trapped by the plant's slippery, waxy surface. It then fell into the pool of enzymes and acid that is housed at the base of the pitcher. Large pitcher plants often eat rats and frogs, and can completely devour a piece of meat in just a few days.

PLANT LIFE The South Atlantic's arid and volcanic Ascension Island received its diverse plant species in the 1850s when the British Royal Navy populated it with annual shipments of plants from around the world.

DOOMSDAY VAULT Millions of seeds taken from more than 500,000 different crop varieties are stored in a special vault situated 425 ft (130 m) inside a frozen mountain on a remote Norwegian island near the Arctic Ocean. The location for the Doomsday Vault, as it is known, was chosen because it is thought to be about the safest place on the planet to protect the world's seed collections from nuclear war or other disasters.

ORANGE GOO A strange, sticky, orange goo made up from millions of rust fungal spores washed ashore near Kivalina, Alaska, in 2011.

SKELETON VIEW A five-bedroom house in Visby on the Swedish island of Gotland has a medieval tomb and skeleton in the cellar. The house was built in 1750 on the foundations of a Russian church. The kitchen rests on the presbytery, and the tomb containing the skeleton of a Russian man who died about 800 years ago is visible through a glass panel.

WILD ORCHID A single Lady's Slipper orchid growing on the Silverdale Golf Course in Carnforth, Lancashire, England, is the last of its kind growing wild in all of Britain and is protected by police patrols. The orchid, which is more than 100 years old, attracts hundreds of visitors each year, with people traveling over 200 mi (320 km) just to see it.

LONG STREET A single street in central Brazil stretches for 311 mi (501 km). Lined with houses for the whole length, it is almost the equivalent to a street running all the way from San Francisco to Los Angeles.

WATERPROOF VAULT The Crypt of Civilization—a waterproof vault beneath Oglethorpe University in Atlanta, Georgia—was sealed in 1940 and contains objects and information of the day. Its stainless steel receptacles are filled with inert gases and so are designed to last 6,000 years.

TWIN TOWN About 1.5 percent of all human births are twins—but they are over three times more common in the town of Igbo-Ora, Nigeria. The reason for the high level of multiple births is a mystery, but some doctors believe it could be linked to the large amount of the tuberous vegetable yam eaten by the local people.

LONG AND WINDING ROAD

Drivers compete on the twisty 24 Crankle Stilwell Road (also known as the Burma Road) during a hill-climb rally in Guizhou Province, China. The road is 717 mi (1,154 km) long and runs from Yunnan Province, China, to Burma. Over 2,300 laborers lost their lives while building the Chinese section of the road in 1938.

FLYING HIGH The city of Calipatria, California, sits at an altitude of negative 184 ft (56 m), but its flagpole is just high enough for the U.S. flag to fly right at sea level.

HOLY STALAGMITE India's ice "Shiva Lingam," a stalagmite that is worshiped by Hindus, was melting in August 2011 because of warmer weather and a record number of vistors generating too much body heat. Over a 40-day period that summer, 620,000 people went to see the holy stalagmite at Amarnath caves in Kashmir.

CONNECTICUT CORNER If you travel directly North, South, East or West from the city of Stamford, Connecticut, you will enter the state of New York.

DRIVE-THRU MORTUARY There is a drive-thru mortuary in Compton, California. Robert L. Adams Mortuary has a drive-thru viewing option where mourners can see the open casket of a dead relative displayed behind a long bulletproof glass window without getting out of their car.

COLOSSAL CAVE At more than 650 ft (198 m) high and almost 500 ft (152 m) wide, Hang Song Doong, a cave in Vietnam, is large enough to contain several 40-story buildings.

Buddhist Body

Inside a large pot at a temple in Fujian Province, China, construction workers found the body of a Buddhist nun that had been buried for 32 years. Although Chen Zhu's corpse had not been embalmed, it was so well preserved that it has been wrapped in gauze and coated in black lacquer and gold foil to make a permanent human body statue. Buddhists say the nun's vegetarian diet kept her body in a good state.

VOODOO SUPERSTITIONS

- If a woman visits you first thing on a Monday morning, it is bad luck for the rest of the week.
- If you shake a tablecloth outside after dark, someone in your family will die.
- To keep her husband faithful, a woman should add a little of her blood to his coffee.
- Laying a broom across the doorway at night keeps witches at bay.
- To stop a widow remarrying, cut all of her husband's shoes into small pieces as soon as he is dead.
- Borrowing or lending salt is bad luck.
- Turning someone's picture upside down automatically gives them a headache.

VOO

Voodoo is a traditional religion from West Africa. It is based on a belief that animals and inanimate objects, known as fetishes, have spiritual powers. These fetishes are used in voodoo rituals. Powders made from various animal parts are administered by voodoo priests, or *bokors*, which can seemingly send people into a trance. Traditional West African voodoo was transported to Haiti in the Caribbean and the southern U.S.A., particularly Louisiana, where it mixed with Catholicism. Voodoo concoctions have been linked to reports of real-life "zombies" in Haiti, with victims supposedly stuck in a trance for years.

Voodoo healers claim to be able to cure a vast range of sicknesses by slicing open human flesh and inserting into the wound a black powder made from the body parts of dead animals. Akodessewa Fetish Market in Togo, West Africa, is a voodoo supermarket—an outdoor pharmacy where thousands of animal body parts, including crocodile heads, monkey testicles, snake skins and elephant's feet, take the place of conventional medicine. People from all over the region descend on the market—the biggest of its kind in the world—to buy fetishes, to cure family illnesses or simply to enhance any of their particular abilities.

To concoct these magic charms, voodoo priests grind up the animal parts with herbs and burn the mixture on a fire to create a black powder. Three incisions are made in the patient's back or chest into which the powder is then rubbed. During this ritual the priests often work themselves into and out of trances, as if possessed by spirits.

The different animal body parts are said to correspond with the human body. So the hand of a dead chimpanzee might be ground down and inserted into the flesh of a soccer goalkeeper to help with his agility, while marathon runners are given powder made from the head, heart and legs of a horse to increase their speed. Powdered monkey testicles are sometimes used to help women conceive.

The market also sells animal-bone statues to ward off evil spirits and protect homes.

The heads of dead leopards are used by voodoo priests to make a powdered medicine to cure human head and brain conditions.

DOO

A voodoo witch doctor, known as "King Fox," poses in a ceremonial animal hide costume in Africa.

Cats with their stomachs ripped open line the market stalls at Lomé, Togo. The stench from the market is described as foul.

In Haiti, voodoo dolls, or fetishes, can be seen in graveyards. Some believe they act as messengers to the spirit world, and to help contact loved ones. This doll, found in the national cemetery in Port-au-Prince, belongs to a voodoo priest who practices in the graveyard.

Visitors to Akodessewa Fetish Market can buy all manner of medicinal skulls, including crocodile heads, vultures, owls, dogs, turtles, rodents and mummified bats.

A voodoo priest caked in mud in Port-au-Prince, Haiti, in November 2011. Haitian voodoo believers bathe in sacred mud pools and sacrifice animals as part of an annual voodoo festival in Plaine du Nord, in the north of the country.

Voodoo medicine is so powerful that voodoo priests, or *bokors*, are believed to have used it to create real-life "zombies." Clairvius Narcisse was declared dead by doctors in Haiti and buried in 1962, only to reappear 18 years later, claiming that he had been poisoned through a skin abrasion by a *bokor* and then brought back to life. He said that soon after his "death" he had been revived by the *bokor*, drugged with plant toxins that impaired his brain function, and put to work as a zombie slave on a plantation. When the poison administered by the voodoo priest was analyzed, it was found to contain puffer fish, one of the world's most toxic creatures. The toxin causes paralysis and a strange coma in which patients claim to retain consciousness despite being unable to move. That was how Clairvius came to be buried alive. When he did eventually reappear, he bore a scar on his cheek that he said was caused by one of the nails in his temporary coffin.

UNDERSEA RIVER Differences in temperature and salt content cause water from the Mediterranean to flow into the Black Sea as an underwater river, complete with waterfalls and a riverbed on the sea floor.

TORNADO RECORD On April 27, 2011, a record-breaking 312 tornadoes were recorded over the U.S.A.'s southern States in a 24-hour period starting at 8 a.m.—more than double the previous record of 148 twisters in a single day in 1974. Four of the April 2011 tornadoes achieved the most powerful ranking possible—EF5 on the Enhanced Fujita Scale—whereas normally such destructive twisters are recorded only once a year or less.

WORLD SIGN A signpost in Lynchville, Maine, points to Norway (14 mi/22 km), Paris (15 mi/24 km), Denmark (23 mi/37 km), Naples (23 mi/37 km), Sweden (25 mi/40 km), Poland (27 mi/43 km), Mexico (37 mi/60 km), Peru (46 mi/74 km) and China (94 mi/151 km). The towns are all in Maine and the distances from Lynchville are genuine.

POPULAR PRESIDENT Indonesian President Susilo Bambang Yudhoyono was re-elected with nearly 74 million votes cast for him in 2009—the most votes ever received by a democratically elected official anywhere in the world.

Rock Face

Photographer Peter Bardsley of Cumbria, England, spotted this creepy face formed by the reflection of a cave in the Hodge Close Quarry, in the Lake District. The skull cave (best seen when the picture is turned through 90 degrees, as in the main photo above) can be seen only by abseiling 100 ft (30 m) down an unstable cliff, or wading through a 260-ft (80-m) mine tunnel. The quarry has not been used for decades, and its flooded tunnels and caves are popular with divers.

NEW ISLANDS New islands regularly appear and disappear off the coast of Pakistan near the Makran Desert over a matter of months. They are created by volcanoes of mud that erupt from deep within the Earth.

LONGEST CONSTITUTION With 444 articles, 12 schedules and 94 amendments totaling more than 117,000 words, India's Constitution is the longest written constitution of any independent country. By contrast, the U.S. Constitution is the shortest, with just seven articles and 27 amendments, giving a total of only 4,400 words.

TSAR BELL The bronze Tsar Bell, which sits in the grounds of the Kremlin, Moscow, Russia, weighs over 200 tons, stands more than 200 ft (6 m) high, has a diameter of 21 ft 8 in (6.6 m) and is 2 ft (60 cm) thick. Cast in 1735, the bell—the biggest in the world—was damaged two years later by fire, the heat from which caused a 12-ton piece to shatter. The bell has been used as a chapel, with people entering and exiting via the broken area.

TREE HOME After graduating from college and with his parents moving to Hawaii, Corbin Dunn built a tree house and lived in it for five years. Located 40 ft (12 m) above ground at the back of the family home in Santa Cruz, California, the tree house had electricity and boasted a fully functional shower and toilet.

NO CANDIDATES When the small town of Tar Heel, North Carolina (population 117), announced vacancies for mayor and three commission seats in 2011, no one bothered to run for election.

CROOKED FOREST

The town of New Czarnowo, Poland, is home to a bizarre forest near the Odra River, where hundreds of pine trees display large bends in the bottom of their trunks, before growing vertically as normal. Surrounding trees are completely straight. The reason behind their deformity is a mystery, and explanations range from man-made techniques used to shape the wood for use in furniture or boats, to extreme environmental conditions when the trees were young.

FINGER FUNERAL

The Dani tribe from the island of New Guinea had an unusual method of mourning their dead relatives. It was customary for females to have one or two fingers chopped off at the first joint when a family member died, eventually leaving some with only shortened stumps. Observers have reported that a tribal elder would numb the arm by knocking the elbow, and then remove the digits with one blow of a stone axe. The finger-cutting ritual has been banned, but you can still see older Dani women bearing the results of the practice.

CAPTIVE ANIMAL STARS
Monkey Business
TIGHT FIT
Tiny Puppy
WILD WOOD WEB
YOUR UPLOADS
HAPPY SNAPPERS
BEST BUDDIES
Rainbow Chicks
PANDA SUITS
Jellyfish Survivor
Giant Croc
LARGEST CROC EVER CAPTURED

Animals

HAPPY SNAPPERS

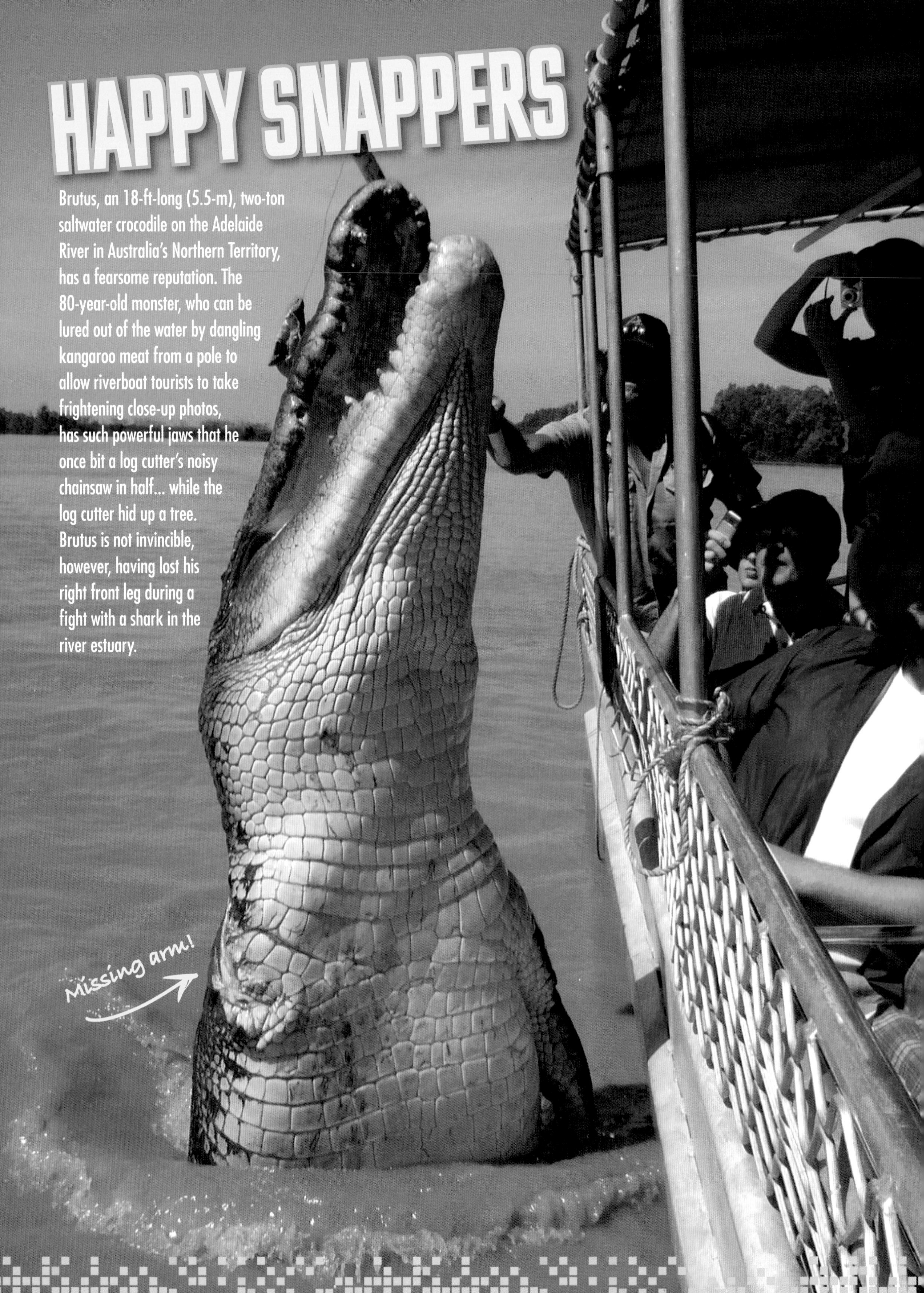

Brutus, an 18-ft-long (5.5-m), two-ton saltwater crocodile on the Adelaide River in Australia's Northern Territory, has a fearsome reputation. The 80-year-old monster, who can be lured out of the water by dangling kangaroo meat from a pole to allow riverboat tourists to take frightening close-up photos, has such powerful jaws that he once bit a log cutter's noisy chainsaw in half... while the log cutter hid up a tree. Brutus is not invincible, however, having lost his right front leg during a fight with a shark in the river estuary.

CONFUSED CAT Overcoming her natural tendencies, a female cat named Niu Niu acted as a mother to 30 newborn chicks. Her owner, farmer Lao Yang of Suibin County, China, was amazed to see the cat licking, embracing and playing with the chicks, who responded by following her everywhere.

BEST BUDDIES

In a real-life version of Timon and Simba from the movie *The Lion King*, Marcell Tournier's pet meerkat Bob cuddles up to Zinzi the lion cub at his home in Sun City, South Africa. Zinzi was rescued by safari-park owner Marcell after being abandoned by her mother, and she and Bob have since become inseparable.

> AIRPLANES IN THE U.S.A. COLLIDE WITH AN AVERAGE OF ONE ALLIGATOR A YEAR ON RUNWAYS.

BEST FRIENDS A mynah bird and a dog have become so inseparable that their owner has built a special perch for the bird that can be attached to the dog and enables them to go for walks together. Qiao Yu of Shandong Province, China, says the mynah combs the dog's fur and plucks fleas off it, while the dog responds by barking loudly whenever someone goes near the bird.

POOPED PARK A campground in Cornwall, England, faced a $15,000 clean-up bill in February 2011 after a huge flock comprising tens of thousands of starlings covered it in a layer of bird droppings that was 7 in (18 cm) deep in places.

UNINVITED GUEST After floodwaters receded from her home in Parauapebas, Brazil, in February 2011, a woman was shocked to find an alligator behind the couch in the living room—and her three-year-old son happily patting the 5-ft-long (1.5-m) reptile on the head.

LONG CAT Stewie, a five-year-old Maine Coon cat owned by Robin Hendrickson and Erik Brandsness of Reno, Nevada, measures more than 4 ft (1.2 m) long from the tip of his nose to the tip of his tail.

TRACTOR LOVE For more than three years, a swan in the grounds of a luxury hotel in Velen, Germany, has been madly in love with a big blue tractor and follows the vehicle around wherever it goes. The swan—named Schwani—also finds diggers and machines on the building site next door interesting. Animal behaviorists believe the bird probably had contact with machines as a cygnet and therefore sees the tractor as a likely mate.

Rainbow Chicks

Chickens are dyed with artificial coloring to make them more appealing to buyers at a market in Semarang, Central Java, Indonesia.

PANDA SUITS

To prepare captive-born giant panda cubs for life in the wild, keepers at the panda conservation centers in western China dress up in fluffy black-and-white panda costumes. They wear the suits whenever approaching the cubs so that the pandas have only minimum contact with humans. Here, baby panda Tao Tao is being transferred to a large wilderness area where it is planned he and his captive-bred mother, Cao Cao, will start their reintegration into the wild.

SKINNY SCAVENGERS Hagfish are primitive, tubelike scavengers that eat using their skin. On finding a carcass on the ocean floor, the hagfish burrows into the dead body, where it not only uses its mouth to eat, but also absorbs nutrients through its skin and gills.

BLIND SHEEPDOG Liz Edwards, a farmer in Cheshire, England, bought Jack, a sheepdog that was so good at his job it took several months for her to realize the dog had gone blind. "He's such an inspiration," she said. "He carried on as if nothing had happened. He must have had our farm mapped out in his head. He knows exactly where everything is." She discovered he had lost vision in both eyes only when he ran straight into a wooden peg sticking out of the ground.

MUCUS COCOON Some species of parrotfish spend up to an hour each night preparing a cocoon of mucus, which they wrap around themselves like a sleeping bag.

DOLPHIN SCAN Tapeko, a female bottlenose dolphin, had her pregnancy confirmed by undergoing a human-style ultrasound scan at Brookfield Zoo, Illinois. The dolphin was happy to float belly-up for the scan—in return for a fish reward.

NATURAL PRAWN KILLERS The Mantis shrimp of the Indian and Pacific oceans has a sting as powerful as a shot from a .22-caliber bullet. They kill prey by dismembering or spearing it with their claws, but can also stun it with their fearsome sting.

SAVIOR LILLY After suffering a bad epileptic fit, Nathan Cooper of Bournemouth, England, came close to death—but was saved by his cat Lilly, who alerted Nathan's parents. She can detect the weekly fits her owner experiences before they happen, and once resuscitated him by licking his mouth. Experts think cats' and dogs' acute sense of smell helps them detect minute chemical changes within the human body prior to a fit.

JURY SERVICE Tabby Sal the cat was summoned to do jury service in Boston, Massachusetts, even after his owner Anna Esposito told the court he was "unable to speak and understand English" and was "a domestic short-haired neutered feline."

THE LARGEST JELLYFISH EVER CAUGHT HAD TENTACLES 120 FT (36 M) LONG!

GATOR DRAG Ten-year-old Michael Dasher of Rockledge, Florida, dragged a live alligator, measuring 5 ft 9 in (1.8 m) in length, home from a nearby canal. The boy was fishing with friends when the alligator snapped at the line and ran at him. He hit it with sticks and jumped on its back before dragging it home, suffering just minor scratches on his arms and hands.

Giant Croc

A huge saltwater crocodile weighing more than a ton is thought to be the largest specimen ever captured. The 21-ft-long (6.4-m) monster weighed 2,370 lb (1,075 kg), that's well over a ton, and had been hunted by villagers in the Philippines for nearly a month following a spate of attacks on humans and animals. It may have eaten a farmer who went missing in July 2011, along with several water buffaloes near the town of Bunawan, where the head of a 12-year-old girl was also bitten off by a crocodile in 2009. The record-breaking croc was so big that it took 30 local men to secure its capture, and its enormous size means that it could fit three men inside it at once.

WEIRD RECORD • RIPLEY'S WEIRD RECORD • RIPLEY'S WEIRD RECORD

LARGEST CROC EVER CAPTURED

WEIRD RECORD • RIPLEY'S WEIRD RECORD • RIPLEY'S WEIRD RECORD

Ripley's Research

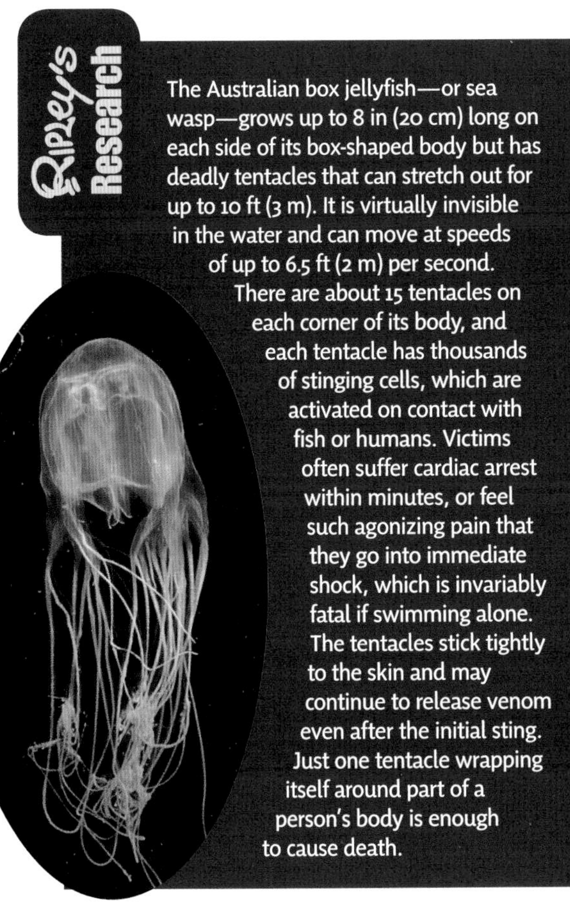

The Australian box jellyfish—or sea wasp—grows up to 8 in (20 cm) long on each side of its box-shaped body but has deadly tentacles that can stretch out for up to 10 ft (3 m). It is virtually invisible in the water and can move at speeds of up to 6.5 ft (2 m) per second. There are about 15 tentacles on each corner of its body, and each tentacle has thousands of stinging cells, which are activated on contact with fish or humans. Victims often suffer cardiac arrest within minutes, or feel such agonizing pain that they go into immediate shock, which is invariably fatal if swimming alone. The tentacles stick tightly to the skin and may continue to release venom even after the initial sting. Just one tentacle wrapping itself around part of a person's body is enough to cause death.

Jellyfish Survivor

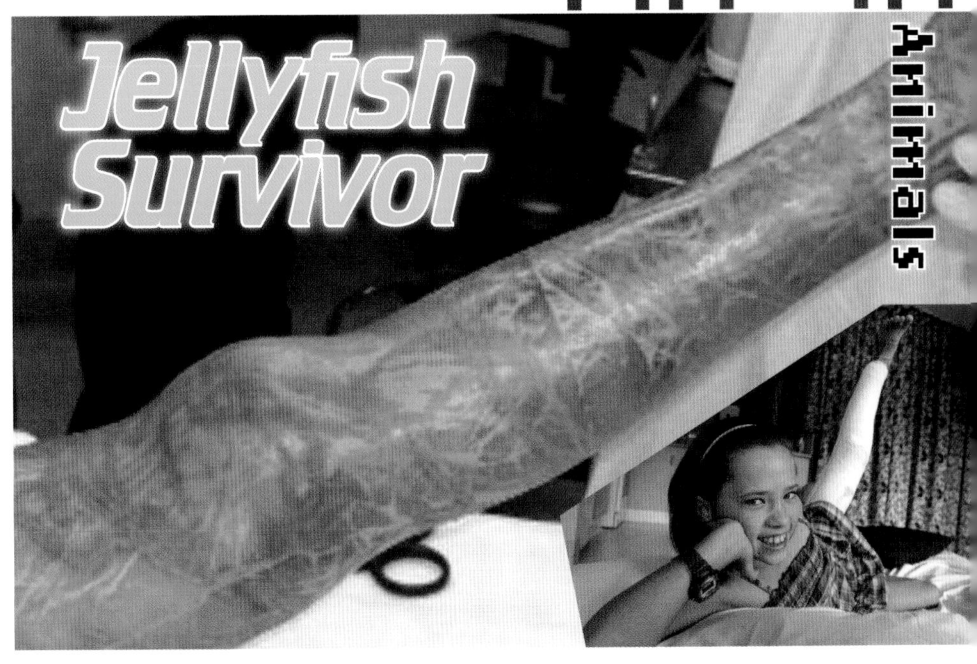

Ten-year-old Rachael Shardlow is the first person known to have survived an extensive sting from a box jellyfish—one of the world's most venomous creatures. She was stung while swimming in the Calliope River, Queensland, Australia, and after her brother pulled her from the water, she fell unconscious with the jellyfish's lethal tentacles still strapped to her limbs. Rachael required six weeks of hospital treatment before being allowed home.

SECRET DRINKER After checking the plumbing of hot tubs that appeared to have been leaking water, workers at the Etali Safari Lodge in North West Province, South Africa, discovered the culprit wasn't in fact a water leak—but actually a thirsty elephant. They nicknamed the elephant "Troublesome."

LONG-DISTANCE SWIM A migrating humpback whale swam 6,200 mi (10,000 km) from Brazil to Madagascar—a quarter of the way around the world. She was spotted off the coast of Brazil in 1999 and just over two years later, identified by the distinctive markings on her tail, she was seen in the Indian Ocean off the East coast of Madagascar.

SELF-SUFFICIENT The spiny-shelled species of deep-sea snail, *Alviniconcha hessleri*, lives near geothermal vents and gets its food from bacteria that live within its own gills.

SNAKE ISLAND Although Shedao Island, China, covers only 180 acres (73 ha), it is home to over 15,000 poisonous pit vipers.

Gargantua the Great was billed as "the world's most terrifying living creature" and was described by noted journalist Heywood Broun as "the fiercest looking thing I have ever seen on two legs." An African lowland gorilla, he was said to be the largest gorilla ever exhibited, weighing some 600 lb (272 kg)—a whopping 160 lb (72 kg) heavier than the average lowland gorilla.

Gargantua was captured as a baby in the Belgian Congo in the late 1920s and given to a sea captain as a pet. He traveled with the captain and was popular with the crew until a drunken sailor threw acid in his face on the voyage from Africa to the U.S.A. The attack not only left him with a scarred face, it also made him increasingly aggressive.

Unable to cope with him, the captain presented the young gorilla to eccentric animal lover Gertrude Lintz who cared for sick creatures in Brooklyn, New York. She named him buddy and nursed him back to health, including chewing his food for him, and even arranging for plastic surgery on his scar, leaving him with a permanent sneer. She used to drive around Brooklyn with the gorilla, dressed in clothes, in the passenger seat. However, one night a thunderstorm panicked Buddy, who smashed his way out of his cage and went looking for his "mother" for comfort. By then he weighed about 460 lb (209 kg), so Mrs. Lintz sold him to the Ringling Bros. and Barnum & Bailey Circus for $10,000 in 1938. At the circus, Buddy was renamed Gargantua the Great on account of his size and mean disposition and went on to become its star attraction. Visitors were not allowed to go near his cage because, with a reach of 5 ft (1.5 m), he could grab people to whom he took a dislike. The most feared ape in the Western world, Gargantua died of pneumonia in 1949.

Gargantua the Gorilla, with his trademark sneer, which was the result of plastic surgery to repair acid-burn scars on his face.

A circus poster advertising the spectacle of the enormous gorilla

Gargantua was fed a host of medicines to keep him healthy during winter

TWO-HEADED SNAKE

Beating odds of more than 10,000 to one, a two-headed albino Honduran milk snake was hatched by a Florida conservation group. A few days later, the snake's right head ate its first meal—a small mouse—while the left head watched.

X-ray showing where the snake's spines are fused together

CAPTIVE ANIMAL STARS

Jumbo the elephant

Standing 11 ft 6 in (3.5 m) tall and weighing 6.5 tons, Jumbo was the star attraction at England's London Zoo for 17 years. He was sold in 1882 to the Barnum & Bailey Circus in the U.S.A. for $10,000, prompting outrage from the British public. He died three years later, hit by a train while trying to lead a younger elephant to safety.

Chi Chi the giant panda

When she arrived at London Zoo from China in 1958, Chi Chi was the only giant panda in the Western world and a source of great curiosity. She inspired the World Wildlife Fund logo, but repeated attempts to get her to mate with Moscow Zoo's giant panda, An An, failed.

Clarence the cross-eyed lion

TV producer Ivan Tors discovered Clarence, a cross-eyed lion, at "Africa U.S.A.," a wildlife park in Soledad Canyon, California. The gentle beast went on to star in his own 1965 movie Clarence the Cross-Eyed Lion *and the TV series* Daktari.

Congo the chimpanzee

A chimpanzee at London Zoo from 1954 to 1964, Congo was a talented artist and had completed 400 paintings by the age of four. Pablo Picasso was a fan of Congo's work and hung one of the chimp's paintings on his studio wall.

Bart the Kodiak bear

Trained in Utah by Doug and Lynne Seus, Bart was a male Alaskan Kodiak bear, standing 9 ft 6 in (2.9 m) tall and weighing 1,500 lb (680 kg), who appeared in several movies—opposite the likes of Brad Pitt, Alec Baldwin and Anthony Hopkins. Bart died in 2000 at age 23 while filming the documentary Growing Up Grizzly.

NEW EYES When seeing-eye dog Edward lost his eyesight, he got his own seeing-eye dog! Edward the Labrador had helped partially sighted Graham Waspe of Suffolk, England, for six years but then suffered glaucoma and had to have both eyes removed. So another dog, two-year-old Opal, joined the family and now helps both Graham and Edward to get around.

CHATTY CHIMP Kanzi, a mature bonobo ape, has a vocabulary of around 450 words, up to 40 of which he uses daily. Dr. Sue Savage-Rumbaugh of Des Moines, Iowa, has taught Kanzi to "speak" by pointing at different symbols on a computer.

FOUR-FOOTED DUCK A duck born in China's Guangxi Province had three legs and four feet. Behind its normal two legs, the duckling had a third leg with two feet, probably the result of a genetic mutation.

RAIN ALLERGY Researchers in the remote mountain forests of Burma have discovered a species of snub-nosed monkey that sneezes whenever it rains. To avoid getting rainwater in its upturned nose, the monkey spends wet days sitting with its head between its knees.

TITANIUM TEETH Axel, a prison guard dog from Melbourne, Australia, was fitted with titanium teeth after losing his real ones when they shattered as he bit into a bed board.

MINI MARVEL Weighing just 2½ lb (1.1 kg), Nancy the Chihuahua has a natural talent for herding sheep several times her size. Owner Ali Taylor says that Britain's tiniest sheep dog learned her trade from watching border collies in action.

HIGH LIFE During construction of the Shard skyscraper in London, England, a fox was found living on the 72nd floor—944 ft (290 m) above the ground. The animal entered the building through a central stairwell before climbing to the top, where for over two weeks it lived on scraps left behind by builders.

BIG MOUTH Owing to its loosely hinged mouth, a gulper eel can swallow prey with a volume ten times the size of its own body.

SMOKING CHIMP A chimpanzee that became addicted to smoking cigarettes died in 2010 at age 52—ten years longer than the life expectancy of an average chimp. Charlie the Smoking Chimp picked up the unhealthy habit from visitors to Manguang Zoo, near Bloemfontein, South Africa, who threw him lit cigarettes through the bars of his enclosure.

RABBIT HEATING Up to 6,000 nuisance rabbits in Stockholm, Sweden, are culled each year and taken to an incinerator in Karlskoga where their carcasses are burned and processed for biofuel to heat nearby homes.

Pugs Might Fly

On August 15, 2011, in the skies above California, Otis the skydiving pug made his 64th jump with his master, veteran skydiver Will DaSilva. Otis has been skydiving in a special tandem harness with his owner for more than nine years and seems to love every minute of the ride.

CAT IN A VAT

Ksyusha, a white-haired Himalayan kitten, can somehow squeeze herself into a small glass jar. Her owner, Yuriy Korotun of Moscow, Russia, says the kitten—nicknamed "Mewdini"—loves to curl up in confined spaces but always manages to escape unharmed.

DIVING GEAR Gannets dive headfirst into the sea at speeds of up to 90 mph (145 km/h) and can reach depths of 30 ft (9 m) below the water surface. To withstand the impact as they hit the water, the birds have extra-thick skulls that act as crash helmets, as well as throat pouches that inflate like little airbags to protect their bodies during the plunge.

WORKING MONKEYS Two baby monkeys, Nehime and Rakan, work as station masters at Hojomachi station on the Hojo railway line in Japan's Hyogo Prefecture in an attempt to boost visitors to the rail line. The monkeys wear special blue uniforms and miniature hats.

NATURAL DAREDEVILS To avoid predators, barnacle geese build nests high on mountain cliffs—and at just three days old, the tiny goslings must jump from nests as far up as 300 ft (90 m) to reach food on the ground.

KEEP AWAY Mandrill monkeys have leaned how to perform sign language to tell other group members to keep away. They place one hand loosely over their eyes, but with their fingers parted slightly so that they can still see. While the hand is in place, the other mandrills at Colchester Zoo, England, keep their distance.

CLEAN SWEEP A golden retriever uses a specially made small broom to sweep the streets of Changchun, Jilin Province, China, while walking with his owner Xu Ming. The dog takes the broom everywhere and, under Xu's instructions, runs in a zigzag pattern to sweep away dust and debris.

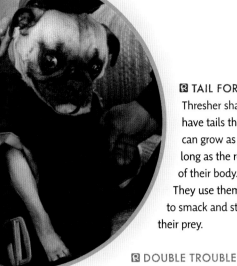

TAIL FORCE Thresher sharks have tails that can grow as long as the rest of their body. They use them to smack and stun their prey.

DOUBLE TROUBLE Oscar the Labrador and his 53-year-old master both survived with just broken bones after plunging 200 ft (60 m) over the edge of a cliff in North Yorkshire, England. After Oscar fell off the cliff, his owner was desperately trying to work out how to reach his pet when a strong gust of wind blew him over the edge, too.

DANGEROUS DANCE As part of their courtship ritual, pairs of bald eagles perform a cartwheel dance, soaring high into the air, locking their talons together, then spinning out of control toward the ground, breaking off at the very last second to fly upward again.

VERSATILE SWIMMER The black ghost knifefish, found in the rivers of South America, is able to swim forward or backward equally well and navigates by emitting a small electric charge.

MAIL MISERY Toby, a Jack Russell terrier belonging to Gill Bird of Hampshire, England, chewed up his owner's mail—and the combination of the envelope glue and wet paper glued his mouth shut.

FISH OUT OF WATER A 1-ft-long (30-cm) sturgeon dropped at night from the sky (probably by a heron) on a lawn in Worcester, England, was found the next morning, having survived thanks to the moisture on the grass.

DANCING DOLPHINS Wild dolphins are teaching themselves to "walk" using their tails on the ocean surface. Researchers in Australia say dolphins have developed the art of tail-walking, which seems to have no practical use and has been compared to dancing in humans.

GATOR SNATCH After a 6-ft-long (1.8-m) alligator snatched his Jack Russell terrier Lizabeth while walking along the Hillsborough River in Tampa, Florida, Tom Martino fired shots into the water to force the reptile to release the dog. He then performed CPR on Lizabeth until she started breathing again.

TOMBSTONING MONKEYS

Mimicking the human tombstoning craze of jumping from great heights into water, these thrill-seeking macaques in Jaipur, India, climb a 12-ft-high (3.6-m) lamppost and then hurl themselves into a shallow trough of water—apparently just for fun. Even a ring of barbed wire around the lamppost could not stop their crazy antics. Macaques have also been seen jumping from 9-ft (2.7-m) rocks into the sea off Thailand and are one of the few primates that are not scared of water.

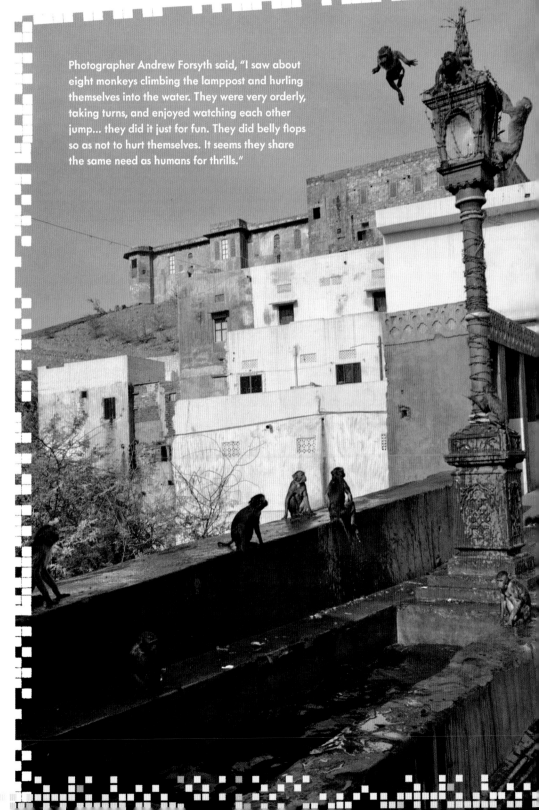

Photographer Andrew Forsyth said, "I saw about eight monkeys climbing the lamppost and hurling themselves into the water. They were very orderly, taking turns, and enjoyed watching each other jump... they did it just for fun. They did belly flops so as not to hurt themselves. It seems they share the same need as humans for thrills."

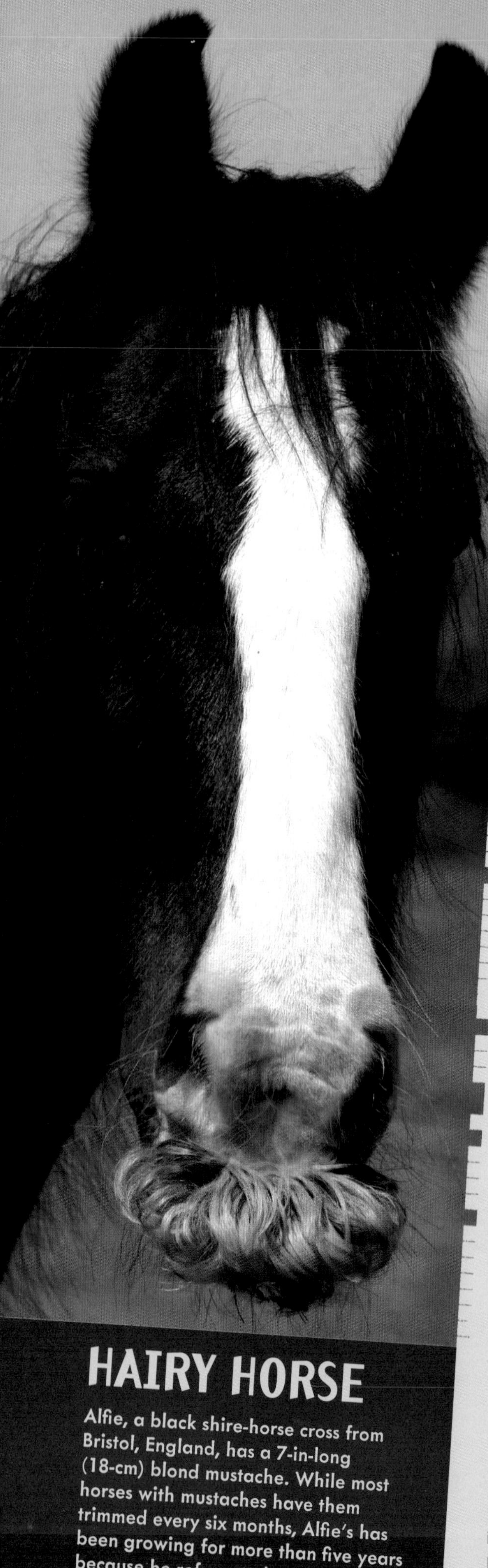

HAIRY HORSE

Alfie, a black shire-horse cross from Bristol, England, has a 7-in-long (18-cm) blond mustache. While most horses with mustaches have them trimmed every six months, Alfie's has been growing for more than five years because he refuses to let the stable hands get close enough to shave it off.

SWEET REVENGE Oystercatcher birds have bladelike beaks for prying open shellfish—but sometimes their prey does get the better of them, holding their beaks in place until the birds drown.

SHORT LEGS The Munchkin breed of cats has a mutation that gives it short legs and a stature similar to dachshund or corgi dogs. Although short-legged cats were known in the early 20th century, the breed was not rediscovered until 1983 when Louisiana music teacher Sandra Hochenedel found two pregnant cats. Half of the kittens in one litter were short-legged, and today's Munchkin cats are descended from that line.

BIRD RESCUE When his pet dog carried a limp goose that had been hit by a car into the yard of his home in Urumchi, China, Yu Yanping thought the dog would eat it. Instead, the dog licked the bird until it recovered, and the two went on to become inseparable, feeding from the same bowl and even sharing the dog's kennel.

STOWAWAY KITTEN Amy Bindman of Calgary, Canada, found a kitten in a shipping container sent from China. It had survived being sealed away without food or water for nearly 45 days.

ROBBERS ATTACKED Two armed robbers who held up a tobacco store in Altadena, California, fled after being attacked by the owner's pet Chihuahua. Little Paco refused to be intimidated even when one of the robbers pointed a shotgun at him, and chased the men out of the shop and down the street.

HORSE FALL A horse stumbled through an open window and landed in the basement of her owners' home in Elbert County, Colorado. It took rescue teams four hours to get the mare—named Summer—out of the house.

SPEEDING HORSE A police roadside camera designed to catch speeding drivers in Meppen, Germany, caught something different on film in July 2011—a runaway horse. The horse had escaped from a paddock and galloped off down a busy main road into the town. The speeding driver who triggered the picture pleaded to be excused the automatic fine because he claimed he was simply trying to get away from the horse.

VULTURE ARRESTED Finding a griffon vulture in Hyaal, Saudi Arabia, carrying a GPS transmitter and a tag from Tel Aviv University, Saudi security services held the bird in custody on suspicion of spying for the Israeli intelligence agency Mossad. However, wildlife experts pointed out that the vulture was simply part of a migration study and the bird was eventually released without charge.

COLD COMFORT When the Arctic ground squirrel goes into hibernation during long Arctic winters, its body temperature drops below the freezing point of water to 26.4°F (–3°C). Scientists have yet to discover another mammal that survives with such a low body temperature.

HOUND HOTEL Alongside its normal rooms for human guests, the Riverside Hotel in Evesham, England, has three dog suites that provide luxury accommodation for pets. Dogs staying there can feast from a special canine menu, swim in a spa pool and have their portrait done.

CONSTANT COMPANIONS Jane Hartley of Loughborough, England, loves her pet parrots Fiz and Buzz so much that she takes them shopping, cycling, walking and even skiing. The small birds sit on her hand while she cycles, and nestle in her pocket as she hurtles down Alpine mountains during skiing vacations.

OCTOPUS SPRAY A common octopus at an aquarium in England has been called Squirt because he deliberately aims a jet of water at visitors. The inquisitive octopus learned to lift the top part of his body above the water in his tank so that he could look around and then realized that if he breathed out while he was doing it, he could fire a stream of water like a hose. Octopuses draw water into their body to absorb the oxygen from it and then pass it out again through special tubes alongside their beak.

ROTTEN LOOK *Nimbochromis livingstonii*, a fish found in Africa's Lake Malawi, has the blotchy appearance of a rotting fish and lies motionless on the lakebed to attract the scavengers on which it preys.

SPIN CYCLE An eight-week-old kitten named Princess survived an hour-long spin in a washing machine after creeping unnoticed into the drum. It was only when her owner, Susan Gordon of Aberdeen, Scotland, was removing the clean items from the machine that she spotted the sodden kitten.

BUNNY CART The O'Rourke family of Tucson, Arizona, discovered an abandoned baby rabbit in their garden that could not use his hind legs. They built a little cart on wheels and strapped it to the rabbit's rear so that he no longer had to drag his legs behind him.

HOURGLASS FIGURE Debbie Pearson of New Orleans, Louisiana, cares for a turtle that grew with a plastic ring from a milk jug around the middle of its shell. When it was a tiny hatchling, it crawled into the ring which proceeded to grow around it so that its shell now resembles a figure eight.

RESCUE CENTER Ha Wenjin gave up her job and sold her house, car and jewelry to adopt more than 1,500 stray dogs at her rescue center in Nanjing, China. She employs 12 people to care for the dogs and to look after 200 adopted cats at a second center nearby.

SLEEPY BIRD

After eating a hearty meal of ants, a green woodpecker appears to have been caught dozing against the branch of this tree in Worcestershire, England.

TO KEEP FROM DRIFTING AWAY FROM EACH OTHER, SEA OTTERS HOLD PAWS WHILE THEY SLEEP.

WIDE WINGS Queen Alexandra's Birdwing—a butterfly found only in Papua New Guinea—can grow to have a 1-ft-long (30-cm) wingspan.

BODY HEAT Sea otters lack blubber to insulate themselves, so they must eat up to one-quarter of their body weight every day in order to generate enough heat to keep warm.

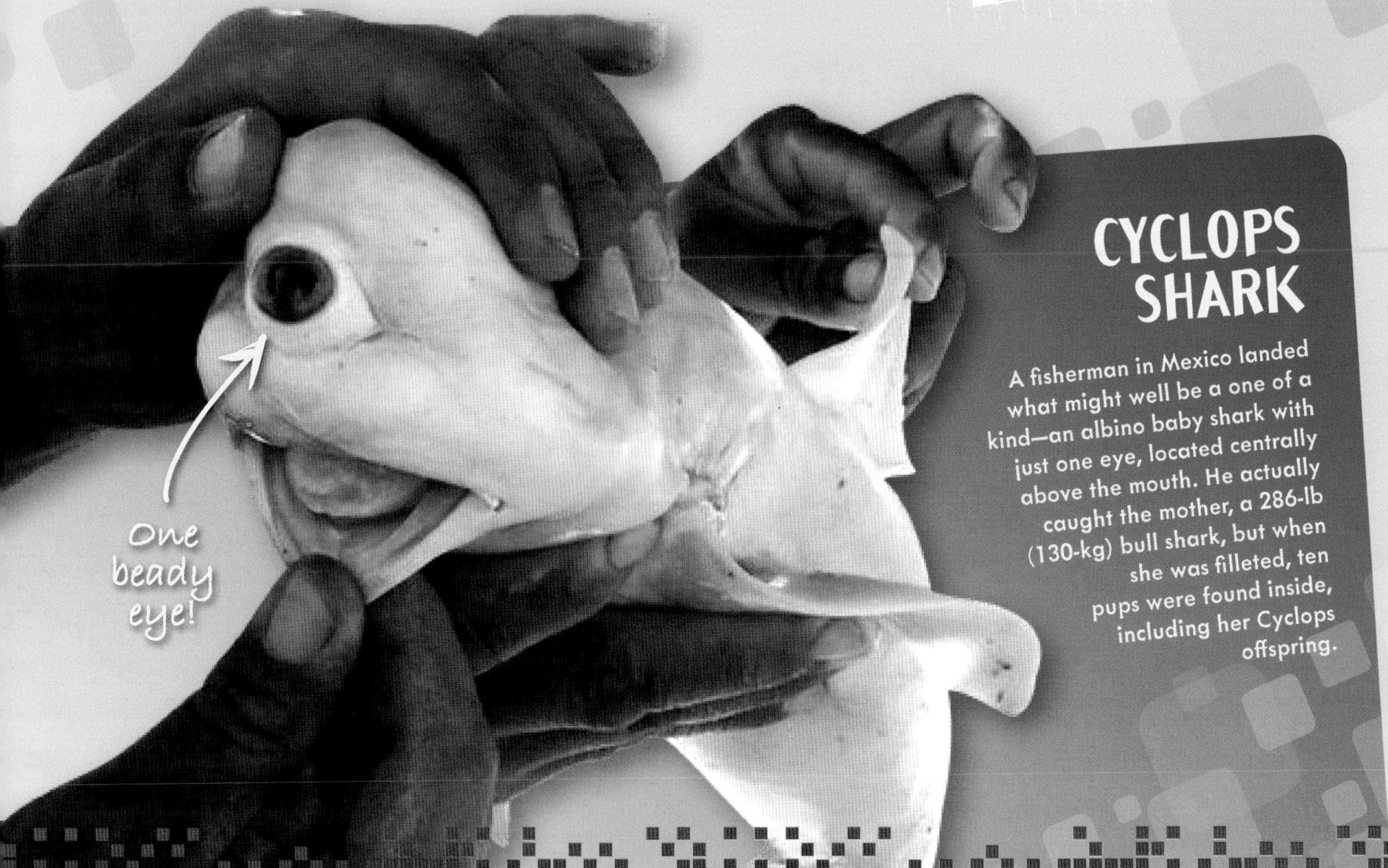

One beady eye!

CYCLOPS SHARK

A fisherman in Mexico landed what might well be a one of a kind—an albino baby shark with just one eye, located centrally above the mouth. He actually caught the mother, a 286-lb (130-kg) bull shark, but when she was filleted, ten pups were found inside, including her Cyclops offspring.

TATTOOED FISH

Tattooed goldfish are sold at a pet market in Changchun, China, for around $12 each. Laser-inscribed decorations on the fish include flowery patterns and the Chinese characters for sentiments such as "wealth," "longevity" and "happiness." Personalized messages are also available.

KEYCHAIN CREATURES

Live fish, tiny tortoises and young giant salamanders, all sealed in plastic pouches, are sold as keychains at a roadside stall in Beijing, China. The vendor says that a special liquid inside the pouches provides all the necessary oxygen and nutrients for the creatures.

HIDDEN MENACE People swam about in a public pool in Darwin, Australia, unaware that a 20-in (50-cm) baby saltwater crocodile was lurking in the deep end. The reptile, which was thought to be a rubber toy until it tried to bite a handler, was rescued and released back into the wild.

REINDEER REFLECTIONS In an attempt to reduce the number of car crashes that kill around 500 reindeer each year in Norway, 2,000 of the animals were fitted with reflective yellow collars or small antler tags, making them more visible in the dark.

FISHY TALE Two goldfish survived 134 days without food or electricity to power their tank filter following the 2011 earthquake in Christchurch, New Zealand. Shaggy and Daphne—named after *Scooby Doo* characters—spent over four months left unattended in an accountants' reception area, but pulled through by eating algae growing on the side of the tank.

DRUNKEN OWL A brown owl was spotted sitting by the side of a busy road in Pforzheim, Germany, seemingly oblivious to passing traffic. The feathery friend did not appear to be injured, but one of its eyelids was drooping noticeably. Looking around, police found two empty bottles of Schnapps nearby and realized that in fact the bird was drunk. So the police took the owl into custody and gave it plenty of water until it sobered up.

SHAGGY DOG STORY

Norman, a shaggy Briard dog owned by the Cobb family of Canton, Georgia, has been riding a scooter since he was a puppy. He balances on the scooter unaided with his front paws resting over the handlebars while he pushes himself along using his hind leg. Videos of his tricks have been a massive hit on YouTube, and he even has his own Facebook page.

ODD SCAN

COPYCAT SQUIRREL Jim Watkins of Carthage, Mississippi, rescued a stranded baby squirrel that his pet cat and her kittens then adopted. The squirrel soon learned how to purr for affection like a cat.

ALBINO ACTORS Showbiz manager Tom Beser has set up the world's first acting agency for albino animals. From his base in Rheinfelden, Germany, he leases his collection of albino creatures—including lizards, minks and a raccoon—to moviemakers for films and TV commercials.

CRACKING CROWS Crows in Japan have been seen placing walnuts on roads, waiting for cars to drive over them to crack open the shells, and then flying back to feast on the nuts' contents.

ANCIENT TORTOISE Jonathan, a giant tortoise on the South Atlantic island of St. Helena, is at least 178 years old. His life has spanned eight British monarchs and 37 U.S. Presidents, yet he still has the energy to mate with three younger females. The St. Helena five-pence coin has a picture of Jonathan on its reverse.

MIMICKING MOM A keeper at China's Wuhan Zoo has to wear a black-and-white-striped T-shirt every day to persuade a newborn, orphaned zebra that he is its mother. Chen Nong realized that whenever he wore black and white the baby zebra became excited, and soon it would take milk from him only if he wore that zebralike shirt.

VEIRD RECORD • RIPLEY'S WEIRD RECORD • RIPLEY'S WEIRD RECORD

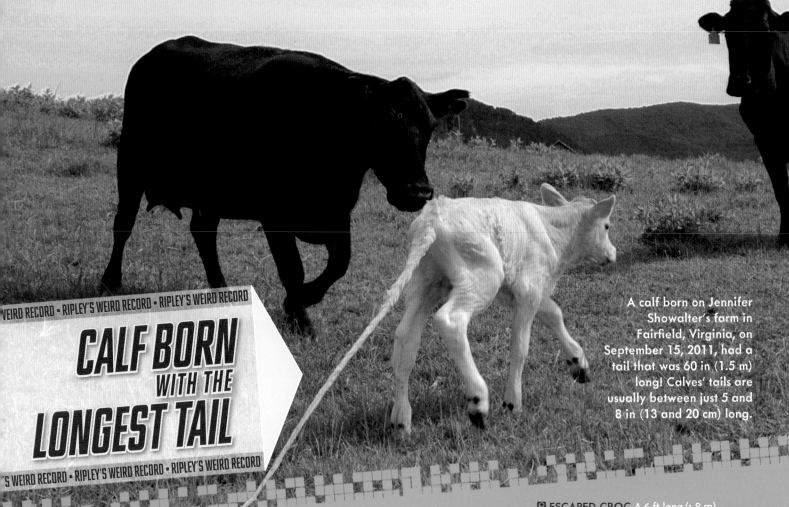

CALF BORN WITH THE LONGEST TAIL

'S WEIRD RECORD • RIPLEY'S WEIRD RECORD • RIPLEY'S WEIRD RECORD

A calf born on Jennifer Showalter's farm in Fairfield, Virginia, on September 15, 2011, had a tail that was 60 in (1.5 m) long! Calves' tails are usually between just 5 and 8 in (13 and 20 cm) long.

TWO-HEADED TORTOISE Magdalena, a tortoise owned by Roman Gresak from Zilina, Slovakia, has two heads and five legs. Each of the heads has its own nerve system and the tortoise has two brains, which work independently of each other, meaning that sometimes the second head wants to go in a different direction to the first!

COLOR CHANGE *Rhacophorus penanorum*, a species of tiny frog that lives on the island of Borneo, has bright green skin at night but changes color to brown by day—and its eyes match it by changing color, too.

FIVE EARS A cat named Luntya, found wandering the streets of Voronezh, Russia, has five ears. She has two normal ears, two extra ears turned at an angle of 180 degrees and a tiny fifth ear.

SMALL COW Swallow, an 11-year-old cow owned by Caroline Ryder of West Yorkshire, England, stands only 33 in (84 cm) tall at the shoulder, making her shorter than most sheep.

ESCAPED CROC A 6-ft-long (1.8-m) crocodile that was taken by a photographer to Lake Shira, Siberia, to pose for pictures with tourists caused panic when it escaped into the water, terrifying hundreds of swimmers. The reptile bolted for freedom while the photographer was haggling with tourists over the price of a souvenir photo.

COW BEDS Dairy farmers in Norway are required by law to provide a place for their cows to lie down—such as rubber mattresses.

ORANGE FLOCK After losing 200 of his sheep to rustlers, farmer John Heard from Devon, England, took drastic action—he painted his entire flock orange. The harmless dip of orange dye made the sheep so visible that thieves left them alone.

ORANGE CROC

Snappy, an 8-ft-long (2.4-m) saltwater crocodile that lives in captivity in Geelong, Australia, suddenly turned orange. He chewed water pipes in his tank, damaging the filter, which caused pH levels in the water to rise and red algae to form. The combination of the two prompted his startling change in color. He is expected to return to a more crocodilian green over time. Tracey Sandstrom, Snappy's keeper, said, "There's no change in his behavior, his aggression or his territorialism. He's still a really nasty crocodile."

Two-faced Cat

Despite being born with two faces, two mouths, two noses and three eyes, Frank and Louie, a cat owned by Marty Stevens of Worcester, Massachusetts, has set a world record by living to the age of 12. Most Janus cats—named after a Roman god with two faces—fail to survive, often because their two mouths cause them to choke. However, although both of Frank and Louie's noses work, only one mouth does. The nonfunctioning mouth isn't connected to his sole esophagus, meaning that he can't eat with it. Frank and Louie has a single brain, meaning both faces react simultaneously.

Tiny Puppy

Believe It or Not, these Viszla puppies, born in Xuzhou, China, are siblings of the same age. Dwarfed by its normal-sized brother, after 18 days the smaller puppy was still barely more than an inch (2.5 cm) long, and weighed under half an ounce (14 g).

A HELPING PAW Sandie, a Sheltie-collie and Staffordshire bull terrier cross, has performed countless jobs for her disabled owner Sue Line of Coventry, England, including doing the shopping, the laundry and paying for the groceries. On trips to the store, Sandie puts the shopping in a bag, which she carries in her mouth, and at the checkout she can take money from Sue's purse and hand it to the sales clerk. Sandie loads the washing machine, separating the dirty clothes into light and dark piles, and locks the machine door before the cycle begins. She has also learned how to unlock the kitchen door to let herself out to the toilet—and always remembers to close it behind her on her way back.

PRIZE PIGLET A court in Primorye, Russia, seized a woman's piglet in October 2010 to pay her overdue debt after it was judged that the animal was her most valuable possession.

SHOW-JUMPING COW Regina Mayer from Laufen, Germany, has trained a cow on the family farm to jump fences like a horse. Denied a horse by her parents, teen Regina fulfilled her riding ambitions by spending hours training Luna the cow to get accustomed to having a rider on her back and to wearing a halter and saddle. Luna now understands commands such as "go," "stand" and "gallop."

NOSE FOR WINE With a nose that is 2,000 times more sensitive than a human's, bloodhound Louisa Bella has been trained as a wine tester by her owners, wine label proprietors Michelle Edwards and Daniel Fischl of Melbourne, Australia. After just two weeks of training, she could sniff out a tainted wine cork within 30 seconds.

TERRIER TERROR Sucked up by a twister that raged through Birmingham, Alabama, in April 2011, Mason, a terrier mongrel, managed to crawl back to his owners' home three weeks later despite suffering two broken front legs.

CANINE COUPLE Louise Harris of Essex, England, spent more than £20,000 on an elaborate wedding ceremony, complete with outdoor marquee, for her Yorkshire terrier Lola, and Mugly, a Chinese crested dog. On her special day, Lola wore a £1,000 wedding dress customized with 1,800 Swarovski crystals. Her outfit was adorned with a £400 pearl necklace, £250 Swarovski crystal leg cuffs and a £350 Swarovski crystal leash. The groom looked resplendent in a tuxedo before the happy couple and their canine guests wolfed down a buffet of dog-friendly cupcakes.

WILD WOOD WEB

In 2010, spiders in Pakistan's Sindh province were forced from the ground by floodwaters. The arachnids took shelter in thousands of trees and stayed for months because the water did not recede. Eventually their new homes became entirely cocooned in thick webs, which according to locals helped control the number of malaria-carrying mosquitoes in the stagnant waters.

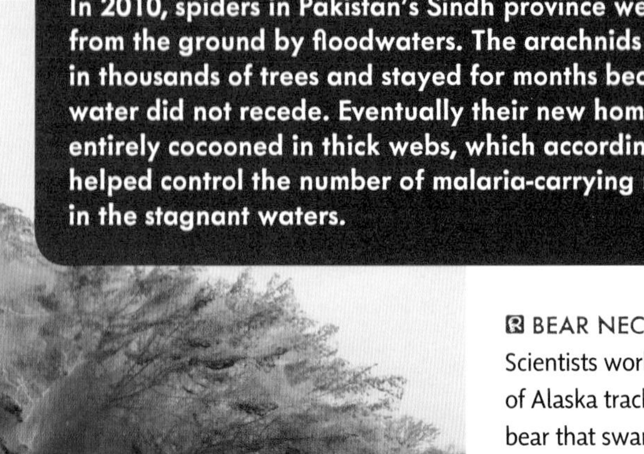

BEAR NECESSITY Scientists working north of Alaska tracked a polar bear that swam for nine days straight, 426 mi (687 km) across the Beaufort Sea to an ice floe. That's the equivalent to the distance between Washington, D.C., and Boston, Massachusetts. Polar bears have been forced to swim longer distances to reach land in areas where the sea ice is shrinking.

YOUR UPLOADS

www.ripleys.com/submit

Is it a bird? Is it a plane? No, it's the spectacular flying Chihuahua. Photographer James Holmdahl of Bend, Oregon, attaches his 5-lb (2.3-kg) dog named Daisy to a cluster of helium balloons and sees her soar into the skies at a Fourth of July Parade.

LONG JOURNEY Four months after disappearing from her home in Cornwall, England, a collie named Lucy mysteriously turned up 500 mi (800 km) away in a garden in Edinburgh, Scotland. Her owners, Sonya and Billy McKerron, made a 20-hour round trip to collect her.

SNIFFER HOGS Believe it or not, wild hogs can detect smells up to 7 mi (11 km) away and 25 ft (7.6 m) underground.

MISSING MATE Pei Pei, a male orangutan at China's Yunnan Wild Animal Park, was so distraught when his mate La Tewhen was moved to an adjoining enclosure while she was pregnant that he started digging a tunnel in the hope of being reunited with her.

POOP FOR GOLD Dog owners in New Taipei City, Taiwan, were given the chance to turn their pets' poop into gold. In an attempt to clean up the streets, anyone handing in a bag of dog poop was entered in a lucky draw, the top prize for which was $2,100 in gold bars.

SEA DOG Just Nuisance, a Great Dane from Simon's Town, South Africa, was inducted into the British Royal Navy in 1939. He never went to sea, but as an official Able Seaman he performed a number of promotional duties ashore and was once taken up in a plane to look for submarines. He was buried with full military honors in 1944 and a statue was erected in his memory. Since 2000, there has been an annual parade of Great Danes in Simon's Town from which the best look-alike is chosen.

JAWS BEACH In September 2010, a fisherman caught a tiger shark off Jaws Beach in the Bahamas and a human left leg fell from its mouth. When the shark's belly was slit open, police found a right leg, two arms and a torso, and were able to use fingerprints to identify the victim as a missing sailor. The beach was used as the location for the 1987 shark movie *Jaws: The Revenge*.

POP STAR Anastasia, a Jack Russell terrier owned by Doree Sitterly of southern California, can pop 100 balloons in 44.49 seconds—that's faster than two balloons per second.

CANINE MAYOR Lucy Lou, a border collie, was elected mayor of Rabbit Hash, Kentucky, in 2008, defeating rival political candidates that included a cat, a jackass, an opossum and several other dogs.

Dogs in Disguise

These canine competitors were participants in a creative dog-grooming competition in Pasadena, California. Creative grooming events are hugely popular in the U.S. Owners trim their poodles to resemble zebras, lions, ponies, snails, and American footballers or movie characters such as Captain Jack Sparrow from *Pirates of the Caribbean.*

TINY POLICE DOG A long-haired Chihuahua has been accepted as a police dog in Japan's Nara prefecture. Momo, who weighs just 6 lb 10 oz (3 kg), passed a search-and-rescue test by finding a person in five minutes after merely sniffing their cap. Momo specializes in rescue operations following disasters such as earthquakes, where she can squeeze her tiny body into places too small for normal rescue dogs.

WIFE ATTACKS TIGER A man who was attacked by a tiger while hunting squirrels near his home in Malaysia was saved when his 55-year-old wife began hitting the big cat over the head with a wooden soup ladle. Han Besau ran to the rescue of Tambun Gediu after hearing his screams and instinctively beat the tiger with the ladle, causing it to flee.

TORTOISE WHEEL A tortoise that lost a front leg after it was severed by a rat while she was hibernating can now outrace other tortoises thanks to a toy tractor wheel being fitted in place of the missing limb. Philip Chubb of Norwich, England, made a brace out of metal and velcro strips to fasten the wheel to the shell of Tuly the tortoise.

A TWO-HEADED CALF WAS BORN IN JANUARY 2011 IN MARTVILI, GEORGIA, THAT COULD EAT WITH BOTH ITS HEADS!

BLOOD POPSICLES To keep its tigers cool during the scorching April of 2011, London Zoo gave them special popsicles made with blood.

EEL POWER Finland's Helsinki Sea Life Center found an environmentally friendly way of powering its Christmas lights—by using an electric eel. Four plastic-encased steel probes were built to capture the eel's 650-volt discharge and filter it through to the lights, which shone particularly brightly at the eel's feeding time.

NO CONTEST In 2010, a 150-lb (68-kg) mountain lion was chased up a tree in South Dakota by Chad Strenge's Jack Russell terrier, Jack, who weighed just 17 lb (7.7 kg).

THICK FUR The furry chinchillas of South America have fur so dense that 50 hairs grow out of a single hair follicle.

SWIMMING WITH BEARS

$1.5M PUPPY A red Tibetan mastiff puppy named Hong Dong was sold for $1.5 million in 2011. Tibetan mastiffs are fierce guard dogs and are rarely found outside Tibet, which makes them highly exclusive and sought-after. Hong Dong was bred in Qingdao, China, and weighed more than 180 lb (82 kg) at 11 months.

TREE-EATING FISH A newly discovered species of armored catfish in the Amazon chews on the wood of fallen trees. Whereas other types of catfish use their teeth to scrape organic matter from the surfaces of submerged wood, this species actually ingests wood. The wood is subsequently expelled as waste, passing through the fish's body in less than four hours.

HIPPO HYGIENE At China's Shanghai Zoo, keepers use giant toothbrushes to clean the teeth of adult hippos. The hippos, whose mouths measure up to 4 ft (1.2 m) wide, are fed on fruit and vegetables, which would clog up their teeth if they weren't brushed three times a week.

WALKING UPRIGHT Treasure, a one-year-old poodle, prefers to walk upright on his hind legs rather than on all four. His owner, Dou Xianhui of Jilin City, China, briefly trained Treasure to walk on two legs when he was a puppy—but now he walks like that for up to 30 minutes at a time.

DOGGIE FACELIFTS Grandmother Amanda Booth from Melbourne, Australia, is using her life savings to pay $15,000 a year on facelifts for Shar Pei dogs to prevent them from suffering eye problems. The designer dogs are bred to have folds of floppy flesh on their face, but the heavy skin forces their eyelids to turn in, causing their eyelashes to scratch their cornea, often leading to blindness.

PIRANHA TERROR More than 15 people swimming off a popular tourist river beach in Cáceres, Brazil, lost toes and chunks of their legs and ankles in November 2011 after thousands of flesh-eating piranhas flooded the river. Piranhas are common in rivers on the outskirts of Cáceres, but this was the first time they had infiltrated the city itself.

Appearances can be deceiving. Children at the Cochrane Polar Bear Habitat in Ontario, Canada, look to be swimming right next to the most feared predators on Earth, but what you can't see is a 10-in-thick (25-cm) plexiglass barrier that separates the humans from the bears, allowing the children to swim in safety.

Diving Champions

Wildlife photographer Charlie Hamilton James has spent thousands of hours taking pictures of kingfishers from a hideout attached to his riverside cottage near Bristol, England. This stunning photograph captures a kingfisher as a vibrant flash of blue as the bird dives into the water to catch a fish. When they dive, kingfishers tuck in their wings and hit the surface of the water at speeds of up to 25 mph (40 km/h), like darts.

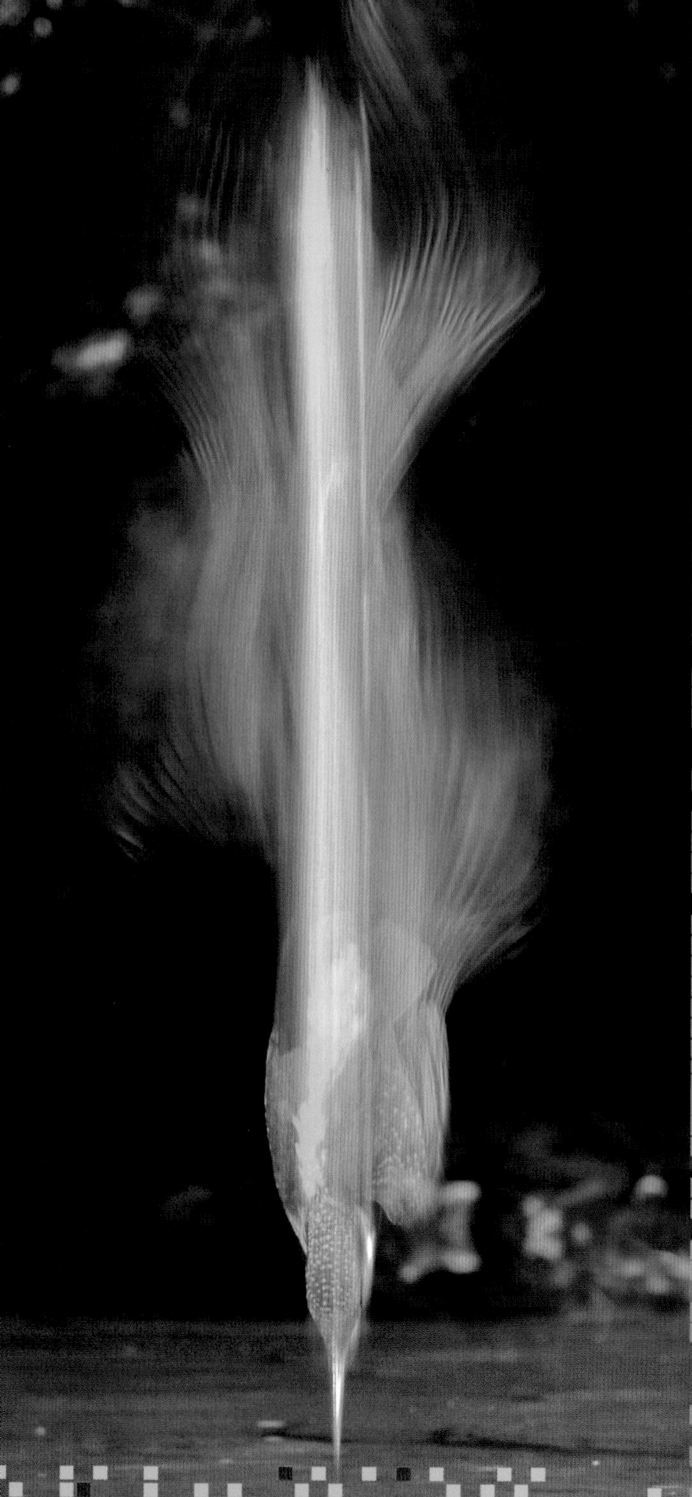

TIGHT SPOT A black bear was released back into a forest near Newport, Tennessee, after spending at least three weeks with a plastic jar stuck on its head. Before being removed by state wildlife officers, the jar had hindered the bear's attempts to feed, as a result of which the animal weighed only 115 lb (52 kg), barely half its healthy weight.

GOLD FISH Curt Carish of Kaua'i, Hawaii, caught a fish that had swallowed a gold watch—and the watch was still ticking and keeping correct time.

BIG BIRD The Newby family from Essex, England, share their home with a 6-ft-tall (1.8-m) pet emu named Beaky. The 196-lb (89-kg) bird was hatched from an egg by dad Iain, who works at an animal rescue center, and Beaky has become so much part of the family that she watches TV with them. She eats 14 lb (6.4 kg) of corn a week, 5 lb (2.3 kg) of fruit and vegetables, plus anything else she can find, including keys, sponges and drill bits.

NEW MOM A wild lynx kitten that had been abandoned by its mother was adopted by a spaniel at a wildlife park in Kadzidlowo, Poland. Kraska the spaniel, who had just given birth to a litter of puppies, readily accepted six-month-old Mis the lynx as one of her own.

GOOSE PATROL A Canada goose and her goslings were given a police escort on a Washington State highway in June 2011. Three police cars closed two lanes of traffic on the busy Seattle highway during morning rush hour while they guided the geese to the nearest exit.

UNDERWEAR THIEF Benji the pet kangaroo escaped from his owner's home in Prague, Czech Republic, and hopped through neighboring gardens collecting women's underwear from washing lines as he did so. He was caught after one victim saw him escaping with her panties.

HOSTILE HOME The most heavily armed border zone in the world—between North and South Korea—has become a refuge for the red-crowned crane, one of the rarest birds on the planet. This is because it is such a restricted area that there is very little human activity to disturb the birds.

EXTRA EARS Shun Shun, a dog in Xinjiang Province, China, has four ears. The extra ears started to grow behind the main pair when the animal was only a puppy but are now more than 4 in (10 cm) long, making them bigger than his original ears.

TIGHT FIT

A bullock in Ayrshire, Scotland, was rescued by animal charity officers after getting its head stuck between the rungs of a ladder in its field in August 2011. The Belgian blue bull was returned to its herd unharmed after the unfortunate incident.

Monkey Business

For Connie Tibbs, her five pet macaque monkeys are part of the family. They play on the trampoline in the back garden of the family home in Pekin, Illinois, join her three children in the swimming pool and even go horse riding. One monkey is so skilled that it can ride a horse unaided. Connie also takes one of the monkeys—dressed in pajamas—to bed every night, much to the amusement of her husband Steve.

Connie baths the monkeys to keep them clean and then dresses one of them in pajamas and takes it to bed with her.

Connie with her much-loved pet macaque monkeys at her home in Illinois.

Connie is so devoted to her pet monkeys that she even takes them out shopping.

BELIEVE IT OR NOT, THE TEXAS HORNED LIZARD CRIES BLOOD

This feisty lizard really pushes the envelope when it comes to warding off attackers. It forces jets of blood from its own eyes when threatened by a predator. It's possible for humans to squirt liquid from their tear ducts, but this is one step further. It can squirt its own blood, which contains an unpleasant-tasting toxin, for more than 5 ft (1.5 m). These lizards are not alone in their disturbing defense mechanisms.

South African armored crickets can not only splash blood from their insect armpits, but also vomit. The Spanish ribbed newt, on the other hand, contorts its rib bones so that they break the animal's skin and become a row of sharp, poison-tipped weapons. Fortunately, stabbing itself multiple times through its own torso does not seem to have an adverse effect on the Spanish newt.

NOISY BUG Although just 0.08 in (2 mm) long, the lesser water boatman, a pond insect that swims upside down using two long legs as paddles, produces 99.2 decibels of noise—louder than any other animal relative to its body size, and the equivalent of listening to an orchestra playing at full volume from the front row.

WONDER WEB The newly discovered Darwin's bark spider of Madagascar builds webs that cover an area of 30 sq ft (2.8 sq m) and span gaps over 80 ft (25 m) across.

ARMY OF CLONES Every insect in a nest of *Mycocepurus smithii* ants from Latin America is a clone of the queen. The species reproduces asexually from a single parent and is entirely male-free, which removes the stress of finding a mate.

RAINBOW ANTS

Dr. Mohamed Babu of Mysore, India, set up this eye-catching experiment whereby ants turned different colors after drinking sugar drops mixed with edible red, green, blue and yellow coloring. As the ant's abdomen is semi-transparent, they absorb the colors as they sip the liquid. His wife gave him the idea after showing him how ants turned white after drinking spilt milk.

DEATH MARCH Army ants that begin marching in a circle can end up marching endlessly by the thousands in the same circle until they all die from exhaustion or starvation.

MONSTER MOLARS In proportion to its body size, the deep-sea fangtooth fish has the largest teeth of any sea creature—its skull has special sockets to hold the teeth and allow it to close its mouth. The fish itself is only 6 in (15 cm) long, but its teeth can reach nearly ¾ in (2 cm) in length. If these proportions were replicated in a great white shark, it would have teeth 2 ft 6 in (76 cm) long.

STICKY PROBLEM An estimated 14 million bees got loose in July 2011 after a delivery truck carrying more than 400 hive boxes and honey overturned on a highway in Fremont County, Idaho. Trying to avoid being stung, crews worked throughout the day to remove all the honey from the road.

TRAIN CRASH On April 27, 2011, termites chewed through a tree branch that then fell onto train tracks, causing a crash in Taiwan that killed five people and injured around a hundred others.

BELLY FLOP New Zealand's Maud Island frogs don't croak, they don't have webbed feet and when they hop they land on their bellies instead of their feet.

LIGHT MEAL *Atolla wyvillei*, a deep-sea species of jellyfish, starts glowing brightly when being attacked by its prey in an attempt to attract other predators that will attack its assailant. Its glow is so bright it can be seen from 300 ft (90 m) away.

SPEED BUG The fastest species of tiger beetle can run at 5.6 mph (9 km/h), which, relative to its body length, is the equivalent of a human running at 480 mph (770 km/h)—about 17 times the speed of Usain Bolt. The beetles move so quickly that their eyes and brain are unable to process vision in sync with their movement and they momentarily go blind, needing to stop and start several times while in hot pursuit of prey.

MICE CROSSING A council in South Wales has spent £190,000 on building bridges for dormice. The three overhead walkways were put up so that the little rodents could cross a busy road safely.

14 in (35 cm) long

Bat Killer

The Amazonian giant centipede is so powerful and agile that it can catch and eat bats. An adult centipede reaches 14 in (35 cm) long—the length of a man's forearm—and is able to climb the walls of caves. BBC cameraman Tim Green spent two weeks in a cave in Venezuela waiting to film this unique event. Eventually, he witnessed this fearsome beast hang down from the cave ceiling, grab a passing bat with some of its 46 legs and kill it with its venom. It then devoured every piece of bat flesh over the next hour.

RARE BABY

A farmer in Hebron, Palestine, feeds milk to a newborn goat with two heads. The extremely rare condition, in which animals are born with more than one head, is called polycephaly.

HASTY HIPPOS With a top speed of around 25 mph (40 km/h), an adult hippo can outrun a person in a short sprint. Hippos keep fit by walking up to 6 mi (10 km) a night foraging for food.

MONKEY BOUNTY In October 2010, Yuki Yoneyama of Mishima, Japan, claimed a 200,000-yen ($2,600) bounty for capturing a wild macaque monkey that had bitten more than 100 people.

TOXIC MUD The bearded goby fish of coastal Africa thrives in toxic mud, can live for hours without oxygen and eats jellyfish.

AGILE GOAT When Yang Yang the goat was born without hind legs in Liaoning Province, China, farmer Lu Shanlu trained the animal to walk on its forelegs. Within three months, Yang Yang could run around his yard several times on two legs without stopping.

RODENT COUTURE In May 2011, New York City staged a fashion show with a difference—the models were all rats. The sociable rodents showed their loveable side, dressed in miniature tutus, wedding dresses and other flattering outfits. Rats have become popular pets in recent years.

GUARD GOAT Zhao Huaiyun of Sichuan Province, China, has trained his pet goat to act as a guard dog. As well as warding off stray dogs from his owner's property, the goat makes sure Zhao answers his cell phone, if he hasn't heard it, by running up to him, putting its forelegs on his arms and baaing nonstop.

BIRD'S-EYE VIEW In a case of real life imitating art, Bobby Haas took a stunning aerial photograph of a colony of hundreds of flamingoes off the coast of the Yucatán Peninsula, Mexico, that had arranged themselves into the shape of a giant flamingo.

NO EYES Rowan, a German Spitz dog owned by Sam Orchard of Bedfordshire, England, was born without eyes but is able to navigate its way around by echolocation, using its barks.

SAY CHEESE!

This 14-day tadpole appears to be smiling for the camera. Snapped by British science photographer David Spears using a high-powered electron microscope, the baby frog displays facial features that are normally invisible to the naked eye.

SCREAMING TADPOLES Scientists in Argentina have discovered tadpoles that can scream. The larvae of the Argentine horned frog, which are carnivorous and eat other species of tadpole, emit a short, audible "metallic-like" sound.

FEATHERED FIEND Shanna Sexton of Devon, England, became so annoyed by what she thought was a faulty smoke alarm sounding nonstop for seven days that she called in workmen to try to locate the problem. Then she discovered the culprit was an African Gray Parrot named Sammi, who had escaped from a neighbor's house and spent the week hidden in Shanna's garden mimicking the beeping sound of an alarm.

RARE FLY The Terrible Hairy Fly is a flightless species of fly that breeds in bat feces and has only been found in a single Kenyan cave. A specimen collected in 2010 was the first to be tracked down since 1948.

COOL ROOSTERS To prevent fights breaking out between rival roosters, farmers in Chengdu, China, clothed the birds in plastic John Lennon-style sunglasses. The eyewear made it difficult for them to see each other clearly and so made them less aggressive.

ROLLING TOADS Venezuela's pebble toad flees predators by rolling like a ball down the rocky inclines of its mountainous home—without coming to any harm. Pebble toads breed communally, and a single nest has been found to contain 103 toads and 321 eggs.

Master of Disguise

The Satanic leaf-tailed gecko is a lizard with a devilish disguise that enables it to adjust its body color to blend in with its surroundings. With its coiled shape, its camouflage is so effective that it is barely visible against these dead leaves in a national park in Madagascar.

BEAVERING AWAY Beavers within Wood Buffalo National Park in Alberta, Canada, have spent decades building and maintaining a massive dam that measures a staggering half a mile (800 m) long.

BIG SCHOOL Schools of Atlantic herring can stretch for more than 25 mi (40 km) and number millions of individual fish.

FIGHTING SPURS Several species of South American birds called screamers have spurs on their wings that they use for fighting. The spurs can break off in another bird's body, but will grow back.

LIGHT SWARM A worker honeybee weighs about 1/300th of an ounce (90 mg), meaning that a swarm of 50,000 bees weighs only 10 lb (4.5 kg).

YOUR UPLOADS

www.ripleys.com/submit

Poultry breeder Diane Kolpin from Lake Placid, Florida, sent us this picture of a baby chicken without any eyes. The bird had no eye sockets at all—just skin and feathers where its eyes should be—yet, given loving care, it has grown into a healthy, if blind, bird.

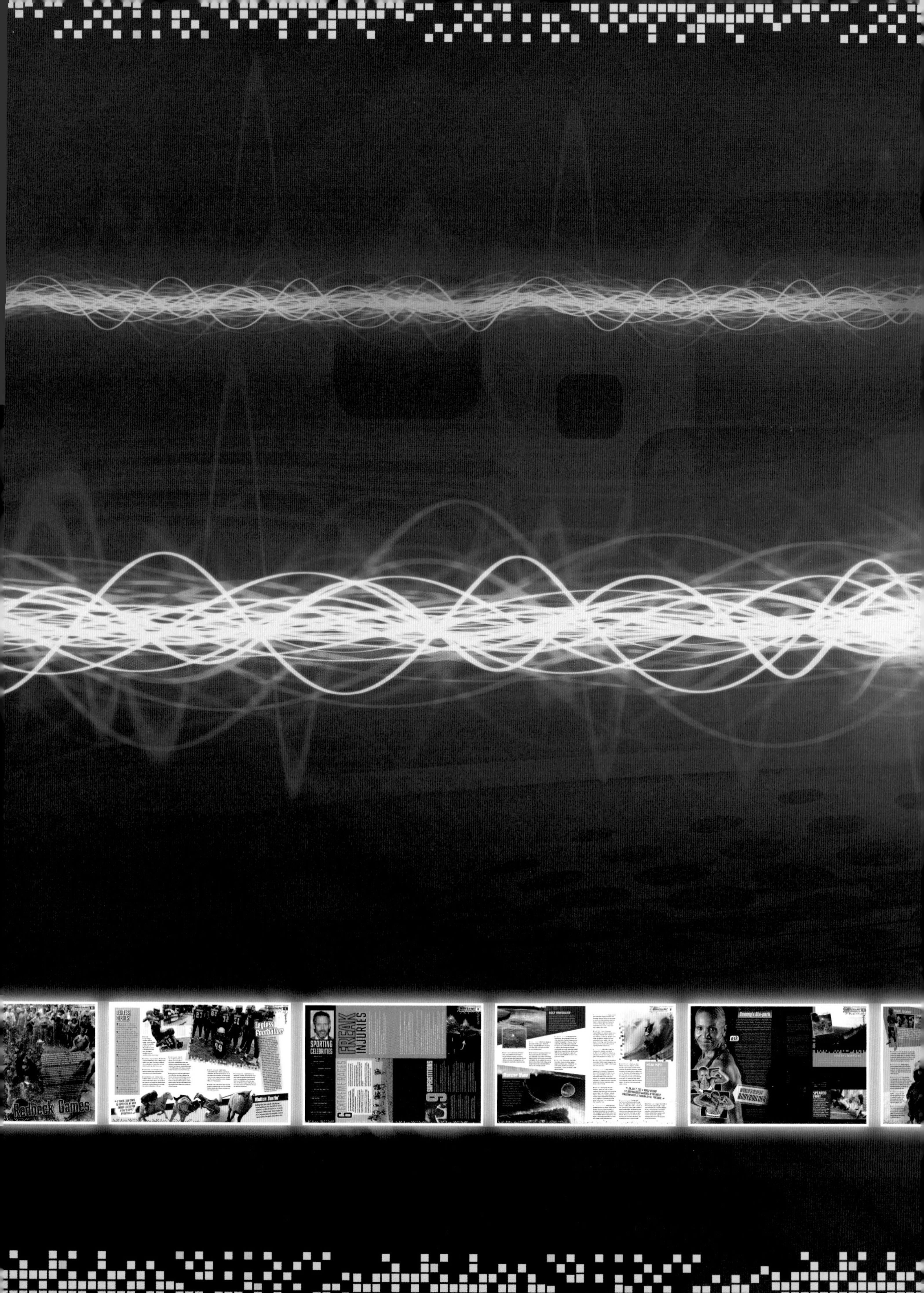
Redneck Games
LEGLESS HEROES
Legless Footballer
Mutton Bustin'
SPORTING CELEBRITIES
FREAK INJURIES
6 EXTREME RACES
9 SUPERSTITIONS
GOLF HANDICAP
Monster Wave
Granny's Six-pack
WORLD'S OLDEST BODYBUILDER
SPEARED FOOT

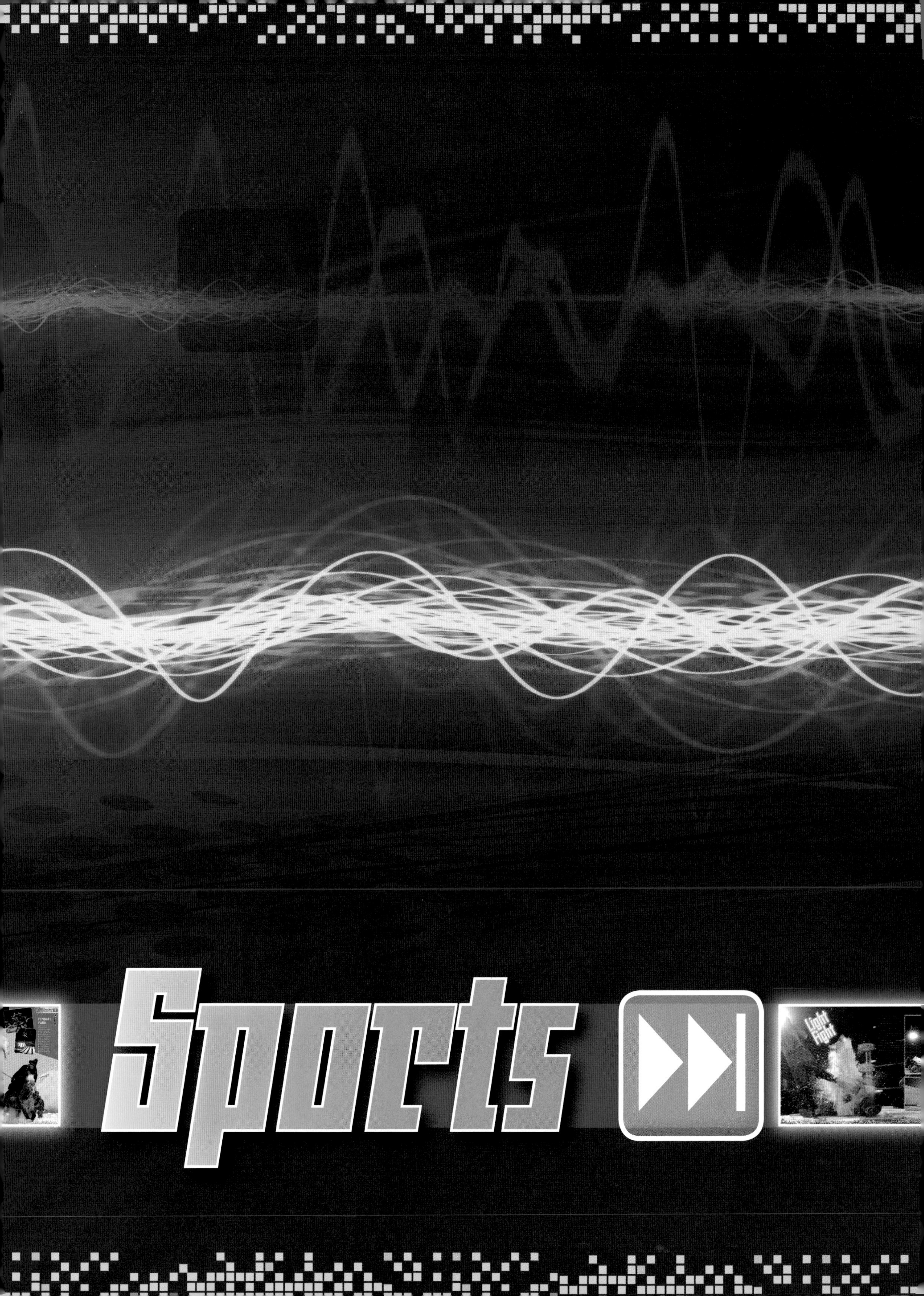
Sports
Light Fight

Light
Fight

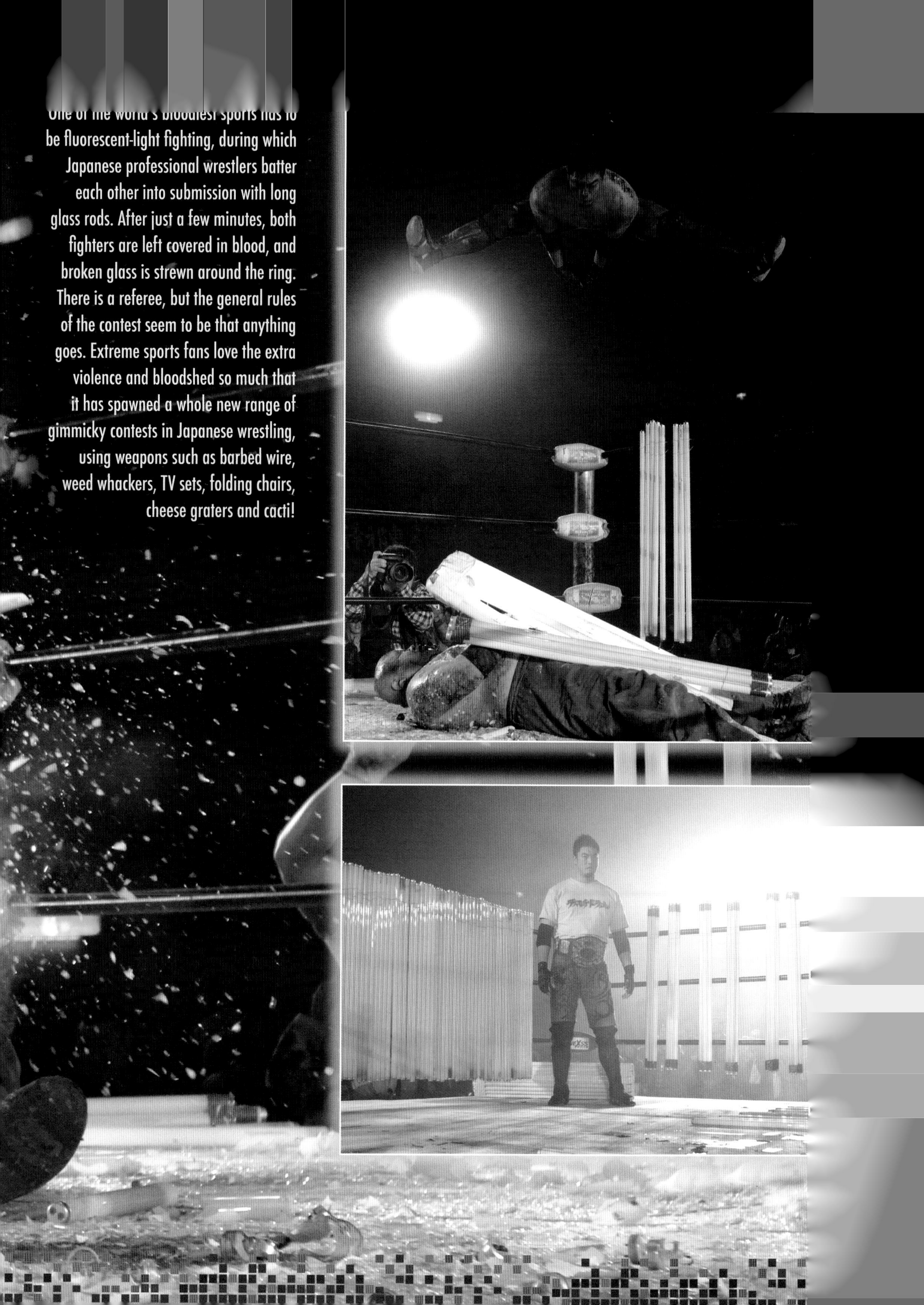

One of the world's bloodiest sports has to be fluorescent-light fighting, during which Japanese professional wrestlers batter each other into submission with long glass rods. After just a few minutes, both fighters are left covered in blood, and broken glass is strewn around the ring. There is a referee, but the general rules of the contest seem to be that anything goes. Extreme sports fans love the extra violence and bloodshed so much that it has spawned a whole new range of gimmicky contests in Japanese wrestling, using weapons such as barbed wire, weed whackers, TV sets, folding chairs, cheese graters and cacti!

LEGLESS HEROES

- Despite being born with only one leg, Anthony Robles of Arizona State University became a national wrestling champion in his weight class.
- Born without legs, Vinod Thakur learned to walk on his hands at his home in Delhi, India, and became a worldwide sensation as a legless hip-hop dancer on the TV show *India's Got Talent*.
- Legless Montana State photography student Kevin Connolly took 32,000 pictures while traveling through 15 countries on a skateboard capturing the expressions on people's faces when they first saw him. He wears a body shoe to protect his torso while taking pictures.
- Huang Jianming climbed the Great Wall of China for two hours in 2006, using the strength of his arms to push himself up the steps. His legs had been amputated in 1994 after he fell from a speeding train carriage.
- Amputee athlete Lance Benson of Raleigh, North Carolina, uses a skateboard to compete in marathons, and finished the New York City Marathon in just 3 hours 37 minutes in 2005.
- Xu Yuehua lost both legs when she was 12 but, balancing her torso on two stools and using them to move around, she has spent more than 37 years raising over 130 children in a social welfare institute in Xiangtan, China.
- Losing his legs as a teenager has not stopped Brazilian skateboarder Italo Romano performing gravity-defying stunts in tournaments across the world.

RECORD SCORE During a marathon 8½-hour innings, 13-year-old Indian cricketer Armaan Jaffer smashed 498 runs off 490 balls in a match in Mumbai in December 2010—the highest individual score ever recorded in Indian school cricket.

FOOTBALL FASHIONISTAS The University of Oregon football team wears a different style uniform every game. They have 512 different color combinations to choose from and only decide on game day which one to wear.

UNBROKEN RUN From 1992 to 2010, National Football League quarterback Brett Favre started in 297 consecutive games.

DANGEROUS HAIR Australian Rules footballer Nathan van Someren, who plays for Victorian side Simpson Tigers, was sent off by the umpire in 2011 because his gelled mohawk haircut was considered dangerous and might have poked another player in the eye.

HIGH BASKET From the top of a light tower that was almost 220 ft (67 m) above the ground, basketball stunt team How Ridiculous (comprising Derek Herron, Brett Stanford, Scott Gaunson and Kyle Nebel) sank an incredible basket at the Western Australia Cricket Association Ground in Perth in 2011.

ARMLESS PITCHER Born without arms, Tom Willis from San Diego, California, has thrown out the ceremonial first pitch at more than a dozen Major League baseball games. He throws the ball with his right foot, and his pitches usually make the entire distance from the mound to home plate (60 ft 6 in/18.4 m) without bouncing.

IT TAKES 3,000 COWS TO SUPPLY THE NFL WITH ENOUGH LEATHER FOR A YEAR'S SUPPLY OF FOOTBALLS.

Legless Footballer

Although he was born with no legs and stands just 3 ft (90 cm) tall, Bobby Martin of Dayton, Ohio, is a formidable opponent on the football field. Encouraged by coaches, he played as a defensive tackle for his high-school team and has since gone on to play at his local college. Far from being a handicap, the 24-year-old father, who suffers from a rare condition called Caudal Regression Syndrome meaning his body ends at his pelvis, says his size actually helps him play football. "My arms are like my legs, so they are very strong," he says. "To hit well in the tackle you have to be low, and how can you get lower than me?" He uses a skateboard to get around and is so strong that he can lift three times his body weight—over 330 lb (150 kg). The only problem he has ever encountered playing football was when he was sent off in a game in Cincinnati because he wasn't wearing thigh pads, kneepads or boots. The ruling was later overturned.

ODD SCAN

BRAVE SWIMMER Despite losing nearly half his body in China's 2008 Sichuan earthquake, Dai Guohong has become one of his country's top swimmers. He lost both legs when they were crushed under tons of rubble after the roof of his Beichuan school collapsed, killing 26 of his classmates.

HUMP JUMP In the Yemeni sport of camel jumping, competitors leap over rows of camels lined up side-by-side. Whoever can jump over the most is the winner.

HARE-BRAINED A greyhound race in Shepparton, Australia, descended into chaos after a real hare sprinted across the track in front of the speeding dogs. One greyhound, Ginny Lou, in third place at the time, gave chase, but the hare escaped. Although Ginny Lou's detour meant she finished last, the race was declared void anyway.

Mutton Bustin'

Budding rodeo riders typically under the age of six and weighing no more than 60 lb (27 kg) try to hold on to a 180-lb (81-kg) ewe for six seconds in the sport of Mutton Bustin' that is sweeping the U.S.A. To prevent injury, the young riders wear ice-hockey helmets, face guards and protective vests.

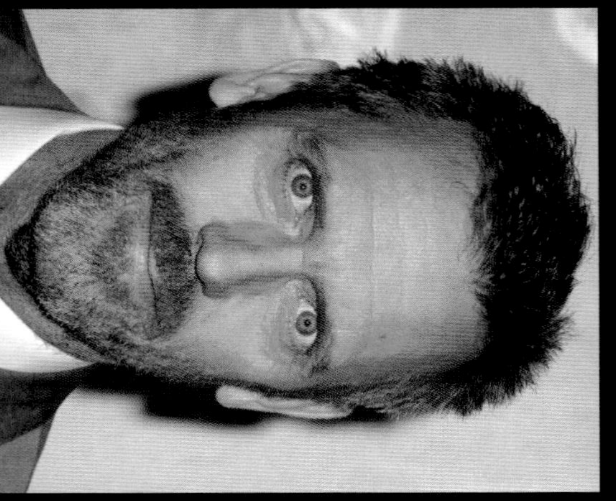

SPORTING CELEBRITIES

Singer **BILLY JOEL** was a welterweight boxing champion in his youth.

Actor **HUGH LAURIE** rowed for the defeated Cambridge crew in the 1980 Oxford–Cambridge University Boat Race.

In 1955, singer **JOHNNY MATHIS** was ranked tied for 85th in the world for the high jump.

Actor **RYAN O'NEAL** boxed as a teenager in Golden Gloves contests, finishing with a record of 18–4, including 13 knockouts.

Actress **GEENA DAVIS** narrowly missed out on being selected for the U.S. archery team to compete at the 2000 Olympics.

Writer **EDGAR ALLAN POE** once held the University of Virginia long jump record of 21 ft 6 in (6.5 m).

Iron Maiden frontman **BRUCE DICKINSON** was once ranked 7th in the U.K. for the foil discipline of fencing.

Actor **CHUCK CONNORS** played professional baseball for the Chicago Cubs and Brooklyn Dodgers, and basketball for the Boston Celtics.

SIR ARTHUR CONAN DOYLE, creator of Sherlock Holmes, played soccer for Portsmouth and cricket for the M.C.C., once bowling out the great W.G. Grace.

6 EXTREME RACES

The YUKON ARCTIC ULTRA is a grueling 430-mi (692-km) marathon on mountain bike, skis and foot where temperatures can drop to –58°F (–50°C) plus windchill, making it the coldest race on the planet.

Crossing mountain routes through Germany, Austria, Switzerland and Italy for eight days, the 200-mi (320-km) TRANSALPINE RUN has a vertical ascent of over 49,200 ft (15,000 m).

The six-day MARATHON OF THE SANDS covers 150 mi (240 km) of Moroccan desert, one-fifth of which is run over strength-sapping sand dunes in 122°F (50°C) heat.

Competitors in the NORTH POLE MARATHON run on ice for 26.2 miles (42 km) around the North Pole in temperatures of –22°F (–30°C).

The BADWATER ULTRAMARATHON is run over 135 mi (217 km) in California's Death Valley, starting at 282 ft (86 m) below sea level and ending at an altitude of 8,360 ft (2,548 m). Temperatures top a blistering 120°F (49°C) in the shade.

Brazil's seven-day JUNGLE MARATHON is run over a distance of 150 mi (240 km) through the treacherous Amazon rain forest. Competitors sleep in hammocks along the route.

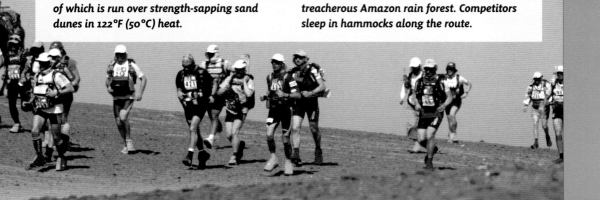

FREAK INJURIES

- Toronto Blue Jays baseball player **GLENALLEN HILL** badly cut himself after falling out of bed and crashing into a glass table while having a nightmare about being covered in spiders.
- British cyclist **MARK CAVENDISH** was snowboarding on a Nintendo Wii video game when he fell off the board and injured his calf.
- Chicago Cubs baseball player **SAMMY SOSA** strained a ligament in his back as a result of a violent sneeze.
- Scottish golfer **SAM TORRANCE** cracked his sternum after colliding with a large plant pot in his hotel room while he was sleepwalking.

WEIRD SPORTS EVENTS

Held annually in Finland, the Wife-Carrying World Championships are raced over an obstacle course, the winner receiving his wife's weight in beer.

For the Great Klondike Outhouse Race, teams steer decorated outdoor toilets around the streets of Dawson City, Canada. One person has to sit on the toilet throughout the 1.5-mi (2.4-km) run.

At Australia's Sheep Counting Championships, hundreds of sheep run across a field as competitors count them.

The World Gravy Wrestling Championships take place annually in Lancashire, England.

At the Emma Crawford Coffin Races, colorful coffins containing a living person are wheeled by teams along a course in Manitou Springs, Colorado.

Sydney, Australia, stages a race solely for women wearing stiletto-heeled shoes.

In the World Bog Snorkeling Championship, competitors wear snorkels and flippers to race in a Welsh peat bog.

The International Cherry Pit Spitting Championship at Eau Claire, Michigan, sees competitors spit their pits distances of more than 90 ft (27.4 m).

9 SUPERSTITIONS

The night before every game, basketball player ***JASON TERRY*** goes to bed wearing the shorts of the next day's opposing team. He also plays in five pairs of socks.

South African golfer ***GARY PLAYER*** would only play with even-numbered balls; he left the odd-numbered ones in his bag.

Tennis player ***SERENA WILLIAMS*** always bounces the ball five times before her first serve and twice before her second serve.

Between hockey periods, one-time Philadelphia Flyers goaltender ***PELLE LINDBERGH*** would drink only a Swedish beverage called Pripps—and only if it had exactly two ice cubes in the cup and was delivered by the same trainer.

Baseball player ***WADE BOGGS*** always ate chicken before each game, took batting practice at 5.17, did running sprints at 7.17, and drew the word *Chai* (Hebrew for "Life") in the dirt before coming up to bat.

U.S. golfer ***JACK NICKLAUS*** always carried three pennies in his pocket for luck.

Basketball star ***MICHAEL JORDAN*** wore his lucky University of North Carolina shorts under his Chicago Bulls uniform in every game. To cover them, he started wearing longer shorts, which inspired an NBA trend.

Former New York Mets baseball star ***TURK WENDELL*** used to brush his teeth between innings, chew black licorice, and draw three crosses in the dirt then wave at the center fielder before he pitched.

Whenever he won a tournament match, Croatian tennis champion ***GORAN IVANISEVIC*** would repeat everything from the previous day—such as going to the same restaurant, eating the same food and talking

- Detroit Tigers baseball player **BRANDON INGE** strained a muscle while placing a pillow behind his son's head.
- Former Manchester United goalkeeper **ALEX STEPNEY** dislocated his jaw after yelling at his teammates during a match.
- Competing in Rome, Italy, long jumper **SALIM SDIRI** was speared in the side by a wayward javelin thrown by Finland's Tero Pitkamaki who had slipped at the end of his run-up. The javelin penetrated 4 in (10 cm) into Salim's flesh.
- Detroit Tigers' pitcher **JOEL ZUMAYA** missed three games after straining his arm playing Guitar Hero on a PS2.
- U.S. boxer **DANIEL CARUSO** broke his own nose while psyching himself up for a fight by pounding his gloves into his face.
- Celebrating a goal he had helped to set up for Swiss club Servette, soccer player **PAULO DIOGO** lost a finger after his new wedding ring caught in the wire fence surrounding the field. To add insult to injury, the referee yellow-carded him for excessive celebration.
- Boston Red Sox baseball player **WADE BOGGS** hurt his back when he lost his balance while trying to put on cowboy boots.
- New Zealand cricketer **TREVOR FRANKLIN** was ruled out of action for 18 months after being run over by a motorized luggage cart at an airport.
- San Diego Padres baseball player **ADAM EATON** accidentally stabbed himself in the stomach with a knife while trying to open some DVD packaging.

- In an infamous WBA Heavyweight Championship fight on June 28, 1997, **MIKE TYSON** bit off a chunk of Evander Holyfield's right ear and spat it on the ring floor.

Granny's Six-pack

At 75, grandmother Ernestine Shepherd of Baltimore, Maryland, is the world's oldest competitive female bodybuilder. She wakes up at 3 a.m. every day to meditate, and then clocks up runs totaling 10 mi (16 km) before lunch. She started working out when she reached the age of 56, but has since won two bodybuilding contests and run nine marathons.

Ripley's ask

Have you always been into fitness and health? *I didn't get into the fitness and health industry until I was 56, when my sister and I were invited to a church picnic, and they told us we could wear bathing suits. We put our bathing suits on and she said "Wow, we don't look good, we need to do something." She was 57 and I was 56—we started exercising and noticed the change in our bodies, and we loved it.*

You started an online fitness program in 2006 at the age of 71—tell us how things developed from there. *I had always wanted to become a bodybuilder, but I didn't know how to go about it. I was introduced to trainer and former Mr. Universe Yohnnie Shambourger and he developed a special training program for me. Over the next seven months my body made an incredible transformation and I was ready to compete against women half my age.*

How does it feel to hold the world record? *It feels great, because so many people have come to me and said "Wow! How did you do that?" Just to have people ask me that question is wonderful to me.*

Tell us what your daily routine consists of? *I wake up every morning at 3 a.m. Then I have my devotions, eat my breakfast, get dressed and I am out that door getting ready to run. When I get back, I eat breakfast again and prepare to go to the gym. I have classes that I train in during the day, so I am at the gym until maybe about 8 or 9 o'clock at night. But I come home in between and rest.*

Do you have a specific diet to accompany your routine? *I have a very strict diet that I have been following for about ten years—without cheating! First thing in the morning I eat a banana, then I go out and run and drink water. When I get back, I eat four boiled eggs—one with the yolk in it and the other three without. Then, I will have crushed pineapples. I also eat a lot of chicken, tuna fish, turkey, frozen vegetables, brown rice, white potato and sweet potato. My most important drink is liquid egg whites four or five times a day.*

RIPLEY'S WEIRD RECORD • RIPLEY'S WEIRD RECORD • RIPLEY'S WEIRD RECORD • RIPLEY

WORLD'S OLDEST FEMALE BODYBUILDER

RIPLEY'S WEIRD RECORD • RIPLEY'S WEIRD RECORD • RIPLEY'S WEIRD RECORD • RIPLEY'S

What is your motto for a healthy life? *My motto for a healthy life would be to remember that you need to strength train each day, do at least one hour's worth of cardio, drink plenty of water, and of course five to six small meals a day. That's how I do it, and that's how I have stayed healthy.*

FITNESS FANATIC At 102 years old, former postman Shi Xiaochun of Xiaoshan, China, still worked out every day, doing pushups on his fists and even on one hand.

WRONG VENUE Serbian tennis player Bojana Jovanovski faced a mad dash to get to a tournament in Carlsbad, California, after flying instead to Carlsbad, New Mexico, 900 mi (1,450 km) away.

LONGEST JUMP On July 2, 2011, Algerian-born Taig Khris set a new world record for the longest jump on rollerblades when he leaped 95 ft (29 m) in front of the Sacre Coeur Basilica in Paris, France.

KUNG FU GRANNY Zhao Yufang, an 82-year-old grandmother from Beijing, China, is a master in Shaolin kung fu. She had wanted to learn kung fu as a girl, but her local master would not teach her. So she taught herself, went back to the school and defeated the master, forcing him to apologize.

FOOTBALL ON WHEELS Founded in 2008 in San Marcos, Texas, the Unicycle Football League features teams playing American football while balancing atop unicycles. Players wear bike helmets but no shoulder pads.

SUMO RUNNER Weighing in at 400 lb (180 kg), American sumo wrestler Kelly Gneiting became the heaviest man ever to complete a marathon when he finished the 2011 Los Angeles Marathon in 9 hours 48 minutes 52 seconds. Battling heavy rain and strong winds, he jogged the first 8 mi (12.9 km) and walked the last 18 mi (29 km).

CHEESE REMEDY Nursing a badly bruised shin that left her participation in the 2010 Winter Olympics in Vancouver in doubt, U.S. alpine skier Lindsey Vonn tried cream and painkillers to no effect before deciding to smear the wound with soft cheese. The cheesy remedy was so successful that a few days later she won gold in the downhill event.

10TH DAN Standing only 4 ft 10 in (1.47 m) tall and weighing just 100 lb (45.4 kg), Sensei Keiko Fukuda of San Francisco, California, became the first woman in history to reach the highest rank of 10th dan black belt in judo. Only three other living judokas have reached that level—and they're all men. She became a judo instructor in 1937, and in 2011 was still teaching judo three times a week—at age 98.

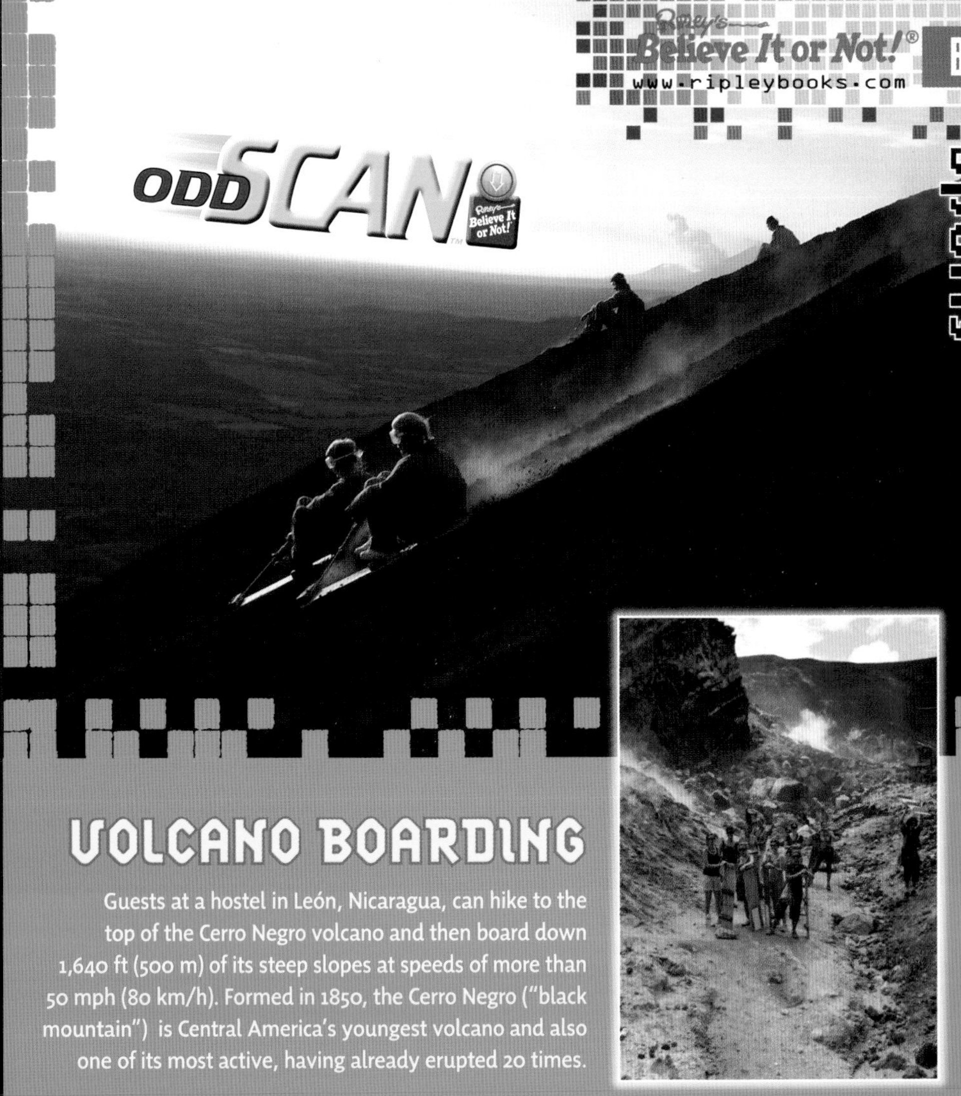

VOLCANO BOARDING

Guests at a hostel in León, Nicaragua, can hike to the top of the Cerro Negro volcano and then board down 1,640 ft (500 m) of its steep slopes at speeds of more than 50 mph (80 km/h). Formed in 1850, the Cerro Negro ("black mountain") is Central America's youngest volcano and also one of its most active, having already erupted 20 times.

LOST DIAMOND For an hour, at least nine Miami Dolphins NFL players crawled on the field and searched in vain for a diamond belonging to defensive end Kendall Langford who had forgotten to remove his $50,000 earrings before a practice session.

BIRTHDAY BATTER Arizona Diamondbacks baseball star Mark Reynolds hit home runs on his birthday, August 3, both in 2009 and 2010.

JET-SKI RECORD Reaching top speeds in excess of 69 mph (110 km/h), Jeremy Burfoot of Auckland, New Zealand, covered a world record 1,421 mi (2,287 km) on a Jet Ski in 24 hours on Lake Karapiro on February 8, 2011.

CHESS CHALLENGE Israeli grandmaster Alik Gershon played 523 games of chess simultaneously in Tel Aviv on October 21, 2010—and defeated 454 of his opponents.

SPEARED FOOT

Track and field judge Lia Marie Lourenco receives medical aid after a competitor's javelin speared her foot during the warm up for the Troféu Brasil championship in São Paulo. She was rushed to hospital, where she underwent surgery to remove the javelin tip.

GOLF HANDICAP

Carbrook Golf Club in Brisbane, Australia, has some unique obstacles on its course—sharks. A dozen or so bull sharks circle the waters in the lake alongside the 12th to 15th tees, their fins poking through the water proving a distraction for even the most hardened pro. The 9-ft-long (2.7-m), 330-lb (150-kg) man-eaters spilled into the lake in the mid-1990s during a flood from nearby rivers that source in coastal Moreton Bay, some 5 mi (8 km) away—and have happily since bred in the lake's waters.

EASY CATCH Jason Kresse of Freeport, Texas, was out fishing for red snapper in the Gulf of Mexico in March 2011 when a 375-lb (170-kg) mako shark leaped into his boat without provocation, thrashing about and damaging the vessel before dying hours later.

DEADLY GAME Football was a dangerous game in its formative years—during the 1905 U.S. college football season, 18 players were killed while on the field and another 150 were seriously injured.

PIER PRESSURE Harnessing winds of more than 60 mph (96 km/h) on November 11, 2010, kiteboarder Lewis Crathern of Worthing, England, became the first person to jump clean over Brighton Pier. He navigated the waves for about two hours before finally finding one big enough to launch him on his death-defying leap over the 50-ft-high (15-m) pier.

CARELESS HANDS Goalkeeper Maarten Stekelenburg, who is regarded as having one of the safest pairs of hands in European soccer, tarnished his reputation in May 2011 when he accidentally dropped the League trophy off the top of a bus as it drove through Amsterdam to celebrate Ajax winning the Dutch title. Coincidentally, just weeks earlier, Real Madrid's Sergio Ramos dropped the Copa del Rey trophy off the top of an open-top bus in Spain and could only watch helplessly as it was run over by the bus's wheels.

TIED FINISH Five runners—Brad Weiss, Chris Solarz, Terence Gerchberg, Stephen England and Francis Laros—finished the 2011 God's Country Marathon in Coudersport, Pennsylvania, in 3 hours 26 minutes—while tethered together.

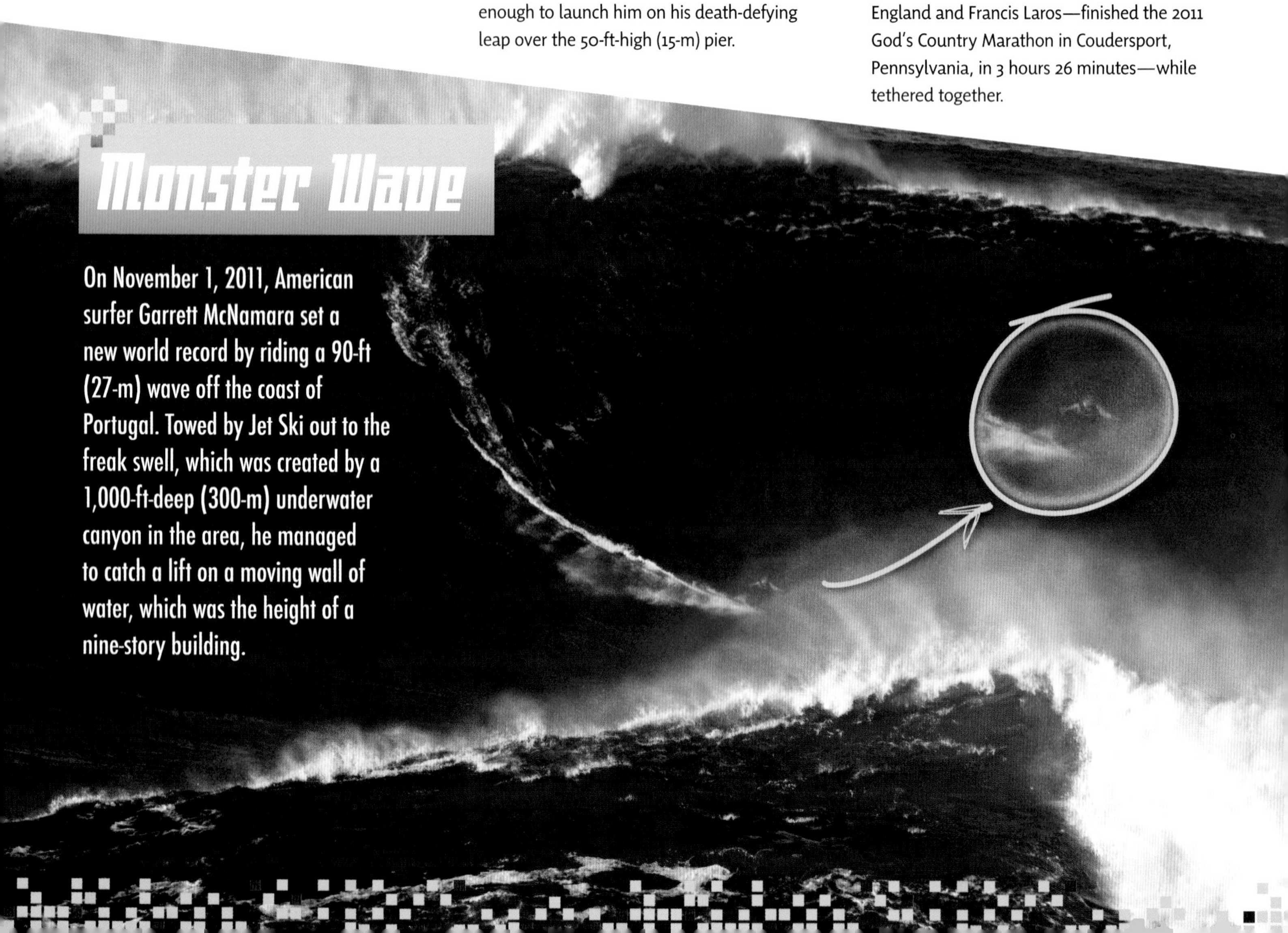

Monster Wave

On November 1, 2011, American surfer Garrett McNamara set a new world record by riding a 90-ft (27-m) wave off the coast of Portugal. Towed by Jet Ski out to the freak swell, which was created by a 1,000-ft-deep (300-m) underwater canyon in the area, he managed to catch a lift on a moving wall of water, which was the height of a nine-story building.

KITEBOARD CROSSING Russian extreme sport enthusiasts Yevgeny Novozheev and Konstantin Aksyonov became the first people to cross the 60-mi (97-km) Bering Strait from Russia to Alaska by kiteboard. During their seven-hour journey, they survived water temperatures of 34°F (1°C), a fierce storm and a collision with a whale.

FAKE TEAM A team of imposters masquerading as the Togolese national soccer team played a friendly match in Bahrain in 2010 and lost 3–0. Before the deception came to light, the Bahrainis said they had been surprised by the poor quality of the Togo players. Former Togo coach Tchanile Bana was later banned from soccer for three years for organizing the fake national team.

DOUBLE ACE Golfer Adam Smith from Aberdeenshire, Scotland, beat odds of 67 million to one by getting two holes-in-one in the space of seven holes during a round of golf at nearby Stonehaven in January 2011.

EXTRA LARGE Former Welsh international soccer player Robbie Savage managed to wear soccer shirts from all 72 English Football League clubs at the same time.

BASEBALL ROBOT A robot created by engineers at the University of Pennsylvania threw out the ceremonial first pitch at a 2011 Major League baseball game between the Philadelphia Phillies and the Milwaukee Brewers. The one-armed, three-wheeled robot was based on a Segway and used a pneumatic cylinder and a burst of compressed carbon dioxide to throw the ball.

IRON MAN Seventy-year-old pastor Bob Kurtz—known as "Golf's Iron Man"—completed 1,850 holes of golf over a seven-day period at Quail Creek Golf Resort, Hartselle, Alabama, in June 2011. Despite playing for 16 hours a day in temperatures touching 100°F (38°C), he still shot an average score of just 74 (par for the course is 72), and shot better than his age four times.

DUMPLING DUMPED Pittsburgh Pirates baseball team fired one of their *pierogi* mascots (the guys who race around the stadium in dumpling costumes) after he criticized the team management on Facebook. Andrew Kurtz was immediately offered employment as a hot dog by a minor-league team before the Pirates had a change of heart and rehired him.

NEAR MISS

This is the moment when Raimana van Bastolaer nearly lost his head to a flying Jet Ski during a surfing contest in his native Tahiti. As the waves in the region are so big, surfers are towed out by Jet Ski, but Van Bastolaer's friend, Reef McIntosh, lost control of the machine, which was pulled over the lip of the 12-ft (3.6-m) wave, missing the surfer's head by inches.

PUNTER'S JOY In March 2011, Steve Whiteley from Devon, England, used his bus pass to get to Exeter racecourse for free, entered for free through a promotion, and then proceeded to win more than £1.4 million from a £2 bet. The 61-year-old heating engineer, who goes to the races only twice a year, backed the winning horse in all six races at total odds of 879,138 to one. Making his wager all the more remarkable, Jessica Lodge, the victorious jockey in the last race, had never previously ridden a winner.

ON JULY 2, 2011, A WORLD-RECORD 272 BODYBOARDERS GATHERED IN THE WATER SIMULTANEOUSLY AT FIGUEIRA DA FOZ, PORTUGAL.

ENDURANCE RACE The 2011 Hoka Hey Motorcycle Challenge traveled through 48 U.S. states and part of Canada, from Mesa, Arizona, to Sydney, Nova Scotia—a journey of over 14,000 mi (22,530 km). Entry is limited to Harley-Davidson bikers, and during the event riders must never sleep more than 10 ft (3 m) away from their bike, which rules out nights in hotels. The race was won for the second successive year by Florida's Will Barclay, who completed the course in just two weeks.

SURPRISE CATCH Angler John Goldfinch from Exmouth, England, fought to reel in what he thought was a huge fish pulling on his line—only to find that it was in fact a scuba diver he had landed instead. He had been casting his line hoping to catch mackerel, but his hook caught the submerged diver between the legs some 50 ft (15 m) from shore.

REDNECK EVENTS

- ARMPIT SERENADE
- CIGARETTE FLIP
- BOBBIN' FOR PIGS' FEET
- MUD PIT BELLY FLOP
- WATERMELON SEED SPITTING
- HUBCAP HURLING
- BUG ZAPPING BY SPITBALL
- TOILET SEAT THROWING (REDNECK HORSESHOES)
- BIG HAIR CONTEST
- DUMPSTER DIVING

BOBBIN' FOR PIGS' FEET

Caitlin Craft plunges face first into a trough of water and uses her mouth to grab a frozen pig's trotter during the 2010 bobbin' for pigs' feet contest. Whoever retrieves the most feet in the allotted time wins the coveted beer-can trophy.

TORCH BEARER

Proudly carrying the beer-can torch, Elbow, the official mascot of the Redneck Games, prepares to light the ceremonial grill to get proceedings underway.

MUD-PIT BELLY FLOP

Another competitor makes a splash and gets down and dirty in the mud pit belly flop—for many people the blue riband event of the Redneck Games. Self-proclaimed redneck grandma Barbara Bailey has won the special event on several occasions.

ARMPIT SERENADE

2009 armpit serenader Aubrey Matthews delights the crowds by performing his winning song. Youngsters excel at this event as excess armpit flesh is not considered conducive to rattling out a good tune.

TOILET SEAT THROWING

A medal-winning contestant in the toilet seat throwing contest (redneck horseshoes) hurls away.

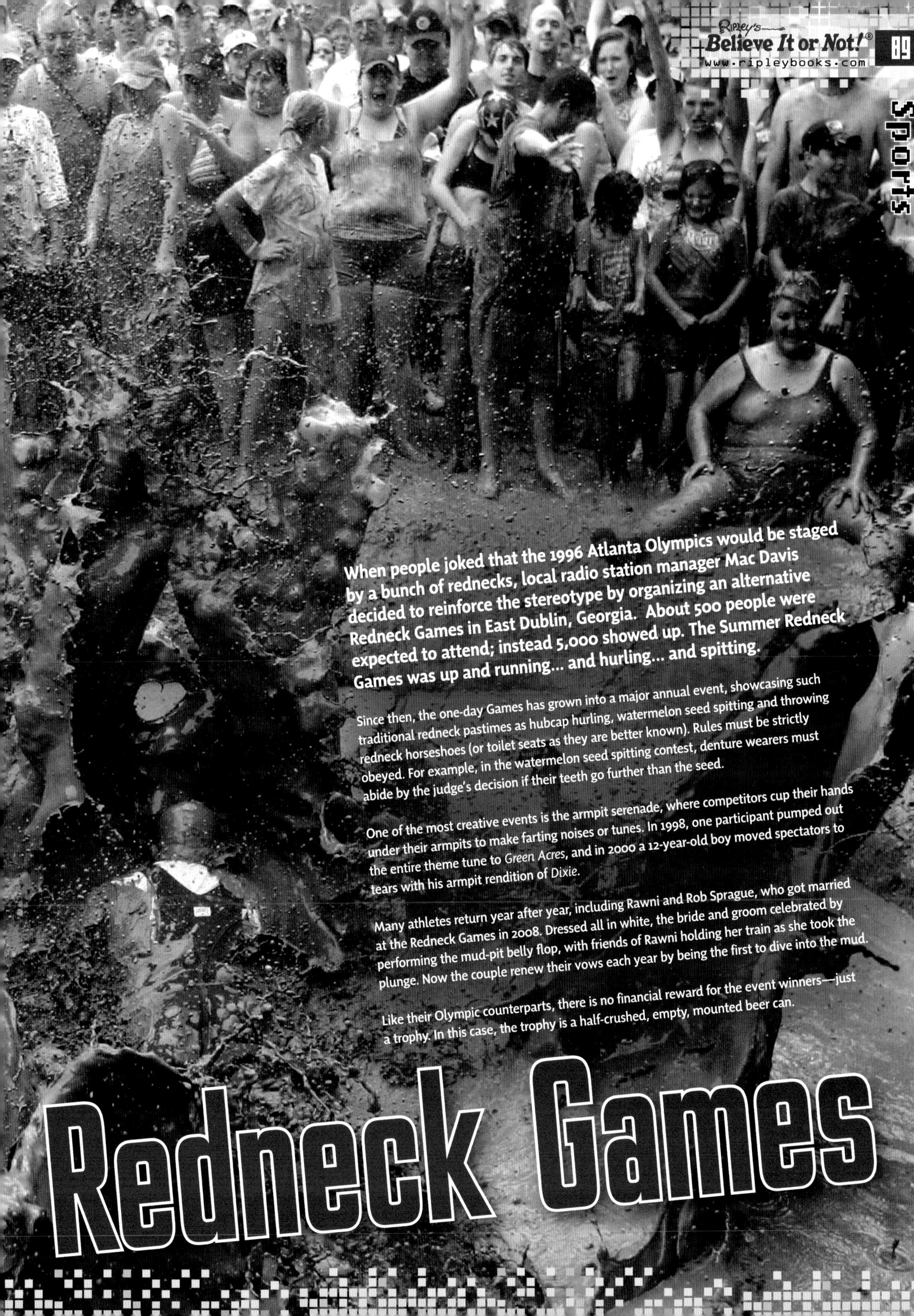

Redneck Games

When people joked that the 1996 Atlanta Olympics would be staged by a bunch of rednecks, local radio station manager Mac Davis decided to reinforce the stereotype by organizing an alternative Redneck Games in East Dublin, Georgia. About 500 people were expected to attend; instead 5,000 showed up. The Summer Redneck Games was up and running... and hurling... and spitting.

Since then, the one-day Games has grown into a major annual event, showcasing such traditional redneck pastimes as hubcap hurling, watermelon seed spitting and throwing redneck horseshoes (or toilet seats as they are better known). Rules must be strictly obeyed. For example, in the watermelon seed spitting contest, denture wearers must abide by the judge's decision if their teeth go further than the seed.

One of the most creative events is the armpit serenade, where competitors cup their hands under their armpits to make farting noises or tunes. In 1998, one participant pumped out the entire theme tune to *Green Acres*, and in 2000 a 12-year-old boy moved spectators to tears with his armpit rendition of *Dixie*.

Many athletes return year after year, including Rawni and Rob Sprague, who got married at the Redneck Games in 2008. Dressed all in white, the bride and groom celebrated by performing the mud-pit belly flop, with friends of Rawni holding her train as she took the plunge. Now the couple renew their vows each year by being the first to dive into the mud.

Like their Olympic counterparts, there is no financial reward for the event winners—just a trophy. In this case, the trophy is a half-crushed, empty, mounted beer can.

WAX CHAMP

World light-heavyweight boxing champion Bernard Hopkins was cast for a full-size wax figure at Ripley's Believe It or Not! world headquarters in Orlando, Florida, in August 2011. Hopkins became the oldest boxer ever to win a world title when he defeated Jean Pascal on May 21, 2011. The process of immortalizing him in wax, however, was not a quick one, taking more than two days to complete.

First, Hopkins had a thick layer of special silicone applied to his head. When this had set, cast strips were added and left to dry. Then the entire piece was removed and the process repeated for the rest of his body—taking two days. With the body casting complete, artists at Ripley's had an exact blueprint of Hopkins to use for the clay modeling and wax figure-making process. The silicone molds were precise down to his wrinkles, whiskers and even the pores in his skin.

STRAIGHT OLLIES On July 16, 2011, Eric Carlin, 18, of Mount Laurel, Pennsylvania, strung together a record 247 straight ollies on a skateboard without his feet ever touching the ground. An ollie is a trick where the rider and skateboard leap into the air without the rider using his or her hands.

HIGH GROUND Pakistan stages a polo tournament high up on the Shandur Mountain Pass—12,251 ft (3,734 m) above sea level—in which teams from the towns on either side, Gilgit and Chitral, play each other every year.

SNOWSHOE RACE The midwinter La Ciaspolada foot race in Italy has been held annually since 1972, with its contestants wearing snowshoes from start to finish. It is run over a 5-mi (8-km) course in the Dolomite Mountains and attracts up to 6,000 entrants each year.

FISHERMAN'S FRIEND Heather, a 40-year-old, 52-lb (23.6-kg) carp living in a pond in Hampshire, England, had been caught and released hundreds of times before she was found dead in 2010.

MULTINATIONAL MATCH The English Premier League soccer match between Blackburn Rovers and West Bromwich Albion on January 23, 2011, featured players representing 22 different countries.

TRIPLE BACKFLIP On May 28, 2011, BMX rider Jed Mildon landed the world's first triple backflip at Unit T3 Mindtricks BMX Jam in his hometown of Taupo, New Zealand. He nailed the record-breaking jump by riding down a 66-ft-high (20-m) ramp carved into a hillside.

MONKEY SECURITY Indian authorities used 38 trained gray langur monkeys during the 2010 Commonwealth Games in Delhi to frighten away other monkeys from the athletes' village.

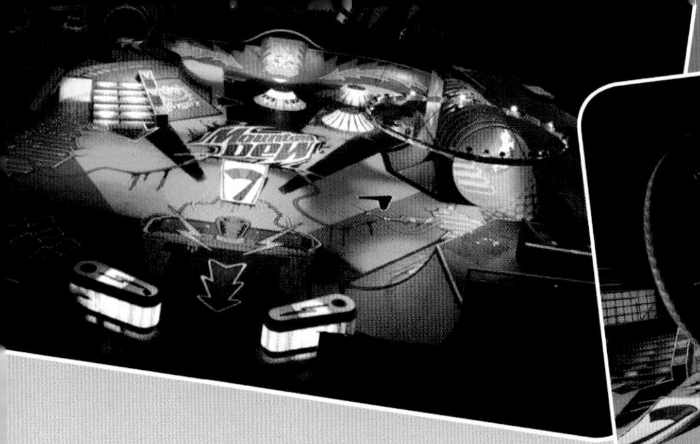

PINBALL PARK

Skateboarders and BMX riders ride around a giant pinball machine at a park in Auckland, New Zealand, as if they are tiny pinballs. They are given a push down the first hill by a huge "arm" and, just like in a real pinball game, they can build up points by jumping over bleepers and bouncing off flippers.

GOAT GRABBING

Buzkashi is a traditional Central Asian sport—and the national sport in Afghanistan—that uses a headless goat carcass as a ball. Teams on horseback try to grab the carcass from the ground and pitch it into a scoring area. The winning team gets to boil and eat the carcass.

Body

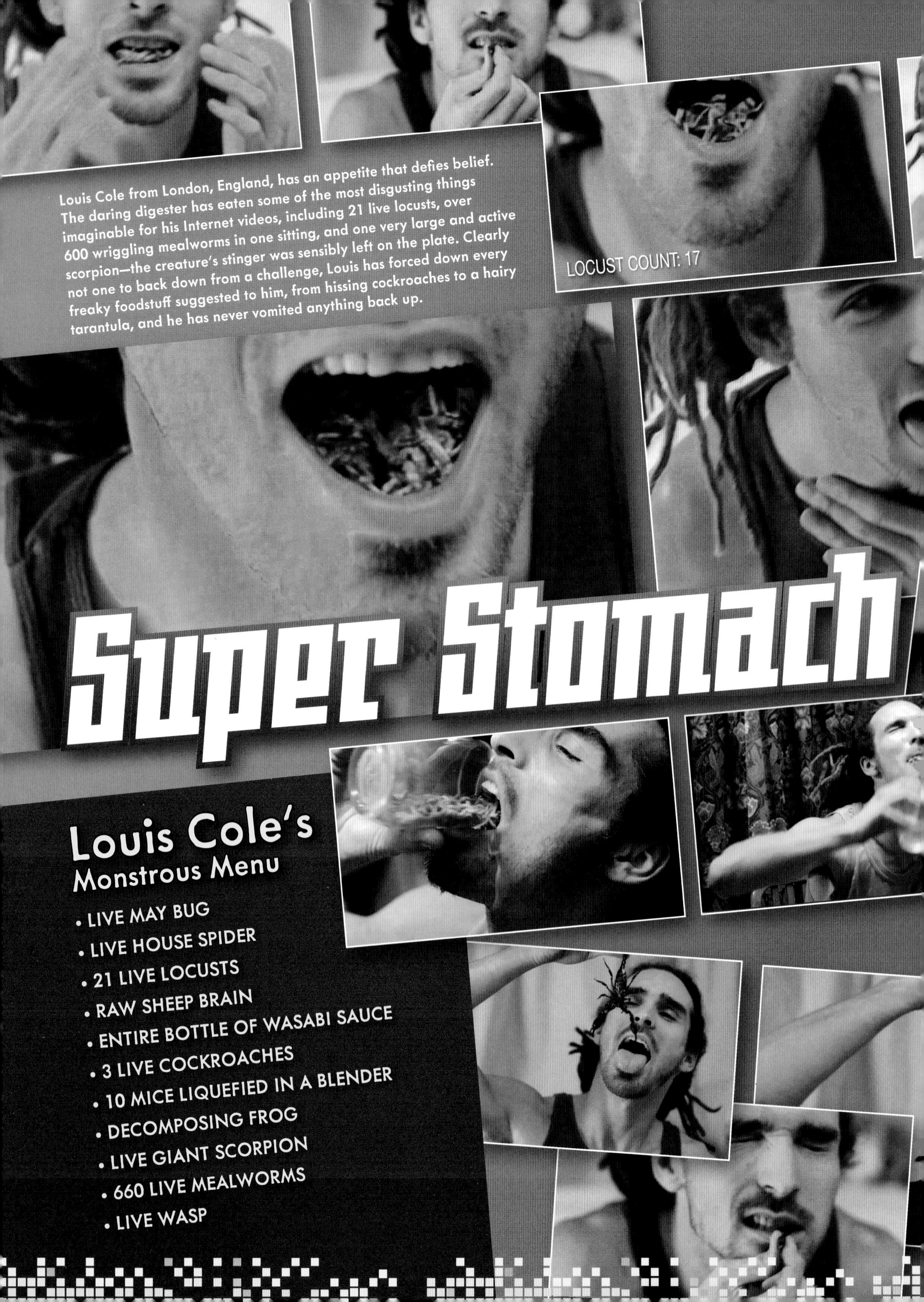

Louis Cole from London, England, has an appetite that defies belief. The daring digester has eaten some of the most disgusting things imaginable for his Internet videos, including 21 live locusts, over 600 wriggling mealworms in one sitting, and one very large and active scorpion—the creature's stinger was sensibly left on the plate. Clearly not one to back down from a challenge, Louis has forced down every freaky foodstuff suggested to him, from hissing cockroaches to a hairy tarantula, and he has never vomited anything back up.

Super Stomach

Louis Cole's Monstrous Menu

- LIVE MAY BUG
- LIVE HOUSE SPIDER
- 21 LIVE LOCUSTS
- RAW SHEEP BRAIN
- ENTIRE BOTTLE OF WASABI SAUCE
- 3 LIVE COCKROACHES
- 10 MICE LIQUEFIED IN A BLENDER
- DECOMPOSING FROG
- LIVE GIANT SCORPION
- 660 LIVE MEALWORMS
- LIVE WASP

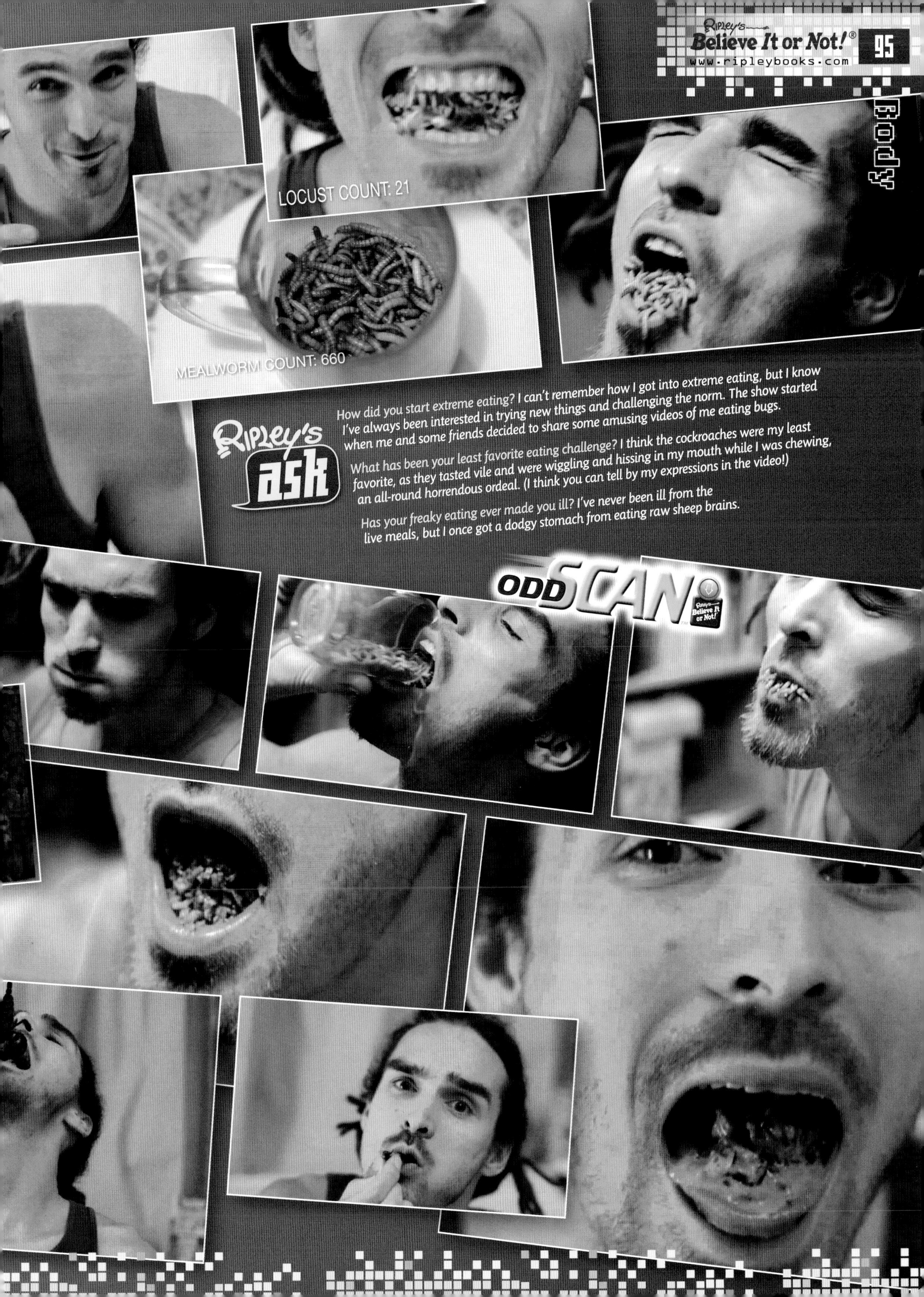

Ripley's ask

How did you start extreme eating? I can't remember how I got into extreme eating, but I know I've always been interested in trying new things and challenging the norm. The show started when me and some friends decided to share some amusing videos of me eating bugs.

What has been your least favorite eating challenge? I think the cockroaches were my least favorite, as they tasted vile and were wiggling and hissing in my mouth while I was chewing, an all-round horrendous ordeal. (I think you can tell by my expressions in the video!)

Has your freaky eating ever made you ill? I've never been ill from the live meals, but I once got a dodgy stomach from eating raw sheep brains.

TOE SWAP

Li Zicheng of Huiyang, China, has a toe on his hand! After the thumb of his right hand was severed beyond repair in a work accident, doctors cut off one of his toes on his left foot and transplanted it onto the hand in place of the thumb.

BLUE GLOW Angel Glow is a rare battlefield condition where an injured soldier's wound begins glowing blue. It is caused by glowing bacteria that typically inhabit the guts of worms.

FALSE TOES Two artificial big toes dating back over 2,600 years to Ancient Egypt were probably the world's first functional prosthetic body parts. One of the false toes, made from wood and leather, resides at the Egyptian Museum in Cairo while the other, made from a mix of linen, glue and plaster, is on display at the British Museum in London, England. Replicas of the artificial toes were tested on modern volunteers, whose big right toe had been lost, in order to prove that the limbs had a practical use and had not simply been attached to the foot during mummification for religious or ritualistic reasons.

ALIEN HAND

For nearly 20 years, Karen Byrne of New Jersey has suffered from Alien Hand Syndrome, a rare neurological disorder in which she is frequently attacked by her own hand. Her left hand repeatedly tries to slap and punch her, it takes items out of her handbag without her permission and it stubs out cigarettes that she has just lit with her right hand. The condition affects even her feet. Sometimes when she wants to turn right, one leg decides it wants to go left, leaving her walking round in circles. Karen's problems started when she underwent surgery to control her epilepsy. Her surgeon cut the corpus callosum, a band of nerve fibers, which keep the two halves of the brain in constant contact. While the procedure cured her epilepsy, it created a power struggle inside her head. A healthy brain consists of two hemispheres. The left hemisphere controls the right arm and leg while the right hemisphere controls the left arm and leg. Usually the left dominates, having the final say in the actions we perform, but in Karen's case after the cutting of the corpus callosum, the right side of her brain refused to be dominated by the left, leading to Alien Hand Syndrome.

PULLING HER LEG While fishing on Lake Ida in Alexandria, Minnesota, Beth Krohn caught a prosthetic leg that Pam Riley had lost while swimming in the lake three years earlier. Krohn returned the leg to Riley after tracking her down through a local prosthetic limb manufacturer.

OLDEST WOMAN? Antisa Khvichava, a woman from a remote mountain village in Georgia, claimed to have celebrated her 131st birthday on July 8, 2011. Although her original birth certificate has been lost, documents and evidence from her family support her age claim. If true, she would be the oldest person in recorded history.

TWO UVULAS Ben Duvall of Missouri was born with not one uvula—the small piece of soft tissue that hangs down from the soft palate over the back of the tongue—but two.

ATE TOES As 61-year-old diabetic James Little slept in his home at Roseburg, Oregon, his dog ate three of his toes. The dog was thought to have been acting instinctively to help remove diseased flesh, and Mr. Little felt nothing because numbness in the hands or feet is a symptom of diabetes.

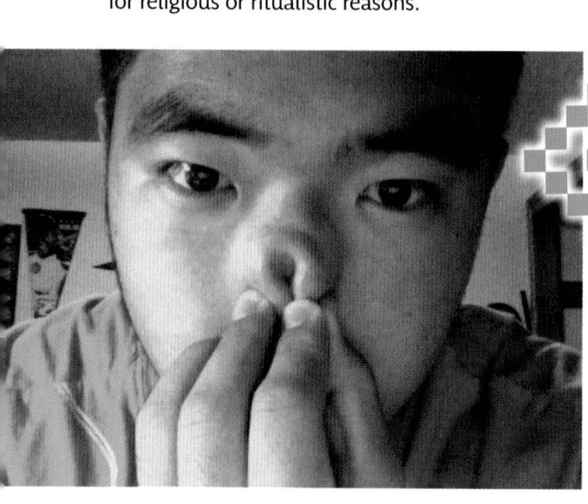

YOUR

www.ripleys.com/submit

Ricky Nakamura from Seattle, Washington, wrote to tell us about his curious nasal ability. He is able to crack, flatten and fold the cartilage in his nose without feeling any pain.

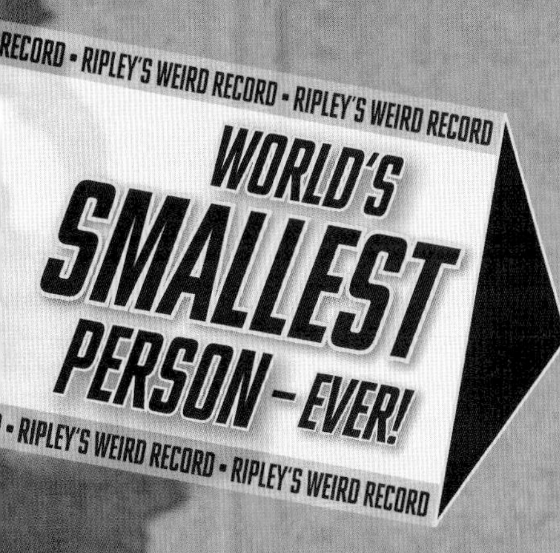

Tiny Mexican

Mexican Lucia Zarate (1864–90) stood just 20 in (50 cm) tall, weighed 5 lb (2.3 kg) and had a 14-in (35-cm) waist, making her one of the smallest adults in history. Weighing only 8 oz (225 g) at birth and measuring just 7 in (18 cm) long, she stopped growing when she was one year old.

At the age of 12 she went to the U.S.A. and became a major draw in sideshows, where she appeared as the "Mexican Liliputian" and earned an average of $700 per week—as much as $20 per hour—a small fortune in those days. With her earnings, Lucia was able to buy her own ranch.

Lucia wore tiny jewelry to match her tiny frame and one museum at which she appeared offered a diamond ring to any baby who could fit a ring the same size as one of Lucia's on its finger.

Sadly, Lucia died of hypothermia at the age of 26 when the circus train she was traveling in got stuck in a blizzard. It took a week to dig the train out of the snow and Lucia did not survive the ordeal.

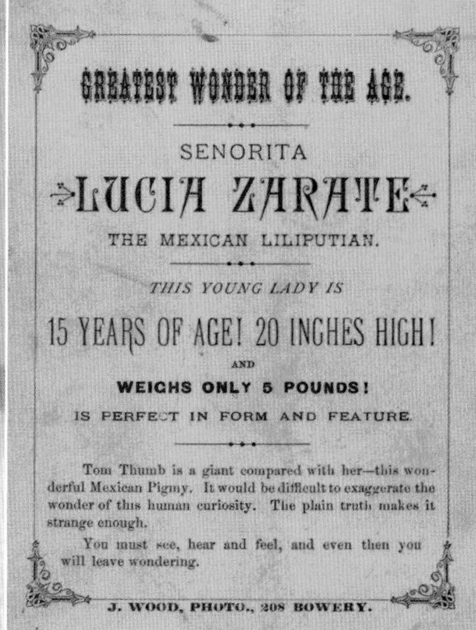

GREATEST WONDER OF THE AGE.

SENORITA

LUCIA ZARATE

THE MEXICAN LILIPUTIAN.

THIS YOUNG LADY IS

15 YEARS OF AGE! 20 INCHES HIGH!

AND

WEIGHS ONLY 5 POUNDS!

IS PERFECT IN FORM AND FEATURE.

Tom Thumb is a giant compared with her—this wonderful Mexican Pigmy. It would be difficult to exaggerate the wonder of this human curiosity. The plain truth makes it strange enough.

You must see, hear and feel, and even then you will leave wondering.

J. WOOD, PHOTO., 208 BOWERY.

COLORED POOP

Based on medical research, Alexandra Daisy Ginsberg and James King's design piece *Scatalog* demonstrates how special *E. chromi* bacteria can be used to change the color of a person's poop to indicate the presence of disease in the body. A team of biologists from Cambridge University genetically engineered the bacteria which, on detecting disease in the human gut, secretes a color signal—red, green, yellow, brown, blue or violet—that is visible in the feces. Each color denotes a different disease.

DIED TWICE A woman died from shock after waking up to find that she was at her own funeral. Fagilyu Mukhametzyanov, 49, of Kazan, Russia, had been wrongly declared dead by doctors, but she died for real after hearing people praying for her soul.

SKELETON FOUND Hanged in 1821 for murdering his former girlfriend, John Horwood finally received a proper burial 190 years later after his family tracked down his skeleton to the University of Bristol, England, science laboratory where it had been displayed with the noose still around its neck. Following his execution, Horwood's body had been publicly dissected, and the skin removed and used to bind a book about the case.

LIFE SAVER Days away from death because of a muscle-wasting disease called Duchenne syndrome, a 15-year-old Italian boy became the world's first child to be given a permanent artificial heart—an implant that should give him at least another 20 years of normal life. His new heart is powered through a plug positioned behind his left ear and is connected to a battery that he keeps on a belt. The battery is charged during the night like a mobile phone.

TWINS SEPARATED A team of British doctors at London's Great Ormond Street Hospital for Children successfully separated Sudanese-born twins Rital and Ritag Gaboura who were born joined at the head—a condition where the chances of survival are just one in ten million. Although the twins did not share brain tissue, they did share vital arteries and nerves. The blood flow between their brains made the operation particularly difficult.

MODERN STYLES A study of hair samples of mummies showed that Ancient Egyptians used to style their hair like Marilyn Monroe and Rihanna. They used fat-based products as gels, tried to curl their hair with tongs and even plaited it in extensions.

MISSING YEARS For almost two months in 2008, 28-year-old Naomi Jacobs of Manchester, England, was convinced that it was 1992 and that she was a 15-year-old schoolgirl about to take her exams. Mobile phones and the Internet were a mystery to her, and she had no idea who her 11-year-old son Leo was or any recollection of giving birth to him. She was suffering from Transient Global Amnesia, a form of memory loss brought on by stress. Her memory started to return after eight weeks, but it was another three years before she fully recovered.

NEW SKILLS Before losing half her brain in a 2008 car crash in St. Petersburg, Russia, Taisia Sidorova was right-handed and displayed no artistic talent—but since the accident she has become a skilled artist who paints with her left hand.

BACK LAWN

Chinese performance artist Yang Zhichao had grass from the Suzhou River surgically implanted into his back without anesthesia. The surgeon made two incisions in Yang's shoulder before planting the freshly picked grass into the deep cuts. Owing to his ability to withstand intense pain, Yang has also had objects surgically implanted in his leg and stomach and had his ID number branded on his back with a red-hot iron.

Body

Vampire Woman

FEATURED ARTIST: MARIA JOSE CRISTERNA ★ FEATURED ARTIST: MARIA JOSE CRISTERNA ★ FEATURED ARTIST: MARIA JOSE CRISTERNA ★

Ripley's ask

Ripley's talks to Maria José Cristerna, the Mexican tattoo artist who has transformed herself into Vampire Woman.

Can you tell us how you began your transformation? *I started with a piercing. I was 12 years old, and it was the gouged ears, and, well, if it's strange now to see it on a 12-year-old girl, imagine in my times... even more! The black star tattoo on my left shoulder was my first. When I was 14, I convinced my dad to take me to get it, and from there on out, it's been a gradual modification, my whole life.*

Would you ever have any tattoos removed? *None. Because they are a part of me. It would be like trying to erase something that's already been lived, and, well, it's impossible; everything is a story. The one most meaningful to me is the one on my knee, because it symbolizes the four eyes that represent my kids. Why eyes? Because they are always going to be watching me, they will be copying my actions... you have to try and be better. And the broken heart [on her right thigh] symbolizes my parents. They both died of a heart attack, ten years apart, but they will always be on my mind... and this is so they will always live on here.*

How many tattoos do you have? *I've stopped counting... they cover 95 percent of my body, and the remaining space is used to contour them, as if I were a painting.*

What do you hope to achieve by your unusual appearance? *Well, to be no one but me, really. Never, never did I want to please nor displease anyone, simply be free to express and feel what I want. I feel that I'm a responsible mother, that I love my children very much and my appearance is of the least importance. We classify beauty like we want and we look for the stereotype we want; beauty is subjective... because I feel beautiful. For other people, it's not so.*

Turn the page

ODD SCAN
Ripley's Believe It or Not!
RIPLEY'S WEIRD RECORD • RIPLEY'S WEIRD
MOST BODY-MODIFIED WOMAN!
RECORD • RIPLEY'S WEIRD RECORD • RIPLEY'S

Vampire Woman

Maria Jose Cristerna is not actually a vampire, but she could probably pass for one after such extensive body modification. The Mexican tattoo artist has transformed herself with numerous tattoos, titanium implants under the skin, a large number of piercings, stretched earlobe tunnels and permanent fangs. Cristerna, a mother-of-four who is trained in law, reinvented herself as a vampire as a sign of strength after troubles in her life.

26 years old!

RAPID AGING

A young Vietnamese woman looked like she had aged 50 years in just a few days following what she thinks was an allergic reaction to eating seafood. Nguyen Thi Phuong suffered the rapid aging affliction in 2008, leaving her with sagging, wrinkled skin all over her face and body. At age 26, she looked like a woman in her 70s and is so upset by her appearance that she wears a mask in public. Doctors are baffled by the exact cause of her sudden aging and have yet to reach a diagnosis.

SENIOR TEACHER Gladys Morris of Oldham, England, was still teaching yoga four times a week at the age of 89. She had three great-grandchildren and had been practicing yoga for nearly 50 years.

CRAMPED CELL A Dutch prisoner, serving a two-year sentence for fraud, went to court in 2011 to complain that his cell was too small for him. At 6 ft 9 in (2 m) and 504 lb (229 kg), he claimed he was unable to use the toilet in his cell at Krimpen aan den Ijssel and could not sleep properly for fear of falling out of bed. The judge ruled against his claim.

YOUNGEST GRANNY In 2011, 23-year-old Rifca Stanescu of Investi, Romania, became the world's youngest grandmother. She was just 12 when she had her first child, Maria, who gave birth to a son, Ion, when she was just 11 years old.

OVARIAN CYST Jane Alexander from Fife, Scotland, had a 21 lb (9.5 kg) ovarian cyst removed from her body. The cyst, which was so big it made her look pregnant, began growing at a rate of 2 in (5 cm) a week until it had grown to twice the size of a soccer ball.

TONGUE STRETCHED Rhiannon Brooksbank-Jones, a language student from Nottingham, England, had her tongue lengthened by almost half an inch (about 1 cm) so that she could pronounce South Korean more fluently. She underwent a lingual frenectomy to have tissue removed from under her tongue, which had previously been too short to say the Korean letter "L" properly.

STRANGER DELUSION Fregoli delusion, which can be triggered by brain damage, causes a person to suspect that strangers are actually people they already know—just acting in disguise.

EYE LIFT In July 2011, Rakesh Kumar of Ludhiana, India, broke his own world record by lifting a 22-lb (10-kg) weight using a hook placed in one of his eye sockets. He can also lift a 178-lb (81-kg) weight with one ear and pull a school bus with his teeth.

SHAVED BEARD Teacher Gary Weddle, of East Wenatchee, Washington State, vowed not to shave his face until Osama bin Laden was killed or captured. He kept his promise and left his beard untouched from 2001 until Bin Laden's death on May 2, 2011.

ARTIFICIAL HEART Charles Okeke became the first person to live outside a hospital with an artificial heart. Fitted at a clinic in Phoenix, Arizona, his mechanical heart was powered by a 13-lb (5.9-kg) backpack that ran on batteries. He wore it at home for 263 days until eventually a suitable donor was found to give him a new human heart.

BIGGEST TONSILS A tonsillectomy performed on 21-year-old Justin Werner of Topeka, Kansas, revealed that one tonsil was 2.1 in (5.25 cm) long, 1.1 in (2.75 cm) wide and 0.7 in (1.75 cm) thick, while the other measured 1.9 in (4.75 cm) long, 1 in (2.5 cm) wide and 0.7 in (1.75 cm) thick, breaking the record for the world's largest tonsils by a total length of 1.4 in (3.5 cm).

SHORTEST WOMAN At just 2 ft 3 in (69 cm) tall, 22-year-old Bridgette Jordan from Sandoval, Illinois, is the world's shortest living woman. She and her 20-year-old brother, Brad, who is 3 ft 2 in (97 cm) tall, have a disorder that affected their growth while they were still in the womb.

BIGGEST BREASTS

With a bra size of 102ZZZ, American Annie Hawkins-Turner (who goes under the stage name Norma Stitz) has the biggest natural breasts in the world. They weigh a combined 112 lb (51 kg)—a third of her total body weight. Her cleavage is 3 ft 6 in (1.07 m) long... and still growing.

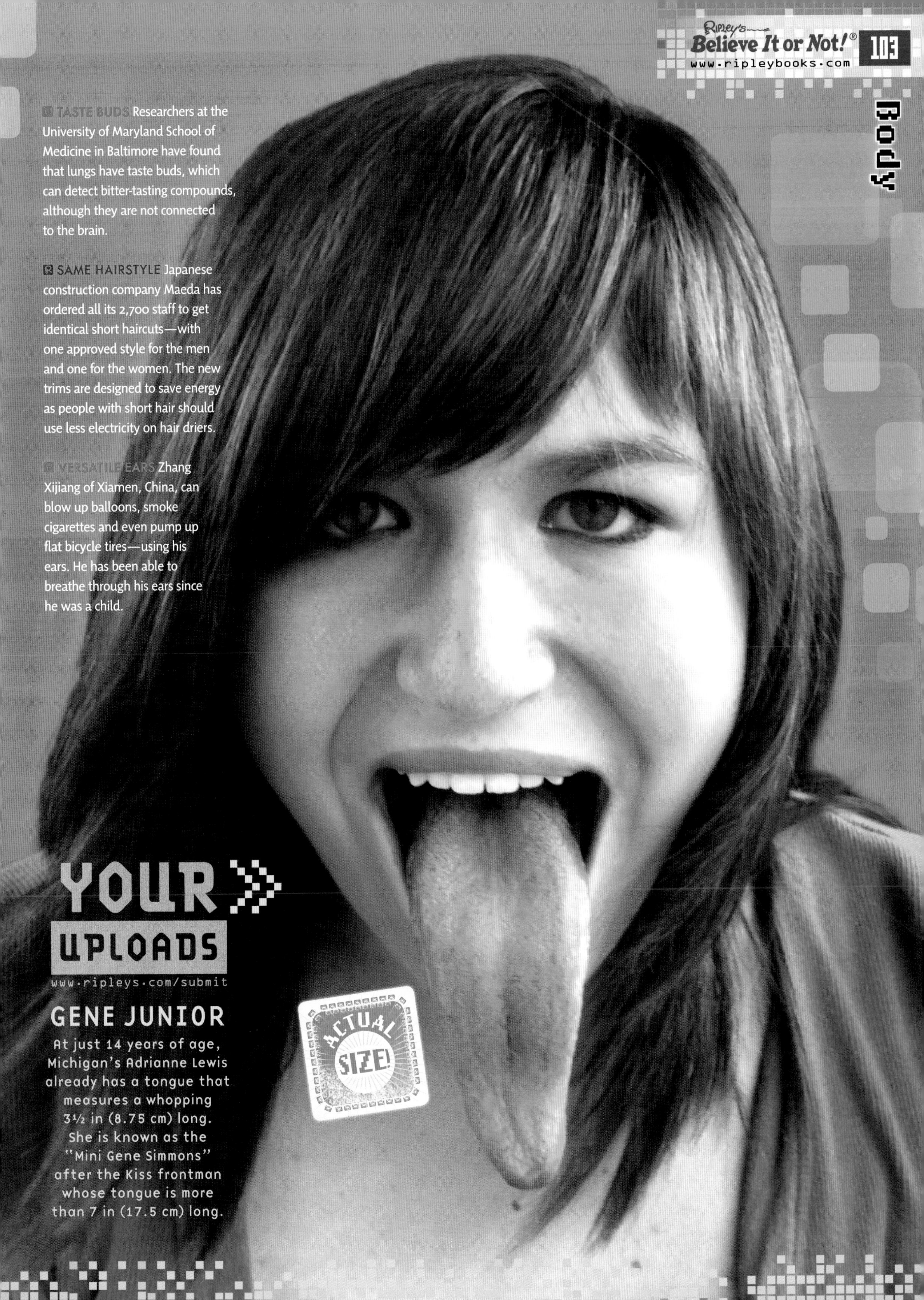

TASTE BUDS Researchers at the University of Maryland School of Medicine in Baltimore have found that lungs have taste buds, which can detect bitter-tasting compounds, although they are not connected to the brain.

SAME HAIRSTYLE Japanese construction company Maeda has ordered all its 2,700 staff to get identical short haircuts—with one approved style for the men and one for the women. The new trims are designed to save energy as people with short hair should use less electricity on hair driers.

VERSATILE EARS Zhang Xijiang of Xiamen, China, can blow up balloons, smoke cigarettes and even pump up flat bicycle tires—using his ears. He has been able to breathe through his ears since he was a child.

YOUR UPLOADS

www.ripleys.com/submit

GENE JUNIOR

At just 14 years of age, Michigan's Adrianne Lewis already has a tongue that measures a whopping 3½ in (8.75 cm) long. She is known as the "Mini Gene Simmons" after the Kiss frontman whose tongue is more than 7 in (17.5 cm) long.

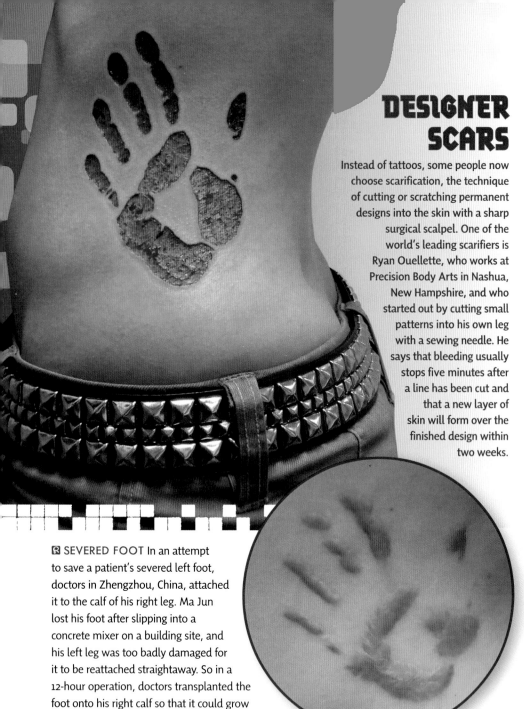

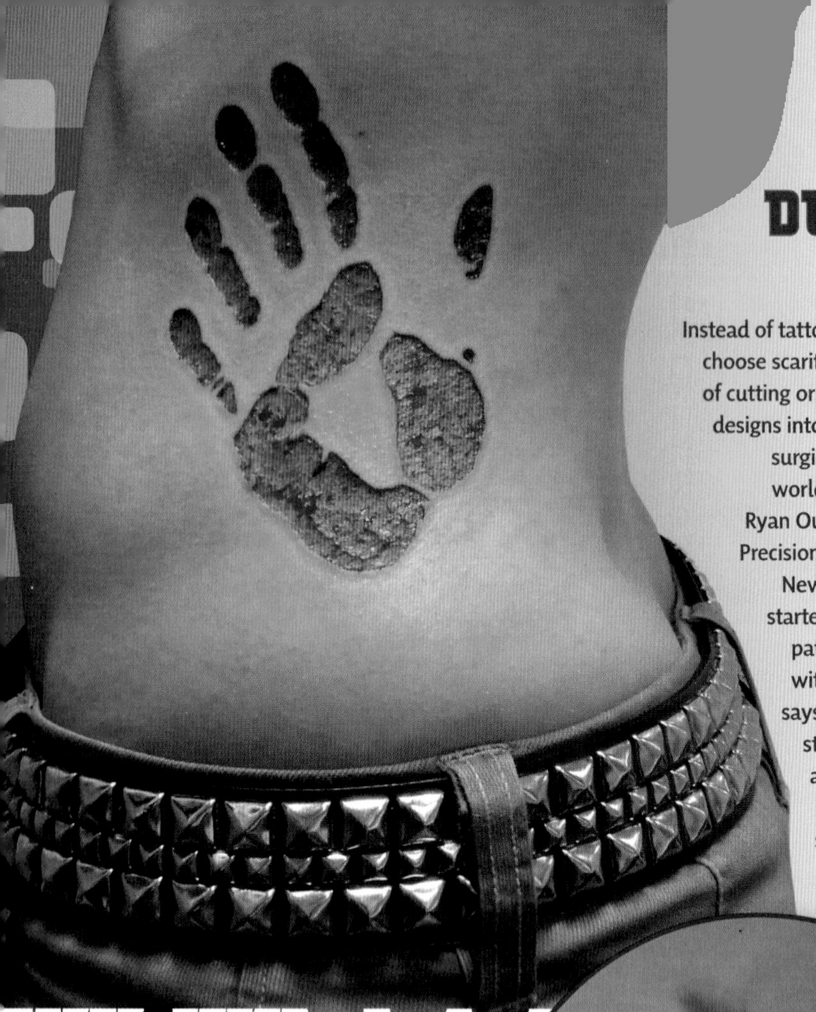

DESIGNER SCARS

Instead of tattoos, some people now choose scarification, the technique of cutting or scratching permanent designs into the skin with a sharp surgical scalpel. One of the world's leading scarifiers is Ryan Ouellette, who works at Precision Body Arts in Nashua, New Hampshire, and who started out by cutting small patterns into his own leg with a sewing needle. He says that bleeding usually stops five minutes after a line has been cut and that a new layer of skin will form over the finished design within two weeks.

PROPHETIC TATTOO? When he was arrested in May 2011 on suspicion of assault, Robert Kennedy of Horry County, South Carolina, had a tattoo on his forehead that read: "Please forgive me if I say or do anything stupid. Thank you."

SMELLY URINE Thorpe Park theme park in Surrey, England, asked visitors to provide smelly urine samples so that the foulest odor could be re-created for a new horror attraction alongside the smells of burning hair and rotting meat. To stand a chance of winning the $750 first prize for the smelliest pee, participants were advised to drink alcohol or coffee and to eat garlic or asparagus.

HER HITLER! During World War II, British scientists devised a plan to smuggle female sex hormones into the food of German dictator Adolf Hitler to make him turn into a woman! They hoped that by slipping undetectable estrogen into the Nazi leader's meals, he would become more feminine and generally less aggressive.

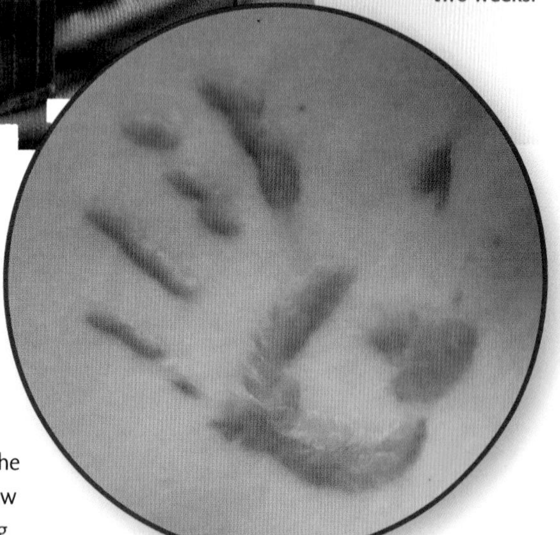

SEVERED FOOT In an attempt to save a patient's severed left foot, doctors in Zhengzhou, China, attached it to the calf of his right leg. Ma Jun lost his foot after slipping into a concrete mixer on a building site, and his left leg was too badly damaged for it to be reattached straightaway. So in a 12-hour operation, doctors transplanted the foot onto his right calf so that it could grow new skin, tissue and muscles before being reattached in its rightful place.

BIONIC FINGERS After losing fingers on both hands to blood poisoning when she was a toddler, 15-year-old Chloe Holmes from Swindon, England, has been fitted with a full set of bionic digits on her left hand, enabling her to pick up things for the first time. The false fingers are controlled by electronic signals from the nerve endings in her hand.

DRIVER SKEWERED Andrew Linn of Las Vegas, Nevada, survived being speared through the face with a 2-in-wide (5-cm) metal pole after falling unconscious at the wheel of his car, veering off the road and plowing into a chain-link fence. The pole tore through his face just below the right side of his nose, ripping out some of his teeth, before exiting through the back of his neck.

TELLTALE TATTOOS Grant Dey of Christchurch, New Zealand, has his face covered in flame tattoos—and in September 2011 he was convicted of deliberately burning down his neighbor's house.

COLORED SWEAT Exposure to certain dyes, foods and chemicals can cause chromhidrosis—colored sweat that usually appears on the face and underarms in a variety of bright hues—red, blue, green, yellow or black.

SILENCE ON COURT! The grunts and screams that famously accompany every tennis shot hit by Russian player Maria Sharapova regularly reach 101 decibels—that's louder than the roar of a freight train at full speed.

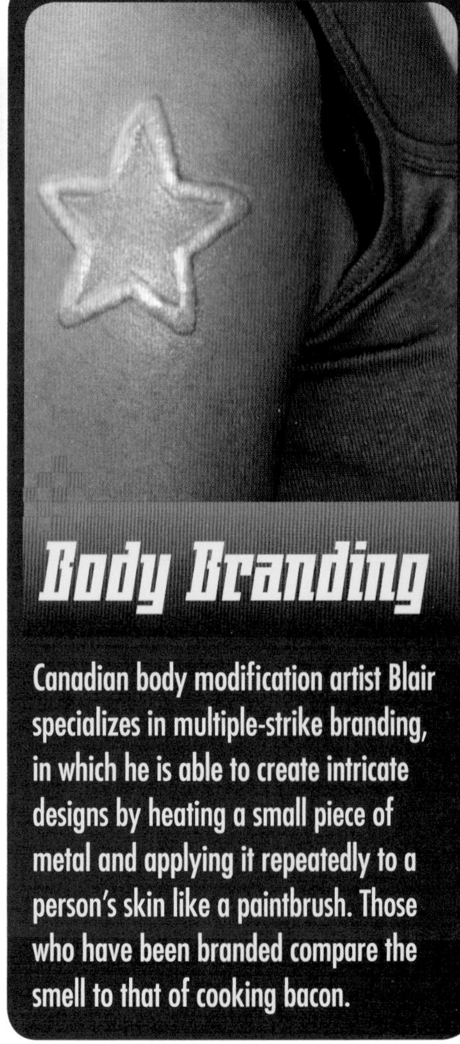

Body Branding

Canadian body modification artist Blair specializes in multiple-strike branding, in which he is able to create intricate designs by heating a small piece of metal and applying it repeatedly to a person's skin like a paintbrush. Those who have been branded compare the smell to that of cooking bacon.

KING'S HEAD In 2010, scientists identified the long-lost head of King Henri IV of France, who was assassinated in 1610 and whose head had been stolen during the French Revolution. Scientists used forensics to identify the head, which had passed between collectors, by features visible in portraits, including a lesion near his nose, a pierced ear and a healed facial wound from a previous assassination attempt.

THREE GENERATIONS Kathryn Crills of Ephrata, Pennsylvania, is the proud matriarch of three generations of identical twins—her own daughters Karen and Sharon (who were born August 7, 1959), her granddaughters Melanie and Michelle (who were born September 22, 1973) and her great-granddaughters Maleah and Makelah (who were born April 16, 2010).

BODY METAL Rolf Buchholz, a 52-year-old computer expert from Dortmund, Germany, has 453 rings and studs on his body.

CORPSE DISPLAY Cancetto Farmica, a U.S. carnival worker, died in 1911, but when his father failed to collect his son's body, the funeral home at Laurinburg, North Carolina, put him on display as an attraction until 1972.

What inspired you to modify your ears in this fashion? *I had been wearing prosthetic elf ears for years, the way other people would wear a necklaces or clothes. It was part of my unique "look" and a statement I was making about who I am and what I am about. I also walked around town wearing a crushed velvet cape and carrying a quarter staff—literally I was a modern-day elf!*

Did it hurt? *The procedure itself was painless. Anesthetic was used and I had a huge grin on my face the entire time. When the anesthetic wore off, the pain kicked in and I had to be very careful how I slept. Even when no pressure was on my ears, there was a constant pain for two weeks.*

How long did it take to heal? *The stitches came out after a week or so. However, I had to use surgical tape for another two weeks to help convince my body to hold this new, foreign shape in my ears. Then it took almost a full year before my ears settled into the shape they are now.*

What kind of reactions do you get to your new ears? *Almost all the reactions I get are positive. Sometimes people post negative things on websites, but that never bothers me. These people don't know me, whereas people who know me have been fantastically supportive. As Russ Foxx said: "I'm not modifying your ears, I am fixing them." This whole process seemed like part of the journey of making myself into exactly who I want to be—who I've always been. When people say that my ears will make me unemployable, I can't help but laugh. Since I got the body modification, I have worked for the B.C. government, as a nanny, and with adults and kids with mental and physical disabilities. I also teach martial arts and history, and have a successful band—The Figures.*

How do you feel about your ears now? *I love them, plain and simple! I love the subtlety of them and the fact that Russ did such an amazing job that most people can't tell they have been modified—they assume I was just born with them. This mod is just an accent to my lifestyle; it's a part of who I am and goes hand in hand with the amazing life I have chosen to live.*

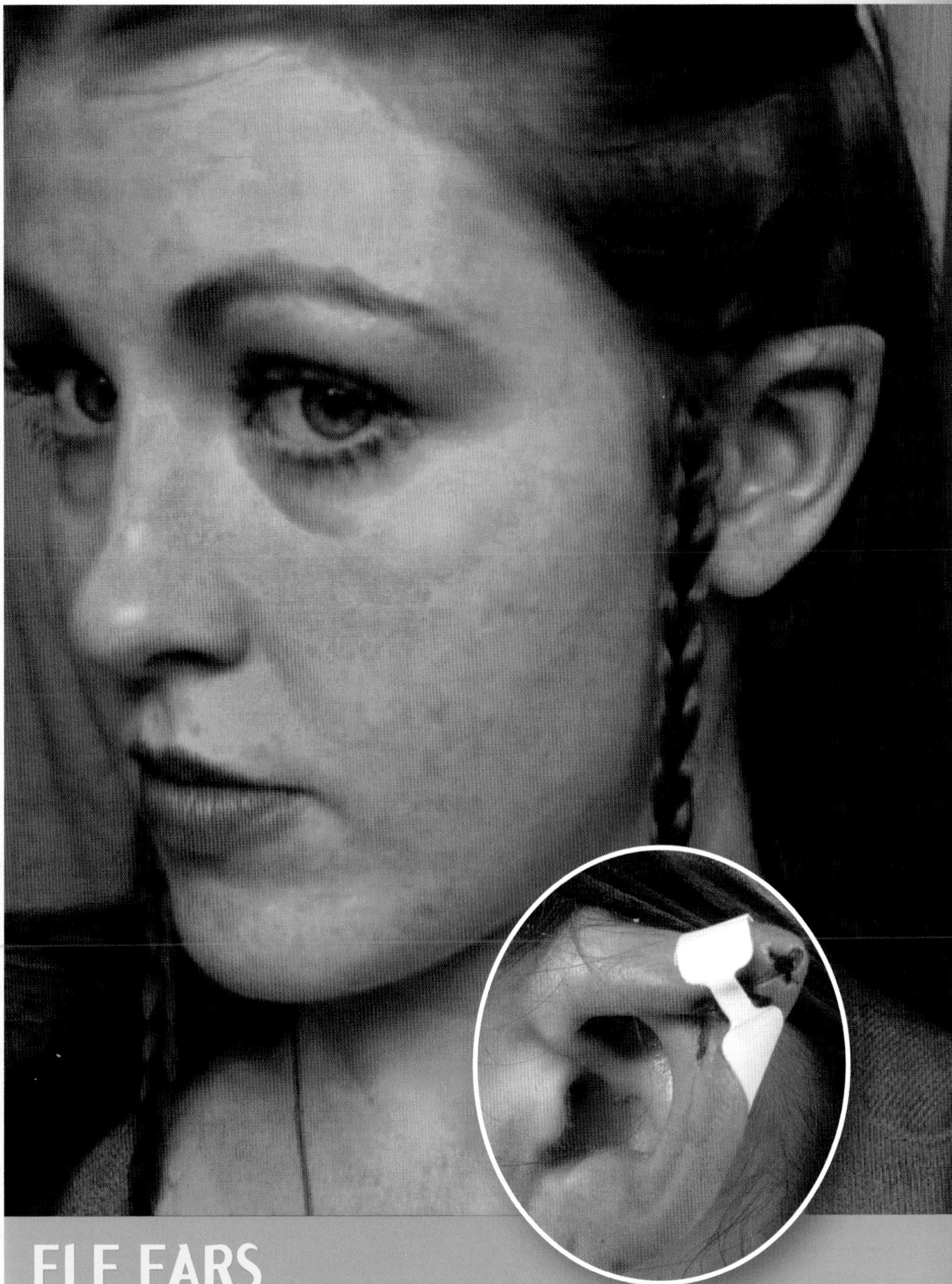

ELF EARS

Kimberleigh Smithbower Roseblade of Vancouver, Canada, underwent complex surgery to acquire a pair of genuine pointy elf ears. Body modification artist Russ Foxx carried out the procedure by removing a piece of Kimberleigh's ear, then folding the ear over and stitching it shut. Kimberleigh had previously worn prosthetic elf ears as a fashion statement, but is now delighted to own the real deal.

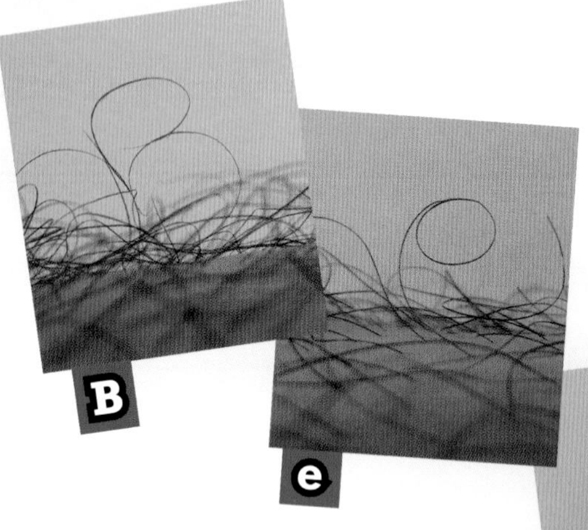

SELF-SERVICE After badly cutting his leg in an accident at home, a 32-year-old man became so frustrated at having to wait an hour at Sundsvall Hospital in northern Sweden that he picked up a needle and thread and sewed up the cut himself.

SUM GIRL! A 15-year-old schoolgirl with a love of math was awakened from a coma when her father began asking her simple sums. Vicki Alex of Northamptonshire, England, had been unconscious for three days and had failed to respond to other attempts to stimulate her brain, but after her father's intervention she soon regained full consciousness.

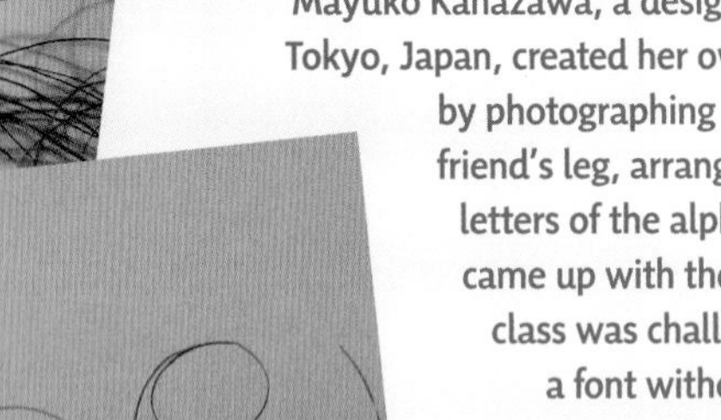

Curly Characters

Mayuko Kanazawa, a design student from Tokyo, Japan, created her own bizarre font by photographing the hair on her friend's leg, arranged to look like letters of the alphabet. Mayuko came up with the idea after her class was challenged to make a font without the aid of a computer, to ensure no digital trickery was involved!

NEW LANGUAGE A 13-year-old Croatian girl woke from a 24-hour coma speaking fluent German, which she had started studying at school only shortly before she fell into the coma. Bizarrely, she could no longer speak Croatian!

EIGHT LIMBS Seven-year-old Deepak Paswan of Bihar, India, was born with eight limbs—having the arms, legs and buttocks of a parasitic twin protruding from his chest. Although the parasitic twin's arms were small and withered, its legs grew at the same rate as Deepak, meaning the youngster had to carry a heavy weight around until he had the extra limbs removed in a complex operation in 2010.

LONG LOBES Jian Tianjin, a farmer from Taiwan, has earlobes that stretch 6½ in (16 cm)—so long and flexible that they reach his shoulders and can be wound around his chin.

LARGE FAMILY After giving birth to two sets of quadruplets (in 2004 and 2005), Dale Chalk from Strathpine in Queensland, Australia, had twins in 2009, giving her a total of 11 children under the age of seven.

SINGLE HANDED Despite being born with just one hand, Kevin Shields from Fort William, Scotland, is an accomplished rock climber and has even managed to master treacherous ice climbs.

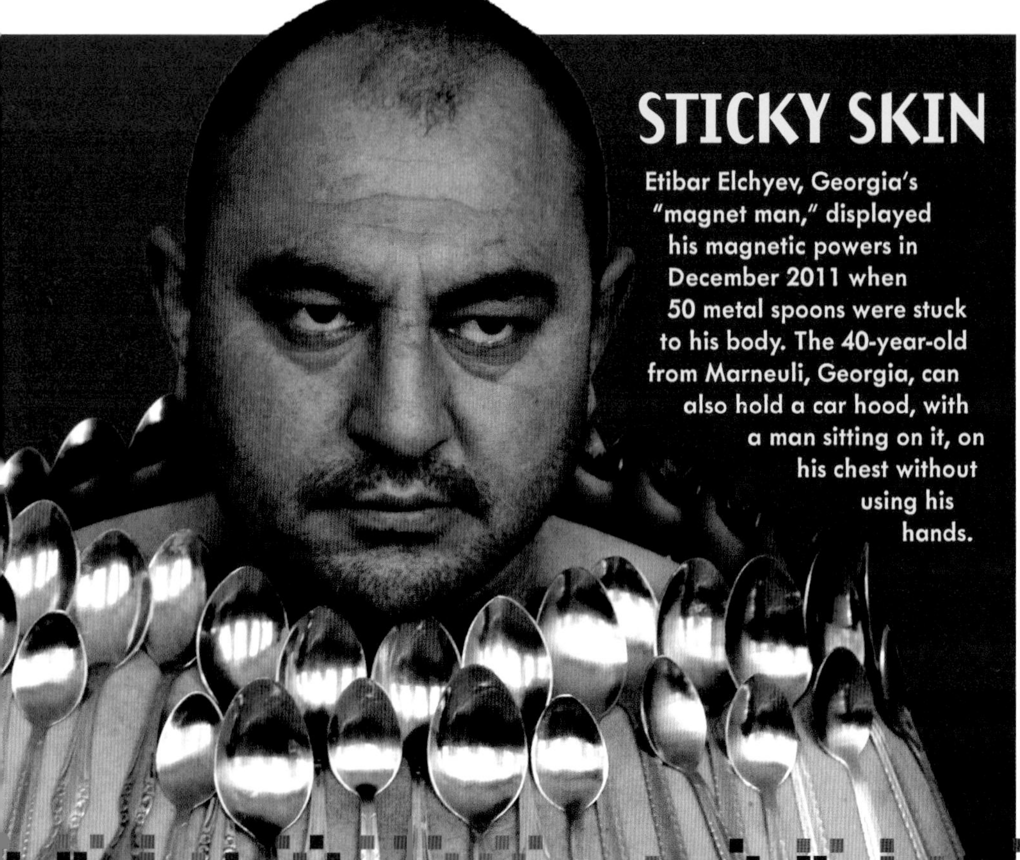

STICKY SKIN

Etibar Elchyev, Georgia's "magnet man," displayed his magnetic powers in December 2011 when 50 metal spoons were stuck to his body. The 40-year-old from Marneuli, Georgia, can also hold a car hood, with a man sitting on it, on his chest without using his hands.

BORN TWICE Doctors in Texas performed prenatal surgery at 25 weeks to remove a grapefruit-sized tumor from Macie McCartney while she was still inside her mother's womb. The procedure involved pulling out mother Keri's uterus and then half of Macie's body. Once free of the tumor, Macie was returned to the womb, where she recovered and grew for another ten weeks before being "born" again.

BABY'S TAIL Surgeons in China performed an operation to remove a 5-in-long (13-cm) tail from the body of a four-month-old baby girl. Hong Hong, from China's Anhui Province, was born with the tail, but it quickly doubled in size. X-rays had shown that it was connected to a fatty tumor within her spinal column.

Long in the Nails

Kathy Hayes from Los Angeles, California, has let her toenails grow over a number of years to what is now an incredible length. The anthropologist keeps her 5-in (13-cm) nails in tiptop condition, always polished and painted. Kathy's devotion to her decorated feet means that she is unable to wear regular shoes; she is restricted to open-toed sandals with platform heels in order to protect her nails.

HAIRY HANDS Since becoming the first American to undergo a double hand transplant, Jeff Kepner from Augusta, Georgia, has noticed that his new hands are considerably hairier than the rest of his body because the donor had more hair than him.

METAL MUNCHER Doctors in Cajamarca, Peru, removed 2 lb (900 g) of metal from a man's stomach, including nails, coins, rusted copper wire and scrap metal. Requelme Abanto Alvarado said he had been eating metal for months and had once swallowed 17 nails that measured 5 in (12.5 cm) in one day.

TODDLER PLUNGE Two-year-old Zhu Xinping miraculously survived after falling from the 21st floor of a tower block in Jianyang City, Sichuan Province, China. She suffered only a broken leg because she landed on a freshly dug pile of soil that cushioned her fall.

SELF-AMPUTATION Trapped by a fallen concrete girder in the rubble of a building that collapsed during a 2009 earthquake in Padang, Indonesia, an 18-year-old construction worker named Ramlan survived by sawing off his own leg.

AUTO DEGREE Mike Needs, a 48-year-old from Canton, Ohio, has been blind for decades, yet is finishing his degree as an auto mechanic.

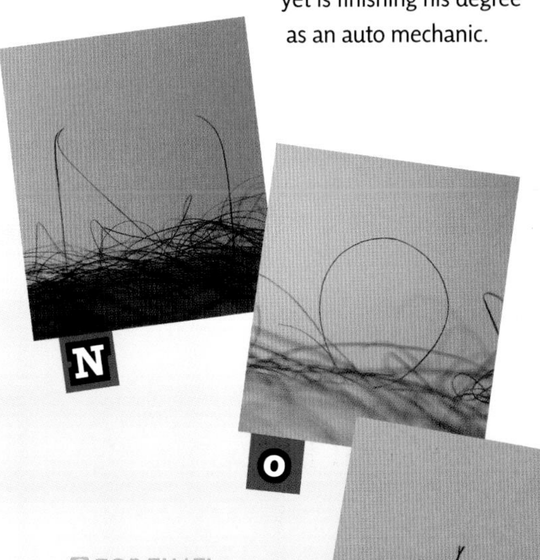

BULLET SURPRISE A 35-year-old Polish man went to the hospital in Bochum, Germany, worried about a small lump on the back of his head, to discover that he had a .22 caliber bullet lodged there. Only then did he remember receiving a blow to the head around midnight at a New Year's Party five years earlier.

THE WIDTH OF BOTH ARMS STRETCHED OUT IS THE SAME AS THE LENGTH OF YOUR WHOLE BODY.

LEGLESS ACROBAT Although he was born without legs, Lv Li from Dengfeng, China, makes his living as an acrobat. The amazing street performer's act includes handstands, snake charming and fire breathing, drawing huge crowds wherever he goes.

ON THE MOVE U.S. President Abraham Lincoln's coffin was moved 17 times after his funeral and was kept under a pile of lumber to hide it from grave robbers.

TOP THAT! George Linn of Lakewood, Colorado, suffered a heart attack in July 2010 and was saved by a pizza deliveryman who applied CPR.

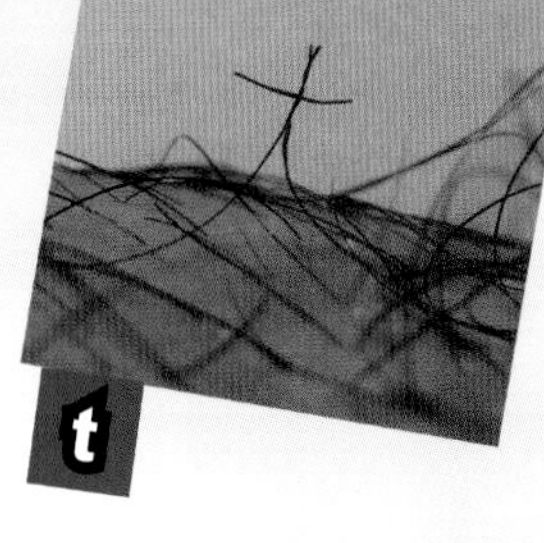

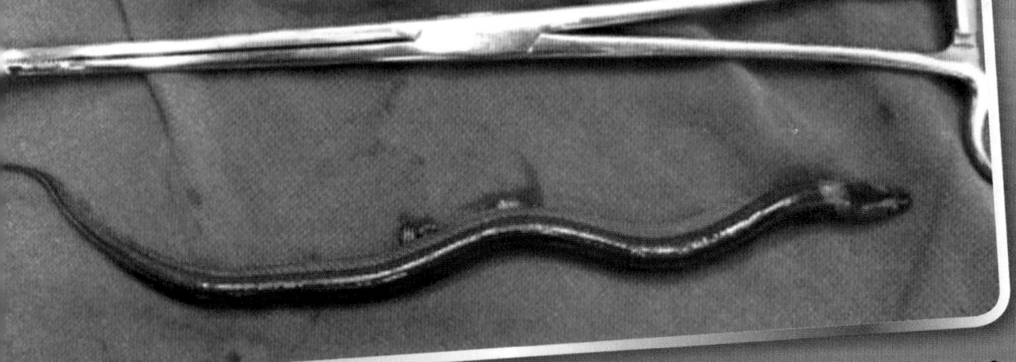

SLIPPERY PROBLEM

Doctors removed an eel from a man's bladder after it had swum up his penis during an unorthodox beauty treatment. Zhang Nan of Honghu, China, climbed into a bath with ten eels after reading on the Internet how they can cleanse the body of dead skin. However, he soon felt a sharp pain and saw one of the eels drilling into his urethra. Unable to stop it because it was too quick and slippery, he then tried to urinate the eel out, but when that failed he went to hospital where the 6-in-long (15-cm) eel was removed in a three-hour operation. With a diameter of less than half an inch (1 cm), the eel was wider than the urethra, but doctors said its slippery nature acted as a lubricant and allowed it to penetrate Zhang's body.

DIY OP A 63-year-old Californian man was taken to the hospital after he tried unsuccessfully to perform a do-it-yourself operation on his hernia by slicing open his stomach with a 6-in (15-cm) butter knife.

HOLE IN JAW Wu Moude, a worker on a building site in Quanzhou, China, survived a fall in which a half-inch-thick (1.2-cm) steel bar penetrated his jaw and embedded itself 6 in (15 cm) into his skull.

BREAKING GLASS American vocal coach Jaime Vendera can shatter a wine glass using only the sound of his voice. He can get his voice box up to an incredible 120 decibels, louder than the roar of a motorbike doing 60 mph (96 km/h).

POINTED EARS New York City cosmetic surgeon Dr. Lajos Nagy offers patients the opportunity to acquire pointed, Mr. Spock-like ears, which he claims improve the experience of listening to music, as pointed ears focus sounds better.

GIANT CYST Anne Warren, 60, of Westport, New Zealand, had a 22-lb (10-kg) ovarian cyst—a tumor the size of triplets. The cyst had been growing for years, but it wasn't until it began to affect her organs that Anne realized something was wrong. It was so big that the incision needed to remove it stretched from her groin to past her belly button.

BLOCKED NOSE

Doctors in Yongkang, China, discovered that a man who had gone to hospital with breathing difficulties had a tooth growing in his nostril. Feng Fujia, aged 21, had experienced nasal problems for five years, during which time his nose smelled so bad that his coworkers would stay away from him. When X-rays were finally taken, doctors were stunned to see a tooth in his nose. They think that when he was young and his teeth were developing, he must have eaten something so hard that it pressed one of his upper teeth into his nostril. The tooth then slowly started to grow.

TOOTHBRUSH TRAUMA

Complaining of severe stomach pains, a woman from Jinan, China, rushed to a hospital where doctors found the cause of her discomfort—a toothbrush lodged in her stomach. It had been there for a month since she arrived home drunk from a party and fell asleep while brushing her teeth. When she woke up, the brush had vanished. "I thought my family members threw it away," she said. "I really don't know how I swallowed the toothbrush."

EMERGENCY CALL On October 17, 2010, three-year-old Vincent Lamitie of North Ridgeville, Ohio, called the 911 emergency line to help his unconscious father—after remembering the 911 number from a cartoon.

SAVED BY TOOTH Walter Davis was shot in the face in New Orleans, Louisiana, in February 2011—but escaped serious injury when the small-caliber .22 bullet ricocheted off his gold tooth.

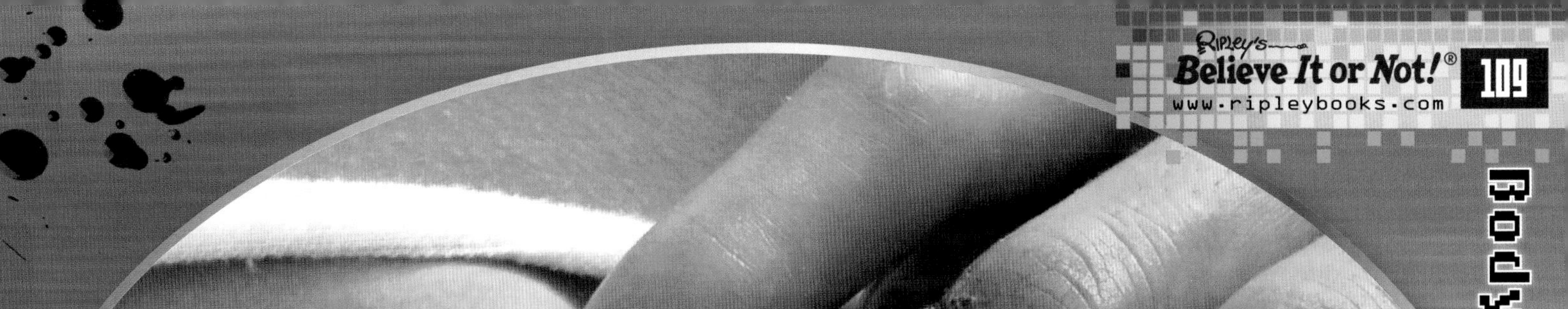

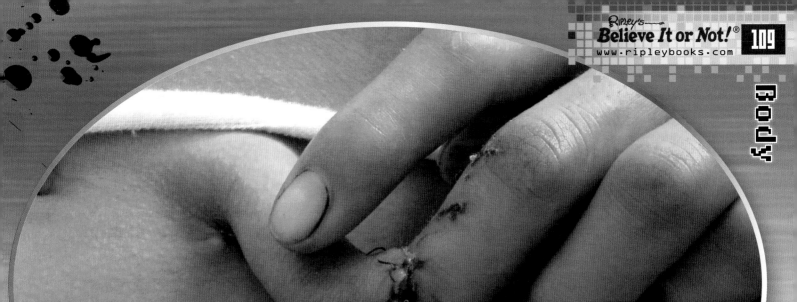

Stomach Growth

Chinese factory worker Wang Yongjun grew a new fingertip... on his stomach. After he accidentally cut off the end of his middle finger with an electric saw, doctors in Liaoyang attached the bony finger to his stomach for over a month so that new skin and muscle could grow around it. Once the fingertip had repaired itself, it was separated from the stomach and reattached to the injured hand.

GUN SHOT A Polish man who was hit in the back of the head by a .22-caliber bullet during New Year's Eve celebrations in the German town of Herne took five years to realize he had been shot. It was only when he went to a doctor after feeling a lump on his head that an X-ray revealed the presence of the bullet.

WALDO TATTOO John Mosley of Norwich, England, has a *Where's Waldo?* scene of 150 characters tattooed on his back. He sat patiently for 24 hours while tattooist Rytch Soddy created the body artwork, which features Darth Vader from Star Wars, cavemen, pirates, Vikings, cowboys and Waldo himself.

SURGICAL SPONGE Helen O'Hagan of Sydney, Australia, lived for more than 15 years with a surgical sponge the size of a grapefruit sewn inside her following an abdominal operation in 1992. She suffered cramps, fevers and bowel problems until an X-ray detected the sponge in 2007.

SAVED BY DENTURES When 81-year-old Zacarias Pacheco de Moraes was shot in May 2011 while working in the bar he owns in Alta Floresta, Brazil, his life was saved by his dentures deflecting a bullet that was headed for his brain. The bullet hit his dentures before lodging in his throat.

WORKER IMPALED Wang Tao from Xian, China, survived after an accident at a concrete factory left him impaled on 13 metal rods. An explosion sent the steel rods spearing into his thigh and hip. Some of them were so long that workmates had to use an angle grinder to sever them so that Tao could fit into the ambulance.

IRON FINGER Some Shaolin monks can do one-finger handstands or "iron fingers." To balance the body on just one finger requires immense strength and concentration—yet Hai-tank, a 91-year-old monk from the Sil Lum Temple in China, can perform the feat.

SPAT BULLET In June 2010, a 39-year-old man was shot in the face while walking down a street in Chicago, Illinois. Incredibly, he spat out the bullet and a tooth, suffering only minor injury.

STOMACH GRIP China's Wu Zhilong has such powerful stomach muscles he can use them to pull a 2.2-ton car a distance of 65 ft (20 m). He is also able to hold an iron pot so firmly in his abdomen that others cannot pull it off.

ARTIFICIAL TEETH Scientists from Tokyo University of Science, Japan, have grown fully formed teeth from stem cells. The artificial teeth, which were grown in mice, looked realistic, could chew food and were sensitive to pain.

ANCIENT BONES A woman in Marathon, Florida, discovered human bones in her garden in October 2010. On inspection, experts estimated that the bones are in fact 2,400 years old.

DIME MUSEUMS

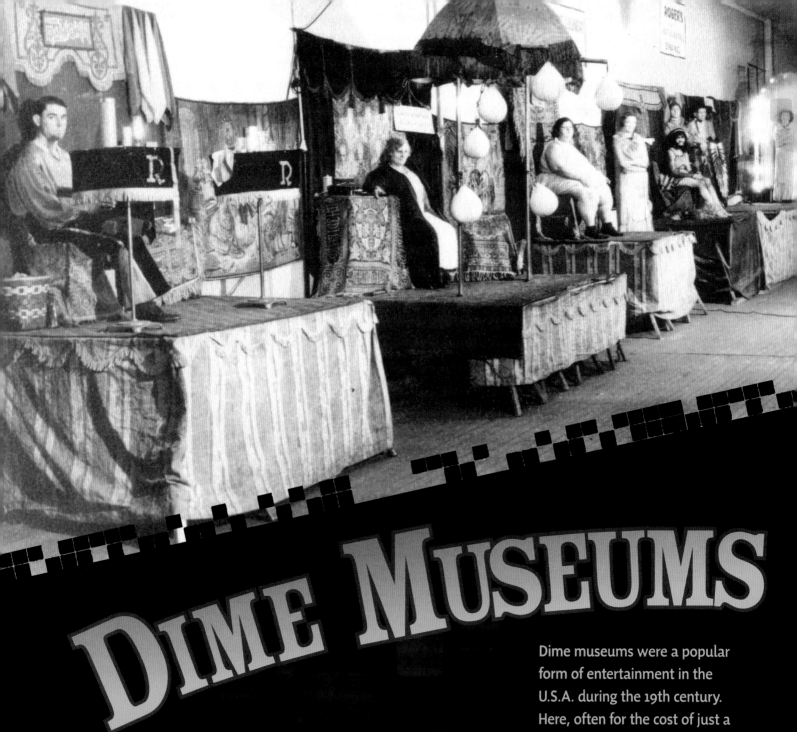

Dime museums were a popular form of entertainment in the U.S.A. during the 19th century. Here, often for the cost of just a dime, visitors could step into a strange world entirely beyond their imagination, populated by midgets, giants, bearded ladies and other incredible sights.

The first dime museum was opened in New York in 1841 by legendary showman P.T. Barnum. As well as showing human oddities, Barnum exhibited many stuffed curiosities, including mummies, mysterious creatures in jars and the famous Feejee Mermaid, which was actually the head of a monkey sewn onto the body of a fish.

Rival entrepreneur George B. Bunnell opened his first dime museum in New York in 1876, employing a variety of performers such as the world's tallest couple—Captain Bates and his wife Anna Swan—and celebrated

P.T. Barnum opened Barnum's American Museum of Curios in New York in 1841. He declared: "I want to make people talk about my museum; to exclaim over its wonders; to have men and women all over the country say: 'There is not another place in the United States where so much can be seen for 25 cents.' " Barnum hired an orchestra to play on the balcony outside to drive in the crowds, and the museum contained an ever-changing mixture of sideshow exhibits and educational displays. The collection comprised 600,000 curiosities in 1849, rising to 850,000 in 1865 when the museum was destroyed by fire.

Percilla Lauther and Emmitt Bejano, billed as "Monkey Girl" and "Alligator Boy" respectively, met on the sideshow circuit in the 1930s and fell in love. Percilla was born in 1911 in Puerto Rico with hypertrichosis (excess hair on the body) and two rows of teeth. Emmitt had hard callouses on his skin and between performances immersed himself in ice water because he could not sweat. They eloped in 1938, but returned several years later to exhibit themselves as the "World's Strangest Married Couple." Eventually tiring of public life, they retired to Florida where they lived together until Emmitt died in 1995. Percilla lived on, clean-shaven for the first time in her life, until her death in 2001.

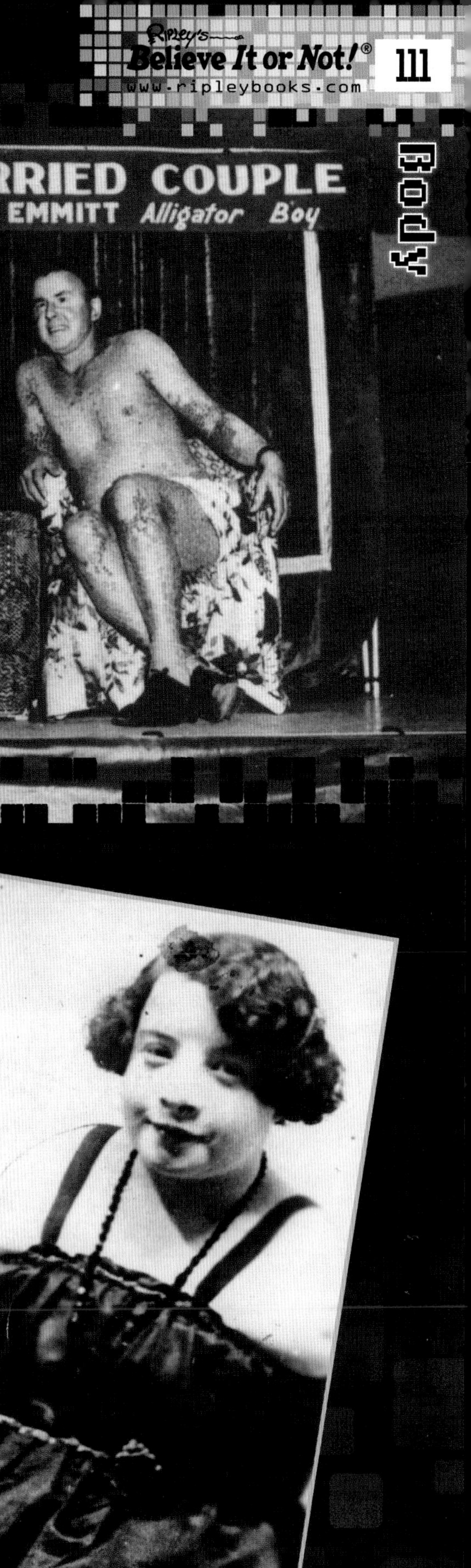

STRANGEST MARRIED COUPLE
PERCILLA Monkey Girl — EMMITT Alligator Boy

Jennie Lee and Elvira Snow, also known as "The Snow Twins" and "Zip and Pip," suffered from microcephaly, a condition characterized by abnormally small craniums. They were commonly known as "pinheads." They performed and traveled for many years.

Martha the Armless Wonder was one of Hubert's Museum acts in New York in the 1920s. She was born in the early 1900s with no arms, and shortened legs protruding from her hips. Her act included eating, writing and typing with her feet.

midgets Admiral Dot and Major Atom, and the Wild Men of Borneo (who were actually two brothers from Ohio). The Wild Men performed acts of strength and earned around $200,000 during their career, a vast sum at that time.

A later establishment was Hubert's Museum that opened in Times Square, New York, in the mid-1920s. Among the acts on display there were sword swallower Lady Estelline, Albert-Alberta the Half-Man Half-Woman, Susie the Elephant Skin Girl, Professor Heckler's Flea Circus, Martha the Armless Wonder, and Zip the Pinhead. Hubert's finally closed in 1965, by which time the admission price had risen to 50 cents. Nevertheless, this was still amazing value for a rare glimpse into another world.

TOENAIL INSECTS

In *Ripley's Believe It or Not! Strikingly True* we featured Rachel Betty Case's bears made from bellybutton lint. Now we reveal "Human Ivory," Rachel's miniature creatures crafted from real human toenails. In 2003, the Pennsylvania artist began collecting the discarded toenails from her art school colleagues and professors, who would leave them in bags outside her door. After gathering two years' worth of clippings, Rachel decided to get creative with her macabre collection. After noticing how people reacted to her work, she was soon "addicted to shocking people, and to making art from the most unconventional materials."

MAGNET BOY Eleven-year-old Paulo David Amorim of Mossoró, Brazil, can stick metal objects such as forks, knives, scissors and cooking pans to his chest, stomach and back.

SURGICAL IMPLANTS Marie Kolstad of Santa Ana, California, had $8,000 breast implants at age 83. She kept the surgery a secret from her four children, 13 grandchildren and 12 great-grandchildren until the day before for fear they might disapprove.

SORE LEG On June 21, 2010, Tracy Durham of Peoria, Illinois, awoke with a sore leg and discovered he had been hit with a gunshot on the night before without noticing it.

ALL'S WELL... When four-year-old Deng Rui from Tengchong, China, tripped and fell to the bottom of a 30-ft (9-m) dry well, he found he had company—a cat that had fallen down the well earlier. Deng was rescued two days later with nothing worse than a few scratches to his face. The cat was also hauled to safety but ran off as soon as it reached the surface.

KNIFE BLADE After being stabbed in a 2006 robbery, Li Fu of Yuanjiang County, China, lived for the next four years with a 4-in (10-cm) blade buried in his face—and he didn't even know it! Doctors found the knife blade, which had penetrated his tongue root, muscles and brain, only when they carried out an X-ray to investigate Li's complaint of headaches and a nasty taste in his mouth.

RUN OVER TWICE A woman from Melbourne, Australia, survived after being run over by her own car—twice. Pulling into the driveway of her home, she forgot to put on the handbrake, whereupon the runaway car knocked her to the ground, running over her abdomen and legs. As she lay injured, the car continued rolling down the slope, hit a fence and rebounded back toward her, running her over again.

BLOOD DONOR John Sheppard of Fort Myers, Florida, has given over 300 pints of blood in 60 years. His 39 gal (150 l) of blood has possibly saved almost 1,000 lives.

SWORD EXTRACTION Surgeons in Hunan Province, China, successfully removed a 20-in-long (51-cm) metal sword from the head of a 15-year-old boy. The sword accidentally stabbed Zhang Bin between his eyes, penetrating at least 2 in (5 cm) into his forehead.

INCRIMINATING X-RAY A thief who stole a diamond from a woman in Marbella, Spain, and swallowed it, was caught when police gave him an X-ray. The X-ray showed the gem in his stomach, and he was charged with theft.

NOISY EYEBALLS For six years, Stephen Mabbutt of Oxfordshire, England, suffered from a rare medical condition that meant he could hear his eyeballs move in their sockets. He first experienced the symptoms in 2005 when he felt a dull ache in the side of his head. He was diagnosed with superior canal dehiscence syndrome, an ear condition in which he could hear sounds inside his body. Until he had an operation to cure it in 2011, as well as hearing his eyeballs move, he could hear his heart beating, and the noise while he chewed food was deafening.

SHEAR HORROR

Eighty-six-year-old Leroy Luetscher from Phoenix, Arizona, survived a horrific gardening accident in which he impaled himself through the eye with a pair of pruning shears. After dropping the shears blade-side down in the ground, he lost his balance as he bent to pick them up and fell face-down on the handle, which penetrated his eye socket and went down into his neck, resting on the external carotid artery. Half the shears were stuck in his head; the other half left sticking out. Surgeons removed the shears and saved his eye.

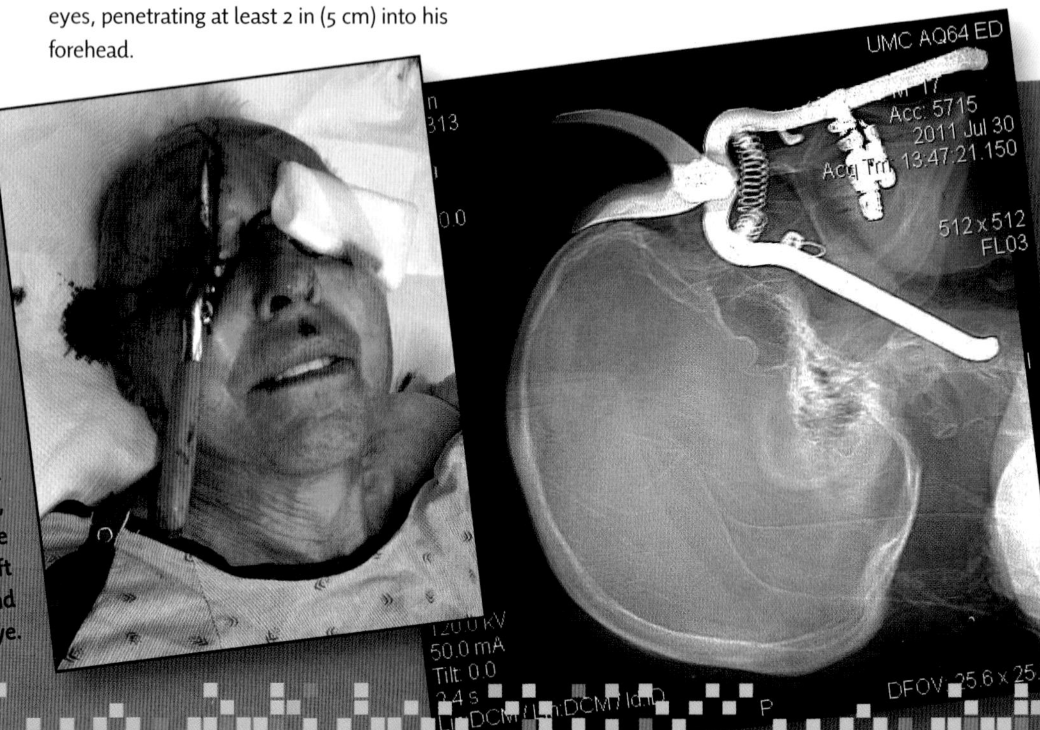

Lucky Fried Chicken

Extreme chef Kann Trichan does away with cooking utensils and retrieves pieces of deep-fried chicken from vats of boiling hot fat that bubble at temperatures of over 400°F (200°C) using his hands! Incredibly, he feels no pain and his hands show no sign of burns. Trichan discovered his strange ability seven years ago when he emerged unscathed after being sprayed with hot oil. It's possible that Trichan's feat is explained by the Leidenfrost effect, when water on the skin vaporizes on contact with the hot oil, providing a protective layer for a short period of time. However, don't try this in your own kitchen!

PIERCING TALES

METAL RAILINGS Nick Blossom survived after falling from a third-floor New York City balcony and impaling his head on metal railings. He was taken to hospital with part of the railing still attached to his head.

STEEL BAR Ezra Bias of Spokane, Washington, survived after a 2-ft-long (60-cm) piece of steel construction bar shot through his windscreen as he was delivering pizza.

IRON RODS Indian construction worker Anil Kumar amazingly survived after two 1.2-in-thick (3-cm) iron rods fell from a truck and impaled him while he was riding home on his motorbike. The rods pierced his abdomen, ripped apart his small intestine and exited through the back of his body.

BUTTER KNIFE Thrown by another boy, a butter knife lodged 4 in (10 cm) deep above the right ear of 11-year-old Tyler Hemmert of Vancouver, Washington, but miraculously only grazed his skull.

TREE BRANCH Michelle Childers was in a car in northern Idaho when an 18-in-long (45-cm) tree branch flew through the open window and impaled itself in her neck, just missing her windpipe and jugular vein.

METAL HOOK Seventeen-month-old Jessiah Jackson of Leland, North Carolina, survived after he fell off a chair and onto a metal hook lying on the ground beneath him, penetrating 2 in (5 cm) into his brain.

BAMBOO SPIKE Thirteen-year-old Dez Heal from Lynchburg, Virginia escaped death in 2011 when a large bamboo spike he was playing with impaled him through the neck.

Merrick's story was not forgotten, and the 1980 David Lynch movie *The Elephant Man*, starring John Hurt, recounted the short, sad life of Joseph Merrick to a new generation. Hurt (*left*) wore a mask and cap identical to that which Merrick used when venturing outside the London Hospital, to avoid shocking the public. Hurt had to sit for seven hours every day while his makeup was applied. The movie was nominated for eight Academy Awards.

Joseph Merrick was born in Leicester, England, in 1862. By the age of 21 months, his lips had started to swell abnormally. His skin became loose and rough, his right arm ballooned alarmingly, and a huge bony growth appeared on his forehead. He also suffered a childhood fall, damaging his left hip and leaving him permanently lame. His mother died when he was 11 years old, and, later, his father found him a job as a door-to-door salesman. However, Joseph's facial disfiguration had rendered his speech almost unintelligible, and in any case, his appearance meant that most women were too scared to open the door to him.

By age 20, the growth from his mouth was some 9 in (23 cm) long, making it difficult for him to eat, so he had part of the lump surgically removed. However, his enlarged head was still so heavy that he had to sleep in a sitting position for fear of breaking his neck if he tried to raise his head from a pillow. Unable to earn a conventional living, he decided that the only way to escape the squalor and poverty of the workhouse was to exhibit himself as a human freak. He toured locally and became a regular performer at a shop in the East End of London, where he was billed as the "Elephant Man," complete with posters depicting a monstrous creature, half-man, half-elephant. He was hidden behind a curtain, and when it was pulled back visitors were visibly horrified by the sight before them, even though they were assured that the Elephant Man was "not here to frighten you, but to enlighten you."

When the authorities clamped down on freak shows in England in 1886, Merrick was forced to ply his trade in Europe, but he was robbed by his new manager of his savings (over $6,000 in today's money) and left to make his own way home. Back in London, he was put in touch with an interested surgeon, Dr. Frederick Treves, who took him to the Royal London Hospital where he lived for the rest of his life.

Despite Merrick's difficult background and problems with communication, visitors to the hospital would remark on his intelligence and sensitivity. He wrote letters and poems about his condition to friends and overcame his deformed hands to build a detailed model of a church that remains in the hospital museum to this day. Merrick became a popular draw for Victorian high society, even hosting the Princess of Wales in his chambers, a meeting that left him "overjoyed." She gave him a signed photograph of herself and sent him a card each Christmas. Sadly, his condition deteriorated. His facial deformities continued to grow and his head became even more enlarged. Finally, on April 11, 1890, he was found dead in his bed. It seems that he had tried to sleep lying down for once, but the sheer weight of his head had, as he had always feared, dislocated his neck causing asphyxia.

Ripley's Research

The precise cause of the Elephant Man's terrible affliction has been subject to speculation for more than a century. At the time, doctors believed that Merrick was suffering from inflammatory elephantiasis, a disease that causes a thickening of the skin and tissue. Now ideas range from neurofibromatosis type 1, a genetic condition causing tumors of the bone and skin, to Proteus syndrome, a genetic disorder that promotes abnormal body growth—or he may have been suffering from a combination of conditions.

MERRICK'S CONDITION

- Thick and lumpy skin
- A large bony lump on his forehead
- A 9-inch (23-cm) protrusion from his mouth, which impaired his speech and made eating difficult
- A twisted torso
- A swollen and deformed right arm, which was much bigger than his left
- Enlarged feet
- One finger that measured a massive 5 in (13 cm) in circumference, which is nearly twice the normal size
- Skin covered in warty growths, some of which exuded an unpleasant odor
- A head that was too heavy for him to sleep lying down

"I AM NOT AN ANIMAL!
I AM A HUMAN BEING!
I...AM...A MAN!"

THE ELEPHANT MAN

Poster from the Hollywood movie *The Elephant Man* (1980), starring John Hurt.

Joseph Merrick was one of the great curiosities of Victorian England. Although apparently healthy at birth, he quickly became hideously deformed, his lumpy, distorted face was so terrifying that in later years he had to wear a mask in the street to prevent passersby fainting at the very sight of him. He was known as the "Elephant Man," his bizarre condition explained by the suggestion that his mother Mary had been knocked over and frightened by a fairground elephant while she was pregnant with him.

Parasites

◀ WORM'S-EYE VIEW

A parasitic loa loa—or African eye worm—wriggles across a human eye. Long, thin and almost transparent, the worm is just beneath the surface membrane (conjunctiva) of the white of the eye. Although the worm does not usually damage a person's vision, it can cause pain when moving around the eyeball.

GIANT ROUNDWORM ▶

This tangle of giant roundworms was found in the intestines of a child from Kenya. The worm begins life when an egg hatches in the host's intestine. The larva then travels to the lungs via the blood vessels, where it continues to develop until it is coughed up and swallowed, ending up in the stomach. The worm, which infects around a billion people worldwide, then travels back in the small intestine where it completes its life cycle.

MORE THAN 100 TYPES OF PARASITIC WORM CAN LIVE IN THE HUMAN BODY.

RED RASH ▼

The red track on the foot of this 33-year-old woman shows the painful movements of the burrowing larvae of nematode hookworms.

◀ BODY LOUSE

Body lice lay their eggs on clothes, and move on to human skin only to feed on blood, causing intense itching. They excrete on skin and clothing and can occur in large infestations where living conditions are cramped and hygiene is bad.

▲ HUMAN TAPEWORM

Tapeworms do not have a digestive tract so they absorb nutrients from the half-digested food of their host through their skin. Different species of tapeworm live in different animals—including humans, fish, rats and dogs.

FOOT FLEA ▶

Found in the tropical Americas and Africa, chigoe fleas (or chiggers) burrow into people's feet, usually through the soles but sometimes—extremely painfully—under the toenails. From 0.04 in (1 mm) long, the pregnant female balloons to ten times that size, causing inflammation of the foot and sometimes ulceration, tetanus and gangrene.

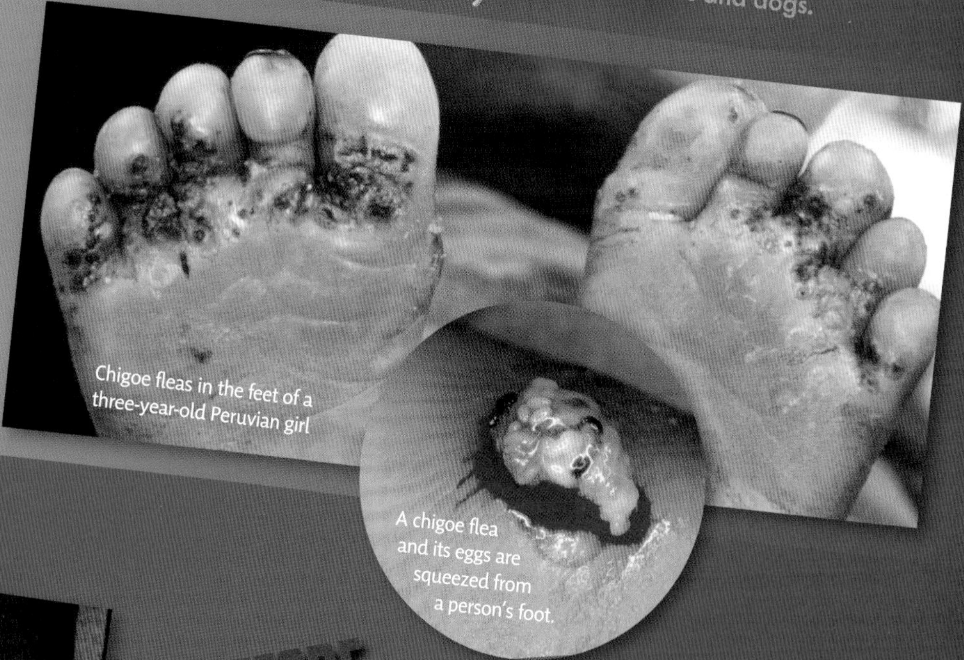

Chigoe fleas in the feet of a three-year-old Peruvian girl

A chigoe flea and its eggs are squeezed from a person's foot.

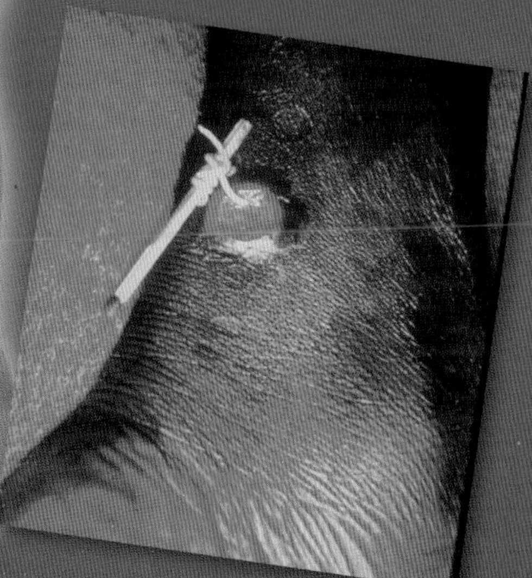

▲ GUINEA WORM

The guine worm parasite is found in contaminated water and, once it infects a host, grows into a worm underneath the skin, often more than 3 ft (90 cm) long.

TICKS ▶

Ticks suck up so much blood that their bodies fill up like balloons. They can't fly or jump, but they carry many diseases that are deadly to humans.

RIPLEY'S WEIRD RECORD • RIPLEY'S WEIRD RECORD

LARGEST AFRO

TOP MOP

Aevin Dugas holds a hair-raising record on top of her head—the world's largest "afro" hairstyle, which has grown to 4 ft 4 in (1.3 m) in circumference and rises to 7 in (18 cm). The 36-year-old social worker from New Orleans has been cultivating her curls for 12 years, but doesn't always wear her hair at its biggest, as it restricts her vision when driving and can get too hot in the Louisiana summer.

HIDDEN GEM When Calvin Wright of Athens, Georgia, went into the hospital with an acute case of bronchitis, an emergency room nurse discovered a pearl inside his ear. It had been in his ear canal for 41 years, after his mother's necklace had broken and his baby sister had playfully stuffed two of the pearls into his ear. Although doctors had managed to remove one immediately afterward, amazingly the other pearl had gone undetected for more than four decades.

TATTOOED GRANDPA Great-grandfather Tommy Wells from Greater Manchester, England, has more than 1,000 tattoos etched across every part of his body. He has spent more than 50 years having tattoos inked not only on his arms, hands, legs, torso, back and head, but also on the soles of his feet, his lips, his butt and even his genitals.

MIGHTY YAWN College student Holly Thomson of Northampton, England, found a lesson in government and politics so tiresome that she yawned hard enough to dislocate her jaw. She remained with her jaw locked open in a yawning position for five hours until a doctor at the local hospital was able to open it even further and unlock it.

SHORTEST MAN In 2011, an 18-year-old from the Philippines, Junrey Balawing, was declared the world's shortest man. The son of a blacksmith from Sindangan on Mindanao Island, he stands just 23.6 in (60 cm) tall—5 in (12.5 cm) shorter than the average one-year-old boy—after he stopped growing when he was two years old.

BRAIN SURGERY Helen Hollis, 47, from Nottinghamshire, England, graduated from the University of Derby in 2011 with a degree in psychology and counseling studies—five years after part of her brain was removed. Part of her right temporal lobe was taken out in a high-risk operation to overcome her repeated epileptic attacks, which used to total around 40 a month.

TWIN CURSE Gladys Bulinya of Nzoia, near Kenya's Lake Victoria, has given birth to six sets of twins over a period of 17 years. Sadly, after the sixth set arrived in 2010, her husband decided she was cursed and left her, and the rest of her family also shun her as many people in her region think twins bring bad luck.

ONCE A YEAR, UP TO 10 TONS OF HUMAN WASTE FROM ANTARCTIC BASES IS SHIPPED TO A LANDFILL IN CALIFORNIA.

NO HANDS Ten-year-old Nick Maxim of Readfield, Maine, won a national award for penmanship—despite being born without hands. He writes fluently by holding the pencil between his arms, which end just above where his elbows should be.

34 DIGITS Akshat Saxena of Uttar Pradesh, India, was born with 14 fingers (seven on each hand but no thumbs) and 20 toes (ten on each foot), giving him 34 digits—more than anyone else in the world. He later had the excess digits surgically removed and doctors made him thumbs from the fingers they amputated.

HAIR-RAISING INSECTS

Artist Adrienne Antonson from Asheville, North Carolina, bends and weaves real human hair into remarkably detailed insect artworks. On her praying mantis, moths and flies, she uses glue to mold the hair and to hold it in place. Adrienne collects locks of different-colored hair from close friends and family, and is interested in using her creations for art therapy, working with people who have lost their hair through illness.

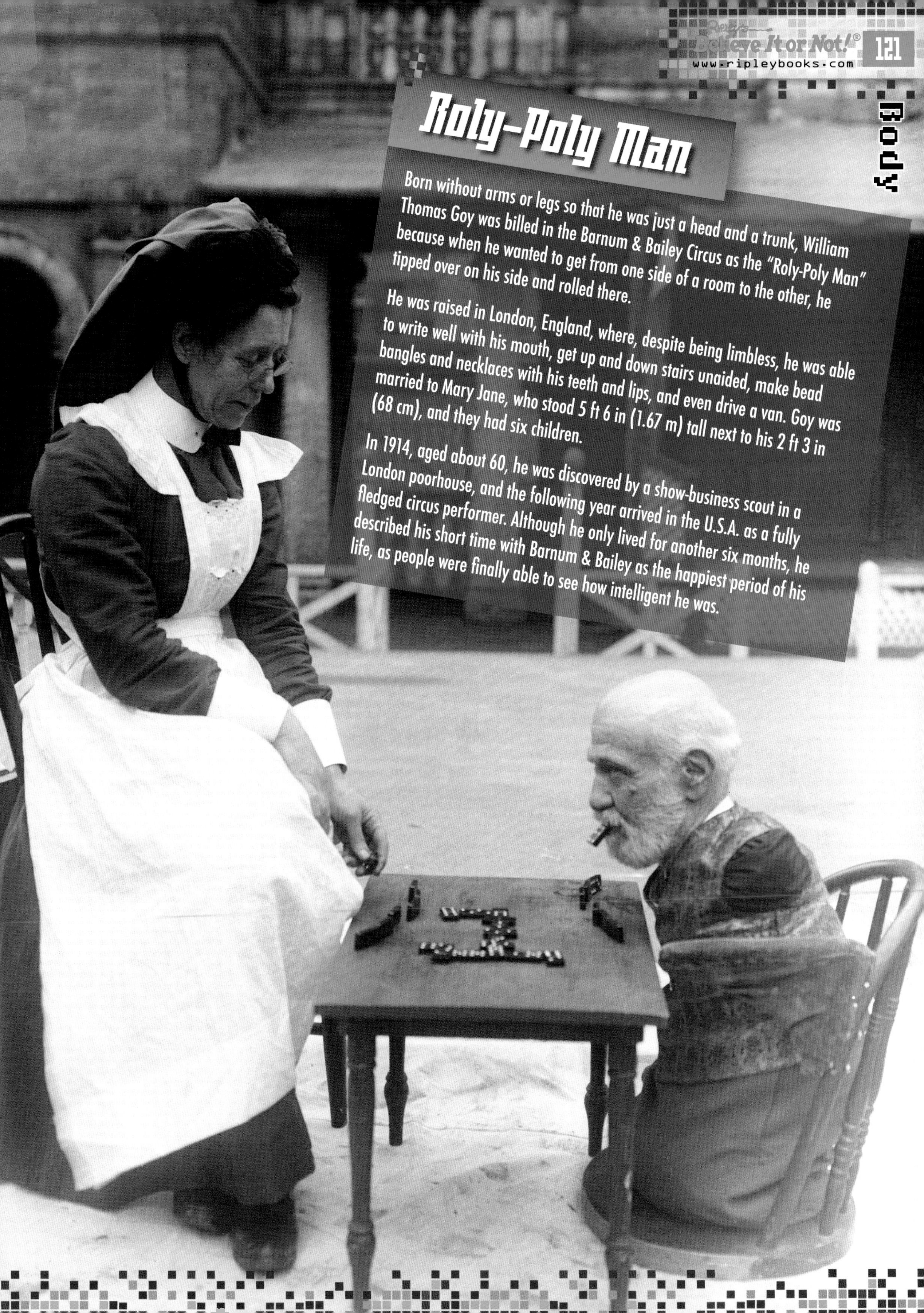

Roly-Poly Man

Born without arms or legs so that he was just a head and a trunk, William Thomas Goy was billed in the Barnum & Bailey Circus as the "Roly-Poly Man" because when he wanted to get from one side of a room to the other, he tipped over on his side and rolled there.

He was raised in London, England, where, despite being limbless, he was able to write well with his mouth, get up and down stairs unaided, make bead bangles and necklaces with his teeth and lips, and even drive a van. Goy was married to Mary Jane, who stood 5 ft 6 in (1.67 m) tall next to his 2 ft 3 in (68 cm), and they had six children.

In 1914, aged about 60, he was discovered by a show-business scout in a London poorhouse, and the following year arrived in the U.S.A. as a fully fledged circus performer. Although he only lived for another six months, he described his short time with Barnum & Bailey as the happiest period of his life, as people were finally able to see how intelligent he was.

SUCKED INTO PIPE Writer Allan Baillie of Sydney, Australia, survived with just cuts and bruises after being sucked feet-first into a drainage pipe and spat out onto a nearby beach seconds later. He was swimming in a pool while a workman was cleaning it, and when the workman pressed the button to open the water valve, Baillie was sucked into the pipe. The circumference of the pipe was smaller than his body, but luckily the tremendous pressure meant that he popped straight out at the other end like a wine cork.

STEADY HAND Performing in Hamburg in 2010, German stuntman Joe Alexander used his elbow to break a record 24 concrete blocks, assembled in three stacks of eight, demonstrating such skill that the egg he was holding in his smashing hand did not break.

HUMAN BLOCKHEADS At the ninth annual Sideshow Gathering at Wilkes-Barre, Pennsylvania, in November 2010, 36 people simultaneously hammered various objects into their noses to create a mass human blockhead.

JUNIOR TEACHER Shruti Pandey was just four years old when she began teaching yoga to adults at a retreat in Uttar Pradesh, India. Her elder brother, Harsh Kumar, had learned all 84 yoga positions by the age of five.

DEXTROUS TOES After losing both of his hands at age three in an accident with electricity lines in his native China, Luo Yanbo has learned to eat, write and brush his teeth with his feet. His grandmother taught him how to use chopsticks with his feet and he has become so adept that he can even use his toes to make phone calls.

FOREIGN ACCENT When Karen Butler of Toledo, Oregon, went for dental surgery to remove several teeth, she came round from the anesthetic with a British accent—even though she has never traveled to Europe or lived outside the U.S.A. She suffers from foreign accent syndrome, a rare neurological disorder caused by an injury to the part of the brain that controls speech. There have been only about 100 known cases since the condition was first reported in the 1940s.

RAISED ARM Sadhu Amar Bharati Urdhavaahu, an Indian holy man, has kept his right arm raised above his head continuously for decades as a sign of his devotion.

THE STRANGE CAREER OF ELMER McCURDY'S CORPSE

Inept at robbing trains, Oklahoma outlaw Elmer McCurdy made more in death than he ever did while he was alive. He was killed in a 1911 gunfight, his last words being the familiar "You'll never take me alive," but it was then that his corpse took on a life of its own. When nobody came forward to claim it, the undertaker had it embalmed with a preservative and exhibited as *The Bandit Who Wouldn't Give Up* with customers inserting a nickel in McCurdy's mouth. The attraction proved so profitable that numerous carnival operators put in bids for the dead outlaw, but the undertaker resisted all offers until being duped by a man claiming to be McCurdy's brother. Led to believe that McCurdy was to be given a proper burial, the undertaker handed him over, only to see him exhibited in a traveling carnival two weeks later.

For the next 60 years, McCurdy's body was sold to various wax museums and carnivals, although one haunted house owner in South Dakota turned it down because he did not think it was sufficiently lifelike. Then in 1976, during the filming of an episode of the TV series *The Six Million Dollar Man* at the Californian amusement park known as "The Pike," a crew member moved what he thought was a mannequin hanging from a gallows and got the shock of his life when the arm fell off to reveal mummified human remains. It was Elmer McCurdy. The following year, Elmer was finally buried in Oklahoma, the state medical examiner ordering that his casket be buried in concrete so that his corpse would never be disturbed again.

SUMO SPLITS Although Matt Alaeddine from Edmonton, Canada, weighs more than 400 lb (180 kg), he is a contortionist. Despite his considerable bulk, he can press the soles of his feet to the cheeks of his face by doing the "sumo splits."

BIKER IMPALED During a motorcycle accident in January 2011, a 20-year-old man in Delhi, India, was impaled through his chest by inch-thick (2.5-cm) iron rods. Doctors saved his life in a four-hour operation.

ASHES TATTOO Brother and sister Andrew and Helen Bird of Stoke-on-Trent, England, created a lasting tribute to their dead grandfather by having his ashes tattooed into their skin. Andrew had an extract from one of grandpa Reginald Alefs' poems etched on to his arm while Helen had a rose inked onto her back. The tattoo artist mixed some of Mr. Alefs' ashes with ink to create the artworks.

INTERNAL DECAPITATION The impact of a car accident jolted two-year-old Micah Andrews' head sideways with such force that his skull separated from his spine—a condition called atlanto-occipital dislocation, or internal decapitation. Surgeons in Phoenix, Arizona, kept Micah's head still by placing sandbags on either side before implanting a titanium loop to reattach the base of the skull to the spine. The rod is held in place with a piece of the boy's rib. Two months later, Micah was released from hospital, able to walk and talk again.

GIANT TUMOR A massive tumor, accounting for one-third of his body weight, was removed from the back of a Chinese teenager in 2011. The 41-lb (19-kg) growth had been expanding on the body of 15-year-old Qiu Sheng, from Yunnan Province, since birth. It started as two bean-sized tumors on his waist, before growing first to the size of a peach, then a coconut and finally a sandbag on his back that grew into his chest cavity and pushed aside his right shoulder-blade.

RUSTY BULLET In 2011, doctors finally discovered why a Chinese farmer had been affected by epilepsy for more than two decades—a ¾-in-long (2-cm) rusty bullet had been lodged in his brain since 1988. Wang Tianqing of Zhangjiakou City remembered being knocked unconscious by a blow to the head, but had no idea he had been shot.

PLAYING TWISTER Chen Daorong from Zhengzhou, Fujian Province, China, at age 80 years is a contortionist. He started contorting his body in 1999 to cure back pains and is now so supple that he can twist his legs around his neck, do the splits and sleep resting his head on one foot, as a pillow.

NASTY SHOCK Joseph Ferrato of Akron, Ohio, sustained only minor injuries after 23,000 volts of electricity burst through the windshield of his car. The damage was caused by a falling power line that had been cut down by copper thieves.

Corset Piercing

Fashion victims must endure an hour of pain and risk permanent scarring to acquire corset piercing, the latest trend in extreme body modification. Small hoops are stuck into the skin and then threaded with ribbon to give a corset effect. The decoration can be applied only to an area of the body where the skin is loose. The most popular locations are the back, the ribs and even the throat. It is only temporary—after a few weeks the hooks grow out, leaving scars in their place.

Transport

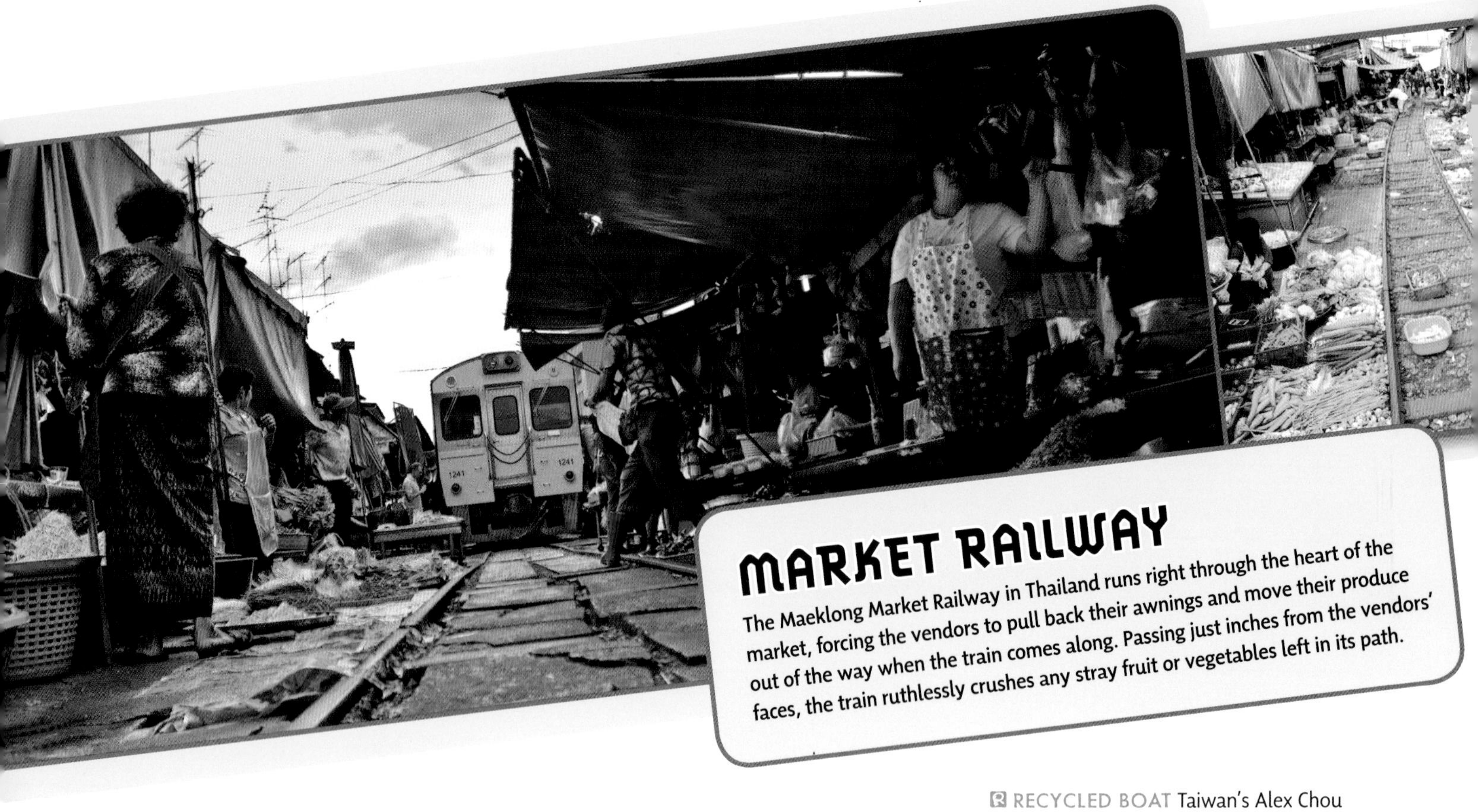

MARKET RAILWAY

The Maeklong Market Railway in Thailand runs right through the heart of the market, forcing the vendors to pull back their awnings and move their produce out of the way when the train comes along. Passing just inches from the vendors' faces, the train ruthlessly crushes any stray fruit or vegetables left in its path.

HIGH SPEED A Chinese passenger train traveling between Beijing and Shanghai can reach the incredible speed of 302 mph (486 km/h). The new high-speed train has halved travel times between the two cities from ten hours to five.

CROWDED TRAINS India's rail system serves about six billion passengers every year—that's nearly equal to the entire population of the Earth.

PIPE DREAM Anthony Smith, an 85-year-old grandfather from London, England, crossed the Atlantic Ocean in 2011 on a 40-ft-long (12-m) raft that was made from lengths of gas and water pipes. He and his three-man crew—all of whom were aged over 55—set sail from the Canary Islands for the 66-day, 2,800-mi (4,506-km) voyage to the Caribbean.

RECYCLED BOAT Taiwan's Alex Chou designed an eco boat made primarily from 700 plastic bottles. The sailboat *Forever*, built entirely from recycled materials and powered by wind and solar energy, made its maiden voyage in June 2011.

RESCUE MISSION After spending nine years building a two-seater airplane in the basement of his home in Lower Allen Township, Pennsylvania, Dan Reeves realized it was too big to get up the steps. So he dug a trench down to the foundation, knocked out a wall and, with the help of neighbors, used a heavy chain to pull the plane up into daylight.

SINKING FEELING

Love, Love, a boat created by French artist Julien Berthier, floats at a constant 45-degree angle to give the impression that it is sinking. Berthier split an abandoned 21-ft-long (6.5-m) yacht, sealed it with fiberglass, repositioned the keel, built a new seat and put two electrical motors underneath the vessel to power it. The effect is so convincing that when the boat appeared on Lake Constance, Germany, dozens of people called the harbormasters to tell them a boat was sinking.

SHOE CAR A Chinese shoe manufacturer has converted a giant shoe into an electric car. The 10-ft-long (3-m), 3-ft-high (90-cm) shoe car has leather bodywork and took six months to create from the hide of five bulls. It can carry two people 250 mi (400 km) at a top speed of 20 mph (32 km/h) on a single charge of the battery, which is located beneath the driver's seat in the heel.

DRY RUN Battling against extreme heat and sandstorms, Reza Pakravan from London, England, cycled 1,084 mi (1,734 km) across the Sahara Desert in 13 days 5 hours, averaging more than 80 mi (130 km) a day. The heat was so fierce that he had to drink around 15 pt (7 l) of water every day to keep hydrated.

ELECTRIC TRIKE Four engineers from Hamburg, Germany, have devised a tricycle powered solely by two 18-volt electric screwdrivers. The 44-lb (20-kg) EX trike, which can reach speeds of 18.6 mph (30 km/h), is driven in a headlong position, the driver operating the brake and gas levers with his hands and the rear wheel with his legs.

$1-MILLION CRASH A woman driver in Monte Carlo caused a $1-million car accident in July 2011 by crashing into some of the most expensive cars in the world as she tried to negotiate her way around the famous Place du Casino. Her $375,000 Bentley Azure scraped the side of a $110,000 Mercedes before hitting a $200,000 Ferrari, a $225,000 Aston Martin Rapide and a $120,000 Porsche 911.

BUS PROPOSAL Romantic British bus driver Phill Openshaw used the digital display on the front of his vehicle to propose to his girlfriend Sam Woodward. He changed the electronic board on his Wilts and Dorset bus to read: "Sam, Will you marry me?" She was waiting at a bus stop in the town of Poole when she saw the sign—and said yes!

Tricky Trike

A man in Jaipur, India, was seen transporting the chassis of an old car attached to the frame of his tricycle. He pushed his trike with his head through the open hood of the car so that he could see where he was going.

EXPLODING MANHOLE An exploding manhole caused by flash floods threw an unoccupied parked car several feet into the air in Montreal, Quebec, Canada, in July 2011. The torrent of water turned the manhole into a geyser which tossed the rear half of the vehicle repeatedly into the air.

PICTURE THIS!

A driver was so preoccupied with getting out of the car to take a picture of the rooftops in Alassio, Italy, that she forgot to put on the handbrake... leaving the vehicle to roll down a hill and plunge through the roof of a house in the street below. The front end of the car ended up wedged in a bathtub, which fortunately was unoccupied at the time.

HARD LUCK

Making a sudden U-turn in an attempt to get out of heavy traffic, a driver in Houston, Texas, found herself in a lane of freshly laid cement. Stuck fast, she had no choice but to sit there in her $70,000 Lexus, while she waited for help.

HANGING AROUND

A New York Department of Sanitation salt-spreading truck dangles precariously over the road below after crashing through a wall on the second floor of a repair shop in Queens. The driver had to be rescued by a fire crew's cherry picker.

BUMPY RIDE

Following a wrongly positioned sign to the parking lot in a shopping mall in Liuzhou, China, Xiang Zhen drove her car down a staircase, where it became stuck. As startled shoppers fled, Xiang abandoned her car halfway down the stairs and phoned a tow-truck company to winch it back up to the street.

MIND THE GAP

Driving at night along a country road in Arnsberg, Germany, this motorist failed to spot that the road ahead had collapsed. Her car fell headlong into the gap, but she escaped unhurt.

DRIVEN CRAZY!

WATER RIDE

In Monterey, California, the driver of this BMW sports car escaped serious injury after accidentally propelling the vehicle off the edge of a parking lot, over a sun deck, and through a fence before flipping into the swimming pool below. It's thought that the driver pressed the accelerator by mistake. Fortunately, the sun deck and the pool were empty at the time, and the driver escaped with only minor injuries.

OVER-THE-TOP

Arturas Zuokas, mayor of Lithuania's capital city, Vilnius, surprised bystanders when he drove over an illegally parked vehicle in a Russian armored personnel carrier, crushing the vehicle beyond repair. The elaborate stunt was a headline-grabbing response to luxury cars being parked illegally in the capital.

MINI MINI Retired mechanic Lester Atherfold from Napier, New Zealand, trimmed over 2 ft (60 cm) off his 1964 Mini car so that it could fit into the trunk of his motor home. He reduced the 10-ft-long (3-m) Mini to 7 ft 10 in (2.4 m) by slicing a chunk from the middle, narrowing the chassis, and fitting a new sub-frame, transmission, clutch and dashboard.

ARMORED CAR The "Popemobile," the Roman Catholic Pope's touring car, is armored with 3-in (8-cm) blast-resistant glass panels and has its own internal air supply for protection against a chemical or biological attack.

QUICK THINKING Duane Innes of Kent, Washington State, deliberately crashed into a truck driven by 80-year-old Bill Pace. The crash stopped Pace's truck, saving his life after he had passed out behind the wheel.

WOODEN SCOOTER Carlos Alberto, a carpenter from Portugal, built a functioning replica of a Vespa motor scooter almost entirely from wood.

TIGHT SQUEEZE In December 2010, 26 members of the New York City-based Pilobolus Dance Company squeezed their bodies into a standard MINI car.

SAFETY BOWL The Longxiang Public Bus Company in Changsha, China, uses a hanging bowl of water in its buses as a visual reminder for drivers to drive calmly and carefully.

STRANGE HYBRID Motorbike-crazy Markus Sell, from Jonschwil, Switzerland, welded the rear half of a Renault Clio car onto the front half of a motorbike. But, as he roared along at 70 mph (115 km/h), police stopped him and claimed the vehicle was unsafe.

PAPER PLANE In October 2010, near Madrid, Spain, a paper airplane fitted with a tiny camera was launched into space to photograph its descent to Earth. For Operation PARIS (Paper Aircraft Released Into Space), it was attached to a weather balloon. When the balloon burst 17 mi (27 km) up, the plane began to fall, taking pictures on its way.

FERRARI FAN Jon Ryder of Sheffield, England, loves his yellow 1996 Ferrari 355 Spider so much he parks it in his living room. He drives it through a garage door at the end of the room so he can admire it from his sofa.

WRONG TURN A British man and his wife drove their Renault into the side of a church near Immenstadt, Germany, after obeying faulty instructions from their GPS. The couple ended up in the hospital with minor injuries, their car was wrecked and $30,000 of damage was done to the church—all because the GPS directed them to turn right where there was actually no road.

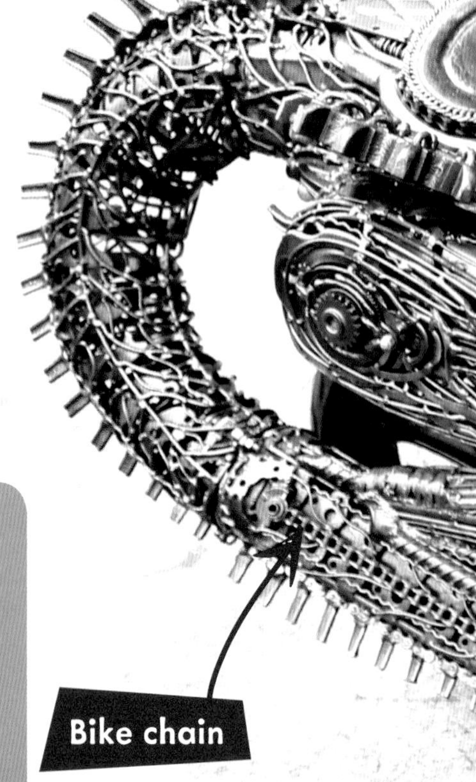

SURPRISE CARGO

When police in Bargteheide, Germany, stopped a van that was driving erratically, they opened the rear doors—and found a car neatly parked on its side in the back. It was the brainchild of two men from Kazakhstan who, after buying a Mazda 626, decided to save on the costs of shipping it home on a trailer by loading it into their van, placing a mattress beneath the car to stop its doors getting scratched on the floor of the van. The police confiscated both the van and the car until the pair found a proper transporter.

HEAVY LOAD A truck carrying steel pipes that increased its total weight to 98 tons was so heavy that it fell through a bridge and landed in a river. The truck was being driven across the Dongrong Bridge in Changchun, China, when the road suddenly collapsed beneath it, leaving a truck-sized hole measuring 46 x 16 ft (14 x 5 m).

KEEP TURNING California's Ridge Route mountain highway—built in 1915 and linking Los Angeles to Bakersfield—has 697 turns in just 36 mi (58 km) of road.

FLOATING VAN An amphibious ice-cream van toured Britain's seaside resorts in 2011. Driven by Dave Mountfield from Brighton, Sussex, HMS *Flake 99* had a top speed of five knots and chimed Rod Stewart's "Sailing" as it took to the water.

ALIEN BIKE

It looks like an alien monster, but it's really a motorbike. This stunning creation was assembled by artist Roongrojna Sangwongprisarn at his workshops in Bangkok, Thailand. Roongrojna builds crazy-looking motorbikes from the recycled spare parts of cars, motorcycles and bicycles—and his awesome metal sculptures can actually be ridden.

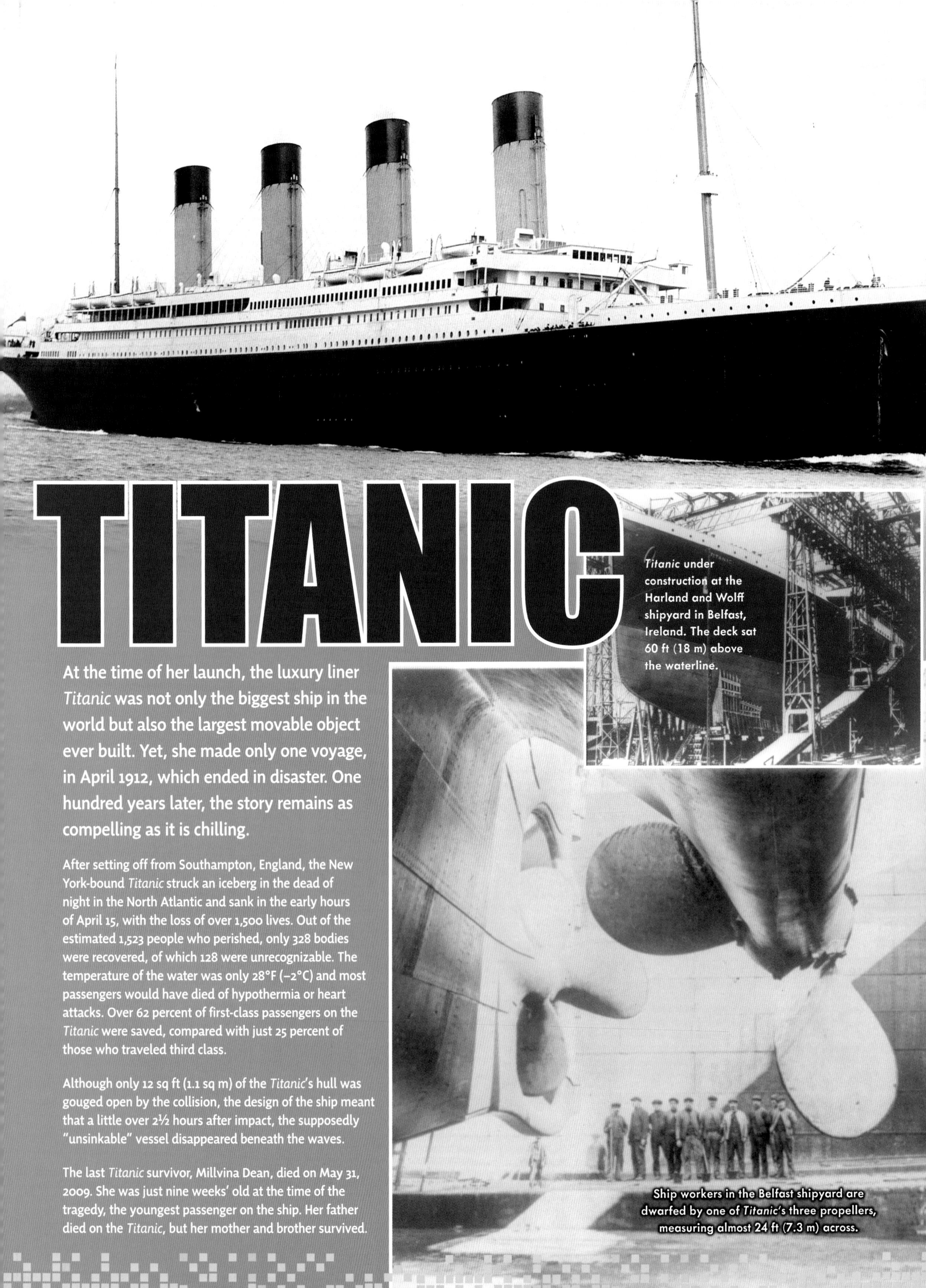

TITANIC

Titanic under construction at the Harland and Wolff shipyard in Belfast, Ireland. The deck sat 60 ft (18 m) above the waterline.

At the time of her launch, the luxury liner *Titanic* was not only the biggest ship in the world but also the largest movable object ever built. Yet, she made only one voyage, in April 1912, which ended in disaster. One hundred years later, the story remains as compelling as it is chilling.

After setting off from Southampton, England, the New York-bound *Titanic* struck an iceberg in the dead of night in the North Atlantic and sank in the early hours of April 15, with the loss of over 1,500 lives. Out of the estimated 1,523 people who perished, only 328 bodies were recovered, of which 128 were unrecognizable. The temperature of the water was only 28°F (–2°C) and most passengers would have died of hypothermia or heart attacks. Over 62 percent of first-class passengers on the *Titanic* were saved, compared with just 25 percent of those who traveled third class.

Although only 12 sq ft (1.1 sq m) of the *Titanic*'s hull was gouged open by the collision, the design of the ship meant that a little over 2½ hours after impact, the supposedly "unsinkable" vessel disappeared beneath the waves.

The last *Titanic* survivor, Millvina Dean, died on May 31, 2009. She was just nine weeks' old at the time of the tragedy, the youngest passenger on the ship. Her father died on the *Titanic*, but her mother and brother survived.

Ship workers in the Belfast shipyard are dwarfed by one of *Titanic*'s three propellers, measuring almost 24 ft (7.3 m) across.

DARING STUNT

A daredevil driver in Florida calmly maneuvered his Mazda car under a moving 18-wheel juggernaut traveling at a speed of around 40 mph (65 km/h)... and stayed there for over a minute. His reckless action, captured on film by a shocked motorist, mimics a scene from the 2001 movie *The Fast and the Furious*, where actor Vin Diesel drives underneath a truck that his gang is trying to rob.

PERFECT PARKING German stunt driver Ronny Wechselberger squeezed his Volkswagen Polo car into a parking space that was just 10¼ in (26 cm) longer than his vehicle. He performed the incredible feat of parallel parking by using the handbrake to flick the car's rear end around.

MINI CHOPPER U.S. company Vanguard Defense Industries has developed a miniature, remote-controlled helicopter that is being used to track pirates off East Africa and tackle crime on the streets of the U.S.A. The Shadowhawk UAV is just 7 ft (2.1 m) long and weighs 49 lb (22 kg), but it has a top speed of 70 mph (112 km/h). It can fire tasers, grenades and shotgun shells, and record and broadcast footage in real time.

JEEP RECORD On August 12, 2011, more than 1,100 Jeeps from across the U.S.A. converged on the Bantam Heritage Jeep Festival at Butler, Pennsylvania, to break the record for the world's largest Jeep parade.

TRAFFIC DIRECTOR Civilian Hugh McManaway spent so much of his spare time directing traffic at a busy intersection that the city of Charlotte, North Carolina, built a statue to commemorate him.

NEW ROADS Although it already has 2 million mi (3.2 million km) of road, placing it third in the world behind the U.S.A. and China, India is building another 15 mi (24 km) of road every day to cater for the nation's rapidly expanding use of cars.

FIRST BAN Venezuela issued its first-ever driving ban in 2011—to a bus driver who was speeding in an overladen, six-wheel passenger bus that was missing one of its rear wheels. Drivers have strong rights in Venezuela, where the first law allowing the ban of motorists was not introduced until 2008, and the bus driver's ban was suspended for 12 months.

BABY DRIVER A seven-year-old Michigan boy, who had to stand up to reach the gas and brake pedals, drove over 20 mi (32 km) in an attempt to see his father. The boy took his stepfather's Pontiac Sunfire and, barefoot and in pajamas, hit speeds of 70 mph (113 km/h) before being stopped by a police patrol.

THINK BIKE Toyota has created a bicycle with gears you can change by using your mind. The rider of the Prius X Parlee (PXP) wears a special "neuron helmet" that uses electrodes to pick up cues from the brain and send signals to a thought-controlled gearbox mounted under the seat of the bicycle.

FIRE DRILL A team of 25 firefighters from London, England, drove 30,000 mi (48,000 km) around the world—in a fire engine named *Martha*. Their nine-month journey took them through 28 countries, including Russia, China, Australia, New Zealand and the U.S.A.

LOW CAR Students from Okayama Sanyo High School in Asakuchi, Japan, built a single-seater electric car that is just 18 in (45 cm) high and runs at speeds of up to 30 mph (50 km/h).

Ferrari Table

French furniture designer Charly Molinelli has encased the wreck of a Ferrari F40 supercar in a coffee table. Asked to build a unique piece and knowing that his client was a motor-sports fan, Molinelli approached a friend who worked at a scrapyard that was crushing a Ferrari and managed to procure it.

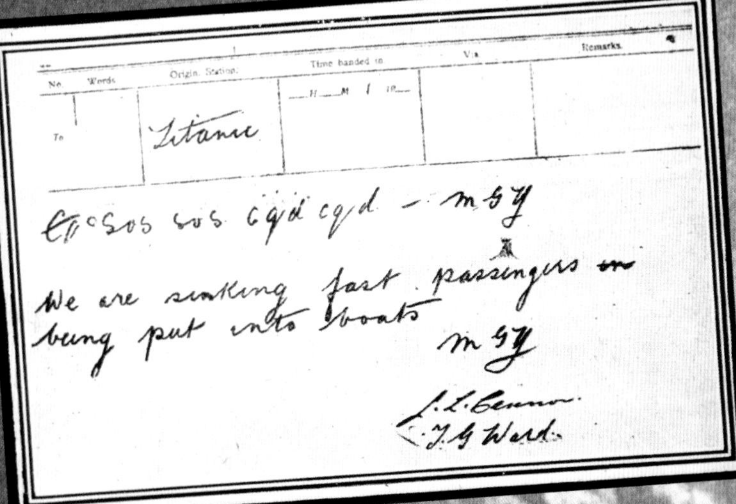

No.	Words.	Origin Station.	Time handed in	Via	Remarks.
To		Titanic			

Ctc SOS sos cqd cqd – MGY

We are sinking fast passengers are being put into boats

MGY

One of the last SOS telegrams sent from the *Titanic* before it sank.

The iceberg that hit the *Titanic* towered about 75 ft (23 m) above the surface of the ocean, approximately the height of a seven-story building. As 90 percent of an iceberg's mass is usually below the surface, it could have extended a further 400–600 ft (120–180 m) underwater.

WEALTHY PASSENGER The wealthiest passenger on board was U.S. businessman Colonel John Jacob Astor IV, who owned a large chunk of Manhattan and whose personal fortune was estimated at $150 million. In today's money, that equates to $102.2 billion, enough to make him the richest man in the world. He did not survive the disaster.

TRAVELING LIGHT? The luggage of wealthy Philadelphian Billy Carter included 60 shirts, 15 pairs of shoes, 24 polo sticks and a new Renault car! Everything, including the car, went down with the *Titanic*, although Carter himself survived.

MISSED THE BOAT At least 55 passengers canceled their bookings on the *Titanic* at the last minute and 22 crew members also missed the boat. They included three brothers, Bertram, Tom and Alfred Slade, who had been taken on as trimmers in the coal bunkers, but stopped for a last-minute drink in a Southampton pub and were prevented from boarding the liner after being delayed by a passing freight train.

DYING VISION In Scotland on the night of April 14, 1912, a dying girl named Jessie predicted to Salvation Army captain W. Rex Sowden the tragedy that would occur three-and-a-half hours later. She spoke of a big ship sinking, people drowning and someone called Wally "playing a fiddle and coming to you." Among those who drowned on the *Titanic* was bandmaster Wallace Hartley, whom Sowden had known as a boy but had since lost touch with.

UNIFORM BILL No members of the *Titanic* band survived, but the Black Talent Agency of Liverpool who hired the musicians sent the family of violinist Jock Hume a bill for $3.50 for the cost of the unpaid and unreturned uniform.

No human remains have ever been discovered on or around the wreck of the *Titanic*. Any bodies that sank with the wreck have been eaten by fish and crustacea. All that remain are the shoes and boots of the victims still lying on the sea floor.

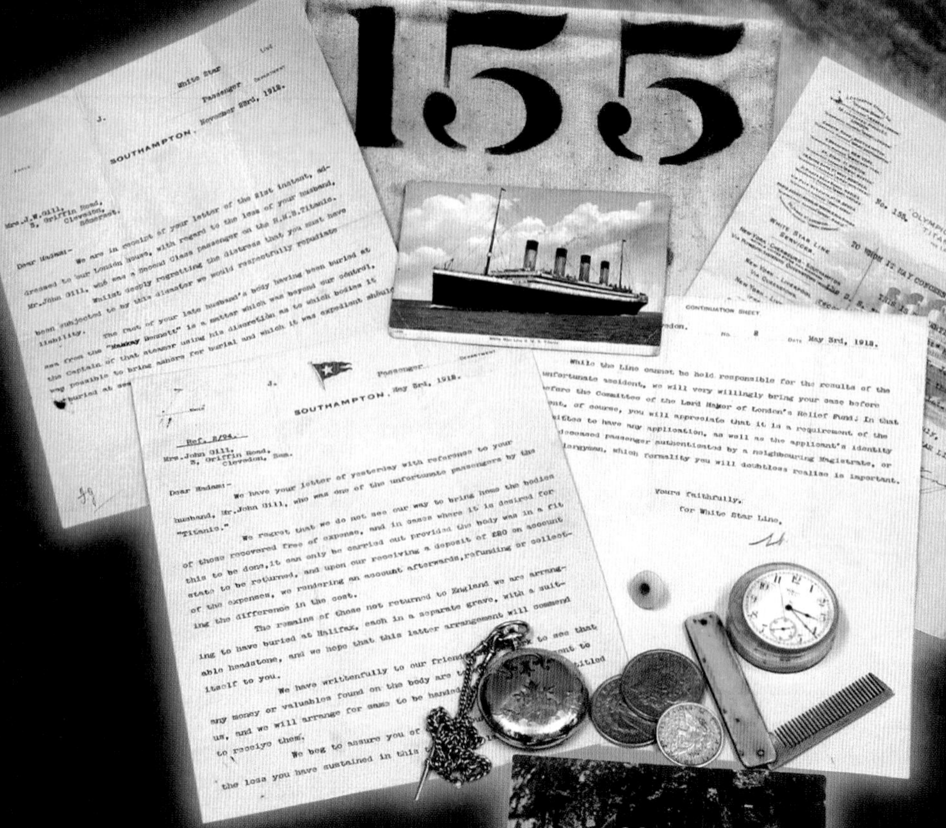

Titanic memorabilia, including a pocket watch recovered from the wreck that stopped one hour after the ship sank.

Realising they would not escape, U.S. mining magnate Benjamin Guggenheim and his valet changed into full evening dress, reappearing on deck to declare: "We've dressed up in our best and are prepared to go down like gentlemen."

On board were 13 couples celebrating their honeymoons.

LOST PROPERTY

Among passengers' insurance claims submitted to the White Star Line following the sinking were:

- Personal property **$177,352.75**, Charlotte Drake Cardeza
- Oil painting **$100,000**, Hakan Bjornstrom-Steffanson
- Renault 35 hp automobile **$5,000**, Billy Carter
- Signed picture of Garibaldi **$3,000**, Emilio Portaluppi
- Champion French bulldog **$750**, Robert W. Daniel
- Four roosters and hens **$207.87**, Ella Holmes
- Set of bagpipes **$50**, Eugene Daly

More than 5,000 artifacts, including china dishes from the dining rooms, have been removed from the wreck of the ship.

SHIP'S STORE

- **75,000 lb (34,000 kg)** of fresh meat
- **25,000 lb (11,400 kg)** of poultry & game
- **11,000 lb (5,000 kg)** of fresh fish
- **40,000** eggs
- **36,000** oranges
- **16,000** lemons
- **20,000** bottles of beer
- **1,500** bottles of wine
- **40 tons** of potatoes
- **1,500 gal (5,700 l)** of fresh milk
- **12,000** dinner plates
- **8,000** cut-glass tumblers
- **45,000** table napkins
- **15,000** pillow slips
- **25,000** fine towels
- **18,000** bedsheets

The wreck of the *Titanic* was discovered on September 1, 1985, by underwater explorer Robert Ballard. It lay largely intact at a depth of 12,000 ft (3,660 m) below the surface of the Atlantic off the coast of Newfoundland. This depth is six times deeper than a human diver has ever descended, and enough to crush human lungs. Using a small submersible craft, Ballard explored the wreck in 1986, but it wasn't until August 1998 that a section of the hull was hauled to the surface.

UNKNOWN IMPOSTOR The mother of Southampton fireman Thomas Hart was distraught to learn that he had gone down with the ship... only for him to return home a month later in perfect health. A drunken Hart had lost his discharge book in a pub, and an unknown impostor had taken his job and had paid for his duplicity with his life.

GIRL POWER With insufficient men to propel her lifeboat containing 28 people, first-class passenger Margaret Brown of Denver, Colorado, took off her life jacket, and began rowing. Her efforts inspired some of the other women to lend a hand and led to her being immortalized by Hollywood in *The Unsinkable Molly Brown*.

Turn the page

1932 — Twenty years

FRIDAY, APRIL 15, 1932.

GREAT SEA TRAGEDY RECALLED IN NEW PICTURES

PASSENGERS on the second-class promenade deck.

APRIL 15! Twenty years ago to-day the mighty liner Titanic sank on her maiden voyage, with the loss of more than 1,500 lives.

Most of these pictures, now published for the first time, were taken by Father Browne, a Jesuit priest, who travelled in the ill-fated ship to Queenstown. Above is the scene on Waterloo Station before the boat-train left, with Colonel J. J. Astor, one of the victims, facing the camera.

The £2,000,000 liner, then the largest ship in the world, left Southampton on April 10. Twenty minutes before midnight on April 14 she crashed into a submerged iceberg and sank in less than three hours; a tragedy unparalleled in the history of sea-passenger service.

TWO of the first-class passengers.

LUNCH in the magnificent dining saloon.

IN THE GYMNASIUM.—Mr. McCawley, the physical instructor, and Mr. Pow, the electrician, both lost their lives.

FAREWELL.—The last glimpse of the Titanic from the coast of Ireland.

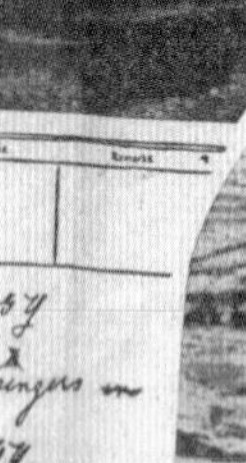

"SPARKS," Mr. Harold Bride, the liner's wireless operator. He was saved.

SURVIVORS arriving alongside the Carpathia. *Left:* The last message received from the doomed ship.

THE FACTS

- **It cost $7.5 million to build**—the equivalent of $400 million today
- Each of the **engines was the size of a three-story house**
- **The four funnels were 62 ft (19 m) high and 22 ft (6.7 m) in diameter**, wide enough to drive two trains through
- The hull was constructed with **three million rivets**
- The **center anchor weighed 15.5 tons** and needed 20 horses to pull it through Belfast to the shipyard
- The ship contained more than **200 mi (320 km) of electrical wiring**
- The ship was lit by **10,000 lightbulbs**
- *Titanic*'s whistles could be heard from a distance of **11 mi (18 km) away**
- The ship was fitted with 29 boilers and 159 furnaces, and carried more than **8,000 tons of coal**
- **16,800 gal (63,645 l) of drinking water** were consumed on board every day
- If the 882-ft-long (269-m) ship had been stood on its end, it would have been **taller than any building in the world at that time**
- **Sixty chefs** and chefs' assistants worked in five kitchens providing food for the passengers

YOUR UPLOADS

www.ripleys.com/submit

Joe Pires of Geneva, Florida, has a home with a stunning trick up its sleeve; it doubles as a hangar large enough to fit an airplane. The façade of the building hinges electronically to reveal a large hangar for various flying craft. Joe can jump into a gyrocopter or microlight without leaving his home, and taxi straight out onto the runway, which also doubles as his lawn.

VERTICAL PARKING

Heralding today's multistory parking lots, in the early 1920s cars were hoisted up on individual platforms to form elevator-style parking lots in order to save space.

Feats

Nailed It!

Xu Tiancheng can do a headstand on a nail for 30 minutes—and he has the dent in the top of his head to prove it! The 56-year-old performs his unusual ritual as part of his daily morning exercise routine at a park in Changsha, China—a pain-defying display of endurance that attracts large crowds.

PLANE SWAP

In an incredible midair stunt, Austrian skydiver Paul Steiner climbed from one glider to another 6,560 ft (2,000 m) up in the air while both planes were traveling at 100 mph (160 km/h). He climbed out of the cockpit, crawled along the wing, somersaulted under the wing and then stepped onto the wing of the second glider flying below. Then, while the first glider turned upside down and flew overhead, Steiner reached up to form a human link between the two planes.

Steiner sits on the wing of the first glider

KNIFE EXERCISE Xie Guanghai, a 57-year-old physics professor in Luoyang, China, does 4,000 push-ups a day—on upturned chopping knives. By developing thick calluses on his palms, he feels no pain from the blades of the knives, which are held in place on a wooden board.

BUNNY HOPS Polish stunt cyclist Krystian Herba bunny-hopped his way up the 48 flights of the 656-ft-high (200-m) Millennium Tower in Vienna, Austria, in 18 minutes 9 seconds.

BUNGEE JUMPS Scott Huntly from Edinburgh, Scotland, made 107 bungee jumps in just nine hours from a bridge 702 ft (214 m) above the Bloukrans River in the Western Cape region of South Africa.

THE CZECH TECHNICAL UNIVERSITY HAS DESIGNED A ROBOT THAT CAN JUGGLE FIVE POOL BALLS AT ONCE.

CROSSING AMERICA In 2010, six British and U.S. servicemen ran 3,530 mi (5,648 km) from New York to Santa Monica, California, on a Gumpathon, named after the movie *Forrest Gump* in which the hero runs across the U.S.A. Their eight-week journey took them through three deserts, four time zones, ten mountain ranges, 16 states and 789 towns. Among the team, which ran in relays, was British Royal Marine Mark Ormrod, a triple amputee who lost both legs and one arm when he stepped on a land mine in Afghanistan on Christmas Eve 2007.

Benji Williams

SENIOR SKYDIVER In March 2011, Fred Mack of Newtown Square, Pennsylvania, celebrated his 100th birthday by performing a tandem skydive at an altitude of 13,000 ft (3,960 m) in the skies over New Jersey. He made his first skydiving jump aged 95 and vowed to repeat the feat if he lived to be 100.

YO-YO HERO James Buffington, founder of the Chicago Yo-Yo Club, has built a working yo-yo with a string length of 39 ft 9 in (12.1 m). He demonstrated it from the roof of a store in the city, where it hung down over three stories.

POLE POSITION Israeli stuntman Hezi Dean stood on a small platform on top of a nine-story-high pole in Tel Aviv for more than 35 hours in May 2011. A crane hoisted him to the top of the pole and he descended at the end of the endurance test by jumping into a pile of cardboard boxes.

CAREFUL CLIMB In December 2010, the Czech Republic's Anatol Stykan climbed the 235 steps leading up to the famous Sacre Coeur church in Paris, France, while balancing his partner Monika on his head.

Ripley's REVISITED

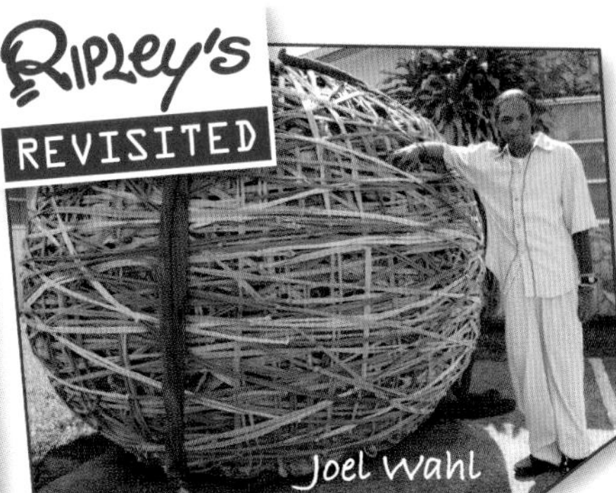

Joel Wahl

YOUR UPLOADS

www.ripleys.com/submit

Benji Williams of Los Angeles, California, has been making rubber-band balls since he was six. He went to Orlando, Florida, on vacation to visit Ripley's warehouse to see the world's biggest rubber-band ball, made by Joel Waul and weighing 9,432 lb (4,282 kg). Benji's ball is already well over 100 lb (45 kg)—and growing fast.

UNDERWATER CARD GAME A group of 16 German scuba divers played a card game underwater for 36 hours in March 2011. The divers sat on the bottom of a pool in Geiselhoering, playing a traditional Bavarian card game called "Sheep's Head."

STAR SWIMMER Four-year-old Tae Smith from Poole, England, swam 101 lengths of a pool (1¼ mi/2,000 m) just five months after learning to swim. She was meant to swim 30 lengths, but kept going until she had swum more than triple the distance.

He somersaults under the wing

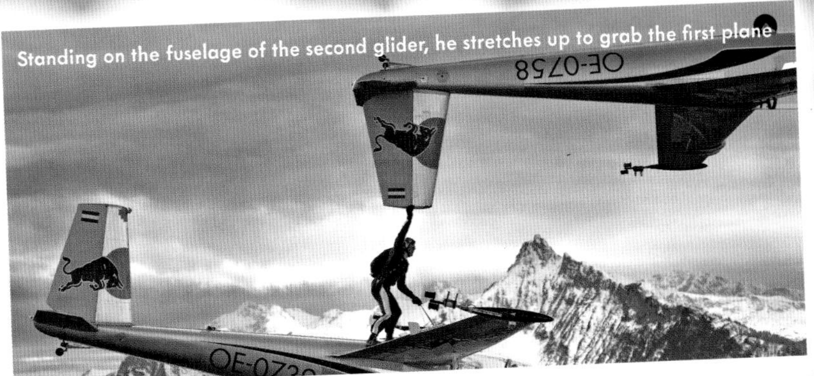

Standing on the fuselage of the second glider, he stretches up to grab the first plane

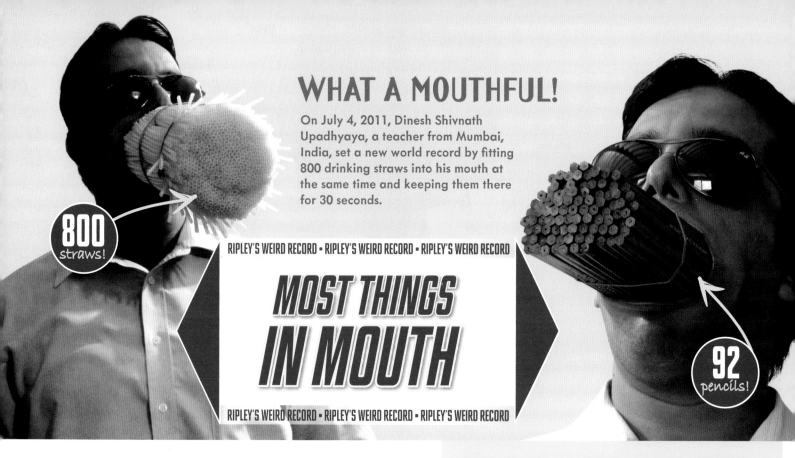

WHAT A MOUTHFUL!

On July 4, 2011, Dinesh Shivnath Upadhyaya, a teacher from Mumbai, India, set a new world record by fitting 800 drinking straws into his mouth at the same time and keeping them there for 30 seconds.

800 straws!

RIPLEY'S WEIRD RECORD • RIPLEY'S WEIRD RECORD • RIPLEY'S WEIRD RECORD

MOST THINGS IN MOUTH

RIPLEY'S WEIRD RECORD • RIPLEY'S WEIRD RECORD • RIPLEY'S WEIRD RECORD

92 pencils!

BOTTLE-CAP CHAIN Students and teachers at Seaview Elementary School in Linwood, New Jersey, created a chain from 10,714 bottle caps.

CANADIAN CROSSING In 2011, Kevin Robins of Fort McMurray, Alberta, Canada, cycled across Canada from Vancouver, British Columbia, to St. John's, Newfoundland, in just over 22 days, beating the previous record by a day and a half. He covered a total of 4,500 mi (7,200 km), clocking up an average pace of 200 mi (323 km) a day.

LARGEST KILT Ordering 170 sq yd (142 sq m) of material, Steve Campbell, a Scotsman living in the U.S.A., made the world's largest kilt and used it to dress the 80-ft-tall (24-m) *Golden Driller* statue in Tulsa, Oklahoma, for the 2011 Oklahoma Scottish Festival. The supersized kilt was 25 ft (7.6 m) long and had a waist measuring 48 ft (14.6 m), nearly 14 times bigger than a U.S. extra-large size.

MOUTHWATERING RECORDS

- 800 DRINKING STRAWS — Dinesh Upadhyaya (India)
- 159 CIGARETTES — Jim Mouth (U.S.A.)
- 109 LIVE BEES — Dr. Norman Gary (U.S.A.)
- 92 PENCILS — Dinesh Upadhyaya (India)
- 57 GRAPES — Shobhit Keshvdass (India)
- 41 CIGARS — Jim Mouth (U.S.A.)
- 22 LIVE SCORPIONS — Maged Almalki (Saudi Arabia)
- 11 LIVE RATTLESNAKES — Jackie Bibby (U.S.A.)
- 11 LIVE COCKROACHES — Travis Fessler (U.S.A.)
- 5 TENNIS BALLS — Augie (U.S. dog)

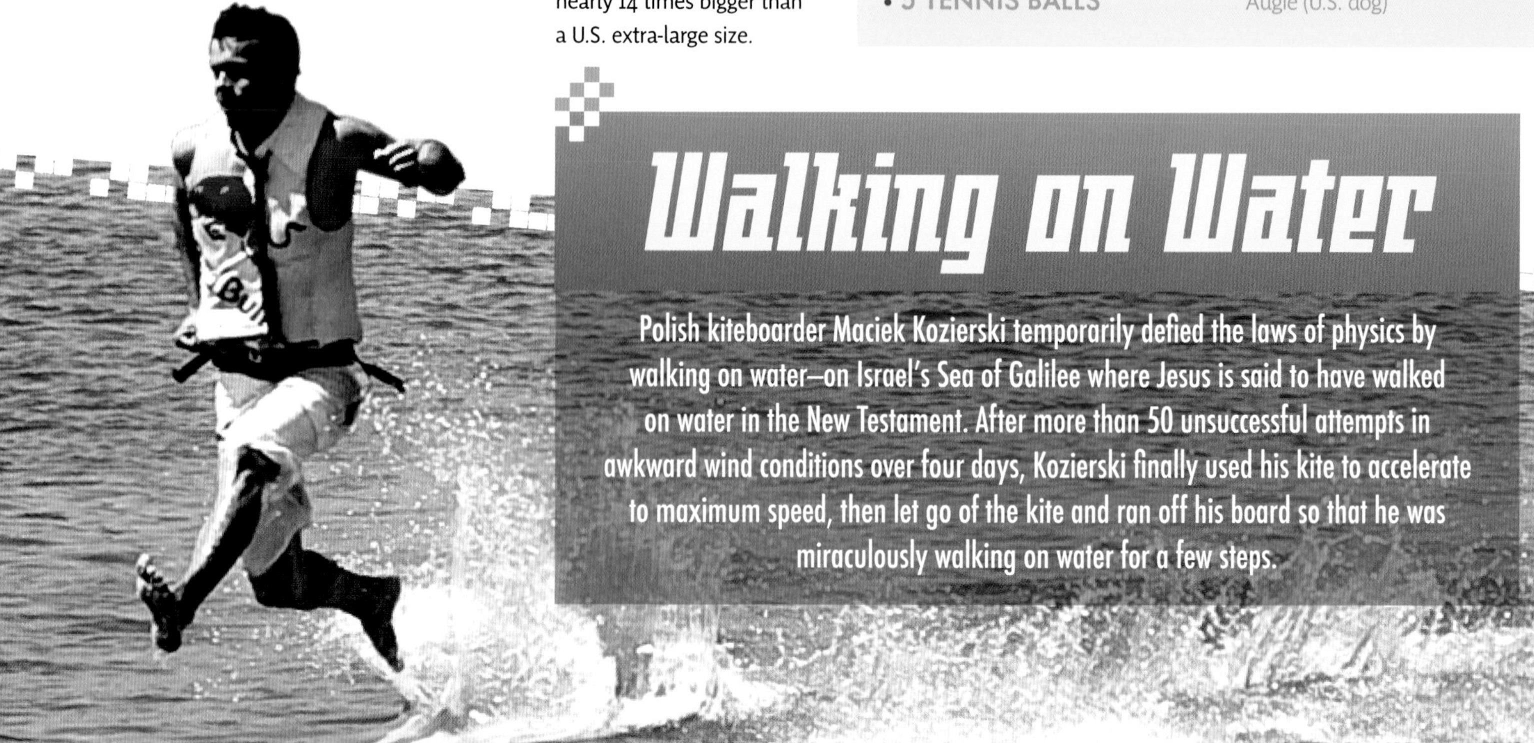

Walking on Water

Polish kiteboarder Maciek Kozierski temporarily defied the laws of physics by walking on water—on Israel's Sea of Galilee where Jesus is said to have walked on water in the New Testament. After more than 50 unsuccessful attempts in awkward wind conditions over four days, Kozierski finally used his kite to accelerate to maximum speed, then let go of the kite and ran off his board so that he was miraculously walking on water for a few steps.

WONDER WHEEL On June 18, 2011, the Lilly fireworks factory in Mqabba, Malta, lit the world's biggest pinwheel (Catherine Wheel) firework. With a diameter of 105 ft (32 m), it was 45 times the size of the average car wheel.

ARMY MEDIC At 76 years old, U.S. Army medic Dr. John Burson, an ear, nose and throat specialist from Villa Rica, Georgia, was posted to Afghanistan to take his fourth tour of duty in war zones since 2005.

UNDERWATER ESCAPE U.S. entertainer Thomas Blacke escaped from a pair of handcuffs underwater in a world record time of 8.34 seconds on October 27, 2010, in Yarmouth, Massachusetts.

WILD WALK In windy conditions in August 2011, Austrian daredevil Michael Kemeter completed a death-defying walk for 148 ft (45 m) along a ¾-in-wide (2-cm) slackline at an altitude of 2,600 ft (793 m) on Austria's highest mountain, the Grossglockner. He had a safety rope but wore no shoes and despite the cold went topless to reduce wind resistance. A week earlier, he crossed a 525-ft-long (160-m) slackline—the longest in the world—over the Gruenen See in Styria, Austria. In slacklining, the thin nylon line is anchored between two points, but unlike a tightrope it is not taut and is allowed to sway around in the air.

SOLO PILOT On June 4, 2011, nine-year-old Bobby Bradley of Albuquerque, New Mexico, became the youngest solo hot-air balloon pilot when he flew a balloon for 26 minutes over his home state before making a perfect landing. Bobby already had 30 hours' flying experience with his parents—both keen balloonists—and started taking control of the burner when he was just four.

UNDERWATER WALK On August 5, 2011, pool supervisor Joe Wilkie of Tonawanda, New York, walked a record 241 ft 6 in (73.6 m) underwater on a single breath in 1 minute 15 seconds while carrying a 25-lb (11.3-kg) weight to hold him down.

CARTON REGATTA Thirty-six teams used 45,000 empty milk cartons to make rowboats to take part in the 2011 milk carton boat regatta over a 165-ft-long (50-m) course on Latvia's Lielupe River.

POGO HOPS Chef Ben Hoyle from Sudbury, England, completed 75 successive pogo hops on the back wheel of his trail bike in September 2011.

BEER LABELS Since 1955, Charles Johnson of Cuyahoga Falls, Ohio, has collected more than 108,000 beer-bottle labels from all over the world.

500-MILE CRAWL In 2010, two Buddhist monks crawled 500 mi (800 km) on their knees to visit a statue in China's Putuo Mountains—a journey that took them two months.

SEVEN SUMMITS At just 16 years old, George Atkinson from London, England, reached the summit of the world's highest mountain, 29,029-ft (8,848-m) Mount Everest, and in doing so completed his challenge of conquering mountaineering's famous Seven Summits. Despite his young age, he had previously climbed Tanzania's Mount Kilimanjaro, Russia's Mount Elbrus, Indonesia's Carstensz Pyramid, Argentina's Mount Aconcagua, the U.S.A.'s Mount McKinley and Antarctica's Mount Vinson.

Lizardman Feats

FEATURED ARTIST: ERIK SPRAGUE ★ FEATURED ARTIST: ERIK SPRAGUE ★ FEATURED ARTIST: ERIK SPRAGUE ★ FEATURED ARTIST: ERIK SPRAGUE ★ FEATURED ARTIST: ERIK SPRAGUE

Ripley's ask

Ripley's Believe It or Not! met up with Erik Sprague to ask him about his extreme transformation.

Why did you decide to transform yourself into the Lizardman? *Originally, I was working on ideas for body-based art pieces that explored transformation and how we use the term "human." This, combined with my interests in body modification and the sideshow, came together as a single project idea. I chose a lizard partly due to the cross-cultural symbolic significance of reptiles but also because I thought it would look good.*

Do your modifications get a lot of attention from the public? *Since the beginning my modifications have drawn a lot of attention, mostly double takes and staring, but over the years the attention has shifted from "What is that?" to "Hey, that's the guy from TV"—due in no small part to programs like Ripley's.*

What is your favourite modification? *My split tongue is the one I am most known for, but my favorite might be one that people rarely see—my septum piercing. The piercing is stretched to half an inch in diameter and I wear a small plug in it. It was done by a dear friend, Keith Alexander, who has since passed away and it has huge sentimental value to me.*

Can you eat normally with your modified tongue and teeth? *Yes, the only thing that has changed for me is that when I eat apples I no longer just bite into them because my sharp teeth simply tear off thin strips, so I have to slice them up first now.*

Are you "completed" yet? *I am not quite complete yet, with over 700 hours of tattooing on my body I still have about another 100 or so to go. Once all my scales are filled in green I will think of myself as complete, but that doesn't mean I won't come up with new additions in the future.*

Turn the page

Lizardman

As a young boy

As Best Man

Wedding day

Performance artist Erik "The Lizardman" Sprague, from Austin, Texas, has spent years transforming himself into a reptile-man hybrid. Since 1994, he has undergone almost 700 hours of tattooing in order to achieve a full head and body of green scales. To complete his unique look, four of his teeth have been filed into sharp crocodile-like fangs, he has had his tongue bifurcated and five Teflon horns have been subdermally implanted above each eye to form horned ridges. This last procedure was the most painful to endure—five hours with his head cut open, followed by swelling and soreness. He has also had his septum (the piece of skin that separates the nostrils) pierced and the hole stretched to ½ in (1.25 cm) in diameter.

During Erik's act, he inserts razor-sharp scissor blades in the fork of his tongue and through his nostrils, threads a metal corkscrew through his nose and mouth, and sticks a running power drill up his nostrils. He also swallows swords, eats and breathes fire, and acts as a human dartboard. On several occasions he pulled cars with his 1-in (2.5-cm) pierced earlobes, which at the time were the strongest earlobes in the world, but he had to stop wearing jewelry in them in 2009 following an adverse reaction.

Erik, who has a degree in Philosophy, estimates that it would cost around $250,000 for anyone wanting to achieve the same unbelievable look as The Lizardman.

The scissors carefully go right into his nasal passage!

He corkscrews through his nose, out of his mouth and then through his ear!

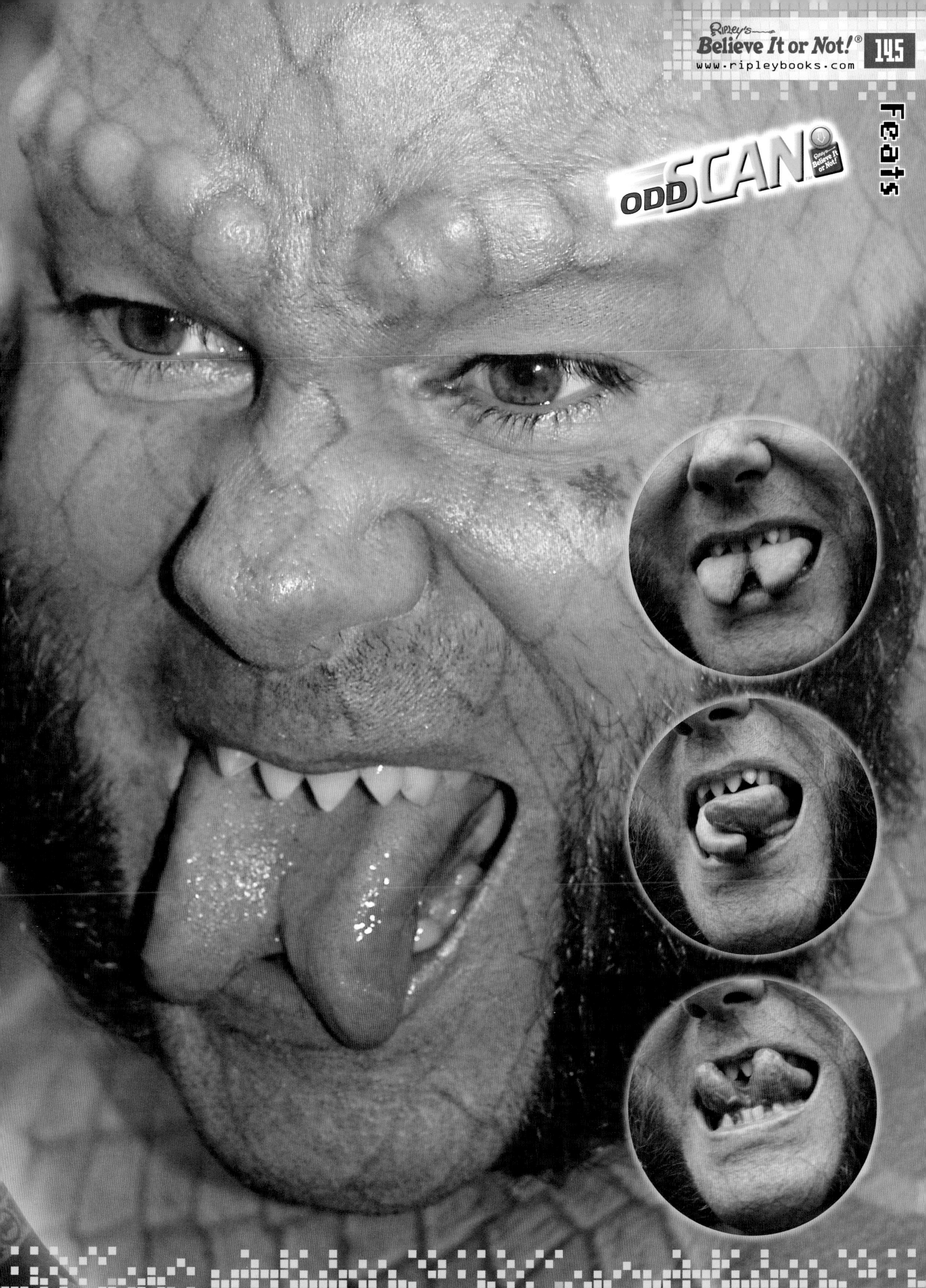
ODD SCAN

SKYSCRAPER CLIMB

In a six-hour climb, Alain Robert, or "Spiderman," the French freestyle skyscraper climber, scaled the 2,717-ft-high (828-m) Burj Khalifa building in Dubai, United Arab Emirates, in March 2011. He has climbed over 70 of the world's tallest buildings, including New York's Empire State Building and Chicago's Willis Tower.

WORLD WALK Jean Béliveau of Montréal, Canada, walked around the world for 11 years. He set off on his 45th birthday and traveled 46,940 mi (75,543 km) through 64 countries, wearing out 53 pairs of shoes on the longest-ever uninterrupted world walk. He ate insects in Africa, dog in South Korea and snake in China, and carried his sleeping bag, clothes and a first-aid kit in a three-wheel stroller.

HAT MOSAIC The New Era Cap Company of Buffalo, New York State, created a hat mosaic made up of 1,875 official Major League Baseball caps.

ICE ORDEAL Two Chinese men stood encased in ice for two hours in Zhangjiajie, Hunan Province, in 2011. Wearing only their swimming trunks. Chen Kecai, 52, and Jin Songhao, 54, lasted 118 and 120 minutes respectively standing in transparent boxes with ice right up to their necks. Jin was even able to write Chinese calligraphy during the challenge.

SENIOR WORKER Hedda Bolgar Bekker, who runs her own psychotherapy clinic in Los Angeles, California, still works at age 102, giving lectures and seeing patients for up to 20 hours a week.

FEATURED ARTIST: WILLARD WIGAN

Willard Wigan

Willard Wigan, a sculptor from Birmingham, England, makes amazingly detailed microscopic sculptures. In 2011, Ripley's managed to acquire 97 pieces of his work to showcase in their museums. The Ripley's team spoke to Willard:

Ripley's ask

"I work in a closet 4 ft across to minimize air disturbance, and often at night when the vibrations from traffic are less. It's a messy space with bottles and tiny boxes containing ground diamond and glass, platinum, dust, those plastic clothes tags that I carve shapes into, cloth fibers, eyelashes, flies' hairs—all the materials I work with.

I can be in there for 20 hours or so at a time. I have trained myself to increase my concentration—when I started doing this sort of work 40 years ago I used to put tiny ball bearings at the ends of my fingers and hold them there for three hours. I would thread a needle 200 times to increase my attention span. I now find I can concentrate to such an extent that I enter a semi-meditative state.

I once wanted to carve a stately home small enough to fit in the eye of a needle and at about 3 p.m. one day I went into a U.K. grocery store and started looking in a magazine for inspiration. The next thing I knew, a sales assistant tapped me on the shoulder and said the store was closing. It was 5 p.m. and I had been staring at one picture for two hours! Another time, I was hollowing out a hair to make a space for a train I wanted to insert inside and held my breath—until I heard a loud bang. That was the sound of me hitting the floor. I'd held my breath too long and passed out.

After concentrating for a few hours, my movements are slow for a while when I stop. I have to train myself to see again that some things are big and don't need such a gentle touch. I don't enjoy doing my work because it's so demanding, but I love finishing a sculpture and seeing peoples' reaction to it.

If I'm making something to fit in the eye of a needle, I'll carve the sculpture outside the needle first. I have to watch out for the catapu action. I have a clamp that holds the model and if I press too hard it'll catapult off, or stati electricity might make it jump. I made a whol scene of Miss Haversham, Estella and Pip, from Great Expectations, *complete with cobwebs ar cakes, but it catapulted away. That was three months work lost. I was pretty upset. Another time, a bead of sweat ran down my fingers on a wet sculpture as I painted it and entombed i Ruined. And sometimes I might inhale work, a I did once with* Alice in Wonderland.

After that, if the model has, say, two legs, I drill two tiny holes in the needle and fill the holes with honey. I drop the feet in and surface tension holds the model enough for me to paint it, after which it hardens. I've dropped sculptures on the floor before and people shrie and panic that it's broken, but it never does. I an ant falls off your house roof, it won't die. It' too small. A speck of dust on your shirt will sti be there even if you jump up and down. Same with the models.

Paint has to be worked on before I can use it because the pigment molecules in it can be too big for the sculptures. I drop a speck of paint on a microscope slide and grind down the molecules with a ball bearing for two to three hours until the paint becomes smoother. There no second chance with the painting. You can't wipe it off and start again.

My aim is to create smaller and smaller artworks. My next project will be to capture the "Old Woman Who Lived in a Shoe," complete with 25 children and the shoe... in the eye of a needle!

I think I draw people's attention to the wonde of the minuscule world. After all, everything starts small—even us, as a tiny spec in the womb. Microscopic bacteria can cause massiv devastation and survive against the odds. An atom might be one of the smallest things tha exists, but it produces the biggest explosion."

TO VIEW THE COLLECTION Turn the page

HAIRCUT TOUR Hair salon owner Patrick Lomantini from Wichita, Kansas, did at least 50 free haircuts a day, in all 50 U.S. states in 50 days in 2011—a total of more than 2,500 haircuts. Visiting a different state each day, he traveled between states overnight and cut hair all day.

SWALLOWED SAW On November 14, 2010, U.S. sword swallower Dan Meyer swallowed a 100-year-old handsaw, which belonged to the Bruce Museum in Greenwich, Connecticut, during a presentation on the history of sword swallowing.

Willard Wigan, a sculptor from Birmingham, England, makes amazingly detailed microscopic sculptures, some of which measure just 0.0002 in (0.005 mm) tall—more than three times smaller than the period at the end of this sentence. His figures can be viewed only undera microscope and magnified 400 times. They can fit on a single grain of sand or on the head of a pin, and he has even managed to fit nine camels into the eye of a needle.

Now, 97 of his stunning miniature artworks have been bought by *Ripley's Believe It or Not!*—and most of them, the result of more than 40 years of painstaking carving, chipping and painting, could fit comfortably together inside a single matchbox.

ODD SCAN

Ripley's Believe It or Not!

As a child with undiagnosed dyslexia, Willard had an unhappy time at school and sought refuge in local woods, where he watched ants running about the floor of a shed. "I was four or five," he recalls, "and I thought the ants must be homeless, so I built them houses from splinters of wood. Then I thought the ants needed furniture, so I made little chairs and tables that could fit inside the houses." His mother saw the ant houses and encouraged him to continue. "She told me that I was going to get bigger by getting smaller."

Each nano-sculpture takes up to three months to create. His homemade carving tools consist of tiny shards of diamond attached to a needle, as well as filed-down acupuncture needles. He uses one of his own eyelashes or a hair plucked from the back of a housefly as a paintbrush. To keep his hands still, he enters a meditative state and works in the 1.5-second space between heartbeats, as even the pulse in his finger is enough to cause a mistake.

His stunningly accurate creations include Little Miss Muffet, with spider, in the eye of a needle, Muhammad Ali boxing Sonny Liston on a pinhead, the Statue of Liberty in the eye of a needle, the *Titanic* on a tiny crystal, a church on a grain of sand, and the cast of *Peter Pan* in a fishhook. His work is mentally and physically draining, but he strives to get smaller still. Referring to the nine camels in the eye of a needle, he says: "One day, I'll get 20 in there. It'll probably drive me nuts, but I will do it."

in the eye of a needle

nine camels in the eye of a needle

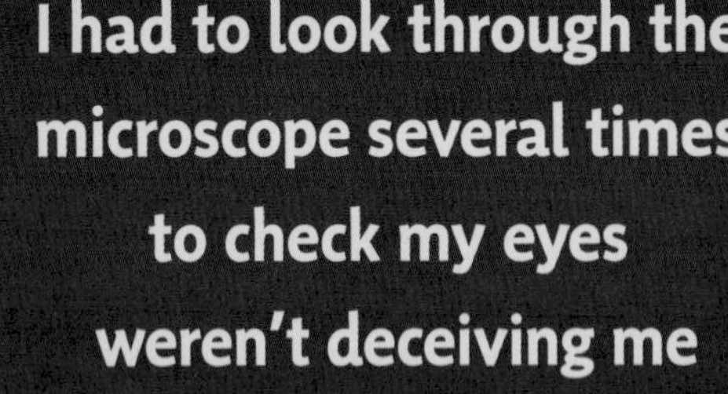

I had to look through the microscope several times to check my eyes weren't deceiving me

~

Lord Richard Rogers

statue of liberty in the eye of a needle

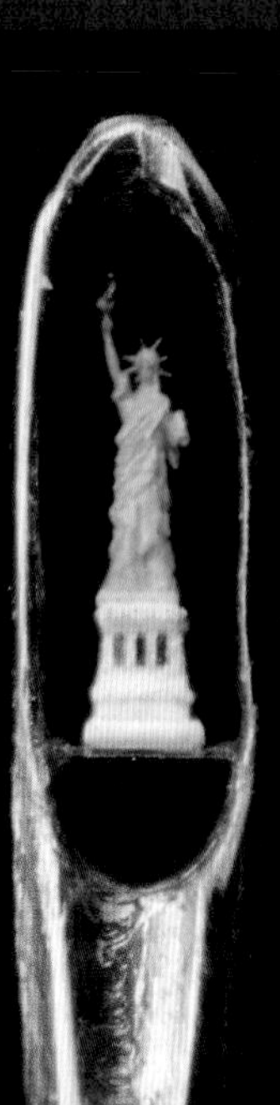

ali vs. liston on the head of a pin

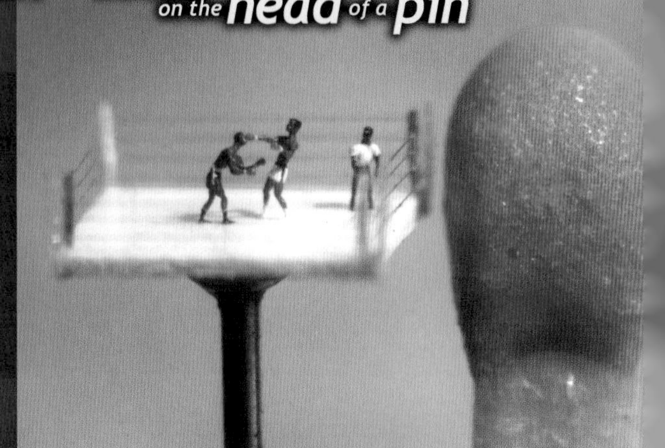

titanic on the tip of a crystal

Ripley's archivist Edward Meyer tells how he acquired the collection

"I had been following Willard Wigan's career since 1999, and when he first sold some of his artworks in 2007 and a website listed several for sale, I realized that maybe Ripley's could obtain a couple. Following dozens of letters and a meeting in a London hotel bar, I decided to try and buy a large number of his works. During negotiations the figure rose to 97 pieces—which was everything not already in private collections or about 85–90 percent of everything he has ever made. The art was delivered by hand in a gym bag to our Orlando HQ, all contained in small jewelry cases inside three small cardboard boxes."

I spy with my little eye...

little miss muffet in the eye of a needle

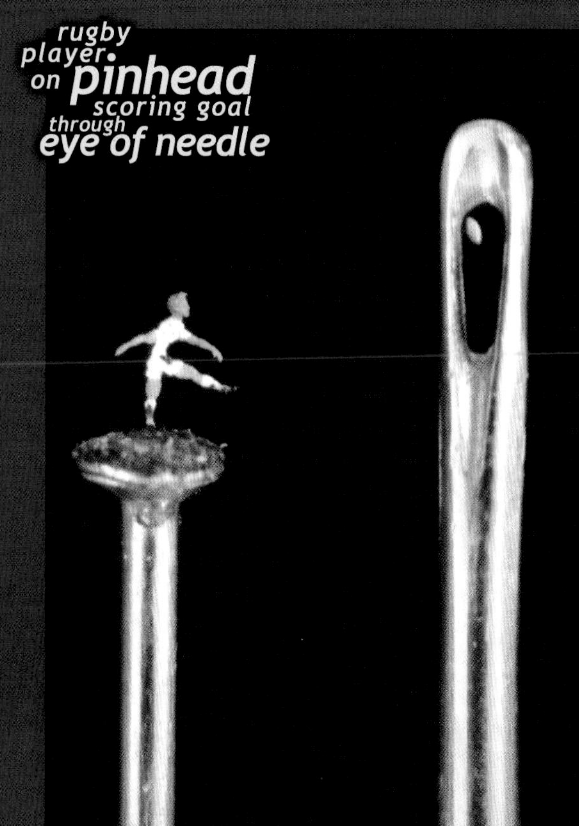

rugby player on pinhead scoring goal through eye of needle

Willard's talents defy description

~

H.R.H. Prince Charles

hairy biker on the head of a pin

BEE SUIT

In May 2011, Zhang Wei from Zizhou County, China, wore a suit of bees weighing a staggering 184 lb (83.5 kg)—that's approximately the weight of an adult American man. Wearing a pair of goggles, but leaving his face and hands unprotected and holding a tube in his mouth for breathing, he sat in a foliage-covered frame as thousands of bees were released next to him.

ROCKET RACER Students at the Joseph Leckie Community Technology College in Walsall, England, designed and developed a rocket-powered scale model car that reached a speed of 88.92 mph (143.1 km/h)—that's an equivalent speed of 259 mph (417 km/h) in a regular-sized car. The 21-in (53-cm) car was fitted with D-Class Estes rocket motors and fired 328 ft (100 m) along a high tensile wire.

DELAYED GRADUATION Leo Plass of Redmond, Oregon, dropped out of college in 1932 to take up a job in logging when he was less than one semester away from graduating—but in 2011 he finally received his diploma from Eastern Oregon University at the age of 99.

LOTTA BOTTLES Over a 25-year period, Steve Wheeler has collected more than 17,500 milk bottles in different shapes and sizes from around the world, some dating back to the 19th century. He has built a giant shed to house the collection, which weighs 15 tons, behind his home in Malvern, England. Ironically, Steve doesn't even like milk!

SOCK LINE As part of National Red Sock Day—in memory of yachtsman Sir Peter Blake who used to wear red socks for good luck—New Zealanders donated more than 30,000 socks, which, when stretched out on a line, extended for over 1.8 mi (3 km).

WIRE BALL Starting in 2001, landscaper Rick Fortin of New Boston, New Hampshire, has created a copper wire ball that now measures over 3 ft (0.9 m) in diameter and weighs more than 922 lb (418 kg).

DANCING BALLOON

Australian entertainer Bruce Airhead uses a voice-activated vacuum cleaner to inflate a 6-ft (1.8-m) balloon—and then he slides his entire body inside, bit by bit, and starts dancing. As a final twist, although he enters the balloon wearing only lycra shorts, he emerges through the burst balloon fully dressed as Elvis.

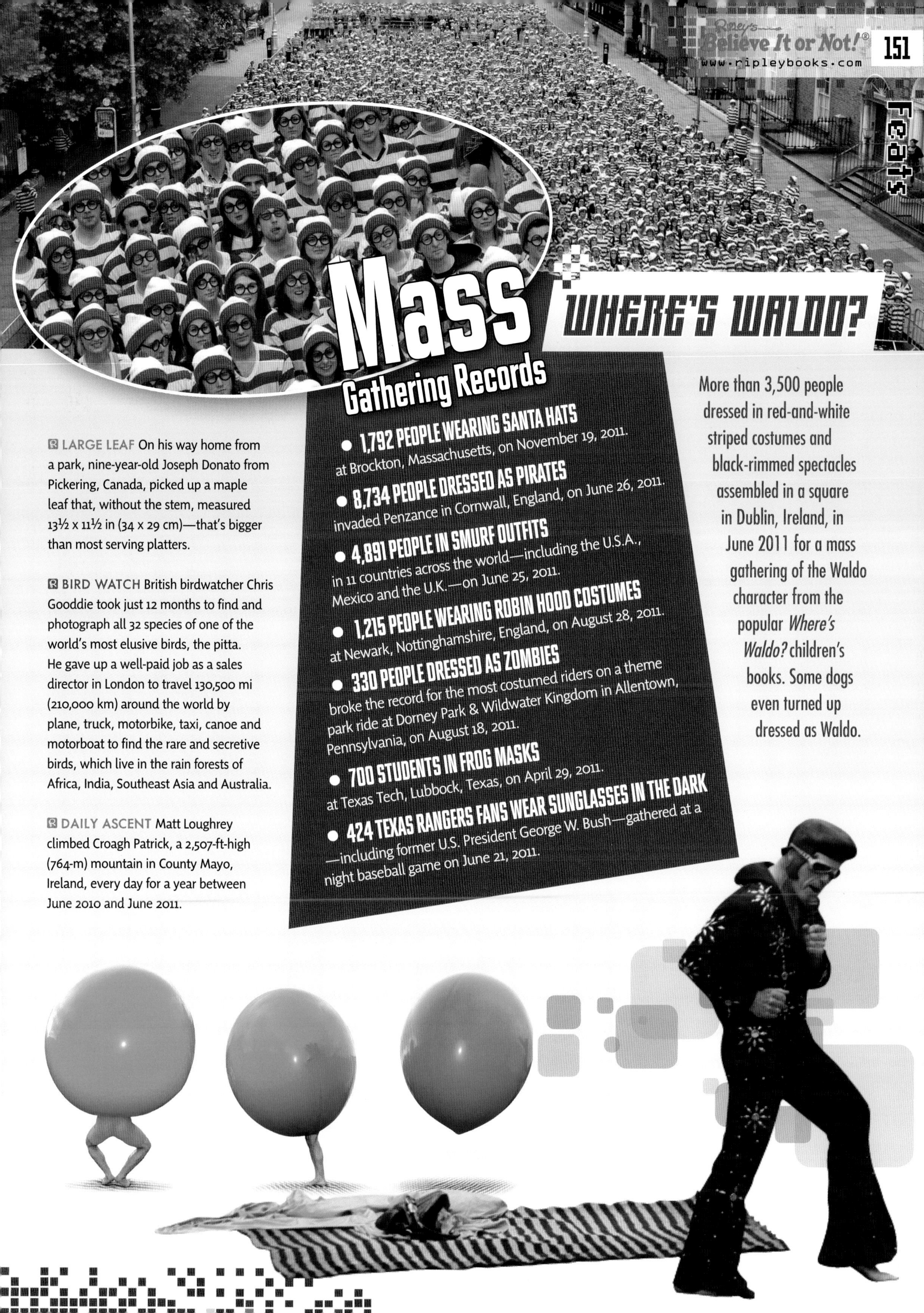

Mass Gathering Records

WHERE'S WALDO?

More than 3,500 people dressed in red-and-white striped costumes and black-rimmed spectacles assembled in a square in Dublin, Ireland, in June 2011 for a mass gathering of the Waldo character from the popular *Where's Waldo?* children's books. Some dogs even turned up dressed as Waldo.

- **1,792 PEOPLE WEARING SANTA HATS** at Brockton, Massachusetts, on November 19, 2011.
- **8,734 PEOPLE DRESSED AS PIRATES** invaded Penzance in Cornwall, England, on June 26, 2011.
- **4,891 PEOPLE IN SMURF OUTFITS** in 11 countries across the world—including the U.S.A., Mexico and the U.K.—on June 25, 2011.
- **1,215 PEOPLE WEARING ROBIN HOOD COSTUMES** at Newark, Nottinghamshire, England, on August 28, 2011.
- **330 PEOPLE DRESSED AS ZOMBIES** broke the record for the most costumed riders on a theme park ride at Dorney Park & Wildwater Kingdom in Allentown, Pennsylvania, on August 18, 2011.
- **700 STUDENTS IN FROG MASKS** at Texas Tech, Lubbock, Texas, on April 29, 2011.
- **424 TEXAS RANGERS FANS WEAR SUNGLASSES IN THE DARK** —including former U.S. President George W. Bush—gathered at a night baseball game on June 21, 2011.

LARGE LEAF On his way home from a park, nine-year-old Joseph Donato from Pickering, Canada, picked up a maple leaf that, without the stem, measured 13½ x 11½ in (34 x 29 cm)—that's bigger than most serving platters.

BIRD WATCH British birdwatcher Chris Gooddie took just 12 months to find and photograph all 32 species of one of the world's most elusive birds, the pitta. He gave up a well-paid job as a sales director in London to travel 130,500 mi (210,000 km) around the world by plane, truck, motorbike, taxi, canoe and motorboat to find the rare and secretive birds, which live in the rain forests of Africa, India, Southeast Asia and Australia.

DAILY ASCENT Matt Loughrey climbed Croagh Patrick, a 2,507-ft-high (764-m) mountain in County Mayo, Ireland, every day for a year between June 2010 and June 2011.

FAMILY RUN Competing in the London Marathon on April 17, 2011, 52-year-old Kelvin Amos and his son Shane, 31, from Stoke-on-Trent, England, finished in a combined time of 6 hours 3 minutes 7 seconds—the fastest-ever father-and-son team to run a marathon.

SNAKE CHALLENGE In 2010, David Jones, a 44-year-old carpenter from Crawley, England, spent four months locked in a room with 40 poisonous snakes, including cobras, black mambas and puff adders, in Johannesburg, South Africa.

MOVIE STATUES Dave Bailey of Middlesex, England, has collected Star Wars memorabilia for over 30 years. His £60,000 hoard includes full-size statues of all the main characters, including a 7-ft-tall (2.1-m) Darth Vader.

WING WALK On November 15, 2010, pensioner Tom Lackey from Birmingham, England, broke his own record as the world's oldest wing walker—at the age of 90. He was strapped to the 32-ft-long (9.7-m) wing of a plane and flown 500 ft (152 m) above the ground in Gloucestershire.

TONGUE TWISTER

China's Li Jinlong used his mouth to balance a tower of three plastic bottles, 12 wine glasses, five glass plates and 16 soccer balls, and then made the entire tower spin using only his tongue. His tongue had to support and spin a total weight of 33 lb (15 kg).

RIPLEY'S WEIRD RECORD - RIPLEY'S WEIRD RECORD - RIPLEY'S WEIRD RECORD

WORLD'S GREATEST TONGUE BALANCING ACT

RIPLEY'S WEIRD RECORD - RIPLEY'S WEIRD RECORD - RIPLEY'S WEIRD RECORD

DELAYED DIPLOMA Eighty-six-year-old James Livingston from Savannah, Georgia, graduated from Screven County High, and was awarded his high-school diploma, on May 28, 2010. His parents had allowed him to leave high school in 1942 to help fight World War II on condition that he earned his diploma when he got back.

JAIL BREAK On August 22, 2011, exactly 25 years after he first performed the stunt of escaping from Waushara County Jail, Wisconsin, Anthony Martin, the "King of Escapists," repeated the feat—and in almost half the time. Despite being placed in a straitjacket, strapped to a ladder and locked behind four steel doors, he was able to complete his escape in just 2 minutes 50 seconds—nearly two minutes faster than in 1986.

ISLAND SWIM Julie Bradshaw from Loughborough, England, swam the 28.5 mi (45.9 km) around New York's Manhattan Island in 9 hours 28 minutes, using only the butterfly stroke.

TOILET MUSEUM In Wiesbaden, Germany, toilet fan Michael Berger has opened a museum devoted exclusively to the lavatory. The unusual attraction contains his personal collection of toilet brushes, toilet roll holders and toilet seats. Among the extraordinary artifacts are a "Mona Lisa" toilet roll holder, a Virgin Mary toilet brush holder and a urinal with Adolf Hitler's face on the inside, which was designed after World War II to show disapproval of the Nazi regime.

HEAVY LOADS

On August 27, 2011, 11 former U.K. servicemen climbed England's highest peak with 100-lb (45-kg) tumble dryers or washing machines on their backs. It took the ex-marines and paratroopers eight hours to climb up and down the 3,209-ft-high (978-m) Scafell Pike.

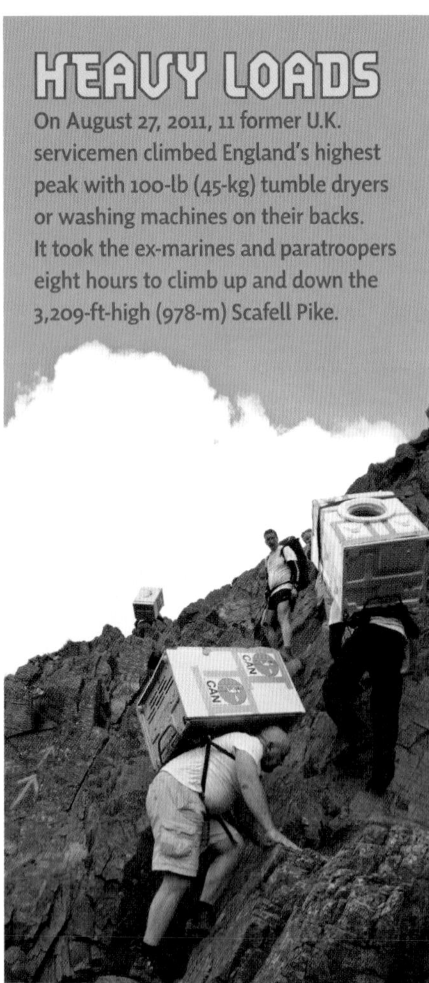

CHANNEL SWIM At the age of 70 years 4 months, Roger Allsopp, a retired surgeon from Guernsey in the Channel Islands, became the oldest person to swim the English Channel when he completed the 24-mi (39-km) crossing from Dover, England, to northern France in 17 hours 51 minutes on August 30, 2011.

BIKE LEAP Chilean base-jumper Julio Munoz roared off a massive cliff in the Andes on his motorbike, free-falling around 3,000 ft (915 m) before opening his parachute. It took him three years to plan the spectacular stunt, during which he had several cameras attached to his body so that he could film the jump from different angles.

WEIRDEST OF THE WEIRD

FEEJEE-TYPE MERMAID	STAIRCASE
ELEPHANT SKULL RIDDEN BY A SKELETON	LIVING ROOM
ANCIENT MUMMY	LIVING ROOM
ALLIGATOR/FISH HYBRID	DINING ROOM
CHANDELIER DECORATED WITH HUMAN SKULLS	DINING ROOM
STUFFED BEAR	PARLOR
TWO-HEADED CALF	PARLOR
ANTIQUE TOASTER COLLECTION	KITCHEN
8-FT-TALL (2.4-M) HUMAN SKELETON	LIBRARY
PICKLED HUMAN FETUSES IN JARS	BEDROOM
SENSORY-DEPRIVATION TANK	BASEMENT
13-FT-TALL (4-M) MINOTAUR BUST	GARDEN

Blade Runner

On March 23, 2011, a man in Chongqing, China, set a record for the highest broadsword ladder climb by scaling a ladder 94 ft 6 in high (28.8 m) built with 168 razor-sharp broadsword rungs... in bare feet.

Steve's Weird House

Every inch of Steve Bard's house is filled with old sideshow artifacts and weird human and animal curiosities. The narrow paths that wind from room to room are just wide enough for a person to walk through. Yet it remains a functional house. The kitchen boasts a microwave, a refrigerator and a burner, all cleverly concealed by human skulls, figures, severed heads and other oddities. The house is not open to the general public, but Steve does sometimes give private tours to those who share his eclectic taste in the freaky and the creepy.

Remember the *Addams Family* house? Well, it looks mundane and suburban compared to Steve Bard's rambling Victorian home in Seattle, Washington, where every room is crammed from floor to ceiling with hundreds of thousands of curiosities, ranging from an 8-ft-tall (2.4-m) human skeleton to two-headed animals and a collection of 100-year-old pickled human fetuses in jars.

Known as "Weird Steve," Bard is in fact just an average guy with a passion for collecting things—the stranger the better. That's why he is happy to share his home with funeral ephemera, monster movie props, sci-fi art, questionable medical devices, weird taxidermy, Victorian hair art, countless skulls and the world's smallest mummy.

A self-confessed sci-fi geek, he started out collecting books, but as he picked up oddities and old sideshow artifacts on eBay and from various other sources, his collection spread out from the library to fill the entire house and garden. He has over 25,000 books (including thousands of autographed sci-fi first editions), more than 150 antique toasters, plus a collection of casket plates, antique funeral caskets, and embalmer and mortician tools.

Then there are the animals. While live birds reside in the kitchen, everything else is dead. There are stuffed gazelles, bears, monkeys and a tiger, as well as preserved curiosities such as conjoined weasels, two-headed kittens, two-headed chicks and a two-headed calf. Many of his exhibits are stored in jars, including a pickled bat, a giant tapeworm and a jar containing a human finger lost in an accident in the 1950s. Among Steve's most prized possessions are his "pickled punks"—Victorian human fetuses preserved in formaldehyde that were once sideshow attractions. They were known as "frog babies" because they were stillborn with anencephaly, a disorder whereby most of the brain is missing owing to a neural tube defect. Steve keeps these in jars on the mantle above his bed!

However, not everything in the house is as it seems. The giant human skeleton is thought to have been made for medical students, while a two-headed baby is actually made of rubber. Steve had to create it himself because, as he acknowledges, it is not easy to obtain real two-headed babies.

Paintings line every wall of the house, and Steve also has hundreds of kinetic art objects and art deco statues. His more unusual artistic exhibits include a series of paintings on the head of a pin and Victorian art woven from human hair.

Adjoining the library is a "Devil Room" devoted to all things Satanic, and the basement has been converted to a glow-in-the-dark "Future Room," decorated in the style of The Jetsons and Barbarella, and containing futuristic furniture in the form of an egg-shaped stereo chair as well as a sensory-deprivation tank.

This shrine of creepy curiosities extends outside, where Steve has set up a Minotaur Garden in his backyard. The garden features a 14-ft-high (4-m) bust of a Minotaur, a 25-ft-tall (7.6-m) Rapunzel Castle Tower and a sinister cemetery. For all the weirdness that surrounds him, Steve claims the weirdest thing of all was the one question that a lady visitor to his house wanted to ask: "How do you dust?"

YOUR UPLOADS

www.ripleys.com/submit

EGGSERCISE!

Darryl Learie of Alberta, Canada, is able to complete one-armed push-ups on the top of a raw egg, without smashing it. Incredibly, Darryl's record stands at 11 repetitions before the egg finally gave way. Darryl explains that the arched top and bottom of the shell enable the egg to withstand the forces he exerts when performing the feat.

REAL EGG!

CHIN UP

Farmer Zhu Baobing is capable of carrying great weights on his chin. Known locally in Guli, China, as "China's First Chin," he successfully held aloft a 90-lb (40-kg) child while filming a TV program in Jiangsu Province in May 2011.

HOT WHEELS Driving down a ramp ten stories high and designed to look like a Hot Wheels toy ramp, Hollywood stuntman Tanner Foust jumped his car across a world-record-breaking 332-ft (101-m) gap before the running of the Indianapolis 500 in May 2011.

DUCK LINE Families from Seattle, Washington State, joined forces to create a record-breaking line of 17,782 yellow rubber ducks that stretched a mile long at the city's Warren G. Magnuson Park.

BLOWING BUBBLES In 2011, British professional bubble-maker Samsam Bubbleman (real name Sam Heath) created a large bubble, 19 in (48 cm) in diameter, with 56 smaller bubbles inside. It took him over two hours to blow and required conditions of low wind, low humidity and no rain. He has been making amazing bubbles since 1989, and once managed to fit 50 people inside a giant bubble.

CHOPSTICK CHAMP Ma Deqi, a farmer from Yuzhou, China, can catch 40 Ping Pong balls with a pair of chopsticks in one minute.

TWO-DAY KISS Husband and wife Ekkachai and Laksana Tiranarat kissed nonstop for 46 hours 24 minutes to celebrate Valentine's Day in Pattaya, Thailand, in 2011.

STILT WALK Wearing specially made 2-ft-high (60-cm) aluminum stilts, Samati Yiming, a 33-year-old physics teacher, walked 65 ft (20 m) on a high wire that was suspended 70 ft (21 m) above the ground at a park in Xinjiang, China. Samati, who has been stilt walking for over 15 years, did not even use a safety rope. In 2004, he walked for eight days on stilts, covering 180 mi (290 km), and the following year he walked for 49 steps on stilts that were an incredible 52 ft (16 m) high.

MOUNTAIN WALK In 2009, 34-year-old Buddhist monk Endo Mitsunaga completed the "Sennichi Kaihogyo"—one thousand days of meditation and walking around Mount Hiei, Japan. During this time he walked 26 mi (42 km) a day, for periods of 100 or 200 days in a row.

EYE RUN Noel Bresland from Manchester, England, ran 26 mi (42 km)—the equivalent of a marathon—on a treadmill inside a capsule of the giant wheel, the London Eye, in 3 hours 51 minutes in London, England, in April 2011.

EXTRA LARGE In June 2011 in Nashville, Tennessee, a manufacturer unveiled a colossal T-shirt measuring 180 x 281 ft (54.8 x 85.6 m)—that's nearly the size of a football field. The T-shirt took six weeks to make and weighed more than two tons.

SCISSOR HAPPY Barber Nabi Salehi of London, England, cut the hair of 526 customers in just 24 hours on June 3, 2011.

STUNNING STOGIE In 2011, Cuba's José Castelar "Cueto" Cairo rolled a massive cigar that measured over 268 ft (81.8 m) long.

MAGIC NUMBER Indian businessman Mohammed Farooque Dhanani from Mumbai, has collected more than 31,000 currency notes from across the world—all ending with the serial number 786. The number has no particular significance—he simply started collecting it over a decade ago as a unique hobby. His biggest surprise since then was finding that the serial number on his new credit card ended in 786.

OPTICAL EXTRUSION

Kung fu expert Dong Changsheng performed an incredible feat at a festival in Hubei Province, China. Reports claim that he swallowed two metal ball bearings, before executing several martial arts moves to move the balls up into the back of his mouth. He then proceeded to force the balls out of one of his eyes, with the help of a chopstick!

Ripley's Research

Dong claims he is able to propel the small metal balls through the narrow tunnels in his head, eventually maneuvering them out of his eyes through the tear ducts. Dong explains "The tear ducts actually connect to other tunnels in the head, and normal people just haven't broken the barrier and made the connection through." At 50 years old, he has been stretching the limits of his eyes for at least 15 years. He began by placing buttons in his eyes to toughen them up, and is now capable of many eye-watering endeavors: Dong was featured in *Ripley's Believe It or Not! Seeing is Believing* after pulling a minibus attached to hooks under his eyelids.

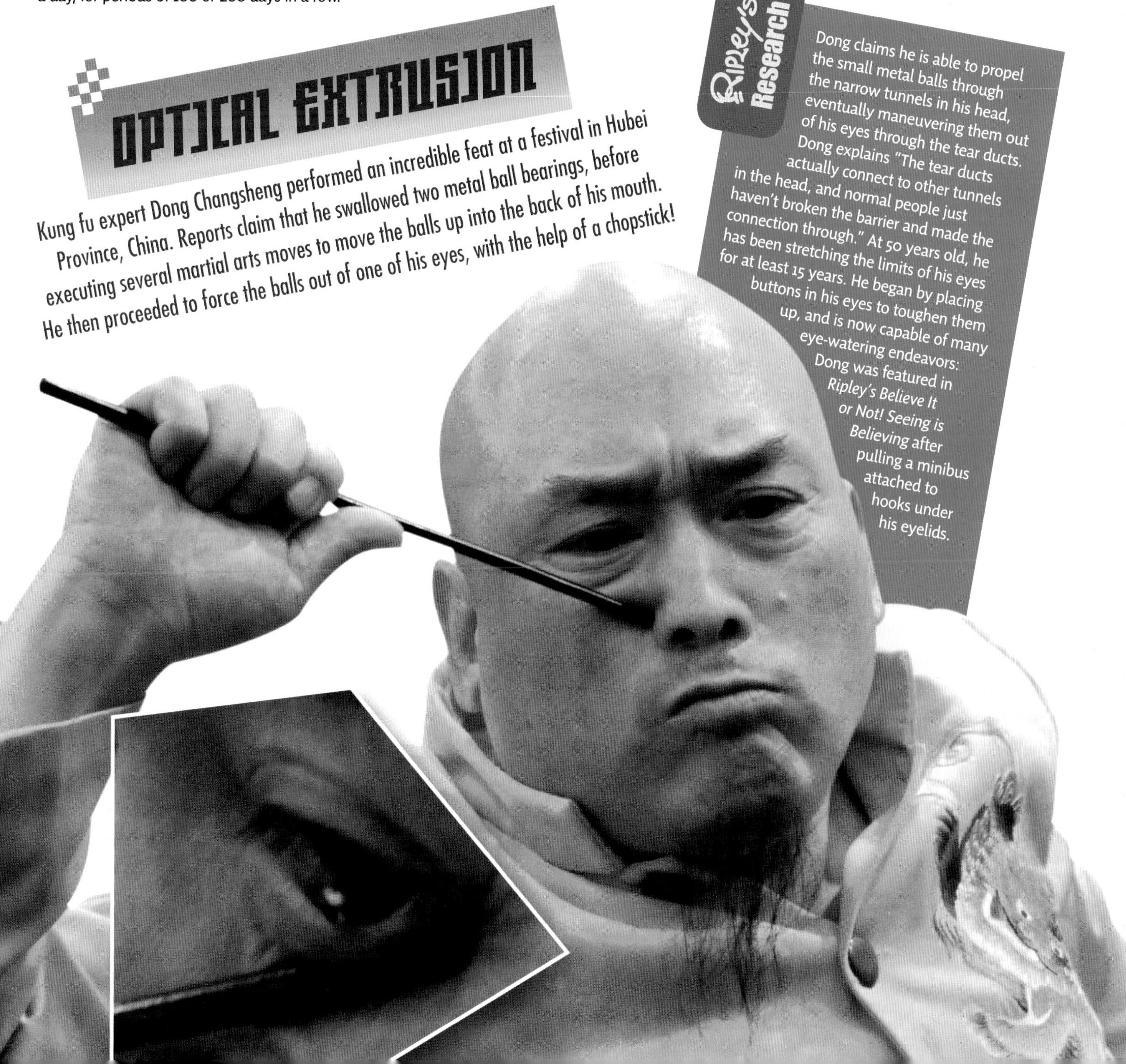

HARD TO SWALLOW

Liang Yuxin from Xia Mei, China, can regurgitate live goldfish, coins and even a 50-in-long (127-cm) chain. He discovered his unusual talent as a boy after accidentally swallowing a ball and finding that he could bring it back up at will.

OLDEST RANGER Betty Reid Soskin is still an active ranger in the U.S. National Park Service—at the age of 90. She works at Rosie the Riveter National Historic Park in Richmond, California, six hours a day, five days a week.

FLAMINGO FAN Sherry Knight of Lecanto, Florida, loves flamingoes so much that years ago she started collecting flamingo-related items—and now has over 619 pieces of flamingo memorabilia.

LOST LEG A year after losing his right leg in a climbing accident, Hungarian climber Zsolt Eross scaled the world's fourth-highest mountain—the 27,940-ft (8,516-m) peak of Lhotse in the Himalayas—wearing his replacement prosthetic leg.

ROUTE 66 Andy McMenemy from Harrogate, England, ran 66 ultramarathons—each 31 mi (50 km) long—on 66 consecutive days in 66 different cities in the U.K.

LOOSE CHANGE Craig Davidson of Phoenix, Arizona, collects loose change he finds as he takes his morning jogs. In 30 years, he has found more than $8,400 in dropped coins.

POLAR FIRST Taking advantage of seasonal melting ice caps in August 2011, a team of six British explorers—Jock Wishart, David Mans, Billy Gammon, Mark Delstanche, Mark Beaumont and Rob Sleep—became the first people to row to the magnetic North Pole. During their 450-mi (720-km), month-long voyage through Arctic waters, they encountered polar bears, collided with icebergs, and Wishart was bitten by a seal.

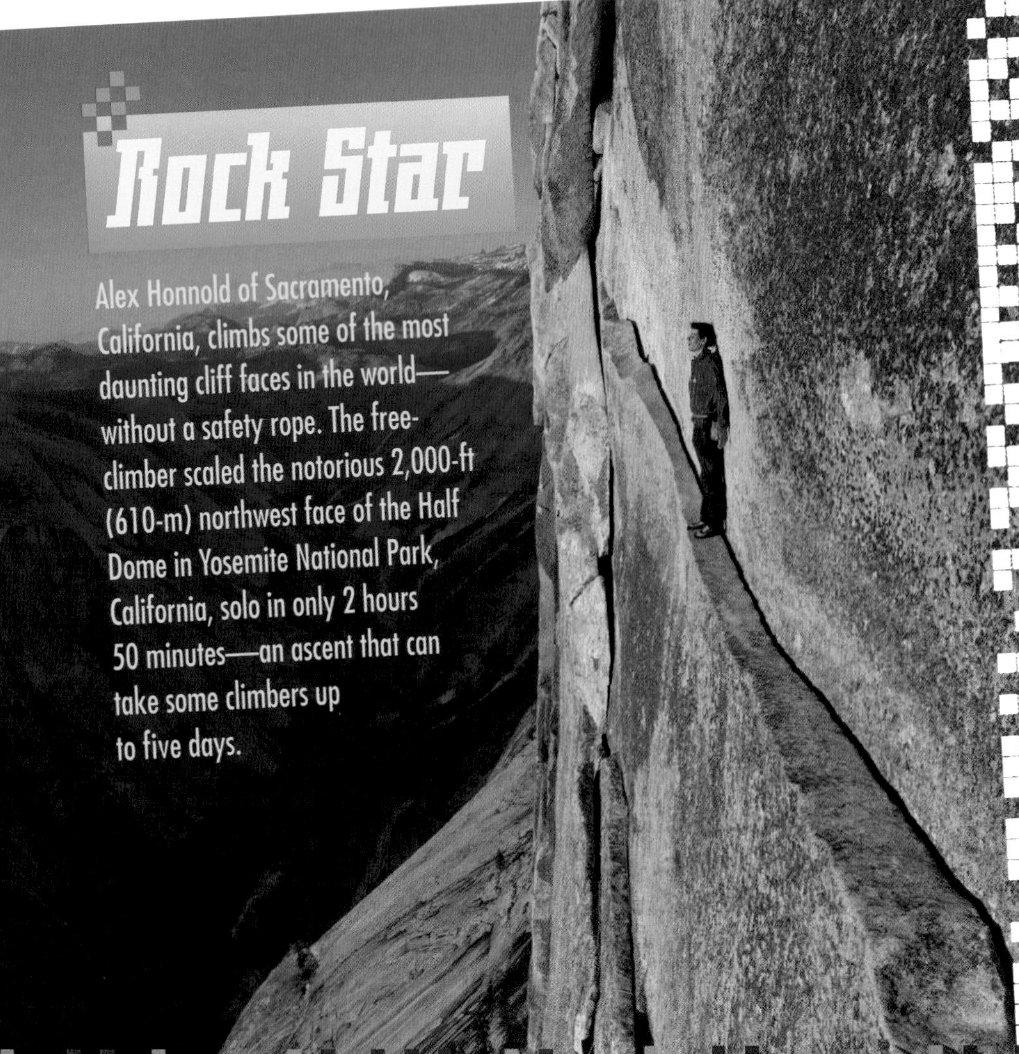

Rock Star

Alex Honnold of Sacramento, California, climbs some of the most daunting cliff faces in the world—without a safety rope. The free-climber scaled the notorious 2,000-ft (610-m) northwest face of the Half Dome in Yosemite National Park, California, solo in only 2 hours 50 minutes—an ascent that can take some climbers up to five days.

GUM COLLECTOR Sarah Maughan of Idaho Falls, Idaho, has collected over 1,400 different packages of gum. She began collecting gum in 1948, beginning with a pack of Popeye bubble gum, and has been adding new types and flavors for more than 60 years.

SCUBA DIVE Diver and scuba instructor Allen Sherrod of Groveland, Florida, spent more than five days 20 ft (6 m) underwater in Lake David to complete the longest ever freshwater dive. He surfaced on September 16, 2011, after 120 hours 14 minutes 32 seconds in the lake, during which time he entertained himself with a waterproof keyboard and monitor that enabled him to watch movies and check Facebook.

EPIC FLIGHT Paraplegic pilot Dave Sykes of Dewsbury, England, flew an ultralight aircraft 13,480 mi (21,700 km) from the U.K. to Sydney, Australia. Sykes, who lost the use of his legs in a motorbike accident in 1993, battled through dust storms, thunder and lightning and baking heat on his three-month solo flight over 20 countries.

MOUNTAIN JUMP In September 2011, stuntman Jeb Corliss of Malibu, California, flew from the 5,000-ft-high (1,524-m) summit of China's Tianmen Mountain wearing a wingsuit—which has extra fabric between the legs and under the arms to help with lift. He glided like a bird down the mountain and across surrounding valleys before landing safely by parachute on a mountain road.

ONE-TRACK MIND A collector of rare vintage toy trains for 50 years, Jerry Greene amassed over 35,000 items, worth a total of more than $50 million. He kept them in the basement of his home in Philadelphia, Pennsylvania. He had about 1,700 locomotives and cars, 700 stations and thousands of accessories. When he decided to sell the collection, it took his family three weeks to unpack just 5,000 of the pieces for display.

LIVING WITH LIONS Ukrainian private zoo owner Alexander Pylyshenko lived for 36 days in a cage with a lioness and her two cubs. He slept on hay on the floor and ate food that was passed through the bars. He installed a toilet and shower inside the cage for personal hygiene, but had to avoid using shampoos and deodorants in case they irritated the lions. An artist by profession, he spent much of his time in the cage painting portraits of roommates.

GOLD COIN Australia's Perth Mint unveiled the world's largest gold coin in 2011, weighing 2,205 lb (1,000 kg) and measuring 31½ in (80 cm) in diameter and more than 4¾ in (12 cm) thick. Made of 99.99 percent pure gold, the supersized coin bears an image of Queen Elizabeth II on one side and a leaping kangaroo on the other, and is worth more than $50 million.

DOUBLE MUSCLE

Strongman pastor Kevin Fast enlisted the help of his 18-year-old son Jacob to pull two fire trucks 100 ft (30 m) down the street in their hometown of Cobourg, Ontario, in June 2011. Combined, the trucks weighed a massive 153,780 lb (69,755 kg). The event was the latest in a long line of strength feats for Kevin. He has also pulled an entire house and a giant CC-177 Globemaster III airplane weighing 208 tons.

EVERY 24 HOURS
Picture Room
Zombie Pranks
TOILET GAMES
EXTREME PLANKING
WACKY WEBSITES
STRANGEST APPS
7 FASCINATING FACEBOOK FACTS
Food Covers
facebook fad
Angry Birds Live
THE STATS

Digital

TWITTER WINNER

Charlie Sheen collected one million Twitter followers in just over a day when he signed up to the site in March 2011, becoming the fastest tweeter to reach seven figures. Sheen gained 60,000 followers before even posting his first tweet; he now has over six million, but that isn't even enough to place him inside the top 20 celebrity tweeters.

VIRTUAL SHOPPING

The world's first virtual retail store has opened in a busy subway station in Seoul, South Korea, where all the goods on display are just pictures. Choosing from over 500 items, ranging from food to electrical goods, smartphone users download an app and make purchases by taking photos of the barcodes. They can order goods on their way into work and have them delivered when they get home.

EVERY 24 HOURS

- **300 BILLION** e-mails are sent
- **22 BILLION** text messages are sent
- **3 BILLION** videos are viewed on YouTube
- **480 MILLION** people log on to Facebook
- **250 MILLION** pictures are uploaded to Facebook
- **250 MILLION** tweets are sent
- **1 MILLION** pictures are uploaded to Flickr
- **58,630** websites are added to the Internet

GPS ERROR

A car transporter became stuck on a mountainside near Greimersburg, Germany, after its GPS had mistakenly directed the driver along a steep forest trail. It took a whole day to recover the truck.

Picture Room

Dutch artist Erik Kessels filled a room with photos after downloading and printing every picture uploaded to the photo-sharing website Flickr in a 24-hour period—that's over one million images.

Zombie Prank

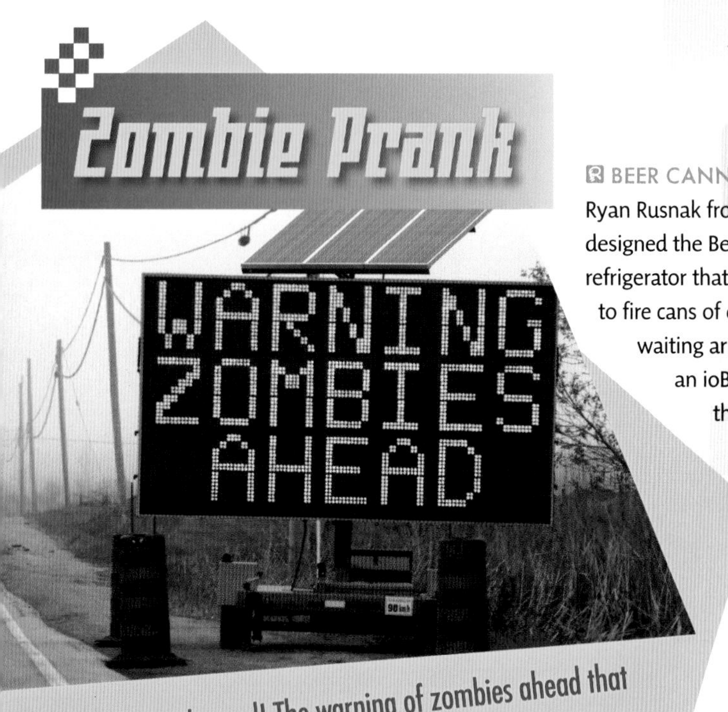

Don't be alarmed! The warning of zombies ahead that greeted drivers in southern Ontario, Canada, in May 2011 was not caused by an invasion of the walking dead but by pranksters hacking into electronic road signs. Similar warnings have appeared on electronic signs in a number of U.S. states, including Illinois where, in 2009, rush-hour motorists near Collinsville were urged to exercise caution because of "DAILY LANE CLOSURES DUE TO ZOMBIES."

PERFECT GAMES Eighty-five-year-old John Bates of Onalaska, Wisconsin, has bowled more than 3,200 perfect games—ones that consist entirely of strikes—in Wii Sports bowling. He plays about 20 games of Wii bowling a day.

PRESIDENTIAL PRANK "Rickrolling" is an Internet phenomenon in which an unsuspecting user who clicks on a link is directed to the video of Rick Astley's 1987 hit "Never Gonna Give You Up." When David Wiggs from Tennessee complained in July 2011 that the White House Twitter feed on U.S. debt was dull, the White House "rickrolled" him by suggesting he click on the link that led to Astley's video.

RINGING CROC A cell phone kept ringing inside the stomach of a crocodile after a woman accidentally dropped it into the enclosure while trying to take a photo. Gena, a 14-year-old croc at the Dnipropetrovsk Oceanarium, Ukraine, refused food and began acting listlessly after swallowing the phone. The woman said she wanted her SIM card back as it contained her contacts.

BEER CANNON Technology consultant Ryan Rusnak from Tyson's Corner, Virginia, has designed the Beer Bot, an iPhone-controlled refrigerator that uses a compressed air cannon to fire cans of cold beer across a room into waiting arms. The fridge is fitted with an ioBridge microcontroller, a device that allows the fridge to link to Ryan's iPhone via the Internet.

ROYAL KISS The royal wedding of Prince William and Kate Middleton on April 29, 2011, in the U.K. had 72 million views on YouTube by people in 188 countries. During the newlyweds' ten-second balcony kiss, the YouTube channel experienced an additional 100,000 requests on top of the already high load—that's an extra 10,000 requests per second.

SCARY NOSE A 2011 YouTube clip of Emerson, a five-and-a-half-month-old baby boy from London, Canada, freaking out at the sound of his mother blowing her nose went viral, racking up over two million views in its first three days online. After just four months, more than 21 million people had watched it.

FACEBOOK FUGITIVE A man wanted in Utica, New York State, used his Facebook page to taunt police, "Catch me if you can, I'm in Brooklyn." NYPD detectives said they tracked Victor Burgos down to a Brooklyn apartment where they found him sitting at his computer with his Facebook page open.

BOUGHT TOWN Maddie and Neal Love bought the entire town of Wauconda, Washington State, on eBay for $360,000. The remote outpost has a gas pump, a restaurant, a small store, a four-bedroom house and its own ZIP code. At its peak in the early 20th century, the former mining town had several hundred residents.

HARDY IMITATION A Canadian Laurel and Hardy fan has been posted on Twitter because of her distinctive name—Laurel-Ann Hardie. A professor at Fanshawe College in London, Ontario, the former Laurel-Ann Hasen realized she would be subjected to attention when she married James Hardie.

SUPER MARIO Born in 1985, the same year that Nintendo introduced the first "Super Mario Bros." game, Mitsugu Kikai from Tokyo, Japan, has since collected more than 5,400 items of Super Mario memorabilia.

TOILET GAMES

Male toilet users in Tokyo, Japan, can play urine-controlled video games. The SEGA game "Toylets" operates via a pressure sensor mounted on the back of the urinal that measures the strength and accuracy of the user's urine jet. A small L.C.D. screen at eye level then allows him to play various games, including using his urine to erase virtual graffiti from a wall, and measuring how much pee has accurately hit the sensor.

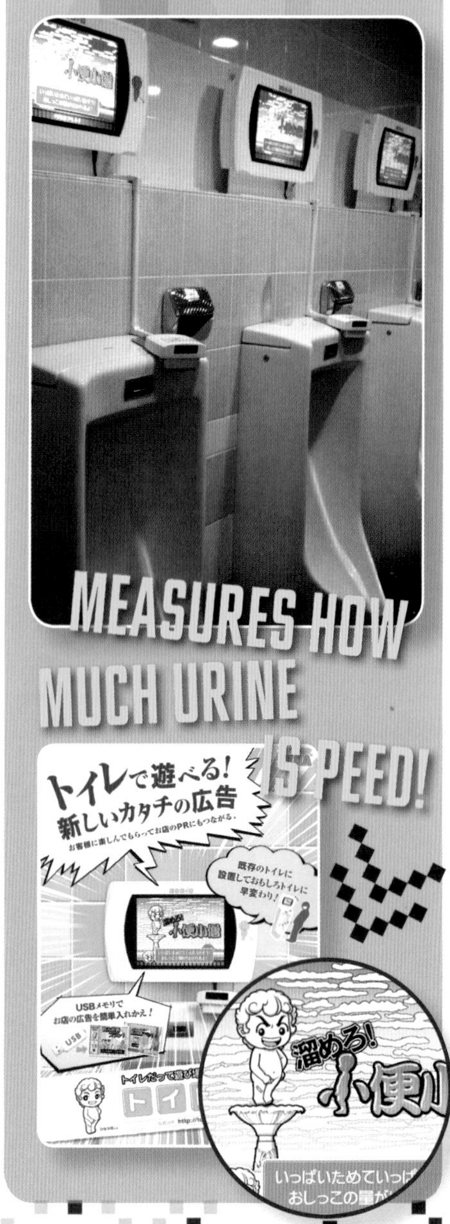

MEASURES HOW MUCH URINE IS PEED!

Claiming to be the inventor of planking, Andy Welch, who now lives in Sussex, England, planks face up as well as face down.

EXTREME PLANKING

Planking is a worldwide craze that has taken off dramatically in recent years due to plankers posting their images on the Internet. The phenomenon involves participants lying face down in unusual locations with their hands touching the sides of the body—mimicking a wooden plank—while someone else takes a picture of the event.

Several people claim to have invented planking, including New Zealander Andy Welch, who says he invented the original craze while on vacation in Croatia in 2006 after he and his girlfriend became bored with striking the usual poses for holiday photos.

Famous plankers include Orlando Magic basketball star Dwight Howard, who planked with 100 fans on a basketball court in Beijing, China, in September 2011 to form the initials "D.H.," and Max Key, son of New Zealand's prime minister John Key, who planked along the back of a sofa with his father standing behind him in May 2011.

Extreme planker Simon Carville from Perth, Australia, once posted a Facebook photo of himself lying naked and rigidly horizontal while being held aloft in the arms of Eliza, a 7.2-ft-high (2.2-m) iconic city statue.

Vincent Migliore demonstrates his planking skills on a tree stump in a city park in Folsom, California, in August 2011.

Reuben Wilson planks on Cairns Esplanade, Queensland, Australia, in May 2011.

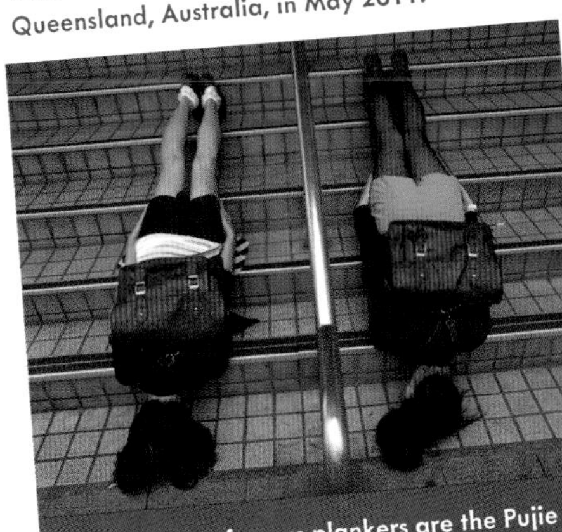

Taiwan's most famous plankers are the Pujie Girls (meaning "Falling on the Street" in Mandarin). They say they wish to use the craze and their associated fame to spread positive social messages.

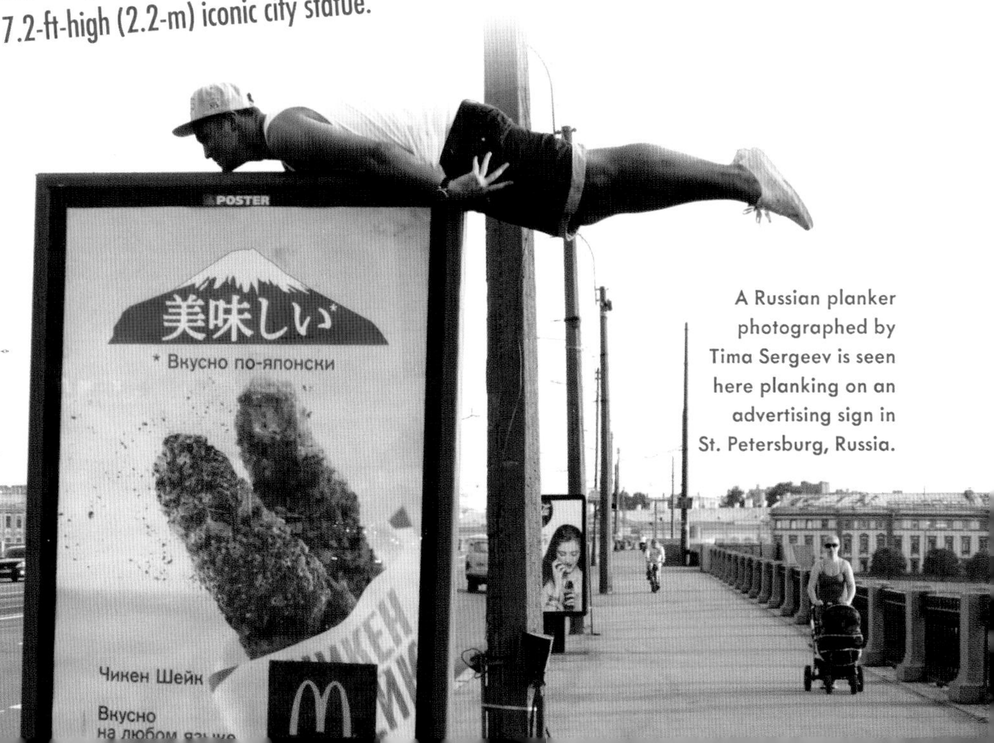

A Russian planker photographed by Tima Sergeev is seen here planking on an advertising sign in St. Petersburg, Russia.

WACKY WEBSITES

Don't like tomatoes? There is a site dedicated to the belief that tomatoes are evil and cannot be trusted.

Loaf of bread cam allows you to watch a loaf of bread slowly going stale.

A toilet paper site enables you to unroll toilet paper for as long as you want without having to wind it up again.

The Iowa State University Entomology Club website offers a selection of tasty insect recipes.

A dancing cows website shows cows doing ballet, disco and other dances.

Like repetition? Try the site that lets you open doors over and over again.

Would your cat look good in a wig? Visit the site catering for all your kitty wig needs.

The University of Virginia has a site that helps you dissect a frog online.

If you like watching paint dry, you might also like the site that enables you to watch paint peel.

Check out the site that helps you to find prison pen pals.

The University of Oklahoma Police Department website has a Citizen's Self-Arrest Form that lets you hand yourself over to the cops.

Does your cat look like Hitler? Check out the site that shows pictures of cats that resemble the Nazi leader.

10 MAJOR TWITTER RUSHES

(number of tweets per second)

August 28, 2011, Beyoncé announces her pregnancy at MTV Video Music Awards 8,868

July 17, 2011, Women's World Cup final (soccer), U.S.A. v. Japan 7,196

July 17, 2011, Copa America (soccer), Paraguay v. Brazil 7,166

January 1, 2011, New Year's Day, Japan 6,939

June 26, 2011, B.E.T. (Black Entertainment Television) Awards 6,436

May 28, 2011, UEFA Champions League final (soccer), Manchester United v. Barcelona 6,303

June 12, 2011, NBA finals, Dallas Mavericks v. Miami Heat 5,531

March 11, 2011, Japanese earthquake 5,530

August 23, 2011, Washington, D.C. earthquake 5,449

GOING, GOING, GONE!

(weird items sold on eBay)

- Ian Usher of Perth, Australia, sold his entire life for **$380,000**. The sale price included his home, his car, his motorcycle, a two-week trial in his job and even his friends.
- Mary Anderson of Indiana put her dead husband's metal walking cane up for sale because his ghost was said to be haunting the house and scaring her grandson. It fetched **$65,000**.
- A ten-year-old half-eaten grilled cheese sandwich bearing a likeness of the Virgin Mary was bought for **$28,000**.
- When Melissa Heuschkel from Connecticut couldn't decide what to name her fourth child, she put the rights up for sale on eBay. Online casino Golden Palace paid **$15,100** to name the baby Golden Palace Benedetto.
- The right to push a button detonating an explosion to demolish a building in Charleston, West Virginia, sold for **$5,207**.
- Justin Timberlake's half-eaten French toast (complete with fork and syrup) sold for **$3,154**.

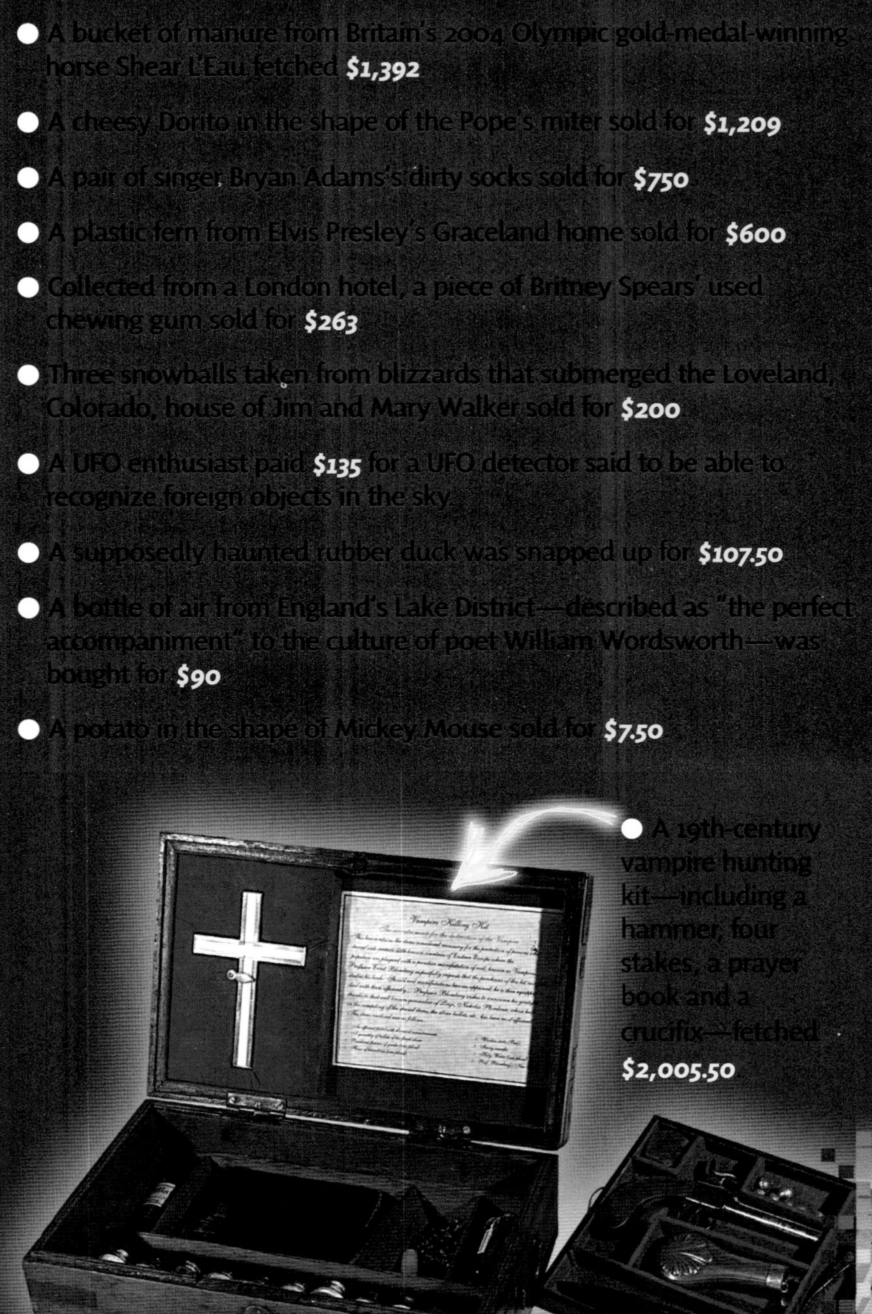

- A bucket of manure from Britain's 2004 Olympic gold-medal-winning horse Shear L'Eau fetched **$1,392**
- A cheesy Dorito in the shape of the Pope's miter sold for **$1,209**
- A pair of singer Bryan Adams's dirty socks sold for **$750**
- A plastic fern from Elvis Presley's Graceland home sold for **$600**
- Collected from a London hotel, a piece of Britney Spears' used chewing gum sold for **$263**
- Three snowballs taken from blizzards that submerged the Loveland, Colorado, house of Jim and Mary Walker sold for **$200**
- A UFO enthusiast paid **$135** for a UFO detector said to be able to recognize foreign objects in the sky
- A supposedly haunted rubber duck was snapped up for **$107.50**
- A bottle of air from England's Lake District—described as "the perfect accompaniment" to the culture of poet William Wordsworth—was bought for **$90**
- A potato in the shape of Mickey Mouse sold for **$7.50**

- A 19th-century vampire hunting kit—including a hammer, four stakes, a prayer book and a crucifix—fetched **$2,005.50**

STRANGEST APPS

- Throw a virtual pie at someone you have a photo of.
- Blow air out of your phone's speaker to snuff out the candles on your birthday cake.
- Convert your phone into a working metal detector.
- Immortalize yourself as a butter sculpture.
- Pop virtual bubble wrap.
- Receive regular messages from an imaginary girlfriend.
- Detect the ripeness of a watermelon.
- Transform your cell phone into a virtual fart machine.
- Play a collection of 16 annoying noises to put your teeth on edge, including a jackhammer, a baby crying and a chainsaw.
- Drink a virtual beer.
- Whistle to call your dog.
- Calculate your time and cause of death on the Death Time Calculator.
- Read about weird genetic diseases.
- Play a trombone.

7 FASCINATING FACEBOOK FACTS

- *Al Pacino's face was on the original Facebook homepage.*
- *One in every 8.3 people on Earth is on Facebook.*
- *Over 60 percent of people use Facebook to find out how ex-partners are doing.*
- *The average user on Facebook has 190 friends.*
- *A Facebook employee hoodie sold for $4,000 on eBay.*
- *There is a medical condition called Facebook Addiction Disorder.*
- *John Watson of New York City was reunited with the long-lost daughter he had been seeking for 20 years after finding her Facebook profile*

Food Covers

A Japanese company has designed a range of iPhone covers that look like food. The plastic cases mimic such dishes as sushi rolls, chocolate desserts, and bacon and eggs.

VIDEO SPOOFS Corey Vidal of Oakville, Canada, makes a living from posting videos on YouTube. He specializes in pop culture spoofs and light-hearted instructional videos, and in just four years his videos have been seen more than 50 million times. "YouTube saved my life," he says.

YOUNG DESIGNER At just 13 years of age, Aaron Bond from Devon, England, has designed and produced an iPhone app video game. Aaron, who set up his own web company when he was only six years old, learned how to write a smartphone game by watching online tutorials. The game, "Spud Run," involves navigating a mutant potato through a maze before it is mashed.

CUTEST DOG After his U.S. owner posted pictures of him on Facebook, Boo, a five-year-old Pomeranian dog, has amassed more than two million "likes," landed a book deal and been named the cutest dog in the world. He acquired the look of a cuddly teddy bear by accident, his natural long hair having become so knotted it had to be shaved off.

AIR PHONE An iPhone app has been designed that blows out air through the phone's speakers. It is powerful enough to extinguish the candles on a birthday cake.

SPEED RECORD On August 22, 2010, Melissa Thompson from Manchester, England, wrote the text message "the razor-toothed piranhas of the genera Serrasalmus and Pygocentrus are the most ferocious freshwater fish in the world. In reality they seldom attack a human" in a record time of 25.94 seconds.

NINTENDO WAS FOUNDED IN 1889—IT STARTED BY MAKING PLAYING CARDS.

SMELLY PHONE The Japanese-produced F-022 cell phone has a detachable fragrance chip that owners can saturate with perfume, which then infuses the entire phone with the chosen scent.

GREAT CATCH A YouTube clip showed a spectator at a 2011 baseball game between the Toronto Blue Jays and the Kansas City Royals catching a foul ball—in his popcorn bucket.

FAST FLIGHT U.S. photographer Nate Bolt posted a video on YouTube showing a flight from San Francisco to Paris, France, in just 124 seconds. Armed with a camera and a time-lapse controller, he took a picture approximately every 20–30 seconds of the 11-hour journey from take-off to landing, a total of 2,459 shots.

EXPERT DANCER On August 29, 2010, nine-year-old Ryota Wada from Herndon, Virginia, became the youngest person to achieve a perfect score on the expert level of the video game "Dance Dance Revolution." He mastered all 223 steps and 16 combinations while dancing to the song "Heavy Eurobeat."

BAD MAPS In November 2010, a Nicaraguan military commander blamed faulty Google maps for an accidental incursion by Nicaraguan soldiers into Costa Rica.

ORIGINAL NAME Lior and Vardit Adler of Hod Hasharon, Israel, named their daughter after a feature on the social networking site Facebook. They called her Like in honour of a button on the site that allows users to express their approval of photographs, links, comments and status updates.

PS2 COLLECTOR A dedicated gamer for more than 19 years, games fanatic "Ahans76" has collected every PlayStation 2 game ever released in North America—a total of over 1,850. He has spent around $60,000 on his collection, but got lucky when, having searched for years for an early, sealed "Moto GP" game, a U.K. user sold it to him for $9 on eBay.

PETS' PAGES One in ten of all U.K. pets have their own Facebook page, Twitter profile or YouTube channel, and more than half of pet owners in the U.K. post about their animals on Internet social networks.

SOCCER TWEETS Japan's penalty shoot-out victory over the U.S.A. in the FIFA Women's World Cup soccer final in Frankfurt, Germany, on July 17, 2011, prompted Twitter users to tweet in overdrive. At their peak, tweeters were sending 7,196 tweets per second.

PLAYING WITH FIRE An enterprising trombone player called Scott, from Jackson, Missouri, has fitted up his trombone with a gas tank so that it also serves as a flamethrower. His YouTube video shows him shooting out 21-ft-long (6.4-m) jets of fire while playing his "Flamebone."

Paul Silviak's head and Robert Mahler's body make up this horsemaning pose with a guillotine, taken by Brent Douglas in Oregon.

Jeffrey Bautista and Paul Riddle from San Jose, California, horsemaning in formalwear.

facebook fad

In the Facebook fad of horsemaning, two people pose for prank pictures to make it look as if one of them has lost their head. The craze for posing for photos as headless horsemen (hence the name) was actually around in the 1920s—long before the advent of the Internet.

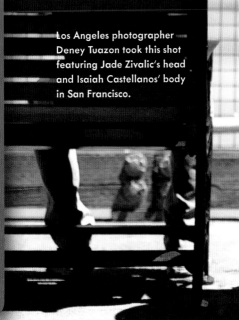

Los Angeles photographer Deney Tuazon took this shot featuring Jade Zivalic's head and Isaiah Castellanos' body in San Francisco.

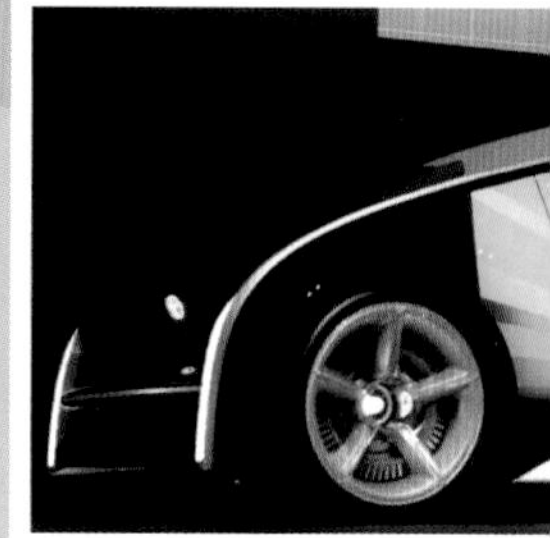

FRISBEE CATCH A video clip of probably the greatest frisbee catch ever notched up 1.5-million hits in just three days on YouTube. Standing on a bridge 50 ft (15 m) above the Swan River in Perth, Western Australia, Brodie Smith hurled the frisbee 500 ft (150 m) out across the water, where Derek Herron leaped 6 ft (1.8 m) from a moving speedboat to make a spectacular one-handed, midair catch.

HOLLYWOOD DEAL Just four days after uploading a short film to YouTube in November 2009, Uruguayan director Fede Alvarez was being courted by every studio in Hollywood—and within a month he had been offered a $30-million contract to make a Hollywood sci-fi movie. His film, *Ataque de Pánico!* (*Panic Attack!*), featured giant robots destroying Uruguay's capital city, Montevideo. Running for less than five minutes, it was made on a budget of just $300. It has had more than 6.8 million views on YouTube.

CELEBRITY CAT The escapades of Maru the cat have been viewed more than 141 million times on YouTube. Described by his Japanese owner as "a little bumbling and a little awkward," Maru has been filmed in more than 200 videos, and has attracted around 190,000 subscribers who have signed up to be notified of his next adventure.

VIRTUAL CITY Kevin Alderman of Tampa, Florida, built a digital simulation of the city of Amsterdam in the online game Second Life and subsequently sold the virtual property on eBay for $50,000.

Angry Birds Live

In 2011, for one day only, Finnish company Rovio—the creators of the mobile app game phenomenon Angry Birds—collaborated with leading telecoms company Deutsche Telekom for a big ad campaign that saw them create a real-life Angry Birds game on a huge scale in Barcelona, Spain. Passersby could play the game as usual on a smartphone, but instead of watching the birds on the screen, an air-cannon propelled giant versions of the Angry Bird characters into a purpose-built fort on the street, and the birds and pigs genuinely exploded.

MAGIC MOTOR

Toyota has created a car that can change its entire appearance at the touch of a button. The body of the hi-tech Fun-Vii is made of touch-screen panels that allow the driver to alter the pattern on display in an instant, like a smartphone. The car even flashes up a greeting message to the driver on the door.

APP TO RESCUE After a Polish trucker was involved in a road crash near Colchester, England, in July 2011, quick-thinking paramedic Nicola Draper downloaded an iPhone app so that she could treat him. When she realized the driver did not speak English, she searched for the online medical Polish translator tool.

JUSTIN'S KLOUT The San Francisco-based social networking index Klout has calculated that Canadian teenage pop star Justin Bieber is more influential online than the Dalai Lama or Barack Obama. Klout adds up tweets, likes, pings, LinkedIn connections, Google mentions, status updates and other social media data to measure a person's importance online.

YELLER PAGES Johnathan "Fatal1ty" Wendel from Independence, Missouri, has won over $500,000 by competing in professional gaming competitions. He set a world record for the game Quake, with a massive 671 kills in 60 minutes.

FAST FINGERS In July 2011, 15-year-old Eduard Saakashvili, son of the President of Georgia, typed the entire English alphabet (A to Z) on an iPad's software keyboard in just 5.26 seconds.

TOTALLY BATTY When a group of students called the "Batman Boilers," from Purdue University, Indiana, posted a YouTube video of themselves hanging upside down by their feet—like bats—from the tops of walls, gates, fences, statues and street signs, it led to a new Internet craze. "Batmanning" was inspired partly by "planking," in which people are photographed face down in unusual places.

THE STATS

- Around one person in 14, globally, has downloaded Angry Birds, equivalent to seven percent of the world's population.
- Worldwide, people spend 300 million minutes every day playing Angry Birds—or 24 years of game play in every hour.
- Angry Birds has had more than 700 million sales (counting downloads as sales), that's more than Call of Duty, Halo, Sonic the Hedgehog, Grand Theft Auto and Mario Kart combined.
- Angry Birds has been the No.1 paid app game in 79 countries.
- In total, at least 400 billion angry birds have been launched at the green pig's castles, and almost 300 billion levels completed.
- Angry Birds cost €100,000 and six months to build. It was the 52nd game developed by Finnish company Rovio.

APPY BIRTHDAY

Mike Cooper from Kent, England, made a spectacular Angry Birds birthday cake for his son Ben when he turned six years old in 2011. Not only was it made from chocolate and sponge, it was a fully functioning Angry Birds game in itself, complete with catapult and sugary birds for catapulting. This swiftly led to a demolition and devouring of the cake, which had taken Mike ten hours to make.

Man Jumps **Speeding Lamborghini**

Videos showing Alassan Issa Gobitaca jumping from a standing start over sports cars traveling at up to 60 mph (97 km/h) have amazed millions of viewers online. To date, Alassan has cleared every speeding car that has driven at him, and the Swedish daredevil has ambitions to leap over even faster cars, perhaps two at once.

MASCOT BRAWL The Duck, mascot of the University of Oregon football team, received a one-game suspension after being involved in a brawl with Shasta the cougar, mascot of the University of Houston. The 20-second YouTube video shows the Duck laying into his opposite number with fists and webbed feet.

VIDEO PROPOSAL Matt Still proposed to his unsuspecting girlfriend Ginny Joiner via the giant screen at a movie theater in Atlanta, Georgia—and the video of his elaborate marriage proposal racked up over 20 million hits on YouTube in its first four months online. Ginny had gone to the theater with her brother expecting to see the action–adventure movie *Fast Five*, when her boyfriend's video suddenly appeared on screen after the trailers had finished. When Matt's mini-movie was over, he appeared for real in the movie theater to place the ring on stunned Ginny's finger.

CHICK RESCUE A visitor to Ireland's Dublin Zoo uploaded a clip to YouTube showing a 210-lb (95-kg) orangutan tenderly rescuing a drowning chick by lifting it from the water using a leaf. Seeing the tiny moorhen chick struggling in the pond of his enclosure, Jorong, a Bornean orangutan, pulled a leaf from a nearby bush and held it out for the bird to cling to. At the second attempt, he managed to save the chick, then placed it down on the grass and stroked its head.

FLATTENED SNOWMAN A bus driver lost his job after his bosses saw a YouTube video of him running over a snowman that had been built in the road at Urbana, Illinois.

DOG BITES SHARK A video clip of a dog biting a shark in the ocean near Broome, Western Australia, has been viewed 4.5 million times on YouTube. Two dogs were swimming in the sea and appeared to be herding several sharks toward shore, when one suddenly ducked under the water and attacked a shark before emerging unscathed.

POPULAR AD As of March 2012, Evian's "Roller-Skating Babies" ad had been watched over 105 million times via video websites, making it the world's most viewed online advertisement.

Break-dancing **Gorilla**

Millions of people have watched this clip of Zola the gorilla dancing at a zoo in Canada. Zola's keepers at the zoo told Ripley's about the video: "Zola, the Calgary Zoo's nine-year-old gorilla is seen here in a shifting area of his enclosure having some playtime in a puddle of water. The keeper was able to capture the action on video and when music was added to the clip, Zola appears to have quite the moves! Western Lowland gorillas are critically endangered and hopefully this bit of video fun can raise awareness of this and of the importance of captive breeding programs. Zola came to the Calgary Zoo three years ago from the Bronx Zoo."

HUMAN CLOUD A video clip of a cloud formation in Canada that appears to show the face of a Roman god notched up over 300,000 hits on YouTube in just four days. The cloud, shaped in a humanlike side profile complete with mouth, nose and eyes, was filmed as a storm gathered over Grand Falls, New Brunswick.

BROOM ROUTINE Beijing road sweeper Zhang Xiufang became a Chinese TV celebrity after performing tai chi in the street using her broom as an exercise prop to keep in shape. A passerby filmed a short video of her routine on his mobile phone and posted it online, where it was such a hit that she was invited to star on a national TV show.

CHEATED DEATH A YouTube clip taken from his helmet camera as he plunged to the ground shows skydiver Michael Holmes somehow surviving a 15,000-ft (4,573-m) fall after both his parachute and reserve chute failed to open on a jump in New Zealand. He escaped with just two broken bones and some bruising.

Jenny the Pug

Jenny the Pug from Portland, Oregon, became a YouTube celebrity after videos of her pushing her puppy stroller around her hometown gained a huge online audience. Probably the most famous pug in the world, Jenny has even made an appearance on *The Tonight Show* with Jay Leno.

David After Dentist

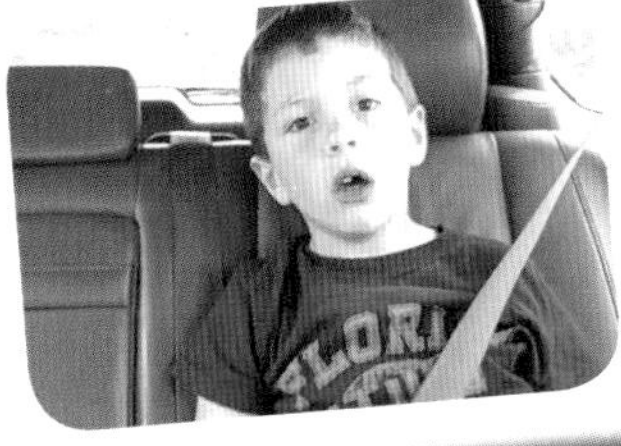

In 2008, David DeVore from Lake Mary, Florida, made a video of his seven-year-old son, David, under the effects of anesthetic after a dental procedure, which had a bizarre effect on his behavior. When David Snr. uploaded the footage to YouTube in January 2009, he was expecting only family and friends to watch it, but the clip has since become a global phenomenon, attracting more than 100 million views, musical remixes and tribute videos. You can even buy T-shirts and stickers printed with David's drowsy "Is This Real Life?" catchphrase. In the picture, top right, David models one of his T-shirts.

LEAPING SHARK An amazing video of a shark jumping over a surfer off New Smyrna Beach, Florida, became an online hit in 2011. Photographer Jacob Langston captured the spinner shark's daring leap while he was filming surfers for the *Orlando Sentinel* newspaper.

HEAD TURNER A YouTube clip shows a Russian waiter named Alexander turning his head and neck 180 degrees to look behind him. It was during gymnastics training that he first realized he had a spinal abnormality, which made his body extremely flexible. He says he has to concentrate energy from his whole body to perform the feat.

Popular

Culture
Inflated Extras

A Cut Above

International pop star Lady Gaga is renowned for outrageous style, designed by her own Haus of Gaga fashion house, but nothing has come close to the genuine meat dress she sported at the 2010 MTV Video Music Awards in Los Angeles. The layered beefsteak number, complete with a meat hat, was designed by Franc Fernandez and Haus of Gaga. The dress was saved from being eaten by the Rock and Roll Hall of Fame in Cleveland, Ohio.

Unbelievable GAGA

In 2010, *Time* magazine compiled a list of the 100 most influential people in the world, based on Twitter and Facebook. Lady Gaga came second, beaten only by President Obama.

By September 2011, Lady Gaga had gathered a remarkable 13.7 million Twitter followers—that's three times the population of Ireland—making her the most popular "tweeter" in the world.

In 2009, Lady Gaga spent over $1,000 on pizza for fans waiting at an autograph signing in Los Angeles.

The 2011 single *Born This Way* achieved one million iTunes downloads in just five days, becoming the fastest ever million-selling song on the iTunes store.

Lady Gaga's YouTube music video *Bad Romance* has been viewed more than 445 million times. That's nearly 1.5 views for every American.

Did you know? Lady Gaga went to high school with Paris Hilton in Manhattan, New York.

The University of South Carolina runs a sociology degree course dedicated to the life and work of Lady Gaga, called "Lady Gaga and the Sociology of the Fame."

SHARK ROCK Matt Waller, a shark tour operator in South Australia's Neptune Bay, has found that great white sharks are attracted by the music of Australian rock band AC/DC. Using underwater speakers attached to diving cages, he pumped rock hits through the ocean, but whereas most had little effect, when the great whites heard AC/DC they quickly swam over and rubbed their jaws against the source of the music.

PSYCHIC POWERS Don Van Vliet, the U.S. rock musician known as Captain Beefheart who died in 2010, could allegedly change TV channels using nothing more than his psychic powers, according to producer Richard Perry. Perry said that Beefheart could do this in unfamiliar environments where he had no opportunity to conceal a remote control beforehand.

DANNY FRASIER, A LEGLESS MAN FROM ALABAMA, PERFORMS AS THE WORLD'S SMALLEST ELVIS.

MONEY TO BURN In 1994, the KLF (a U.K. music duo consisting of Bill Drummond and Jimmy Cauty) burned £1 million in cash of their own money and filmed it as an art project.

TAYLOR MADE All 14 tracks from U.S. singer Taylor Swift's album *Speak Now* charted on the Billboard Top 100. For the week of November 13, 2010, she had no fewer than 11 singles on the Hot 100.

MILKING THE JOKE British comedian Milton Jones performed a stand-up routine to a field of cows on a farm in Hertfordshire, England, to see if they have a sense of humor. His set, called "Pull the Udder One," contained jokes tailored specially for his four-legged audience. Cows are believed to be more productive if they are happy.

UP HOUSE With an asking price of $400,000, U.S. firm Bangerter Homes has built an authentic replica of Carl Fredricksen's flying house from the Disney/Pixar movie *Up* at Herriman, Utah—complete with 1950s' décor.

CHUTE GOWN In 1947, Ruth Hensinger got married in a dress made from the parachute that had saved the life of her husband three years earlier. Major Claude Hensinger was returning from a bombing raid over Yowata, Japan, in August 1944 when his plane caught fire and he had to activate his parachute. Decades after Ruth walked up the aisle at Neffs, Pennsylvania, in her parachute gown, her daughter and her son's bride both wore it at their own weddings.

ROCKY RIDE

Rocky Taylor, the oldest stuntman in Britain, has finally completed the stunt (*left*) that was almost the end of him when he first attempted it in 1985. The 64-year-old leapt from a 40-ft-high (12-m) flaming platform into a vast pile of cardboard boxes at London's Battersea Power Station in August 2011. On set for the 1985 movie *Death Wish 3*, Taylor made the same leap from a burning building, but an explosion sent him crashing into the ground (*above*), inflicting multiple broken bones and burns. The Hollywood veteran made his name in the James Bond movie series and has worked on more than 100 movies, including the Indiana Jones, Pirates of the Caribbean and Harry Potter series.

FIVE DEATHS Hong Kong actor Law Lok Lam died in five different TV soap operas in a 24-hour period in April 2011. One character died in a fight, the second fatally vomited blood, the third succumbed to an illness and although two more died offscreen, their deaths were discussed by other characters.

***FRIENDS* TRIBUTE** A working replica of the *Friends* coffee house, Central Perk, has been created in Beijing, China, because the U.S. TV comedy series is so popular there.

POTTER MAGIC In July 2011, the opening weekend box-office takings of the movie *Harry Potter and the Deathly Hallows: Part 2* were $169 million in the U.S.A. and $307 million internationally, giving it the new opening-weekend record in both categories.

PRECIOUS WORDS The manuscript of an unfinished novel by 19th-century English writer Jane Austen sold for $1.6 million in London in July 2011. Every page of the manuscript—for an 1804 novel entitled *The Watsons*—is littered with crossings out, revisions and additions, and is one of only a handful of Austen's draft works to have survived.

SCENT OF BLOOD

Perhaps inspired by the popular appetite for the *Twilight* vampire movies and the *True Blood* and *Vampire Diaries* TV shows, an Italian company has produced a line of perfume based on the four main blood groups, A, B, AB and O. Although not actually filled with human blood, each fragrance has a hint of the smell of blood. Bottles retail at more than $150.

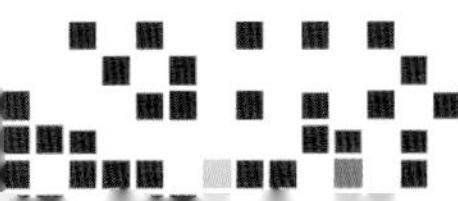

WALL OF SOUND

Joined by his band B-Monster, record-breaking musician John Lee from Vancouver, Canada, showcases his 9-ft-high (2.7-m), 40-ft-long (12-m) wall of speakers, which can channel 2,000 watts of power fed through the world's largest guitar amp. Made up of 168 speakers, it has been dubbed the Wailing Wall of Sound.

CHICKEN COSTUME One of Brad Pitt's first jobs was dressing in a giant chicken costume to lure customers to an El Pollo Loco Mexican fast-food restaurant in California.

CGI PROCESS It took more than 800,000 hours to create the computer-generated images for the 1995 movie *Toy Story*, which worked out at more than a week of computer time for every second on screen.

SOCK IT TO ME! Each year, factories in Datang, China, produce enough socks to give two pairs to every person on Earth.

GUITAR MARATHON On June 17, 2011, Dave Browne from Dublin, Ireland, broke the world record for the longest continuous guitar-playing session after performing a marathon five-day gig lasting 114 hours 20 minutes. He began with Dusty Springfield's "Son of a Preacher Man" and finished 1,372 tracks later with U2's "With or Without You."

TOO LOUD Finding himself surrounded by a pack of four snarling wolves while on his way home from school in Rakkestad, Norway, 13-year-old Walter Acre scared the animals off by playing them a blast of U.S. heavy metal band Megadeth on his mobile phone.

BIG BANJO Richard Ineson of Whitby, England, owns a giant banjo that measures 26½ in (67 cm) across the drum and stands about 5 ft (1.5 m) high. Although the novelty banjo is more than 100 years old, it is still in good working condition.

FLORAL SHOES Florist Nikola Mihajlović of Gornjeg Milanovca, Serbia, provides wedding day shoes for brides that he painstakingly decorates with real flowers. He travels to every wedding with a small battery-powered refrigerator to keep the flowers fresh until the bride is ready to walk down the aisle.

CRUISE CONTROL To film scenes in *Mission: Impossible—Ghost Protocol*, Tom Cruise had to go to the very top of the world's tallest building, the 2,717-ft-high (828-m) Burj Khalifa in Dubai—a journey that required him to take three elevators and then climb more than 443 ft (135 m) of ladders.

HOOF BOOTS

To mark the centenary of England's famous Cheltenham horse racing festival, fashion designers created a pair of ladies' fashion boots and shoes in the style of horses' hooves for a well-known betting company. The footwear was made up of carbon-fiber hooves and some 5,000 individual horsehairs, and was sold for around $2,000.

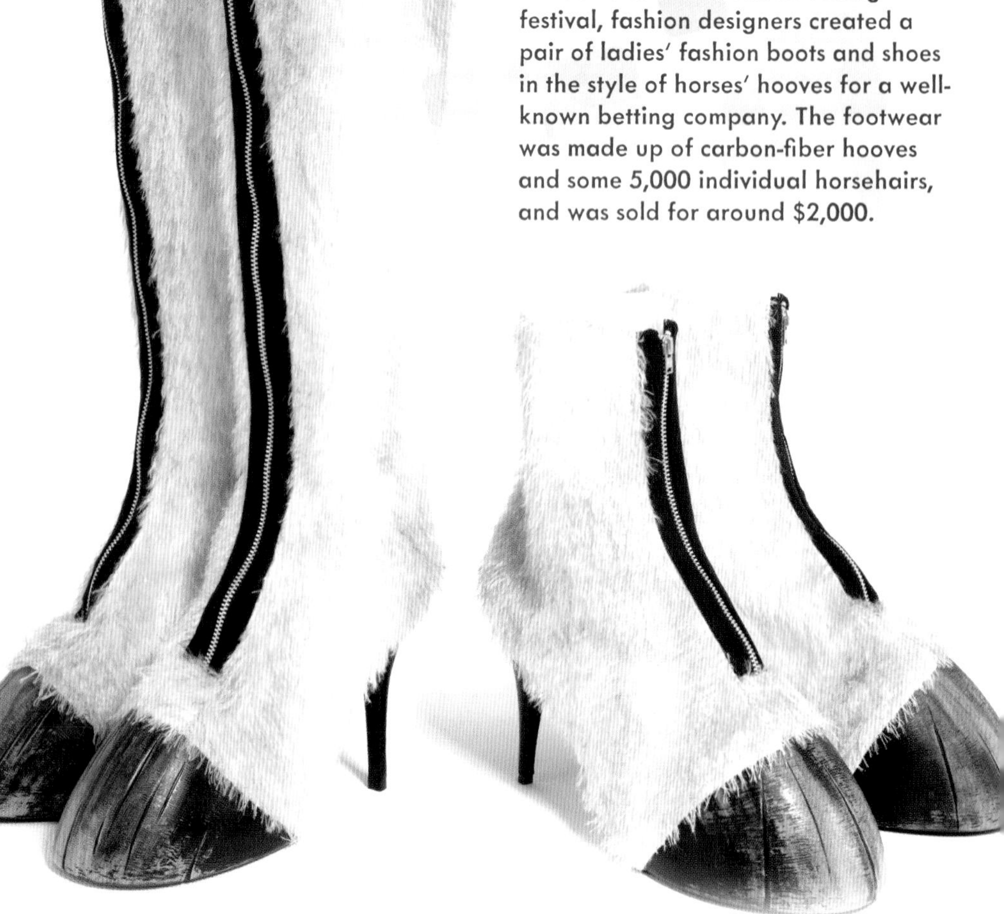

© 2009 Disney/Pixar

Flying House

Inspired by the Disney/Pixar movie *Up*, a house took to the sky near Los Angeles, California, attached to 300 weather balloons, setting a new world record for the largest balloon cluster flight. The 18-ft-high (5.5-m), custom-built, lightweight house was re-created by engineers from *National Geographic* and, with the balloons on top, stood ten stories high. It flew for about an hour, reaching an altitude of 10,000 ft (3,000 m). To lift an average-sized, normal-weight house off the ground would actually require more than 20 million helium balloons.

UP IS THE ONLY BEST PICTURE OSCAR NOMINEE TO HAVE JUST TWO LETTERS IN ITS TITLE.

WAND DAMAGE During the making of the eight Harry Potter movies, actor Daniel Radcliffe (who plays the boy wizard) got through 160 pairs of glasses and wore out nearly 70 wands.

LONG WAIT U.S. actress Romola Remus Dunlap (1900–1987), the first actress to portray *The Wizard of Oz* character Dorothy Gale in film, has only two film credits and they are 77 years apart—1908 and 1985.

SMOKIN' GUITARS Chuck Meyer of New Lenox, Illinois, builds guitars and mandolins from cigar boxes, and spends hours searching flea markets, tobacco shops and eBay for boxes that will give the best sound.

SALSA SENSATION U.K. salsa dancer Sarah Jones won Spain's *You've Got Talent* TV show in 2009—at the age of 75. She won the first prize for an acrobatic routine with her dancing partner Nicko, 40 years her junior.

Bruce Springsteen

WEIRDEST BACKSTAGE RIDERS

Vhen singers and rock bands reach the top :hey demand some strange things backstage, pefore and after performing.

/AN HALEN Van Halen demanded a candy powl of M&M's with the brown sweets picked put and discarded.

AC/DC In 2008, the "Highway To Hell" rockers required the promoter to make sure that three oxygen tanks and three oxygen masks be made available at the U.S. venues they were playing. Additionally, Twinings English Breakfast Tea and a case of bottled beer were two of their ess demanding needs.

THE ROLLING STONES On the Stones' 1997–98 Bridges To Babylon tour rider was a request for a full-sized snooker table (a pool table would not be acceptable) and the necessary accessories, such as cues and chalk. Bizarrely, the band's rider also mentioned that the tour organizers would be providing their own balls.

CHRISTINA AGUILERA A police escort, a large vanity mirror, dressing room plants and flowers, four candles and matches, and the rider staple, honey, are just a few of the demands on Christina Aguilera's four-page tour document from 2000.

BRUCE SPRINGSTEEN Sensibly, "The Boss" likes to have a designated guitar security guard watch over his precious guitar at all times and practical backstage supplies of protein and energy-enhancing products.

50 CENT An all-day supply of peanut-butter-and-jelly sandwiches is what rapper 50 Cent needed to perform to the maximum. Chewing gum and cough drops were also essentials on his 2005 backstage shopping list, together with shrimps on ice.

27 AN UNLUCKY NUMBER FOR ROCK LEGENDS

They didn't all sell their souls to the devil, as legend has it bluesman Robert Johnson did when just 27. So let's just hope it's nothing more than weird coincidence that links all these top music makers who died at that tragically early age. The dearly departed list of seven that died young is...

1911–1938 **Robert Johnson**
died aged 27 years and three months

1942–1969 **Brian Jones**
The Rolling Stones' guitarist, died aged 27 years and four months

1942–1970 **Jimi Hendrix**
died aged 27 years and nine months

1943–1970 **Janis Joplin**
died aged 27 years and eight months

1943–1971 **Jim Morrison**
lead singer with The Doors, died aged 27 years and seven months

1967–1994 **Kurt Cobain**
lead singer with Nirvana, died aged 27 years and one month

1983–2011 **Amy Winehouse**

Winehouse

7 ROCK STARS who caught fire on stage

Michael Jackson—Firework malfunction Jackson was filming a Pepsi commercial in 1984 when a firework display behind him malfunctioned, showering his head with sparks, which set fire to his hair. With audience members wrongly thinking it was all part of the act, Jackson calmly covered his head with his jacket while his brothers rushed to his aid. He suffered second-degree burns and wore a hairpiece when collecting his Grammy awards later that year.

Gene Simmons—Fire-breather The frontman of U.S. band KISS wows the crowds by filling his mouth with kerosene before blowing it out over a flame to create a huge fireball. He has caught fire more than a dozen times doing it, but fortunately one of the crew is always on hand with a wet towel.

James Hetfield—Stepped into shooting flame The frontman of U.S. rock band Metallica was performing before 55,000 fans at Montreal's Olympic Stadium in 1992 when he accidentally stepped into the path of one of the 12-ft-high (3.6-m) special-effects flames that had been rigged to shoot up from the front of the stage. His guitar protected him from the full force of the 3,200°F (1,760°C) blast, but fire still engulfed his left side, searing his hand and arm, burning off his eyebrows and singeing his face and hair. Despite suffering second- and third-degree burns, he was back on stage 17 days later.

MICHAEL JACKSON'S NEVERLAND ZOO

The Santa Barbara County, California, home of Michael Jackson included an amusement park and zoo. Among the menagerie of animals Jacko collected at the 2,600-acre Neverland Valley Ranch where he lived from 1988 to 2005 were:

- One elephant
- One Amazon parrot
- One mouflon
- Two tigers
- Two llamas
- Three apes
- Three crocodilians
- Four giraffes
- 13 flamingos
- Assorted snakes

Travis Barker

TOP 7 TATTOOED ROCK STARS

Pink When the grammy-winning singer's pet bulldog, Elvis, drowned in a swimming pool accident, Pink had a memorial to her pet tattooed on her left arm that read, "A time to weep. A time to mourn. Sleep in peace."

Anthony Kiedis Presumably not a homage to those country-rockers and fellow Californians, the Eagles, an artistic spread eagle adorns the back of the Red Hot Chili Peppers frontman.

Travis Barker A rock star apparently headed toward total tattoo coverage: the former Blink-182 drummer's torso is dominated by a girl and a ghetto blaster, a constant reminder of his passion for break dancing.

Henry Rollins A giant sun topped off with the message "SEARCH & DESTROY" is what the former hard-core Black Flag frontman has chosen to decorate his back.

Eminem The rap legend has a cute portrait of his young daughter Hailie Jade above a Bonnie and Clyde image on his right arm. On his front, a message to his ex-wife reads "ROT IN PIECES."

Tommy Lee The ex-Mötley Crüe drummer removed a 1996 swastika, settling for two roaring lions on a chest topped off with nipple rings.

Billy Joe Armstrong Green Day's lead singer carries tattoos of wife Adrienne and his son's name among almost 20 spread around his body.

Blackie Lawless—Exploding codpiece In the mid-1980s, Blackie Lawless, frontman with U.S. heavy metal band W.A.S.P., decided to wear a codpiece that shot flames into the air. On the first tryout, the codpiece exploded, lifting him nearly 2 ft (60 cm) off the ground and setting his pants on fire.

Arthur Brown—Crown of flames In the 1960s, English rock star Arthur Brown—the "God of Hellfire"—used to appear on stage wearing a burning metal crown. But at a concert in Windsor, England, the methane that fueled the crown spilled over his head and caught fire. Luckily, two members of the audience doused the flames by pouring beer over him.

Bob Bryar—Burning backdrop U.S. rock band My Chemical Romance shot their 2006 video for "Famous Last Words" against a burning backdrop. But it backfired when drummer Bob Bryar sustained burns to the backs of his calves, which required a skin graft.

Tommy Lee—Hanging fire Tommy Lee, drummer with U.S. rock band Mötley Crüe, suffered minor burns to his face and arms in 2005 when a pyrotechnics explosion at a concert in Casper, Wyoming, went wrong. Lee was suspended on a cable 30 ft (9 m) above the stage at the time.

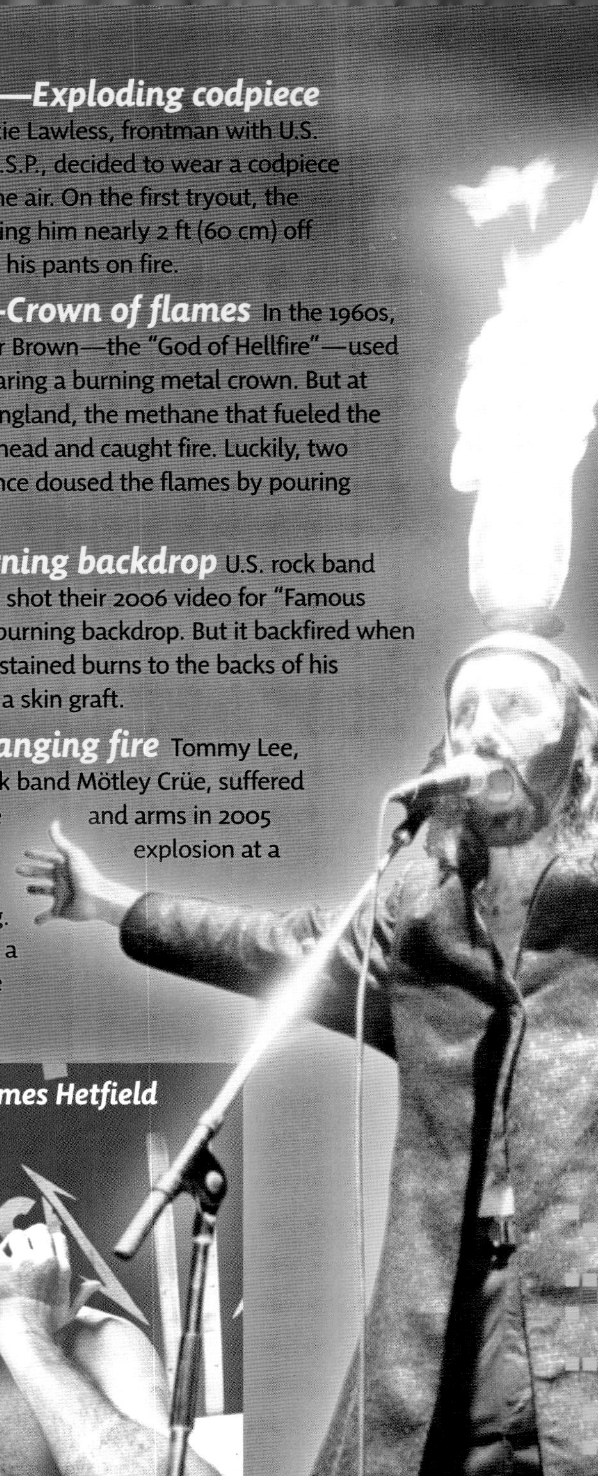

Arthur Brown

James Hetfield

The Blair Witch Project

Rear Window

Guitar Revenge

Japanese artist Yoshihiko Satoh has designed 12-necked guitars that are almost impossible to play. After fretting over his own inability to learn the guitar, he decided to create 72-string monsters that even the most accomplished musician would struggle to play. Each guitar took up to six months to make and some have sold for $90,000.

YOUNG REPORTER As Hurricane Irene battered the U.S. East Coast on August 27, 2011, five-year-old Jane Haubrich from Doylestown, Pennsylvania, became the world's youngest TV reporter by delivering regular weather updates throughout the day via CNN's iReport. Her last report was sent over right before her bedtime.

FAMOUS POSE In 1928, Mexican actor Emilio Fernández was approached by Hollywood art director Cedric Gibbons to pose naked for a full-length sketch. Fernandez agreed reluctantly, but the moment made him immortal as the drawing was used to create the design for the Oscar statuette.

COOL MOVIES A temporary outdoor movie theater in London, England, was built mainly from 150 recycled refrigerators. U.S. design student Lindsey Scannapieco conceived "Films on Fridges," a venue where the screen was surrounded by old fridges, the bar was made of fridge parts, and fridge doors were incorporated into the seating.

PARTY POOPER In their teens, the Followill brothers of U.S. rock band Kings of Leon used to throw parties at their father Ivan's house. When Ivan decided it was time for the party to break up, he would put jalapenos in the microwave, and the fumes burned everyone's eyes so that they quickly left the house.

ORGAN RECITAL Fueled by coffee, vitamins and jellybeans, Jacqueline Sadler of Toronto, Canada, played a church organ continuously for over 40 hours in June 2011.

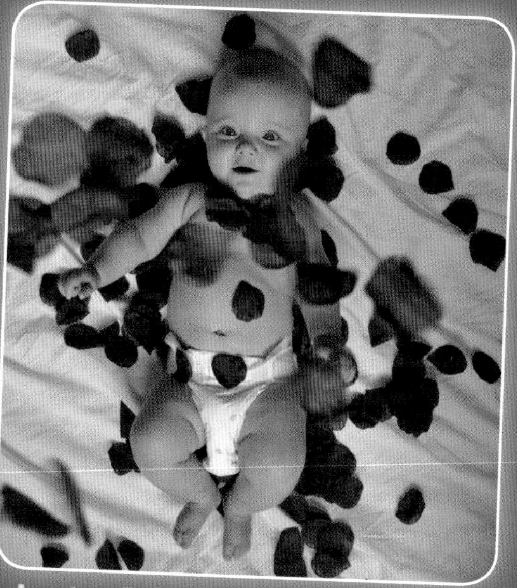

American Beauty

HERE'S LOOKING AT YOU, KID

A six-month-old baby has attracted 50,000 hits a month on his Internet blog by posing with props for pictures that re-create classic movie scenes. With the help of his mother Emily and assorted stuffed toys, Arthur Hammond from Oxford, England, has conjured up iconic images from movies including *Rambo: First Blood*, *American Beauty*, *The Blair Witch Project*, *Jaws*, *Alien* and *The Godfather*.

Rambo: First Blood

DELAYED DOCTORATE Queen guitarist Brian May has a PhD in astrophysics. He completed his thesis on interplanetary dust clouds at Imperial College, London, England, in 2007—36 years after he started, having postponed his doctorate in favor of a career as a rock star.

TWO FUNERALS A month after Michael Jackson died in 2009, a ceremonial funeral was held for him—without the body—in the Ivory Coast village of Krindjabo, where he was crowned a prince of the Agni people while on a visit to the country in 1992.

TOP TOUR U2's 360° Tour (2009–11) grossed $736 million in ticket sales, making it the highest-grossing concert tour of all time. With 120 trucks needed to transport each of the three giant claw sets, the tour cost over $750,000 a day to stage.

VIVID DREAM Released by the Beatles in 1965, Paul McCartney's "Yesterday" has since been covered more than 1,600 times, making it the most recorded song in modern music history. McCartney composed the entire melody in a dream one night and before writing the final lyrics he gave it the working title "Scrambled Eggs."

COMIC COLLECTION Brett Chilman of Henley Brook, Western Australia, has been collecting comic books for more than 30 years and now has more than 68,000. His comics are stored in two houses and are worth an estimated $1.3 million.

GRENADE ATTACK The band La Excelencia was attacked with guns and a grenade—killing two band members—for refusing to play an encore performance after a set in Guadalajara, Mexico, on January 17, 2011.

SUPERMAN'S DOUBLE

Superman fanatic Herbert Chavez, from Calamba City in the Philippines, has undergone more than 13 years of cosmetic surgery to make him look like the comic-book hero. His nose has been reshaped, he has had a chin augmentation to acquire Superman's iconic cleft, silicone injections in his lips to make them fuller, liposuction on his stomach, and thigh implants to make his legs appear more muscular. As he is only 5 ft 6 in (1.67 m) and Superman is 6 ft 2 in (1.88 m), Herbert says: "I wouldn't rule out surgery to make me taller."

Nipple Dress

At the 2011 London Fashion Week, Liverpool designer Rachael Freire unveiled a rose-covered dress made of 3,000 real cow nipples. Created from patches of leather recovered from tanneries, the dress was part of her *Nippleocalypse* collection, which also featured a bra made from layers of protruding nipples.

UNWASHED JEANS Josh Le, a student at the University of Alberta in Edmonton, Canada, wore the same pair of jeans nearly every day for 15 months without washing them. At the end of the experiment, he found that the amount of bacteria on his unwashed jeans was no greater than on a pair that had been worn for only 13 days.

MUSICAL TIE British Conservative Member of Parliament Nadhim Zahawi apologized to fellow members during a debate in the House of Commons after he was interrupted in the middle of a speech by his own musical tie. The red tie emitted a tinny tune that was amplified by a microphone above his head.

RECORD RUN Actor George Lee Andrews played opera house-manager Monsieur André in the same Broadway production of the musical *Phantom of the Opera* for 23 years and a record 9,382 shows. During his run, 12 different actors played the role of the Phantom.

POPPED THE QUESTION For her wedding to Duncan Turner, schoolteacher Rachel Robinson from Lincolnshire, England, wore a dress made from bubble wrap. The dress and train were made out of 13 ft (4 m) of the packing material by pupils and parents from her school. The sheets of bubble wrap were stitched together, attached to an inner lining of cloth, and topped off with white packing foam and candies.

SHORT STORIES A 2005 anthology of fiction called *Meeting Across the River* comprised 20 short stories by different writers based entirely on a song of the same title from the 1975 Bruce Springsteen album *Born To Run*.

CHART GLEE In 2010, the cast of the TV series *Glee* had 80 singles chart on the Billboard Hot 100, the most by any act in a single year in the chart's history.

AUTO ACCIDENT Dutch TV show host Ruben Nicolai was run over while recording a 2011 show designed to find the country's worst driver. The driver was performing a task that involved steering between traffic cones when he lost control and sent the car careering toward a cameraman and Nicolai, who was taken to hospital with a torn lip, shoulder pain and a sore foot.

SHED GIGS Jon Earl has used his garden shed, measuring just 12 x 10 ft (3.6 x 3 m), in Somerset, England, to stage gigs by more than 1,000 musicians from all over the world, including legendary folk-rock band Fairport Convention and a 26-strong gospel choir.

TOTAL FAITH Hollywood executives were apprehensive about casting Leonardo DiCaprio as the Kid in the 1995 movie *The Quick and the Dead*, but co-star Sharon Stone was so confident in his ability she paid his salary out of her own pocket.

INTERVIEW KING From every U.S. president since Gerald Ford to rap star Snoop Dogg, TV host Larry King has interviewed more than 50,000 people in a career spanning over 50 years. That works out at an average of more than three interviews a day.

TV WATCHDOGS Recent research shows that the average dog in the U.K. watches 50 minutes of TV a day, with one in ten watching at least two hours. Labradors are the biggest TV addicts and soaps are dogs' favorite programs.

SQUARE EYES

To mark the 60th anniversary of TV in the Netherlands, six people stayed awake and watched TV nonstop for 87 hours. Fifty-five people started out in the attempt—staged in pods at a studio in Hilversum—but by the fourth evening only six were still glued to their screen.

QUEEN DETHRONED In January 1976, Queen's song "Bohemian Rhapsody," which contains the famous line "mamma mia, mamma mia, mamma mia, let me go," was knocked off the number one spot in the U.K. chart by Abba's "Mamma Mia."

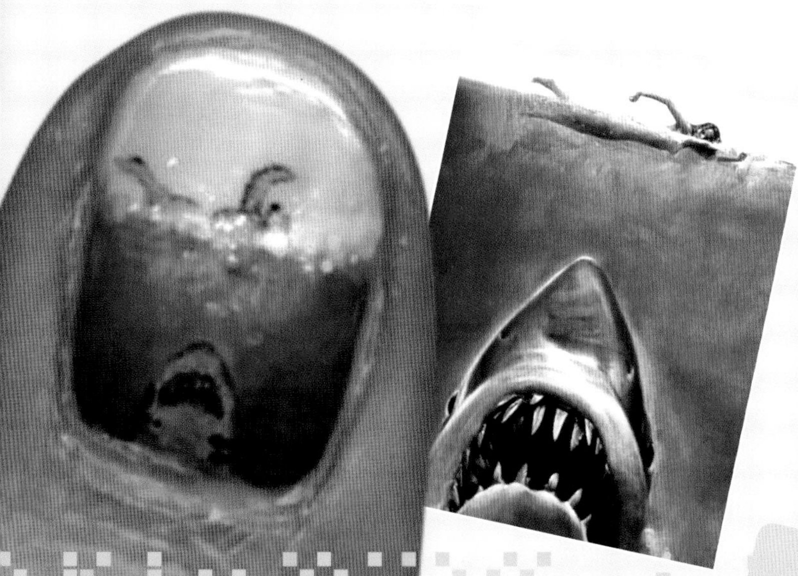

MINIATURE MOVIE SCENES

Spanish artist Maya Pixelskaya has carefully re-created scenes from her favorite movies such as *Jaws*, *Amelie* and *The Wicker Man*—on her fingernails. For each miniature painting, she applies a layer of white nail polish and draws over it with a tiny marker pen to create the basic outline. She then applies up to six layers of nail polish, and because she needs to let each layer dry before proceeding to the next, she has to keep her fingers still for hours on end.

Inflated Extras

Next time you see a big scene in a Hollywood movie, look a little closer at the people in the background, they might not be quite as they appear. You might expect a little computer-generated magic, but perhaps not thousands of individually inflated latex dummies.

The Inflatable Crowd Company, started by Joe Biggins in 2002, provides hordes of rubber dummies to the movie industry, dressed to look like real crowds on screen. Joe's dummies have been fallen soldiers in the Battle of Iwo Jima in World War II (*Flags of Our Fathers*, 2006), victims of a deadly virus outbreak (*Contagion*, 2011), 11,000 fans at a 1930s boxing match (*Cinderella Man*, 2005) and a 7,000-strong horse-racing crowd (*Seabiscuit*, 2003).

Joe was working on the movie *Seabiscuit* when he was asked how to fill the grandstands for the horse-racing scenes in an authentic but economical way. After testing cardboard cutouts, which were the usual method, he realized that the fake figures needed to be portable and three-dimensional. He considered the idea of inflatables, but found that nobody in the industry had done this before so there were none available. He created a prototype torso designed to sit in a stadium and the film's director, Gary Ross, agreed to use 7,000 such inflatables for *Seabiscuit*. Joe started his company after filming had ended.

One year later, there was such demand for the inflatable bodies that Joe and his business partner Richard McIntosh had increased their stock to 30,000 pump-up extras, complete with clothing, masks and wigs.

The first full-bodied inflatables were created for *Flags of Our Fathers* (2006) to act as fallen soldiers at the Battle of Iwo Jima, shot in Iceland. The bodies were modified according to the scene—some were filled with plaster to emulate the reaction of a solid body when it is run over by a tank. Water corpses were also made, weighted to float or sink the way a human body would. In 2006, police were called when a body was found at the bottom of a waterfall in Iceland, rescue teams and a helicopter were deployed, but what they discovered was an escaped member of the Inflatable Crowd Company.

DID YOU SPOT THE THOUSANDS OF DUMMIES USED IN THESE FAMOUS FILMS?

Film	Dummies
CINDERELLA MAN (2005)	11,000
FRIDAY NIGHT LIGHTS (2004)	8,000
WIMBLEDON (2004)	7,000
SEABISCUIT (2003)	7,000
MILLION DOLLAR BABY (2004)	3,000
WE ARE MARSHALL (2006)	2,400
IRON MAN 2 (2010)	2,100
THE FIGHTER (2010)	1,800
THE DAMNED UNITED (2009)	1,800
THE KING'S SPEECH (2010)	1,500
AMERICAN GANGSTER (2007)	1,500
SPIDER-MAN 3 (2007)	1,000
ALVIN AND THE CHIPMUNKS 2 (2009)	550
SALT (2010)	500
CONTAGION (2011)	200
FROST/NIXON (2008)	100

BEHIND THE SCENES

From a distance, the dummies look so genuine when they are fitted with diverse masks and costumes that thousands can be used for one scene, and film producers don't have to hire real-life extras. Each crowd member must be inflated, dressed and placed on their seat, and fitted with individual wigs and masks. At the end of filming they all need to be deflated, packed and shipped to another film or back to storage. Outdoor filming presents the biggest problems. When filming on a beach in Iceland for *Flags of Our Fathers*, the dummies were nearly blown into the sea by strong winds. When the clothed inflatables are soaked from rain, they are twice as heavy. Real-life actors are usually placed in the foreground and randomly throughout the rubber crowd. As the human extras move, they create the illusion of a teeming mass in the background of the scene. The dolls have also been used for commercials, TV shows and music videos.

The Inflatable Crowd Company supplied 200 corpses for a mass grave filmed for *Contagion* (2011).

A boxing scene in *American Gangster* (2007) starring Denzel Washington. If you look closely, the dummies can be seen sitting to the left and right of some of the real-life extras. Fifteen hundred dummies were inflated for the scene.

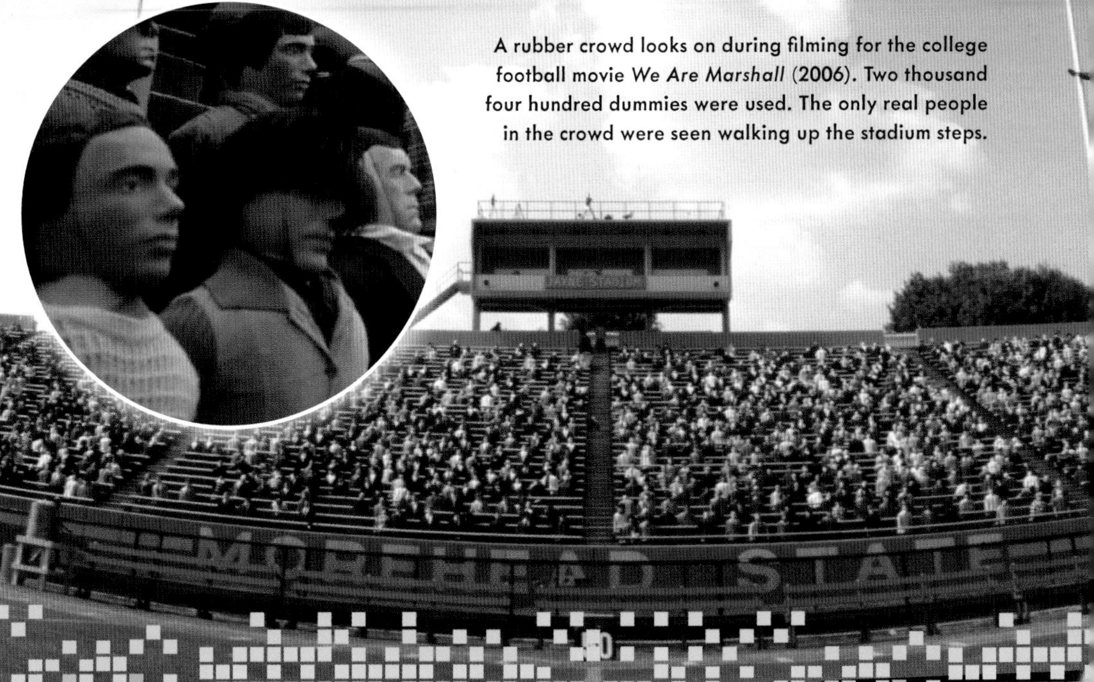

A rubber crowd looks on during filming for the college football movie *We Are Marshall* (2006). Two thousand four hundred dummies were used. The only real people in the crowd were seen walking up the stadium steps.

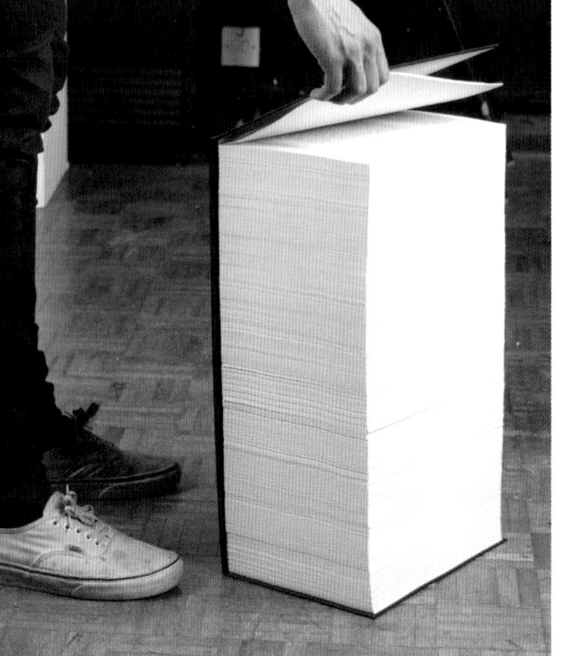

ENCYCLOPEDIA GIGANTICA

Connecticut-based British designer Rob Matthews had a novel idea to highlight how much we rely on cyberspace for information—he published a book made from hundreds of articles from the popular Wikipedia website, and it's 19 in (48 cm) thick. Incredibly, Rob used only 437 articles from the site, just 0.002 percent of the content available. If all the articles on Wikipedia were made into a book, it would be over 225 million pages long, or 13½ mi (21.6 km) thick, and would require a bookshelf the length of Manhattan Island in New York.

NUMBERS BOOK *A Million Random Digits with 100,000 Normal Deviates*, a book containing nothing but a giant list of randomly generated numbers, sold thousands of copies in the 1950s and 1960s.

HUMAN ROBOT Wang Kang, a telecoms worker from Shanghai, China, enjoyed the 2008 movie *Iron Man* so much that he spent nearly three years building his own 110-lb (50-kg) suit of armor and then wore it to the office—to the amazement of his work colleagues. Some froze as he approached them in his robotic suit, and others screamed.

HEALTHY PROFIT Leafing through a pile of old textbooks bought at auction in 2010 for a total of $10, Bill and Cindy Farnsworth of Austin, Texas, found a 25-cent banknote that had been hand-signed in 1843 by the President of the Republic of Texas, Sam Houston. They later sold the note for $63,250.

TIME KEEPER During the making of the 1963 movie *Cleopatra*, Elizabeth Taylor's then husband Eddie Fisher was paid $1,500 a day just to make sure she got to work on time.

MINIATURE MASTERPIECE Collector of miniature books Nikunj Vagadia of Rajkot, India, owns a tiny gold-plated copy of Mahatma Gandhi's autobiography that measures a mere 1.3 x 1.8 in (3.25 x 4.5 cm).

DEAF RAPPER Sean Forbes of Detroit, Michigan, has been deaf since childhood—yet he is a professional musician and rapper who uses sign language for each lyric as he speaks it.

BEST SELLERS With combined sales of more than 450 million copies (and translated into 67 languages), J.K. Rowling's series of Harry Potter books is the fourth best seller of all time, behind only the Bible (3 billion copies), the Quran (1.5 billion) and *Quotations from Chairman Mao* (800 million).

ONE TITLE To boost sales of his 2011 book *Martian Summer: Robot Arms, Cowboy Spacemen, and My 90 Days with the Phoenix Mars Mission*, Brooklyn author Andrew Kessler opened a new bookstore in New York City's West Village and stocked it with 3,000 copies of just one book—his own. The store, Ed's Martian Book, had alien artwork on the walls and was divided into sections including "staff favorite," "self-help" and "best seller," although in each case the recommendation was, of course, the same book.

BOSS TRIBUTE There are more than 60 Bruce Springsteen tribute acts working in the U.S.A. and Europe, including The B Street Band who played at New Jersey governor Chris Christie's inaugural ball after Springsteen himself declined the invitation.

RARE FIND Members of the St. Laurence Church in the village of Hilmarton in Wiltshire, England, found a 400-year-old original copy of the 1611 King James Bible, of which fewer than 200 exist, sitting unnoticed on a church shelf.

CLOWNING AROUND

A bizarre fashion craze swept Mexico in 2011, with young men sporting flamboyant cowboy-style boots with curled toes, some measuring more than 3 ft (1 m) long. The footwear epidemic originated in the town of Matehuala, where a shoemaker was asked by a mysterious customer if he could make him a pair of boots with elongated toes that curved upward. Dancers at local rodeo nightclubs picked up on the impractical fashion accessory and soon the boots had spread to nearby towns and even across the border into the U.S.A. The stretched shoes created such a buzz that people made their own extensions at home, adding flashing lights and glitter.

EUROPE TOUR London, England, music journalist Greg Parmley visited 26 live music festivals across Europe in 30 days. Traveling by motorbike, he journeyed 5,500 mi (8,800 km) through 13 countries and saw over 150 bands playing live.

ENTERPRISING MANUAL In 2010, Haynes, the U.K. publisher best known for its in-depth car manuals, unveiled an unusual addition to its range of workshop titles—a detailed guidebook devoted to the workings of *Star Trek*'s U.S.S. *Enterprise*.

Smurf Alert

For the launch of the 2011 Sony Picture movie *The Smurfs*, the traditional white houses, businesses and even a church in the Spanish village of Júzcar were painted blue, using 1,110 gal (4,200 l) of paint. The locals liked the new color so much they voted to keep it. For the film itself, designers built an exact two-thirds replica of Belvedere Castle in Central Park, New York.

TWIST PARADE During the 2011 Mandan Independence Day Parade in Mandan, North Dakota, 2,158 people lined up on Main Street to dance the Twist.

ELVIS FESTIVAL Over 4,000 Elvis Presley fans flock to the annual Elvis Festival at Collingwood, Ontario, Canada, which ends with over 120 Elvis impersonators competing to become Grand Champion.

ELEPHANT ORCHESTRA Formed by U.S. composer Dave Soldier and conservationist Richard Lair, the Thai Elephant Orchestra has released three CDs of music, which feature elephants playing giant instruments such as xylophones, drums and harmonicas.

ELVIS IMPERSONATOR Simon Goldsmith of Suffolk, England, sang Elvis Presley hits nonstop for more than 35 hours in 2010.

FAMOUS WIGGLE The bottom wiggle that became one of Marilyn Monroe's trademarks was the result of her having weak ankles and bow legs. Once she saw the attention her walk was getting, she emphasized it by sawing a quarter of an inch off the right heel of all of her shoes.

FIRST NOVEL A girl with cerebral palsy who can write only by touching a keyboard with her lips has been offered a contract to have her first novel published. Wang Qianjin, 18, of Zhenjiang, China, is virtually completely paralyzed and has never had a day's schooling in her life—but she taught herself Chinese by watching captioned TV dramas and memorizing the pronunciation and structure of the different characters.

YOUR UPLOADS

www.ripleys.com/submit

Tiffany Tezna, from Virginia, and her best friend sent us these pictures of stylish and vibrant wedding and bridesmaid dresses that they designed and constructed from Marshmallow Peeps candy.

Ripley's ask

Why have you created the story of your persona and background? The idea came about in a strangely organic way. We knew that we wanted to write some songs together, and we already had come up with the band name "Evelyn Evelyn" through wordplay. One idea led to the next, and all of a sudden we'd created an entire world.

Why did you pick the conjoined twins angle? Do you have an interest in old-time circus? Throughout time people have been fascinated by conjoined twins—the idea of having someone so close to you who is a constant confidant and complete companion is both appealing and terrifying to us. As street performers and touring musicians, we have a natural interest in old-time circus, and a lot of our friends are involved in modern circus and new, indie circus. I think the fascination with old-time circus and freak shows is similar. We all, at times, feel like outsiders or freaks.

How does the story relate to your music? Well, all of the music in the Evelyn Evelyn project relates in one way or another to their story. We sat down and figured out the twins' biography and let most of the songs rise up out of the events that happened in their lives. In some cases it worked the other way around, where we had a song idea and we adjusted their story to incorporate it.

Does being conjoined restrict your performance and limit your music? It can be inspiring to have creative limitations, whether those limitations are forced or self-imposed. When performing in costume, it limits us for sure. But that's what is fun about performing these songs. We really have to rethink what we are doing and work together. In a way, it is just like being in a regular band... with the ups and downs and constraints... but different... and weirder. And fun.

EVELYN EVELYN

Dressed identically in connected garments, musical duo Evelyn Evelyn look like conjoined sisters—but in fact they are played by Amanda Palmer and Jason Webley. They even invented a fictional backstory to their characters, claiming that Eva and Lyn Neville were born as conjoined twins on a Kansas farm, sharing between them three legs, two hearts, two arms, three lungs and a single liver.

SWEET MUSIC A Japanese fruit company played Mozart to its ripening bananas for a week in the belief that classical music makes for sweeter fruit.

DOING THE MACARENA A record-breaking total of 2,219 staff and students from schools and colleges in Plymouth, England, simultaneously danced the *Macarena* in July 2011.

LIFE IMITATING ART While filming his role as the Greek god Achilles in the 2004 movie *Troy*, Brad Pitt tore his left Achilles tendon, delaying the movie's final scenes for months.

BACKWARD PIANIST U.S. student Evan Petrone can play music with his back to the piano. He filmed himself sitting down, facing away from the keyboard, before twisting his arms into a seemingly impossible position to play "Clocks" by Coldplay. He suffers from Ehlers-Danlos Syndrome, which gives him unusually loose joints and ligaments. He said he chose "Clocks" because it was simple and repetitive, but it still took him more than five hours to get his brain to adjust to his unusual playing position.

KERMIT COAT For an interview with a German TV station, eccentric U.S. pop singer Lady Gaga wore a coat made from the bodies of *Muppet Show* character Kermit the Frog. The green furry creation by designer Jean-Charles de Castelbajac was draped with dozens of Kermits, and Lady Gaga even wore a Kermit head as a matching hair decoration.

SOLO SESSION Rajesh Burbure, a professional singer from Nagpur, India, sang continuously for 80 hours—that's more than three days—in 2010, during which time he performed nearly 1,000 songs.

BACTERIA FASHION Suzanne Lee from the Central Saint Martins School of Fashion and Textiles in London, England, has designed a range of clothes from bacteria. She has developed a technique for creating a cellulose material from a brew of yeast, bacteria and sweetened green tea, which, when dried, can be shaped into thin shirts and jackets.

HAIR DRESS

Dress designer Thelma Madine and hair stylist Ryan Edwards, both from Liverpool, England, teamed up to create a dress made from 820 ft (250 m) of human hair. It took 300 hours to make, weighs 209 lb (95 kg) and uses hair extensions containing more than 10,000 individual hair wefts. The $75,000 dress also features 1,500 crystals and 12 underskirts.

Dangerous Art
Hair Necklace
Sleepwalkers
Lip Service
Light Paintings

Art

Lip Service

Natalie Irish of Houston, Texas, paints with her lips. Wearing colorful lipstick, she presses her lips against a blank canvas to create amazing portraits of celebrities such as Marilyn Monroe and Jimi Hendrix. She varies the pressure of her kisses to achieve different shades and textures, and applies several layers to achieve darker tones.

1

2

3

4

Ripley's ask

Why did you start to use your lips for art? I love using everyday things in ways that they weren't intended. I learned the thumbprint technique in high school. It was different, and a challenge. I started with lipstick in 2001, and that was so exciting. There was a lot of problem-solving involved.

Are all your lip paintings freehand (free-lip?) or do you use a guide? I sketch an image on paper and then look at that as a reference, but I don't draw on the canvas, only use kisses.

Do you use regular lipstick or special paints? Lipstick. I sometimes use theater makeup as well—it gives me a wider range of colors while retaining the details of the print. I have tried other mediums, but they don't have the same texture as real lipstick.

What problems do you come across in your lip art, compared to more conventional techniques? And what do you like about your unique style? I like that it is such a challenge. My eyes are easily fatigued because of having to try and focus a few inches from my face and then to step back and take in the entire image. Everything is new territory. If I have a problem I must figure it out myself, there are no references.

How long can your portraits take to complete, and do your lips get tired? It varies greatly, on average about two to three weeks. My lips get extremely tired, chapped and swollen. The majority of the Influence video was completed in one sitting for the time-lapse filming. My lips were bleeding by the end of it.

Creature Feature

Andrew Lancaster is an unusually inventive taxidermist from New Zealand. He has turned the traditional skill on its head with his bizarre mutant creations, stitching different dead animals together to make creepy new creatures. Lancaster, an ex-farmer who has been into taxidermy for 14 years, regularly stops his car to pick up roadkill for his projects. Although his pieces might look outrageous, they are made using traditional techniques, taking a few hours to complete before they are dried out over a period of two weeks.

This creature features a possum's body and a doll's head.

ODD SCAN

YOUNG PAINTER At age four, Aelita Andre of Melbourne, Australia, had a solo art exhibition at a gallery in New York City—and her paintings sold for up to $9,000 each. Aelita, who has been painting since she was just 11 months old, specializes in large, colorful, abstract works, which often have children's toys and other small objects stuck to them.

UNDERWEAR EXHIBIT Yi Ci, a student at China's Hubei Institute of Fine Arts, collected several hundred items of underwear to arrange as a piece of art entitled *Privacy* for her graduation exhibition.

BRICK CAR Chinese artist Dai Geng spent over a year making a full-sized model of a BMW car by cementing hundreds of bricks together. Only the windows of the car are not made of brick. The bodywork, tires, steering wheel, exhaust pipe and trimmings are all brick, and he even managed to build brick hinges so that the doors open and close.

FOOD ILLUSTRATOR Graphic designer David Meldrum from Essex, England, kept a record of everything he ate for a year between June 15, 2010, and June 14, 2011, by painting every meal. His illustrations, which were exhibited at a London gallery, revealed that in the course of the 12 months he consumed 1,360 cups of coffee, 305 pints of Peroni beer and 122 Freddo chocolate bars.

LONGEST TRAIN In 2011, after more than 3,500 hours of work, a group of volunteers from Wilmington Railroad Museum, North Carolina, built a model train comprising 31 locomotives and 1,563 freight cars that stretched a record 925 ft (282 m) long, and could move under its own power.

TOOTHPICK LINER Wayne Kusy used a million toothpicks to make a model of the liner *Queen Mary* that was so big it filled his Chicago, Illinois, apartment. The 25-ft-long (7.6-m) model had to be built in six sections so that he could get it out of the building.

MASTER FORGER For decades, experts believed that *The Procuress*, a painting at the Courtauld Institute of Art in London, England, was a prized 17th-century copy of a work by Dutch master Dirck van Baburen. However, in 2011 it emerged that the painting was instead the work of Dutch master forger Han van Meegeren, who died in 1947. Van Meegeren, who specialized in faking great artworks, swindled his buyers out of the equivalent of $100 million in today's money. One forgery fooled the Rijksmuseum in Amsterdam into parting with the equivalent of $18 million, but that painting now languishes in the museum storeroom.

WORLD'S SMALLEST ENGRAVING

In February 2011, after eight months' work, Graham Short of Birmingham, England, completed the world's smallest engraving by human hand. He engraved the motto "Nothing is impossible," measuring just 39/1000 in (0.1 mm), on the edge of a razor blade, the letters being so tiny that they can only be read with the aid of a microscope set at 400-times magnification. He was only able to work at night when there was no vibration from traffic, and did so with his right arm strapped to the arm of his chair to minimize movement. To ensure his body was perfectly still, he used a stethoscope to monitor his heart, and tried to make a stroke of a letter only between heartbeats. Even so, it took him around 150 attempts before he was able to complete the artwork, which later went on sale for £47,500.

ALI TRIBUTE

Californian artist Michael Kalish created a giant tribute to boxer Muhammad Ali out of 1,300 punch bags. Viewed close up, the 26 x 23 x 25 ft (7.9 x 7 x 7.6 m) installation, which was unveiled in Nokia Plaza, Los Angeles, in March 2011, looks like a series of punch bags randomly hung from a metal frame. It's only from a distance that the punch bags morph into a portrait of Ali.

CHANGING COLORS Surendra Kumar Verma and a team of helpers from Kharagpur, India, created a 294-sq-ft (27-sq-m) Rangoli sand artwork, which appears as two entirely different portraits depending on whether green or red light is used to illuminate it.

ART SICKNESS People with Stendhal Syndrome become so overwhelmed in the presence of fine art that they suffer dizziness, fainting and confusion.

CABLE HAT To brighten up the dull gray electrical junction boxes in Leeds, England, local artists gave them a makeover. One box was put behind red velvet curtains that opened to reveal a painting of acrobatic rabbits and hares, while another was covered by a giant wooly hat, hand-knitted from electric cable by Sheffield artist Tony Broomhead.

TRASH HOTEL German artist HA Schult built a temporary hotel in Madrid, Spain, from garbage. The five-bedroom Beach Garbage Hotel opened in January 2011.

SCRAP DINOSAUR Brian Boland of Post Mills, Vermont, built "Vermontasaurus," a 25-ft-tall (7.6-m), 122-ft-long (37.2-m) dinosaur sculpture made from wood. He cut a huge pine tree into four pieces and sank them into the ground as the bases for the feet. He assembled the body from old planks and discarded junk, including the belly of an old guitar and part of a ladder from a child's bunk bed.

NOVELTY TREE The Rocks, a shopping district in Sydney, Australia, erected a Christmas tree made from chairs in 2008, another made from bottles in 2009 and one made of bicycles in 2010.

KNIT WIT

Brooklyn-based, Polish-born artist Olek spends hundreds of hours covering cars and even people in crochet. In 2010, she wrapped Wall Street's famous *Charging Bull* sculpture in crochet. In her most ambitious project yet, she has created an entire crocheted living environment. She covered the floors, walls and all of the furniture in a studio apartment measuring 15 x 14 ft (4.6 x 4.3 m) in bright, acrylic yarn.

TOAST OF HOLLYWOOD Screen legend Marilyn Monroe has been immortalized in Shanghai, China, in the form of a huge toast portrait by New Zealand artist Maurice Bennett, measuring 13 x 12 ft (4 x 3.6 m) and comprising almost 6,000 slices of bread.

BULLET NECKLACE Lovetta Conto, a teenage artist from Liberia, uses disarmed ammunition from her country's 1999–2003 Civil War to make jewelry. Her handcrafted necklaces of spent bullet casings have been worn by the likes of Halle Berry and Angelina Jolie.

LIVING PAINTINGS When Washington, D.C., artist Alexa Meade paints her subjects, she really does paint them. Instead of using a canvas, she paints directly on to the bodies of her models with acrylic paints, making the 3-D subjects appear 2-D. Only the eyes and hair are left untouched. She then photographs the result, which looks uncannily like a conventional painting hanging in a gallery.

SMILEY FACE At Continental Soldier's Park in Mahwah, New Jersey, 2,226 people wearing yellow ponchos gathered to create a huge human-made smiley face.

CART TREES For the 2010 holiday season, Anthony Schmitt of Santa Monica, California, built two giant Christmas-tree statues using 86 shopping carts. The trees, which went on display in his home city and in Emeryville, California, had full-sized carts at the base and smaller ones on the top, all the carts being supported by an internal structure.

FREEHAND CIRCLE Alex Overwijk, a math teacher from Ottawa, Ontario, Canada, can draw a perfect freehand circle about 3 ft (1 m) in diameter in less than a second—and the YouTube clip showing him performing the feat has attracted more than six million hits.

Light Paintings

Scary skeletons with brightly illuminated bones rising menacingly up through the trees make the snow-covered woods of Finland seem really spooky. These light-painting photographs are the work of Helsinki artist Janne Parviainen who creates them by using different light sources during varying exposure times, ranging from a few seconds to several hours. While the camera is exposing, his skeletons and other figures are drawn with LED lights.

Janne's light "mummies" appear in an eerie movie theater—complete with popcorn.

Janne places his skeletons in everyday situations as well as scary ones, as this cool guitarist demonstrates.

MAGGOT ART Rebecca O'Flaherty, an entomologist at the University of California, creates "Maggot Art" from colored trails left by maggots that have been dipped in paint. Using special larval forceps, she dips the squirming maggots in brightly colored, nontoxic, water-based paint, places them on a sheet of paper and watches them crawl.

SOLE SIGNATURE Considered to be one of the greatest artists of all time, Italian Renaissance painter and sculptor Michelangelo (1475–1564) signed only one of his many sculptures during his entire artistic career.

PAINTS WITH TOES Despite being born without hands, Zohreh Etezad Saltaneh of Tehran, Iran, paints so beautifully with her feet that her artworks have been shown in more than 60 exhibitions around the world. Her mother placed a paintbrush between Zohreh's toes when she was young to encourage her painting. She has also learned to weave intricate Persian carpets using her toes.

PICASSO IN WOOL A group of 40 women called The Materialistics, from Tyne and Wear, England, spent months knitting copies of famous works of art. They began by drawing the image of the original artwork on graph paper and then applied a wool finish to pieces such as *The Scream* by Edvard Munch, *Seated Woman in Garden* by Pablo Picasso and *Sunflowers* by Vincent van Gogh.

SQUARE HOLE In June 2011, what appeared to be a giant hole opened up in the middle of the main square in Stockholm, Sweden—but it turned out to be an imaginative work of photographic art. The 3-D optical illusion, measuring 105 x 59 ft (32 x 18 m), was created by Swedish artist Erik Johansson.

GIANT SHOE A giant shoe measuring 18 ft (5.5 m) long was unveiled in Amsterdam, the Netherlands, in November 2010. The shoe was an exact replica of a Converse Chuck Taylor All Star—and was equivalent to a U.S. size 845.

INSTANT CAMERAS Wong Ting Man of Hong Kong, China, owns more than 1,000 instant cameras—including more than 800 Polaroids—at an estimated value of $130,000.

STAR WARS MOSAIC Hungarian artist Zoltán Simon designed a Star Wars mosaic in London, England, in 2011 that covered 1,050 sq ft (97.5 sq m) and was made up of 384,000 LEGO® bricks.

BALLOON SCULPTURE New York artist Larry Moss used balloons to re-create scenes from children's fairy tales, such as *Rapunzel*, *The Frog Prince* and *The Three Little Pigs*. He was even able to build a balloon beanstalk strong enough to support a real child to depict *Jack and the Beanstalk*. He started working with balloons more than 25 years ago, and his previous artworks have included a balloon *Mona Lisa* and four haunted houses, each made from 100,000 balloons.

GIANT COIN Wander Martich of Grand Rapids, Michigan, made a giant replica of a 1-cent coin from 84,000 pennies. Working more than ten hours a day for three months, she glued each penny onto a 10-ft-high (3-m) wooden frame. She used the different natural shades of pennies to create the image and traded in some old coins for shiny new ones from the U.S. Mint to form the highlights. Ripley's saw the coin at an art show and have since acquired it for display in one of its museums.

Bodies appear to lie immobile in the snow with footprints of light walking away into the distance.

FINGER FACE U.S. actress Nikki Reed spent four hours painting the face of her fiancé, former *American Idol* star Paul McDonald, on each of her gold metallic fingernails for the Teen Choice Awards 2011.

CUBIST MOVEMENT Josh Chalom of Toronto, Canada, and a team of eight assistants spent more than 400 hours re-creating Michelangelo's masterpiece *The Hand of God* using 12,090 Rubik's Cubes. The finished work measured 29 x 15 ft (8.8 x 4.6 m) and weighed 2,000 lb (907 kg). The individual cubes, which were bought for $1 each, had to be adjusted by hand so that the colors matched those in the original. *The Hand of God* was the first part of a project to copy the entire ceiling of the Sistine Chapel, in Rome, Italy, using 250,000 Rubik's Cubes. Chalom has also created Rubik's Cube versions of Leonardo da Vinci's famous works *The Last Supper* (which Chalom sold for $50,000) and the *Mona Lisa*.

TOP MARKS Charlie Kratzer used only $10 worth of black permanent markers to create a magnificent mural that covers every square inch of wall space in the basement of his Lexington, Kentucky, home. His cartoon creation features fictional detectives Hercule Poirot and Sherlock Holmes, artists Pablo Picasso and Claude Monet, British Prime Minister Winston Churchill with author and playwright George Bernard Shaw, and TV squirrel Rocky and his moose pal Bullwinkle.

Hand Painted

With their piercing eyes and vivid, colorful markings, Guido Daniele's paintings of animals and birds look incredibly lifelike. Yet they are all painted on human hands. Look closely, and you can see how the different parts of the hand form the animals' features, with the fingers becoming a flamingo's beak, a leopard's head or an elephant's trunk.

The *Handimals* collection—which includes such diverse creatures as a loggerhead turtle, angelfish, leopard, zebra, dolphin, snake and giraffe—started when Guido, from Milan, Italy, was hired by an advertising agency to do a series of body paintings of animals.

Using a human canvas represents a real challenge, and so Guido prefers to use the hands of his son Michael James and daughter Ginevra. He says: "If you're spending hours on end holding someone's hand, I'd rather it be the hand of someone I love. There's nothing worse than working with a nervous, unfamiliar model whose hands are shaking."

Guido says the toughest thing is watching his lovingly created artworks being washed down the drain at the end of the day. "I'm getting used to it," he admits, "and at least I get to start each day with a fresh canvas."

DEATH WATCH BEETLE Artist Mike Libby from Portland, Oregon, customizes real dead insects, spiders and crabs with antique watch parts and electronic components to create intricate sculptures of new hybrid creatures. He was inspired by finding an intact dead beetle, which he thought looked and worked like a small mechanical device. So, he sought out an old wristwatch, and added its screws, springs and gears to the insect's body to create a mechanical beetle sculpture. Each of his pieces takes up to 40 hours to create and can sell for up to $2,000.

SUSHI SOCCER In August 2011, 20 chefs in Bodø, Norway, created a soccer-themed mosaic from 13,000 pieces of sushi over an area of 270 sq ft (25 sq m).

ARTIFICIAL ANIMALS Dutch artist Theo Jansen creates giant artificial animals from plastic pipes and rubber tubes that walk around powered by wind and carry sensors that allow them to change direction. One of his kinetic creatures is so sophisticated that it can anchor itself to the ground if it senses a storm approaching.

ANTLER STATUE Artist Kurt Gordon of Dubois, Wyoming, created a life-size elk statue made entirely of discarded antlers. Gordon, who has been working with antlers for over 35 years, has also sold antler chandeliers to hotels all over the world.

PICASSO'S FIRST WORD WAS "LAPIZ," WHICH IS SPANISH FOR PENCIL.

WORKING MODEL Fernando Benavides from Madrid, Spain, has built a remote-control LEGO™ car that has all-wheel drive, a working seven-speed dual-clutch transmission, a working retractable hardtop, a retractable spoiler and three working differentials. He spent 18 months building the Porsche 911 Cabriolet from 3,500 LEGO pieces.

MARBLE MOSAIC A team of 15 artists from the U.K. and Bahrain spent four months creating a marble mosaic of the Sultan of Oman using 128,274 individual pieces of marble in 90 different natural shades. The mosaic measured 27.2 ft x 17.4 ft (8.3 x 5.3 m) and had to be created using a photograph of the sultan, as he rarely appears in public and did not sit for the artwork in person. His face alone took 40 days to complete, the beard and mustache being made from the sultan's favorite stone, imported all the way from Italy.

LABOR OF LOVE Despite losing the sight in her left eye when she was a child, 69-year-old grandmother Heather Hems, of Hampshire, England, has spent 12 hours a day for more than 17 years creating an embroidery covering 540 sq ft (50 sq m)—the size of 12 table tennis tables. Her creation features important world figures, as well as major global events such as the Moon landing. She has devoted more than 70,000 hours to the tapestry, spending thousands of dollars in materials. The work has also been so physically exhausting that she has had to undergo shoulder surgery.

ON TAPE Ukrainian-born Mark Khaisman from Philadelphia, Pennsylvania, creates amazing artworks—including his favorite movie scenes—from packing tape. By using layers of translucent brown tape on backlit Plexiglas panels, he is able to depict light and shade and even detailed facial features. The darkest sections of his images require up to ten layers of tape, and he uses around three 330-ft (100-m) rolls on each picture.

POST-IT® DRAWINGS Artist John Kenn Mortensen of Copenhagen, Denmark, has drawn over 250 illustrations on humble Post-it Notes. His works, which sell for up to $100 each, often feature spooks and creatures inspired by U.S. horror author Stephen King.

BECOMING VINCENT Artist James Birbeck from Edmonton, Canada, turned himself into a Vincent van Gogh portrait. After friends noted his physical resemblance to the Dutch master, Birbeck bought a jacket like Vincent's and applied paints and makeup to his face to complete the transformation.

FOOT CARVER Pema Tshering of Thimphu, Bhutan, is a professional artist who carves and paints with his feet. He was born with cerebral palsy and congenital deformities in his spinal column, which have rendered both of his arms useless. He also has only limited use of his legs, but carves beautiful wooden dragons, holding the implements between his toes.

Art

Vomit Artist

FEATURED ARTIST: MILLIE BROWN ★ FEATURED ARTIST: MILLIE BROWN

Ripley's ask

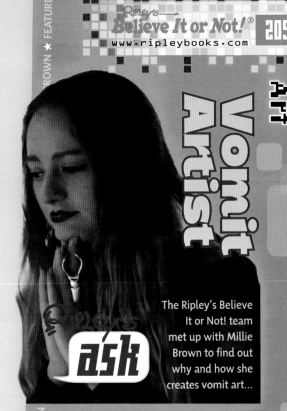

The Ripley's Believe It or Not! team met up with Millie Brown to find out why and how she creates vomit art...

Millie, you create works of art from the unique medium of vomit—how do you do it? *Well, it's a long process that involves drinking dyed soy milk at intervals—one color at a time. I then vomit onto the canvas, pausing between colors so that they retain their true colors and don't mix together.*

How difficult is it to get the paint where you want it to go on the canvas? *I often have a pattern in mind but also let it take its own direction, depending on the mood, you can never fully control it. But that's what I like about the whole process, it makes every piece completely unique.*

Do you need recovery time before you paint again? *I once did a performance where I vomited the whole rainbow, and I don't think I could do that every day. I usually leave a month between performances, so I have enough recovery time.*

Does vomiting as often as you do affect your health at all? *Not really. I am extremely healthy in every other way. I am a vegan and am very into nutrition. My performance clearly isn't very good for me, but I think my overall healthy lifestyle the rest of the time balances it all out.*

You collaborated with Lady Gaga—how did that come about? *Lady Gaga was doing her "Monster Ball Interlude" film with Nick Knight and Ruth Hogben for her Monster Ball Tour when she called me and asked me to vomit on her dress. The video was used as a backdrop throughout the tour. It was amazing to see it projected on huge screens and to hear the crowd's reaction to it.*

Is there a particular statement you are making in your work? *I think it is far more interesting to let people make their own decisions about it. I always find that it means something different to each person.*

Turn the page

Vomit Artist

Millie Brown creates unique works of art by vomiting. Mastering the ability to regurgitate different colors to order, she has established herself as an international "Vomit Artist," and in 2010 even threw up over Lady Gaga's dress for the singer's Monster Ball Tour interlude.

Millie, from London, England, first performed her "vomit art" live at a 2006 art show in Berlin—a daunting feat as she had never made herself sick before and had no idea whether she could.

Vomiting may seem a random exercise, but Millie has got it down to a fine art. First she makes sure that she does not eat for two days before a performance. Then she mixes soy milk with different color food dyes to create the palette she would like for the piece. Next she sits down and slowly drinks the milk before approaching the blank canvas. There, she kneels and begins to make herself sick by sticking her fingers down her throat, and, almost without noise, vomits onto the canvas.

Fountains of colorful vomit fly from her mouth and splash onto the canvas, leaving bits of it dripping from her hands and face. After she has completed the first color, she vomits some more offstage to make sure all of that color is flushed out of her body. Then the process starts over again with color numbers two, three and four.

One of Millie's artworks sold for $2,400, and when she performed exclusively for *Ripley's Believe It or Not!* she stunned the team with her beautiful, yet bizarre, show. Ripley's has since acquired the final piece for display at one of the *Ripley's Believe It or Not!* museums around the world.

Millie uses her fingers to make herself sick and then vomits colored soy milk onto the canvas

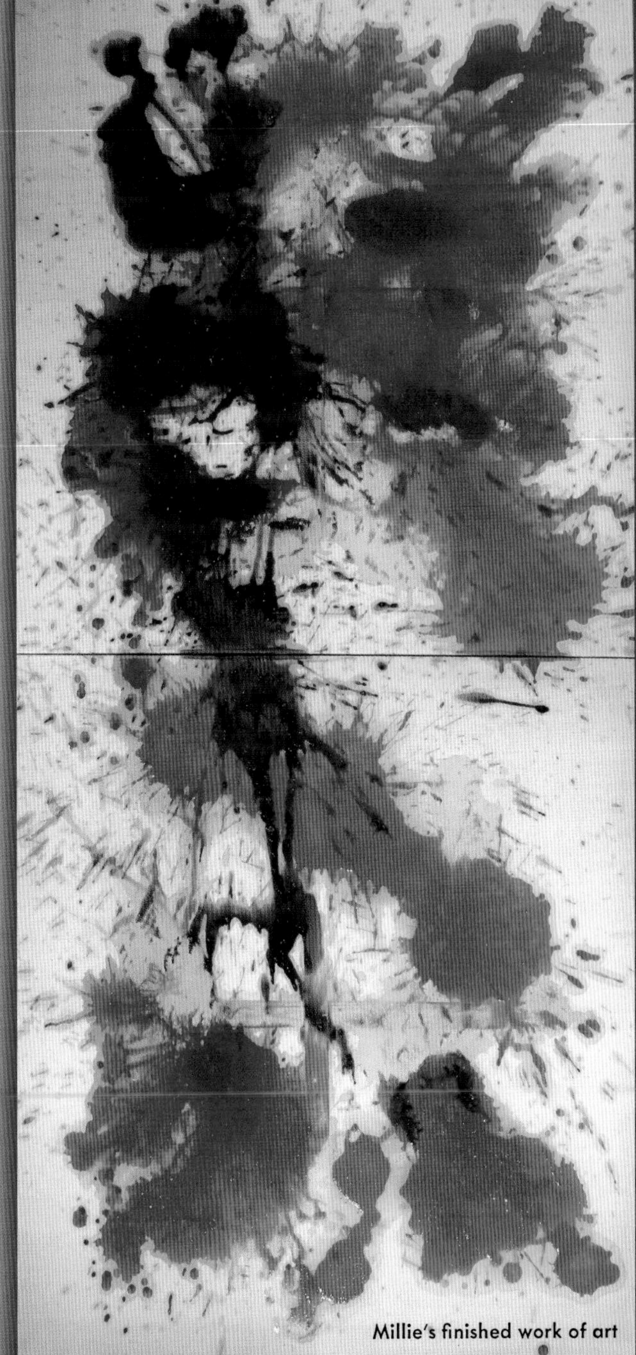

Millie's finished work of art

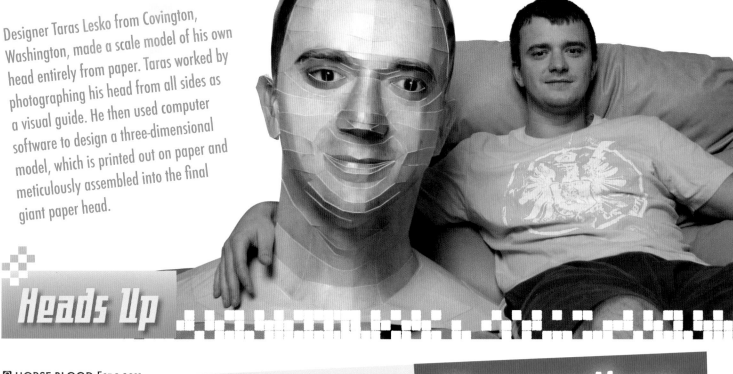

Designer Taras Lesko from Covington, Washington, made a scale model of his own head entirely from paper. Taras worked by photographing his head from all sides as a visual guide. He then used computer software to design a three-dimensional model, which is printed out on paper and meticulously assembled into the final giant paper head.

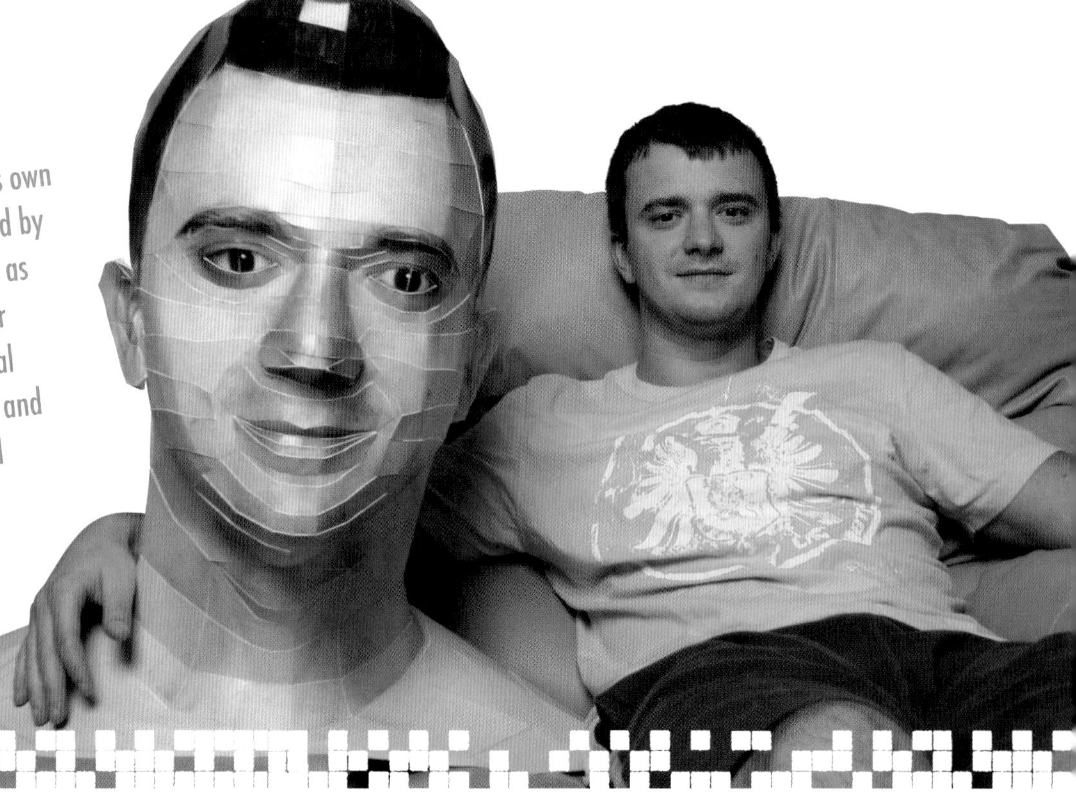

Heads Up

HORSE BLOOD For a 2011 project in Luxembourg exploring trans-species relationships, artist Marion Laval-Jeantet injected herself with horse blood plasma. In the performance piece, titled *May the Horse Live in Me*, she also wore a set of stilts with hooves on the end.

CHOPSTICK TREE To raise awareness of the 100 trees that are felled in China each day to make chopsticks, the China Environmental Protection Foundation assembled 30,000 used chopsticks to create a 16-ft-high (5-m) sculpture of a fallen tree in a Shanghai street.

OCEAN SCULPTURES Artist Andrew Baines stages live "surreal sculptures" in the sea off Australia. In 2011, he persuaded a farmers' group to train a small herd of cows to stand in the ocean for ten minutes so that he could complete his work of art. He had previously posed businessmen reading newspapers in the surf and hired the Adelaide Symphony Orchestra to play tunes in shallow water.

GUN CONVERSION For his work *Palas por Pistolas*, artist Pedro Reyes collected 1,527 guns in the city of Culiacán, Mexico, and transformed them into shovel heads to be used in a tree-planting project.

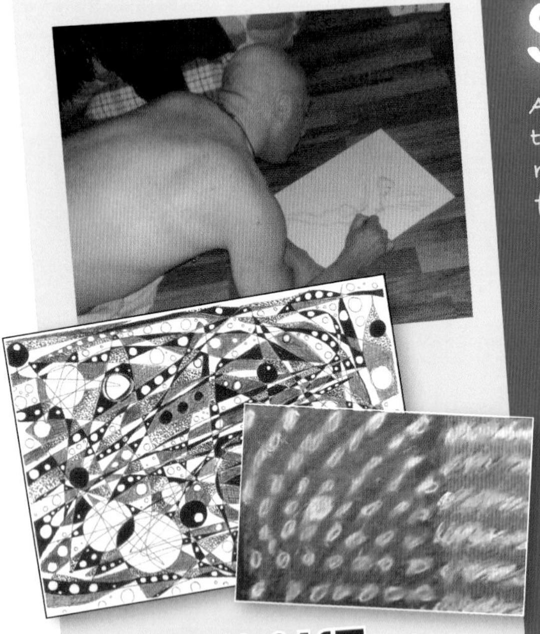

DORMANT TALENT

Lee Hadwin of Henllan, Wales, has created about 200 pictures, including one that sold for over $150,000... in his sleep. While sleepwalking, Lee—dubbed "Kipasso"—draws on walls, tablecloths, furniture and newspapers, but the following morning he has no recollection of what he has done. In fact, when awake he displays no artistic talent whatsoever. Now he prepares for his nocturnal wanderings by leaving sketchbooks and charcoal pencils scattered around the house, particularly under the stairs, his favorite workshop.

Sleepwalkers

A sleepwalking expert at the London Sleep Centre in the U.K. has treated people who have driven cars and ridden horses in their sleep. One patient even tried to fly a helicopter. Here are some other bizarre cases:

- *Crane walking* A teenage sleepwalker was rescued in London, England, after being found asleep on the narrow arm of a crane 130 ft (40 m) above ground. She had climbed the crane and walked along the beam while asleep.
- *Cooking with closed eyes* Robert Wood from Fife, Scotland, is such a good chef he can cook while he's asleep! A sleepwalker for more than 40 years, he heads to the kitchen while asleep and, still sleeping, prepares omelets, stir fries and French fries.
- *Sending e-mails* A 44-year-old woman in the U.S.A. sleepwalked to an adjoining room, turned on the computer, connected to the Internet, logged on and sent three e-mails while asleep. It was only when she received a reply the following day that she realized what she had done.
- *Stepped out of the window* Sleepwalking teenager Rachel Ward stepped out of her bedroom window in West Sussex, England, and plunged 15 ft (4.5 m) to the ground. Although her landing left 6-in (15-cm) divots in the ground, she did not break a single bone.
- *Lawn mowing* U.K. computer engineer Ian Armstrong got out of bed at 2 a.m. and mowed the lawn while naked and fast asleep.

WHALE SONGS Mark Fischer, an expert in marine acoustics from San Francisco, California, captured the sounds of whales and dolphins and transformed their songs into beautifully patterned visual artworks by using a mathematical process known as the wavelet transform.

FILMING EROSION Kane Cunningham bought a clifftop house near Scarborough, England, for a cut-price £3,000 because coastal erosion means that it will soon fall into the sea. He is using it as an art installation, *The Last Post*, rigging rooms with cameras so that he can film its eventual collapse.

ARTWORK CANNED A judge ordered an art storage company from London, England, to pay over £350,000 for accidentally disposing of a sculpture by Indian-born Turner Prize-winning artist Anish Kapoor in a dumpster. The 1984 artwork *Hole and Vessel II* was thrown away during building work in 2004.

HUMAN SPIROGRAPH Illinois-born visual artist Tony Orrico creates huge Spirograph-like artworks using his body as the cog wheel. Holding drawing materials in his hands, he moves his arms in circles while lying straight, bending his knees or standing on his toes to create patterns on a blank canvas. Each artwork can take 12 hours of physical effort.

VALUABLE VASE An 18th-century Chinese vase found by a brother and sister during a clearout of their late parents' modest semidetached house in London, England, fetched over £51.6 million at an auction in 2010. The auctioneers had given the 16-in-high (40-cm) vase a guide price of only £800,000. When the hammer went down after 30 minutes of frantic bidding, the owners had to be led from the auction room in shock.

STAPLE CITY Artist Peter Root from Guernsey, Channel Islands, built a miniature metropolis from 100,000 staples. His 20 x 10 ft (6 x 3 m) city—named Ephemicropolis—comprised dozens of gleaming silver skyscrapers made from staples and took 40 hours to build.

SMALLEST AQUARIUM Russian microminiature artist Anatoly Konenko has devised the world's smallest aquarium—holding just two teaspoons (10 ml) of water. The miniature glass tank measures 1.2 x 0.9 x 0.6 in (3 x 2.4 x 1.4 cm). Even so, it contains miniature plants, stones and several tiny zebrafish, which had to be added with a tiny net. The water was applied with a syringe in order to avoid disturbing the aquarium arrangement.

MAGNETIC STATUE Tim Szeto and Denis Saveliev, the founders of Nanodots—small magnetic toy balls—used over 550,000 gold Nanodots to create a replica of the Golden Globe award that weighed more than 600 lb (272 kg). The statue was created in Canada before being unveiled in Los Angeles, California.

LEGO FROG Dave Kaleta from Chicago, Illinois, made an anatomically accurate model of a dissected frog from LEGO® bricks. The model took him seven hours to build and used over 1,000 pieces.

HARD TO CREDIT

As a protest against what he considers to be the evil of plastic credit cards, Los Angeles-based artist Cain Motter burns and melts old cards down into creative sculptures, which he then sells for up to $1,200 apiece—to pay off his credit-card bill.

Dangerous Art

Some artists go to extreme lengths for their work—don't try this at home!

Blood Painting Australian artist Dr. Rev, whose blood painting was featured in *Ripley's Believe It or Not! Strikingly True*, went a step further in 2011. Rev rigged up a 12-gauge shotgun loaded with lead shot, aimed at his own hand placed on a canvas, and pulled the trigger. The result was a great deal of pain and a seriously extreme artwork—a bloody print of his blasted hand.

Blasted with Flamethrowers The art group Interpretive Arson devised a version of the famous Dance Dance Revolution arcade game in which players are blasted with flamethrowers if they get the dance moves wrong. Dance Dance Immolation performers are protected with fireproof suits but the flames that are hurled at them can reach temperatures of almost 3,600°F (2,000°C).

Cutting Art Performance artist Franko B would cut himself in front of an audience and allow himself to bleed freely, losing as much as a pint of blood during each performance and even blacking out. All in the name of art.

Branded with Hot Iron Chinese artist Yang Zhichao had the I.D. number from his passport branded with a hot iron onto his back in a performance in 2000. He has also enlisted doctors to surgically insert soil into his abdomen, and planted grasses into his own skin (*see page 99*).

FIREWORK ARTIST

Pyro-artist Rosemarie Fiore from the Bronx, New York, creates unique, abstract paintings in her backyard by exploding fireworks onto blank sheets of paper. She makes eye-catching images with colored smoke bombs, firecrackers and lasers, bombing the paper a number of times to create layers. Fiore directs the colorful blasts onto paper with buckets, jars, poles and planks of wood to create a collage effect. The dyes that usually give the aerial explosions their color are then singed across the heavy paper.

Hair Necklace

Artist Kerry Howley from Cambridge, England, makes necklaces from human hair. She spends up to 60 hours creating each necklace, cutting and weaving the strands into abstract shapes. The hair is held in place by tiny specks of glue. Kerry's main source of materials is her mother's Japanese friend, who agreed to have 12 in (30 cm) cut from her waist-length hair.

JUNKYARD GENIUS Retired automobile dismantler Dick Schaefer turns trash into treasure by converting rusty old cars into scary sculptures of monster insects. The yard of his home in Erie, Pennsylvania, houses a giant bee made from a cement truck and a car, as well as a huge spider with the body of a Volkswagen Beetle.

CURTAIN RODS At the Roundhouse venue in London, England, Israeli artist Ron Arad created an installation titled *Curtain Call*—a curtain made of 5,600, 26.5-ft-high (8.1-m) silicon rods. Measuring 59 ft (18 m) in diameter, the curtain formed a 360-degree canvas for screening movies, live performance or audience interaction.

REGAL FIND A couple renovating their home in Somerset, England, uncovered a 6-ft-high (1.8-m), 500-year-old mural of King Henry VIII on one of the walls. Angie and Rhodri Powell had been removing wooden panels from the wall so that they could paint it. The house was once home to Thomas Cranmer, one of Henry's closest advisers.

LIVER OP U.S. actor Larry Hagman—famous for playing ruthless oil tycoon J.R. Ewing in *Dallas*—has an artwork containing a collection of 150 silver staples from his 1995 liver transplant.

MARTIAL ARTS Sixty-year-old Ba Desheng of Kaifeng City, China, uses kung-fu skills to draw giant calligraphy with a 6-ft-6-in-long (2-m) brush that weighs 11 lb (5 kg).

FOIL BALL Dave Mok of Toronto, Canada, created a 20-lb (9-kg) ball made with tinfoil collected from cigarette pack wrappers over a five-year period.

RICE MOUNTAIN On February 23, 2011, a food company from Shizuoka, Japan, made a rice-ball mosaic of Mount Fuji from 22,350 rice balls in five different colors. The mosaic measured 37 ft 5 in x 21 ft 4 in (11.4 x 6.5 m) and later was dismantled to feed rice balls to some 2,000 people.

RAINING HOUSE For a project conceived by Australian artist James Dive, a fully furnished house in Aarhus, Denmark, was destroyed by raining 44 gal (200 l) of water indoors every minute for a month, causing the onset of damp and dry rot.

CD ART

Fascinated by the way light and color reflect off a compact disk, Sean Avery from Ottawa, Canada, makes sculptures of birds and animals—including a rat and a falcon—from old CDs. He cuts up the disks with scissors, arranges the shards according to size and color, and then attaches them to a wire mesh frame using a hot glue gun. Some of his works use 300 disks and take a month to complete.

Cabbage Head
Food
WEIRD CAKES

WORM DELICACY

People in the Philippines eat a saltwater bivalve mollusk that bores into wooden ships, piers and docks. Known as a shipworm, because of its wormlike appearance and taste for wood, it can also be taken with rum as an aphrodisiac—a concoction called tamilok. Filipino Lloyd Lumbania says: "Tamilok is best eaten raw with a dash of lime juice. It tastes like raw oyster, is a bit salty and slimy, and smells like rotten wood."

ACQUIRED TASTES

- **MONKEY BRAINS**
These are eaten, often raw, in some Asian countries.
- **RAW SQUID**
For the Japanese dish of *ika sashimi*, the thinly sliced raw squid is usually so fresh it's still moving when you eat it.
- **STEAMED RATS**
These are on the menu at a wild game restaurant in southern China.
- **TARANTULA SPIDERS**
Deep fried in salt and garlic, these are widely consumed throughout Cambodia.
- **SNAKE WINE**
In Vietnam, you can drink wine with a dead snake still in the bottle.
- **FRIED CATTLE TESTICLES**
In the American Midwest and central Canada, Rocky Mountain Oysters—otherwise known as fried cattle testicles—are consumed.
- **FROG FALLOPIAN TUBES**
Hasma, a popular Chinese dessert, consists of the dried fallopian tubes of frogs.
- **COOKED GOAT BRAINS**
The Mexican dish *cabeza de cabrito* involves eating the cooked brains of a goat directly out of the animal's brain cavities.
- **ASIAN BAT PASTE**
This is prepared by boiling a live bat in milk and then mashing it into a pulp.
- **JELLIED MOOSE NOSE**
In parts of Canada, you can eat jellied moose nose, where the severed nose is boiled into a jelly before being served chilled.

DOG LOVERS In the course of "Hot Dog Season," from Memorial Day to Labor Day, Americans consume an average of 7 billion hot dogs, which works out at 818 hot dogs being eaten every second.

DEVIL'S TOOL In the Middle Ages, the fork was seen as the tool of the Devil. It did not become a popular dining implement until the 17th century, when the French nobility needed something for eating their new

VERY SMELLY FISH Some airlines and Swedish apartment complexes have banned *surströmming*, a delicacy of fermented herring, owing to its intense, rotten odor that makes it one of the world's worst-smelling foods.

LETTUCE LOVER Elsie Campbell of Derby, England, used to eat four whole lettuces a day. She would eat a whole lettuce at work, and then go home and eat more and more, cutting

KEEN GARDENER Thomas Jefferson (1743–1826), the third U.S. president, grew 170 different fruits and 330 types of herbs and vegetables at his Monticello, Virginia, home.

BUTTER SCULPTURES As a tribute to the space shuttle program's 30-year legacy, the 2011 Ohio State Fair displayed butter sculptures of the shuttle and an astronaut, alongside its traditional butter sculptures of a cow and a calf. The exhibit took 475 hours to create and used 1,550 lb (703 kg) of butter —about 6,200 sticks.

TOP POPSICLE The Marquis Los Cabos resort in Baja California Sur, Mexico, has launched a popsicle selling for $1,000. Although served on an ordinary plastic stick the popsicle is made from premium tequila, which sells for $1,500 a bottle, and also

Cabbage Head

Russian artist Dimitri Tsykalov uses an axe, a saw and an electric drill to carve scary human skulls out of fresh fruit and vegetables, including melons, apples and cabbages. With surgical precision, he then uses a scalpel, pincers and cotton-wool pads to add authentic detail. Finally, he waits for his sculptures to rot before photographing them. "The flies let me know when it's time to take a picture," he says.

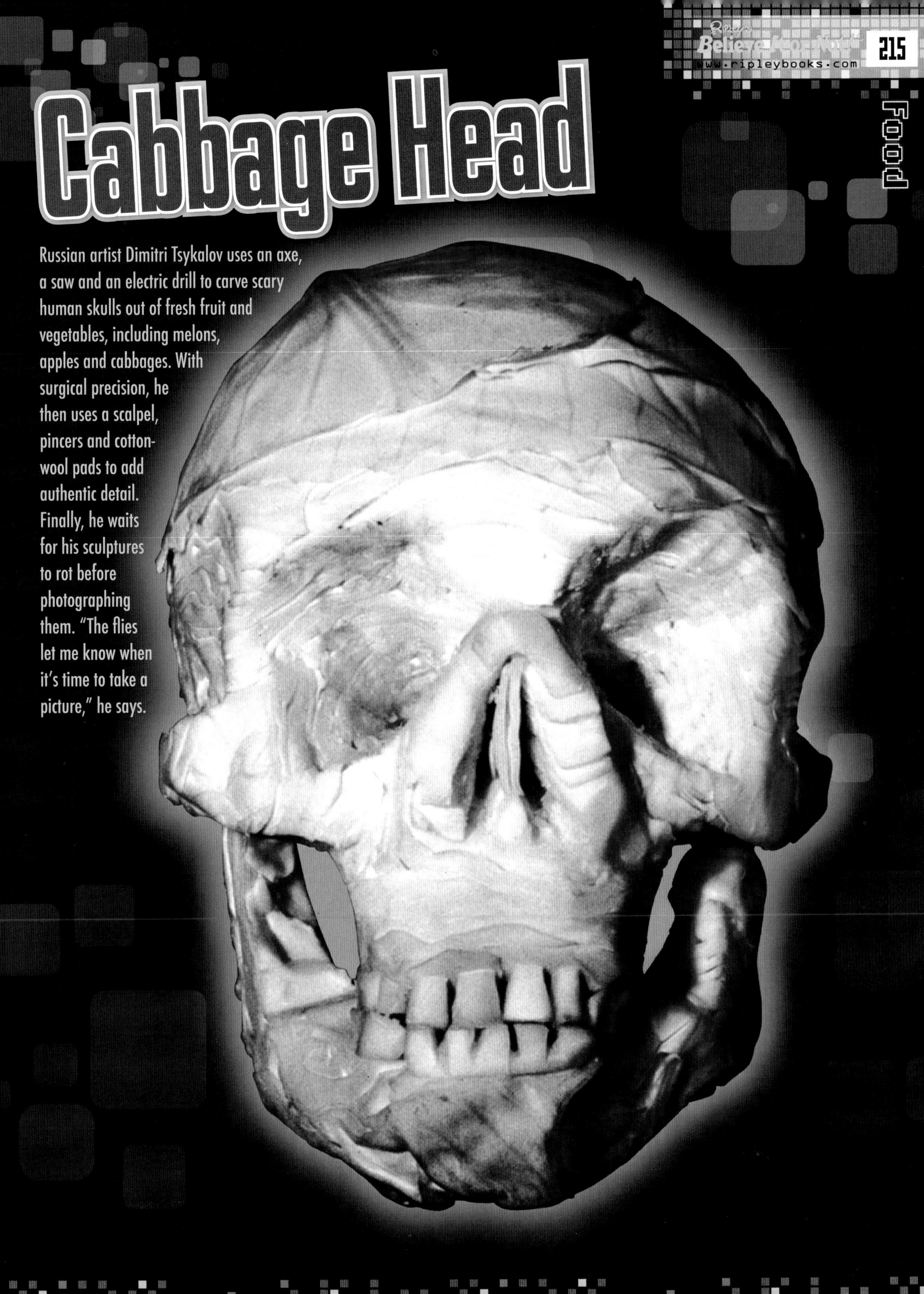

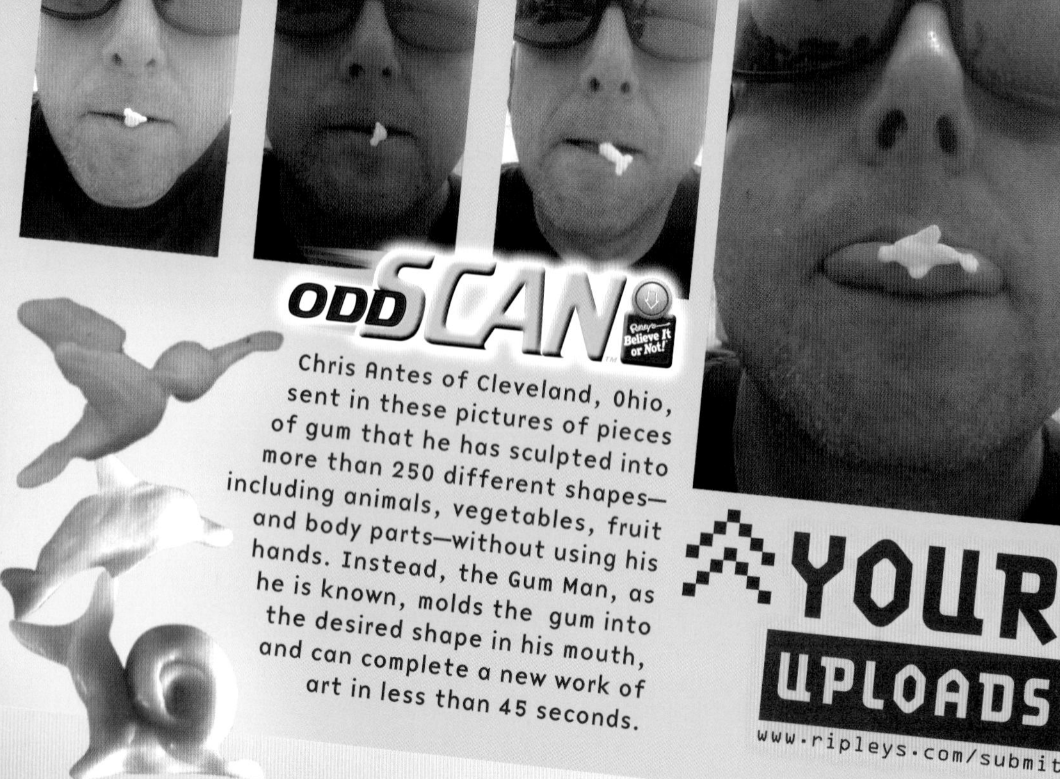

Chris Antes of Cleveland, Ohio, sent in these pictures of pieces of gum that he has sculpted into more than 250 different shapes—including animals, vegetables, fruit and body parts—without using his hands. Instead, the Gum Man, as he is known, molds the gum into the desired shape in his mouth, and can complete a new work of art in less than 45 seconds.

SHELL SHOCK Charlotte Matthews of Rochdale, England, cracked open 29 double-yolked eggs in a row from one carton. Only the 30th and final egg in the box had a single yolk. The odds of cracking open just one double-yolked egg are one in a thousand.

SOUR TASTE Liu Yuejin of Zhenjiang, China, drank three bottles of vinegar in 28 seconds as part of a competition to promote the health benefits of drinking vinegar. After undergoing medical examinations to check they did not suffer from high blood pressure, heart disease or mental illness, contestants had to drink three 12½-fl-oz (375-ml) bottles of local vinegar, one after the other.

POTATO DIET Chris Voigt, head of the Washington State Potato Commission, ate nothing but potatoes for 60 days in 2010 to prove the nutritional value of the starchy vegetable. He lost 21 lb (9.5 kg) on his potato diet, during the course of which he ate around 1,200 potatoes in various guises—baked, boiled, fried, mashed and shredded.

FAST PIZZA Takeout pizza shop owner Alberto Valotta from Hemel Hempstead, England, hired a $225,000 Lamborghini with a top speed of 200 mph (320 km/h) to launch a really fast food service to customers.

KING KEBAB Leon Ekery of El Paso, Texas, prepared a lamb kebab that was 28 ft 7 in (8.7 m) long. He used a 31-ft-long (9.4-m), one-piece stainless-steel skewer, a 30-ft (9.1-m) grill and more than 40 lb (18 kg) of lamb.

COOKING MARATHON In a world-record-breaking cooking marathon, Chef Benno Stewart cooked some 50 dishes—including stews, casseroles, lamb shanks and a pig on a spit—for 31 hours 31 minutes 55 seconds at the Bowen Show in Queensland, Australia, in June 2011.

VINTAGE WINE A 200-year-old bottle of Château d'Yquem white wine was sold to French private collector Christian Vanneque for over $115,000—the most ever paid for a bottle of white wine. Most white wines do not age well, expiring in the bottle after just a few years, but the 1811 Château d'Yquem is an exception because it is sweet. The buyer plans to drink his expensive purchase in 2017 to celebrate his 50 years as a wine expert.

ROCK PIZZAS

Using colorful toppings and herbs, popular U.K. pizza chain PizzaExpress created a slice of rock history by making pizzas replicating the covers of famous albums—including Jimi Hendrix's *Kiss The Sky*, Madonna's *True Blue*, Rihanna's *Loud* and Bob Marley's *Legend*.

Urine Eggs

In Dongyang County, China, buckets of boys' urine are collected from local schools—for use in a culinary dish! Cooking eggs in urine to make Tong Zi Dan (small boy eggs) is believed to ward off ailments and promote energy. The eggs are soaked in boiled urine for an entire day before they are ready to eat, and remain popular with locals, despite advice from doctors in the area who say that Tong Zi Dan is potentially toxic.

SNAKE BLOOD After falling down a 79-ft-deep (24-m) pit in Changshan County, China, while hunting snakes, Yi Guofang survived for two days by killing one of the snakes he had captured, drinking its blood and eating the flesh raw.

UNUSUAL DRINK A $250-million water-recycling device aboard the International Space Station enables astronauts to drink their own urine.

LARGE FRIES Five staff from the Fish and Chip Shop at the Adventure Island fun park in Southend, England, cooked up the world's biggest portion of fries in June 2011, weighing in at 988 lb (448 kg). It took about four hours to peel, cut and fry the potatoes, which were then served in a box measuring 54 x 46 x 30 in (137 x 116 x 75 cm).

PIZZA PASSION There are more than 61,000 pizzerias in the U.S.A. and Americans consume about 100 acres (40 ha) of pizza every day, or 350 slices per second.

EVERYTHING MUST GO Yukako Ichikawa, a chef in Sydney, Australia, gives a 30-percent discount to all customers at her restaurant who eat everything on their plate—excluding only lemon slices, ginger and wasabi.

EDIBLE TABLE Using 14 propane grills and 110 tables, volunteers at Crazy Otto's Empire Diner in Herkimer, New York State, cooked a 2,128-sq-ft (197-sq-m) omelet from 41,040 eggs. Using green food coloring, they turned it into an edible pool table with beach-ball billiards and broomstick cues.

EXPLODING MELONS Thousands of watermelons exploded in China's Jiangsu Province in the spring of 2011 after farmers sprayed their crops too freely with chemicals designed to make the melons grow faster.

COSTLY SMASH A forklift accident smashed hundreds of bottles of Australian wine worth a total of $1 million. All but one of the 462 cases of Mollydooker Wines' Velvet Glove Shiraz bound for the U.S.A. was destroyed. Each bottle sells for around $200.

HOT DOG BET Jim Harrison, a 22-year-old student at McMaster University, Hamilton, Canada, won a $1,500 bet by eating 450 hot dogs in a month—an average of 15 a day.

PIZZA PICKUP David Schuler of Jackson, Mississippi, makes a round trip of more than 2,800 mi (4,500 km)—just for pizza. Unable to find a pizza to his taste in Mississippi, he drives through 16 states to the Town Spa Pizza in Stoughton, Massachusetts. On one trip he bought 150 pizzas at a cost of $1,200.

Fowl Food

Grilled, stewed or fried, a plate of duck tongues is considered one of the most luxurious snacks in parts of the Far East. Devotees of the dish say it's the faint hint of meat, the paper-thin layers of cartilage and the pockets of fat that make the tongues so delicious! The taste of the tongues, barely 2 in (5 cm) long, is like no other duck meat, and the texture is much more creamy. Those who need further convincing might try this recipe for duck tongues—fried.

Fried Duck Tongues

2 tsp soy sauce
1 tsp rice wine, such as sake or Shaoxing
½ tsp white pepper
chili sauce or cayenne pepper
1 lb (450 g) duck tongues
½ of 1 egg white, beaten
1 tbsp cornstarch
2 cups oil

1. *Combine the soy sauce, rice wine, white pepper and a dash of chili sauce in a bowl. Add the duck tongues and mix evenly. Leave them in the marinade for 30 minutes.*
2. *Remove the duck tongues from the mixture and transfer them to another bowl. Add the egg white and cornstarch to the tongues and mix.*
3. *Pour the oil in a wok and heat to 350°F (175°C). Gently slip the duck tongues into the oil and stir to prevent sticking. Deep fry for about 2 minutes, until cooked through.*

RICE CRAZY There are more than 40,000 different types of rice in the world. The Chinese alone eat 130 million tons of rice every year.

STINKING BISHOP After the highly pungent Stinking Bishop cheese—made on a single farm in Gloucestershire, England—was mentioned briefly in the 2005 Oscar-winning animated movie *Wallace & Gromit: The Curse of the Were-Rabbit*, demand for it rose by 500 percent.

SAUSAGE ADDICT David Harding from London, England, has spent nearly £2,000 on counseling and hypnosis to try to beat his addiction for eating an average of 13 sausages a day. The 47-year-old has eaten at least one sausage a day since he was five and spends up to £700 a year on sausages.

JESUS IMAGE Toby Elles of Salford, England, fell asleep while frying bacon—and woke up to find a lifelike image of Jesus Christ, complete with long hair and beard, burned into the pan.

TOP DOG In honor of National Hot Dog Day, on July 23, 2011, the Brockton Rox baseball team of Massachusetts created the world's most expensive hot dog, selling for $80. The dog was deep fried and rolled in truffle oil, then coated with porcini dust, sprinkled with white truffle shavings, and topped with crème fraîche, caviar and roe before being served in a buckwheat blini roll.

view from inside the house

TASTEFUL HOTEL

During the holiday season in December 2011, the Fairmont Hotel in San Francisco, California, put on display a gingerbread house of epic proportions. Constructed out of 7,500 home-baked gingerbread bricks and 1,200 lb (544 kg) of royal icing, the 23-ft-high (7-m) house was decorated with 650 lb (295 kg) of colorful candies and featured a special room where children could write a letter to Santa—with express delivery to the North Pole.

RED HOT CHILI Chili grower Nick Woods of Grantham, England, has grown a new chili, Infinity, with a heat that measures 1.17 million on the Scoville Scale that grades chili heat. That's 300 times hotter than Tabasco sauce, and so hot it carries a health warning. When he first tasted it raw, he was unable to speak or stand up, shook uncontrollably and felt physically sick.

VEGETABLE KING Gardener Peter Glazebrook from Nottinghamshire, England, set a new record for the world's heaviest onion when he exhibited a monster weighing just under 18 lb (8.1 kg) at the Harrogate Flower Show in 2011.

NONPROFIT CAFE In 2010, the Panera Bread Company opened a nonprofit café in Clayton, Missouri, where customers just pay what they can afford and those who are unable to pay can volunteer their time.

RARE MALT A rare 3-pt (1.5-l) bottle of single malt Scotch whisky sold for $460,000 at auction in New York in November 2010. The 64-year-old Macallan malt had been bottled in a one-of-a-kind, handcrafted crystal Lalique decanter.

MICRO BREWERY Bragdy Gwynant, a brewery in Capel Bangor, Wales, is located in a former outhouse and is only 25 sq ft (2.3 sq m) in size. It brews ale for just one customer—the Tynllidiart Arms inn next door.

PRICE OF BREAD At the height of Zimbabwe's economic collapse in 2008, it cost 700 million Zimbabwean dollars to buy a single loaf of bread.

RAVISHING RATS

Finger-licking-good rats are rounded up and sold at almost $1.70 a pound ($3.80/kg) in the markets of Canh Nau, Vietnam. Formerly a food eaten through necessity in times of poverty, the rodents are now a popular, local speciality.

TACO LINE As part of the 2011 Phoenix Phestival in Oregon, a group of taco engineers took just 15 minutes to build a line of tacos measuring 177 ft (53.9 m) long.

SHRIMP COCKTAIL More than 80 chefs in Mazatlán, Mexico, joined forces to concoct the world's largest shrimp cocktail, weighing 1,187 lb (538.5 kg). It was served in a dip containing 127 lb (58 kg) of ketchup and 22 lb (10 kg) of lemon juice.

PERFECT PIE A £3,000 mince pie—the most expensive in the world—went on display in London, England, in 2011. Made by chef Andrew Stellitano from a 17th-century recipe, the mince pie included high-grade platinum leaf, holy water from Lourdes to bind the pastry, vanilla beans and cinnamon from Eastern spice markets, and ambergris sugar harvested from sperm whale secretions.

PRIZE PUFF At the 2011 Wisconsin State Fair, a team of bakers created a cream puff that weighed a whopping 125.6 lb (57 kg). The prize puff measured 7½ in (19 cm) high and 38 in (96 cm) wide.

GRUB PROTEIN The European Union is promoting the nutritional benefits of eating low-cholesterol insects in dishes such as scorpion soup and locust salad. Grasshoppers offer 20 percent protein and just 6 percent fat compared to lean ground beef's 24 percent protein and 18 percent fat. Crickets are said to be high in calcium, termites rich in iron, and a portion of giant silkworm moth larvae provides all our daily copper and riboflavin needs.

METRO BAN The French cheese Epoisses, once a favorite of the emperor Napoleon Bonaparte, has been banned on the Paris Metro because of its strong odor.

CHOPSTICK TRADE A lack of wood in China has led to a U.S. company, Georgia Chopsticks, producing two million pairs of chopsticks a day to export to the country. Until the shortage, manufacturers in China produced 63 billion sets of chopsticks every year.

BEAR FEAST On May 10, 2010, the Union Rescue Mission Shelter in L.A., California, served meals of donated game meat including elk, boar, antelope and black bear.

ACQUIRED TASTES Exotic snacks offered for sale by vendors on Wangfujing Street, Beijing, China, include dried sea-horses, silkworms, sheep's penis, giant grasshoppers, starfish, roasted sparrows, cicadas and inside-out snakes.

HEAD WAITER The Japanese capital, Tokyo, is gaining a reputation for outlandish themed restaurants. The Alcatraz ER restaurant is styled after a prison hospital and has drinks served in a life-sized mannequin head.

ANCIENT SOUP In 2010, archeologists in China discovered what they think is a 2,400-year-old pot of soup. The liquid and bones were in a sealed, bronze cooking vessel near the city of Xian, which was China's capital for over 1,100 years.

1,000 FLAVORS Ice-cream makers Matt and Mike Casarez sold over 1,000 different flavors of ice cream at Crook's Palace, Black Hawk, Colorado. Their more unusual varieties included "Wasabi Sesame," "Popcorn" and "Sweet Pea."

MUMMIFIED LARVA Mummified caterpillar fungus is served with chicken or pork in soups in China and Tibet to improve the flavor. The Thitarodes caterpillar feeds on the roots of a fungus that grows high up in the Himalayas, but the fungus reacts by invading the caterpillar's entire body, eventually killing and mummifying it.

EXPLOSIVE FISH Walu—or Hawaiian butterfish—contains a high level of waxy compounds in its tissue, which when eaten in large amounts can cause severe diarrhea. Native Hawaiians called the fish Maku'u, or exploding intestines. It is banned in Japan and Italy.

JELLY BRAIN

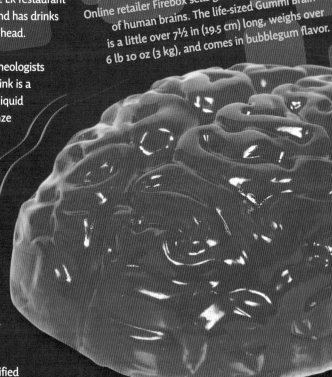

Online retailer Firebox sells gelatin candies in the shape of human brains. The life-sized Gummi Brain is a little over 7½ in (19.5 cm) long, weighs over 6 lb 10 oz (3 kg), and comes in bubblegum flavor.

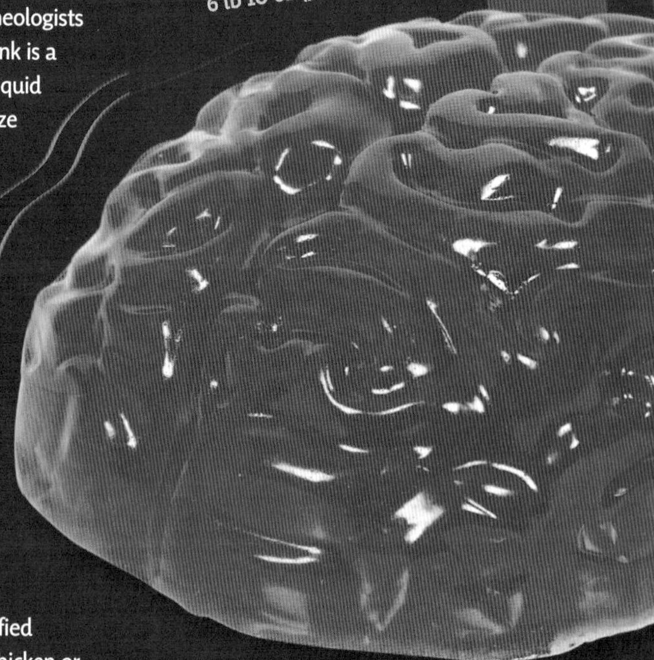

HEALTHY SNACKS Kansas State University nutritionist Dr. Mark Haub lost 27 lb (12.2 kg) in two months on a junk food diet of chocolate bars, potato chips, cookies, pizza, doughnuts and sugary cereals. Despite his diet of sugary, salty and fatty processed food, his body fat and bad cholesterol levels both fell.

BREAKING THE MOLD To mark its centenary in 2011, U.K. chocolate manufacturer Thorntons created the world's biggest chocolate bar at its factory in Derbyshire. The giant bar weighed 12,770 lb (5,792 kg)—around six tons—and measured 172 sq ft (16 sq m). The mold for the bar was set up in the company's parking lot and it took more than 50 bucket-carrying workers ten hours to fill it with liquid chocolate and then another three days for it to cool off and solidify.

SUPERMARKET SURPRISE

Tesco, the U.K.'s leading supermarket chain, is opening stores across China, but the stock is a little different from that usually found on its shelves. Its store in Qingdao caters for local tastes by selling such items as chicken's feet, turtles, dried sea-horse and whole dried lizard! Soaked in a vat of rice wine, dried lizard is said to be a fortifying drink.

EGGSTRAORDINARY Brian Spotts of Dacono, Colorado, balanced 900 eggs on end on the marble floor of a Hong Kong mall in March 2011. He practices egg balancing for half an hour daily and stresses the need for a light touch and the correct grip with the thumb and forefinger of each hand positioned at the top of the egg.

ROBO-NOODLE Robots cook noodles for customers at a restaurant in Nanping, China. The restaurant owner, Fan Ming, paid $1,500 for the robots whose eyes and chest lights flash as they chop the noodles into boiling water.

LONGEST LOG A team of 80 chefs in Shanghai, China, created the world's longest Christmas yule log, measuring more than 0.6 mi (1 km) long and more than five times the length of the previous record. It took 24 hours to make the log using 904 eggs, 2,304 lb (1,045 kg) of flour, 460 lb (209 kg) of sugar, 884 lb (401 kg) of bitter chocolate and 75 lb (34 kg) of vanilla.

STIR-FRY Using a custom-built, 14-ft-wide (4.27-m) frying pan, staff and students at the University of Massachusetts prepared the world's largest stir-fry. The 4,010-lb (1,820-kg) meal included 800 lb (363 kg) of chicken, 500 lb (227 kg) of onions, 400 lb (181.5 kg) of carrots and 300 lb (136 kg) of broccoli.

MONSTER MUSHROOM

Picked from the wild in Shaanxi Province, China, this edible puffball mushroom weighed in at a whopping 10 lb (4.5 kg).

TUNA RECORD The owner of a chain of sushi restaurants in Tokyo, Japan, paid a record $747,000 for a 593-lb (269-kg) bluefin tuna in January 2012, the equivalent of $106 for each piece of sushi.

WINE FLOOD Workers at a liquor store in Sheboygan, Wisconsin, fled for their lives when a 78-ft-long (24-m) shelf collapsed, sending nearly 7,000 bottles of wine crashing to the floor.

GOLDEN CHEESE Cheesemakers in Leicestershire, England, have made a Stilton cheese containing real gold. Clawson Stilton Gold is made from white Stilton infused with a mixture of edible gold leaf and real gold liqueur. The golden cheese sells for about $1,000 per kilo (2.2 lb).

CUPCAKE TOWER Volunteers in Vereeniging, South Africa, baked 21,000 cupcakes that were then arranged into a vast tower 19 tiers high and 11 ft 9 in (3.6 m) wide.

Chinese Treat

The slippery sluglike marine creature the sea cucumber (or sea rat) is a popular delicacy in Chinese cooking. It is considered an aphrodisiac and is used in medicine to treat everything from high blood pressure in humans to joint pain in pot-bellied pigs. The dried ovary of the sea cucumber is eaten in Japan and is called *konoko*.

Sweet Suckers

This slippery customer is actually a cleverly constructed cake. Karen Portaleo of the Highland Bakery in Atlanta, Georgia, is a former clay sculptor who has applied her creative talents to incredible cake decorations. The body and tentacles of the octopus were built with layers of sponge cake before being shaped, covered with fondant and airbrushed. The sponge giant weighed 200 lb (90 kg) and was devoured within two days of being created.

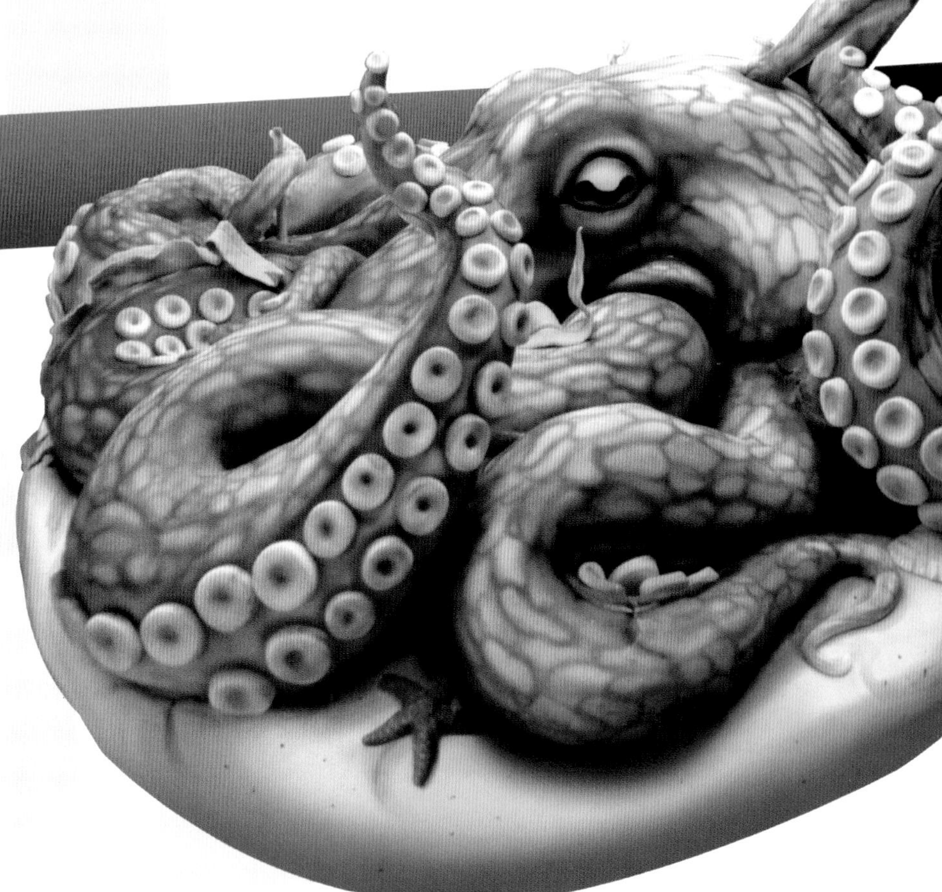

CICADA DESSERT In 2011, an ice-cream shop in Columbia, Missouri, prepared cicada ice cream—and sold out of it within hours. Employees at Sparky's Homemade Ice Cream collected the cicadas in their backyards and removed the wings. They then boiled the bugs and coated them in brown sugar and milk chocolate before adding them to the brown sugar and butter ice-cream base.

COSTLY KEBAB Chef Andy Bates from London, England, served up a £750 ($1,100) kebab, made from expensive purple violet potatoes, *coeur de boeuf* tomatoes, milk-fed lamb, and a mint yogurt topping infused with luxurious Krug champagne.

CHEESY OUTFITS

Students from Bath Spa University, England, spent 1,000 hours making five dresses from a ton of cheese. Their designs included shoes made of cheese and dresses encrusted with heat-molded, scuplted Cheddar.

CHOCOLATE TREE French chocolatier Patrick Roger created a chocolate Christmas tree, 33-ft-high (10-m) and weighing more than four tons, in his Paris laboratory.

BUMPER B.L.T. In Kansas City in 2011, volunteers assembled a bacon, lettuce and tomato sandwich that was 209 ft (63.7 m) long. It took 14 people 42 minutes to prepare the sandwich, using 3,300 slices of bacon, seven cases of lettuce and 750 lb (340 kg) of tomatoes.

BIRTHDAY CAKE To celebrate Canada's 144th birthday on July 1, 2011, three bakeries in Toronto, Ontario, joined forces to create a cake over 5 ft (1.5 m) tall, with 255 layers. The giant confection required 287 lb (130 kg) of sugar and copious amounts of eggs, flour and butter.

OLD CAKE In 2010, Justin Agrella of San Leandro, California, discovered a steamer trunk belonging to his grandparents with a well-preserved piece of their 96-year-old wedding cake inside.

LIZARD LUNCH A lizard commonly eaten in restaurants across southeast Vietnam is an all-female species unknown to science until 2010. *Leiolepis ngovantrii*, which reproduces itself by cloning, was finally discovered on a lunch buffet menu by scientists.

MOUSE MENACE Shopping at a supermarket in Birmingham, England, Liz Wray was horrified to see half a dozen live baby mice fall out of a packet of potato chips she had just picked up.

SQUID BOTTLE An Ika Tokkuri is a Japanese liquor bottle that has been made from an entire sun-dried squid. The cleaned and dried squid skin is often stuffed with rice or grain to help it form a bottle shape, and when sake is poured into it, the drink absorbs the flavor of the squid. The bottle can be reused up to six times, after which it can be eaten!

WEIRD CAKES Other crazy cake creations from around the world include...

- **BABY GIRAFFE**
Debbie Goard of Oakland, California, made a baby giraffe cake 2-ft-tall (60-cm).
- **ST. PAUL'S CATHEDRAL**
George D'Aubney built a 4-ft-tall (1.2-m) fruitcake replica of the famous cathedral in London, England.
- **STATE OF TEXAS**
Gladys Farek from Cistern, Texas, made a fruitcake measuring 5 x 6 ft (1.5 x 1.8 m) in the shape of her home state.
- **BRIDE IN DRESS**
When Chidi and Innocent Ogbuta of Dallas, Texas, renewed their wedding vows, they ordered a 400-lb (180-kg) butterscotch cake that was a life-size model of Chidi in her bridal dress.
- **FULL-SIZE SKODA CAR**
Made by a team of British bakers for a successful ad campaign.
- **LIFE-SIZE HUMAN CHEST ORGANS**
Created by horror fan Barbara Jo of San Jose, California.

SALAD DRESSING To encourage Chinese people to adopt a meat-free diet—meat consumption in the country has quadrupled over the course of the last 40 years—actress Gao Yuanyuan wore a gown made of lettuce and cabbage leaves topped with a necklace fashioned from red chili peppers. Gao herself had stopped eating meat after her pet dog suffered food poisoning two years earlier.

HEAVY CAKE A total of 100 workers from Dairy Queen, Canada, spent 14 hours in a Toronto, Ontario, square in May 2011 assembling an ice-cream cake that weighed more than 10 tons. The cake contained over 20,000 lb (9,070 kg) of ice cream, 200 lb (91 kg) of sponge cake, and 300 lb (136 kg) of icing and crumble. The gigantic dessert was created to celebrate the 30th birthday of Dairy Queen's much-loved ice-cream cake.

SOAP EATER A rare and dangerous medical condition left Tempestt Henderson, a teenage girl from Florida, addicted to eating soap. She used to go through five bars of soap a week, as well as devouring washing powder daily and licking soap bubbles off her skin in the shower. Doctors diagnosed her as suffering from pica, a condition that causes people to eat substances with no nutritional value, such as chalk, metal and sand.

MEALWORM MORSELS

Mealworm quiches and grasshopper spring rolls are among the edible delights created by Dutch scientist Arnold van Huis who has teamed up with a cooking school in Wageningen, the Netherlands, to produce a cookbook of tasty insect recipes. Van Huis believes that bug-eating is the future of nutrition, and that increased bug consumption will help alleviate global food shortages, as well as reduce carbon emissions created by other foodstuffs.

APPLES ARE 25% AIR, WHICH IS WHY THEY FLOAT.

TWINS RESTAURANT New York City's Twins Restaurant is owned by identical twin sisters Lisa and Debbie Ganz and is staffed by 37 sets of identical twins who work the same shift in the same uniform. Even the restaurant's business cards, doorknobs, light fittings, mirrors and bar stools are doubles.

PRISON BAKERY A team of 20 convicts at Rikers Island prison in New York bake 36,000 loaves of bread a week—enough to feed the prison's population of 13,000. The prison bakery covers an area of 11,000 sq ft (1,020 sq m).

ROYAL BEAN When Wesley Hosie of Somerset, England, found a mango-flavored jelly bean bearing what looked like an image of Kate Middleton, Duchess of Cambridge—complete with long hair and smile—he put it up for sale on eBay at a price of £515.

PINEAPPLE PAINKILLER Pineapple is a natural painkiller. The fruit contains enzymes that can reduce the inflammation associated with arthritis and in this way bring pain relief.

STUFFED SHIRT On the U.S. TV show *Late Night with Jimmy Fallon* on March 1, 2011, George Booth stuffed a record 185 hot dogs into his T-shirt in 30 seconds.

CHEESE PLATTER A cheese platter weighing 2,475 lb (1,125 kg) was placed on show at the World Cheese Awards in Birmingham, England. The platter consisted of 139 different wedges, featuring cheeses from every country in Europe as well as from the Americas, Australasia and Africa.

SUPER SUSHI A restaurant in Aichi Prefecture, Japan, serves giant sushi rolls that are wrapped in 6 ft 6 in (2 m) of seaweed and rice. The rolls, which contain 20 foods and cost just under $200, must be preordered two days in advance.

Foodie Fashion

A model shows off a dress made of nori seaweed with a dead octopus necklace at a fashion food exhibition in Berlin, Germany. After appearing on the catwalk, the designs were eaten. Other outfits included a chocolate dress with a quails' egg necklace and a bacon suit topped with a salad headdress.

CUPCAKE KING Competitive eater Tim "Eater X" Janus from New York City ate a record 42 cupcakes in 8 minutes at the Isle Waterloo World Cupcake Eating Championship on April 23, 2011. He has also eaten 141 pieces of nigiri sushi in 6 minutes, nearly 12 lb (5.4 kg) of burritos in 10 minutes, and 7 lb 11 oz (3.5 kg) of boneless buffalo wings in 12 minutes.

ROYAL REBUFF In August 2011, the King and Queen of Sweden were turned away by a German restaurant owner who failed to recognize them. King Carl XVI Gustaf and Queen Silvia called at a 16th-century inn in Ladenburg, but proprietor Nadine Schellenberger was preoccupied with a wedding reception and told them there was no table available. The royal couple and their entourage instead went out for a pizza on the market square.

MINI BAR As part of a campaign to save their local pub, The Plough, residents of Shepreth in Cambridgeshire, England, opened up a village telephone box to serve beer. The Dog and Bone was open for only one night, but in that time it served about 70 customers.

FULLY BOOKED A wall in Brushstroke, a Japanese restaurant in New York City, is made from 12,000 old paperback books.

BOILED EGGS While on board the U.S.S. *Fitzgerald* on August 13, 2011, Adrian Morgan of Baton Rouge, Louisiana, ate 20 hard-boiled eggs in 84 seconds—one every four seconds.

BEAN BARMY Although baked beans originated in the U.S.A., the British are such fans of the food that each year they eat more than 800 million cans—three times more than the rest of the world combined.

SPAM SANDWICH An open sandwich weighing 1,652 lb (750 kg)—including about 1,400 lb (635 kg) of Spam—was produced in Fremont, Nebraska, in 2011.

HIGH TEA In Los Angeles, California, a giant tea bag made from cheesecloth was unveiled measuring 6 x 4 ft (1.8 x 1.2 m) and weighing 151 lb (68.5 kg).

DOUGHNUT DELIVERY In 2011, Voodoo Doughnuts of Portland, Oregon, made a record-breaking box of doughnuts, weighing 666 lb (302 kg), measuring 7 x 7 x 5 ft (2 x 2 x 1.5 m) and filled with about 3,880 doughnuts.

GIANT BURGER A hamburger and bun grilled at the 2011 Alameda County Fair, California, by Brett Enright and Nick Nicora weighed a staggering 777 lb (352 kg). It took 13 hours to cook and measured 5 ft (1.5 m) in diameter and was 3 ft (90 cm) thick, representing a whole cow's worth of beef. The cheese on top of the burger weighed 50 lb (22.7 kg), and was accompanied by 30 lb (13.6 kg) of lettuce, 20 lb (9 kg) of onions, 12 lb (5.4 kg) of pickles, 10 lb (4.5 kg) of mustard and 10 lb (4.5 kg) of ketchup. The bun, which took six hours to bake, weighed 272 lb (123 kg) and was 28 in (70 cm) thick.

DREAM CARS The interior of a restaurant in Surabaya, Indonesia, allows customers to eat in converted classic cars. Dream Cars features a 1949 Mercedes Benz limo that has been modified into a dining table that seats 20 people, and a 1962 Chevrolet Impala, which has been transformed into a smaller table for four. A 1961 brown Cadillac forms a seating area, a 1959 yellow Lotus houses an organ and the restaurant's audio system, while a 1969 red Chevrolet Corvette has been converted into an aquarium holding 100 fish.

FISHY TASTE Japanese scientists who conducted tests to determine why red wine should not be drunk with fish found that the greater amount of iron there is in a wine, the more likely it is to leave a fishy aftertaste when consumed with seafood.

FAST FOOD McDonald's restaurants feed more than 64 million people a day—more than the entire population of the U.K.

BIRTHDAY BASH On September 1, 2011, a 48.6-gal (184-l) bottle of Jack Daniel's Tennessee Whiskey was produced to celebrate what would have been Jack Daniel's 161st birthday. A bottle orchestra played "Happy Birthday" on 475 bottles of Jack Daniel's while fans of the liquor sent Jack a digital birthday card containing 1,075 individual greetings.

DOUGHNUT BURGER The 2011 New York State Fair at Syracuse unveiled the 1,500-calorie Big Kahuna Donut Burger—a quarter-pound burger, with cheese, bacon, lettuce, tomato and onion, in between slices of doughnut.

CUSTARD CHAOS!

Competitors from as far away as Canada, Japan, South Africa and Germany travel to Kent, England, to take part in the annual World Custard Pie Throwing Championships. Points are awarded for throwing pies squarely into opponents' faces and also for the most amusing and original throwing techniques. The event was first held in 1967 and was inspired by a Charlie Chaplin comedy movie.

TOP BANANA

Keisuke Yamada, a 23-year-old Japanese electrician, sculpts ghoulish faces out of bananas, then photographs them and eats them. In 2011, in celebration of the U.K.'s royal wedding, he deviated from his usual grim carvings by attempting to create banana likenesses of Prince William and Kate Middleton. Keisuke said that carving the royal couple was a challenge he relished.

BURGER MILESTONE In May 2011, Don Gorske of Fond du Lac, Wisconsin, ate his 25,000th Big Mac—39 years after eating his first nine in a single day. He says the burgers constitute 90 percent of his total solid food intake, adding: "I plan on eating Big Macs till I die."

DOG BEER Brewers in The Netherlands have devised an alcohol-free beer for dogs so that Man and his best friend can enjoy a beer together. The Dog Beer is made from a special blend of beef extracts and malt.

STRETCH SAUSAGE Chef Alberto Della Pelle created a record-breaking 1,960-ft-long (597.8-m) sausage in the main street of Penne, Italy. Around 1,300 lb (590 kg) of meat was used to stuff the sausage skin, and the end product was sliced to fill 6,000 sandwiches.

CHESTNUT CHAMP On July 4, 2011, Joey Chestnut of San Jose, California, ate 62 hot dogs and buns in ten minutes to win the Nathan's Hot Dog Eating Contest in New York City for the fifth consecutive year. He trains by fasting and by stretching his stomach with water, milk and protein supplements.

LARGE GLASS An enormous wine glass measuring 7 ft 10 in (2.4 m) high and 5 ft 5 in (1.6 m) in diameter was unveiled at a wine festival in Beirut, Lebanon, in October 2010. The giant goblet-shaped container was created by engineers Walid Richa and Moussa Zakharia from Plexiglas, and was only one-quarter full after having 100 bottles of wine emptied into it.

PUB CRAWL A team of 13 people had a drink in 250 Manhattan bars and restaurants in 24 hours on September 3, 2011. One team member drank a half pint at each stop.

SARDINE CURE Patients in Hyderabad, India, eat live sardines coated in masala to cure their asthma. The treatment is administered by 200 members of the Goud family one day in June each year, and several hundred thousand people with respiratory problems line up to eat the 2-in-long (5-cm) spicy fish, the recipe for which is said to have been handed down by a Hindu saint.

ROBOT WAITERS Samurai robot waiters serve customers at the Hajime Restaurant in Bangkok, Thailand. Every 30 minutes the robot waiters stop what they are doing and break into a dance.

RELIABLE REFRIGERATOR A General Electric refrigerator bought in 1952 has enjoyed some 60 years of continuous use in the Oxford, England, home of Doris Stogdale. The fridge—bought for the equivalent of $200 in today's money—has never needed any maintenance or even a single new part.

Lobster Bike

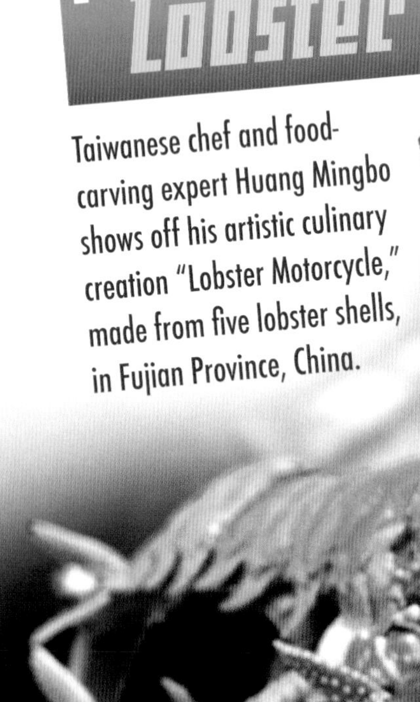

Taiwanese chef and food-carving expert Huang Mingbo shows off his artistic culinary creation "Lobster Motorcycle," made from five lobster shells, in Fujian Province, China.

BAT SOUP

Fruit bat soup is a delicacy on the Micronesian island of Palau. Frozen bats are taken from the freezer and cooked whole—complete with fur, wing membranes and feet—before being ripped apart by hand and eaten. The fur can be chewed until the musky taste has been sucked out of it. Confronted with the dish, Western visitor Benjamin Brown said: "They brought out the bat on a plate with a bow around its neck to show it to me before they cooked it. I had thought at the time that they would be cutting it up after to make the soup. Clearly I was wrong about that!"

Recipe (for those with strong stomachs): serves 4

Ingredients

3 well-washed fruit bats, skinned and gutted if you prefer
1 tablespoon finely sliced fresh ginger
1 large onion, quartered
Soy sauce and/or coconut cream
Chopped scallions
Sea salt to taste

Method

Place bats in a large kettle and cover with water. Add ginger, onion and salt. Bring to a boil, then lower the heat and simmer for 45 minutes. Strain the broth into a second kettle. Remove the bat meat from the bones if you prefer, then return it with any desired innards to the broth. Sprinkle with scallions and season with soy sauce and/or coconut cream.

COLOSSAL CORGI As part of the buildup to the 2011 royal wedding between Prince William and Kate Middleton, British cake designer Michelle Wibowo created a giant cake in the shape of a royal corgi dog. The cake measured nearly 6 x 4 ft (1.8 x 1.2 m) and weighed about 150 lb (68 kg).

RARE WINE At a sale in Geneva, Switzerland, in November 2010, a rare large Imperial bottle of 1947 French Cheval-Blanc white wine—equal to eight standard bottles—was sold to a private collector for $304,375. Labeled "the greatest wine ever made," it is so coveted that enthusiasts have traveled thousands of miles to taste it.

Beyond

Belief

The Greatest

The 1903 lineup at Barnum & Bailey's Circus included a classic Bearded Lady, several "Lilliputians" and many other novelty acts. Founded by showmen P.T. Barnum and James Anthony Bailey in 1881, and billing itself as "The Greatest Show on Earth," the circus enjoyed tremendous success in the U.S.A. and Europe, exhibiting bizarre and unusual performers alongside animal acts such as Jumbo the world's largest elephant, performing geese and musical donkeys.

Show on Earth

1 Mohammed Soliman, Whirling Dervish and Fire-eater 2 Ivy Howard, Contortionist 3 John Hayes, Tattooed Man 4 Leah May, Giantess (8 ft 3½ in/2.53 m) 5 Young Herrman, Expansionist (expands chest measurement by 13¾ in/35 cm) 6 Maxey, Needle Eater 7 George Tomasso, Human Pincushion 8 John/James William Coffey, Skeleton Man 9 Edith Clifford, Sword Swallower 10 James Morris, Elastic Skin Man 11 William Doss, Telescope Neck Man 12 Annie Howard 13 Vera Wren, Female Boxer 14 Billy Wells, Hard-headed Man 15 Hovart family of Lilliputians 16 Beautiful Marie, Human Mountain 17 Hovart family of Lilliputians 18 Krao Farini, Missing Link 19 Hovart family of Lilliputians 20 Lionel the Lion-faced Boy 21 Hovart family of Lilliputians 22 Grace Gilbert, Bearded Lady 23 Charles Tripp, Armless Wonder 24 Hovart family of Lilliputians 25 Albino "Rob Roy," Wild Man of Scotland

BALLOON MAN

In a million-to-one freak accident, New Zealand truck driver Steven McCormack's body was inflated to three times its original size when a compressed air nozzle pierced his left buttock.

The 48-year-old was working on his truck at Opotiki on the North Island in May 2011 when he slipped between the cab and the trailer, dislodging the compressed air hose that feeds the brakes. The nozzle pierced his left buttock, sending air compressed to 100 lb per square inch rushing into his body. As his neck, feet and hands swelled up instantly, he began to scream for fear that he was about to explode. "I had no choice but to just lay there, blowing up like a balloon," he said. Workmates hurried to his aid, and he was rushed to the hospital where his lungs were drained and a surgical drill was used to clear the wound in his buttock, leaving a hole about 1 in (2.5 cm) wide and 2 in (5 cm) deep. Doctors later told him they were surprised the compressed air did not make his skin burst.

PLASTIC BIRDS Keen bird-watchers Ken and Fay Jackson spent an entire day observing two owls on the roof of an apartment block opposite their home in Torquay, England—before realizing that the birds were made of plastic. The couple thought the reason the owls had not moved at all during that time was because they were stalking prey.

FASHION VICTIM Accused of shoplifting from a local store, Stephen Kirkbride turned up in court in Kendal, Cumbria, England, wearing the exact coat he denied stealing.

PEAK CONDITION A 4x4 vehicle was abandoned near the top of the 3,560-ft-high (1,085-m) Mount Snowdon in Wales twice in a month in 2011. On the second occasion—September 29—it had a "For Sale" sign attached to the windshield.

IMPROPER ADDRESS Australian Thomas John Collins was jailed in November 2010 for calling Magistrate Matthew McLaughlin "mate" twice during a hearing in Ipswich, Queensland.

WRONG WARRANT Police searched the home of Rose and Walter Martin of Brooklyn, New York, more than 50 times in eight years owing to a computer error.

TALKING GARBAGE As part of the war on litter, British councils introduced garbage bins that say "thank you," applaud or even burp when trash is dropped into them. In Sweden, a talking bin received three times more trash than a regular one nearby.

WRONG SIDE A senior citizen from Jena, Germany, who wanted to block off the entrance to his cellar, worked from the wrong side of the new partition and ended up accidentally bricking himself into the cellar for several days.

LUCKY LANDING Five-year-old Ye Zixu escaped with just scratches and bruises after falling from the window of a tenth-floor apartment in Chongqing, China. Luckily, her 100-ft (30-m) fall was broken when she landed on a ground-floor awning.

LAUGHING FITS Pseudobulbar affect (PBA) is a neurological condition in which patients are unable to control sudden outbursts of crying or laughter. Episodes can last for several minutes, and a patient might laugh uncontrollably even when angry or frustrated.

LONGEST EARRING U.S.-based Romanian jewelry designer Adrian Haiduc spent eight months creating an earring that is almost a third of a mile (0.5 km) long. The world's longest earring measures 1,550 ft (472 m) in length and is made from crystals, pearls, gemstones and beads, all strung on silk. It features three strings—one worn in the hair, another forming a necklace, and the third hanging as a conventional earring.

FUNERAL CLOWN John Brady of Drimnagh, Ireland, runs a funeral clown company, Dead Happy Ireland, for people looking to put the "fun" into "funeral." The company ad reads: "We bring squirting flowers, we make balloon animals. We can even fall into the grave if you want us to. Let your loved one go down with a smile."

MUMMIFIED PASSENGER Unsure what to do when her homeless friend died in her car, a Californian woman drove the partially mummified corpse around for ten months. On investigating the car, police officers were confronted with a foul stench and a leg poking out from under a blanket.

FLUSHED FRENCHMAN

A high-speed TGV train traveling between La Rochelle and Paris was delayed for two hours after a 26-year-old passenger dropped his mobile phone into the onboard toilet. He attempted to retrieve the device, but his arm became jammed in the toilet system and would not budge. The driver stopped the train, but even French firefighters could not extricate the man's arm from the toilet bowl. In order for the train to continue its journey, the firefighters were forced to remove the entire toilet from the carriage, with the man still attached.

Eye Poppers

Brothers Hugh (left) and Antonio Francis from Essex, England, can pop their eyes out of their sockets. Antonio, who has been able to do this since childhood, has demonstrated his eye-boggling skill on *Britain's Got Talent* and in a music video for electropop act Hot Chip.

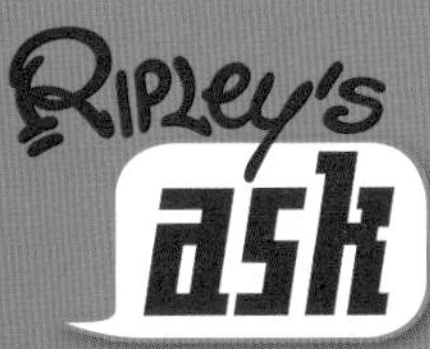

When did you first discover you could pop your eyes out? **Antonio:** *I was seven years old and it was an accident. I was combing through my big Afro hair and the comb got stuck. As I pulled it out, my left eye popped out of its socket at the same time! After it happened this first time, I found I could control it myself and showed my mum, who took me straight to the hospital where they asked me if I could pop the right eye out, too, and I could.*

Hugh: *I discovered I could do it only just over a year ago now, but didn't tell anyone straightaway—it's a fairly new thing for me.*

Does it hurt when you do it? Antonio: *No, not at all. Once when I pushed them out too far they hurt a little, but that was a one-off. My eyes do get tired when I am popping them on a daily basis, but I can see perfectly, so I know it isn't affecting my health.*

Hugh: *It feels uncomfortable because I don't do it all the time like Antonio and it can sometimes make my vision blurry, but Antonio's doctor has said that it is not harmful to my sight, so I am not worried about any long-term effects at this stage.*

How has eye-popping changed your life? **Antonio:** *Since being on Britain's Got Talent, I get stopped in the street and asked to pop my eyes about 200 to 300 times a day.*

Hugh: *When I am walking down the street with Antonio, he often is stopped and asked to pop his eyes out for a picture. They always ask me if I can pop mine out, too, and I say no, but when they take the picture I pop mine, too! Always gets a few laughs, so that is nice.*

Can you explain to us how you do it? Antonio: *Not really! All I know is there are three muscles at the back of your eye and you can compress them, and if you do this and push the eye forward at the same time you get the desired popping result.*

Hugh: *It's tricky! The only way I can explain it, is it is like opening your eye as wide as you can, by pushing your top and bottom eyelids back, and then pushing the muscles at the back of your eye as hard as you can until the eye pops out. But I wouldn't try it at home like us!*

Vast Veil

For her wedding to Ferdinand Pucci near Naples, Italy, bride Elena De Angelis wore the world's longest wedding veil, measuring a staggering 1.8 mi (3 km) long. The white silk veil, which was 6 ft 6 in (2 m) wide, took months to make and needed a staggering 600 people to carry it. The village of Casal di Principe came to a standstill as hundreds of people turned out to help her along the streets to the church. Her veil was so long, it would take Usain Bolt racing at world-record top speed nearly 5 minutes to run its length.

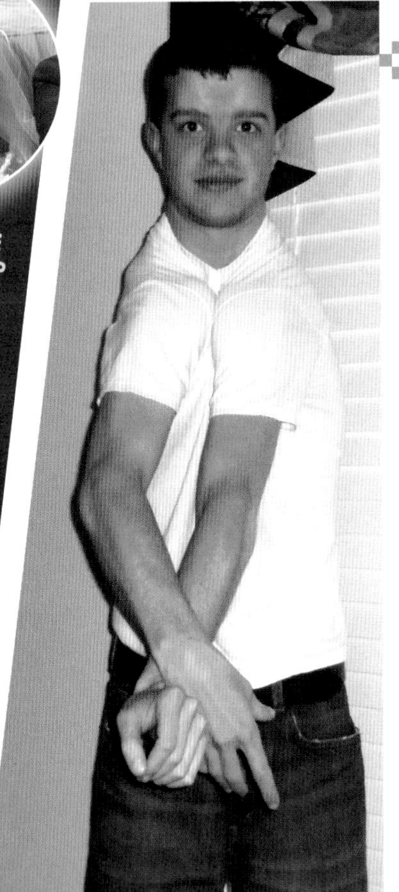

YOUR UPLOADS

www.ripleys.com/submit

Joshua Carter from Leesburg, Georgia, can touch his shoulders together in front of his chest, but don't try this yourself. Joshua was born without collarbones, which means that he has hypermobile, or double-jointed, shoulders. The collarbone normally forms a strut between the shoulder blade and the breastbone, and is the only long bone in the body that lies horizontally. "Having no collarbones is an advantage," says Joshua, "it has allowed me to fit into small spaces and work through a crowd easily!"

HARD LABOR In August 2011, an 11-year-old boy in Aachen, Germany, called police to complain that his mother kept making him do chores around the house during the school summer holidays.

FAMILY TRADITION Four generations of one family have got married on September 9—a tradition stretching back more than a century. Angelynn Perchermeier was wed in Cincinnati, Ohio, on September 9, 2011—100 years to the day that her great-great-grandparents had exchanged their vows. Her great-grandparents and her grandparents also chose September 9 for their weddings.

BUSY LIFE Ancentus Akuku of Kisumu, Kenya, married more than 100 times and sired more than 160 children before his death on October 3, 2010, aged 94.

TIGHT SPOT Prisoner Juan Ramirez Tijerina tried to escape from a jail in Chetumal, Mexico, by packing himself into his girlfriend's suitcase. When suspicious guards opened her bag, they found Ramirez curled up in the fetal position wearing only his underpants and socks.

LEGO TOWER Over a period of four days in April 2011, 6,000 LEGO™ lovers joined forces to build a LEGO tower standing more than 102 ft (31 m) high in Sao Paulo, Brazil. The tower, which was composed of 500,000 LEGO bricks, was stacked up with the help of a crane and was held in place by wire supports to stop it toppling over in the wind.

SEWER ORDEAL In October 2010, Daniel Collins of Collins, Missouri, fell into a sewer and was swept through more than a mile (1.6 km) of pipe before he was rescued. After his safety line had become unhooked, the sheer force of the water pushed him along the 2-ft-wide (0.6-m) pipe, finally dumping him at the bottom of a 12-ft-deep (3.6-m) chamber.

ARROW ATTACK In 2011, New Zealander Matthew Scheurich survived being shot with arrows in a remote jungle area of Papua New Guinea by a tribesman who wanted him dead so that he could marry his French girlfriend. Scheurich sustained an arrow wound to the stomach, which luckily stopped just short of his aorta (the body's most vital artery), and another to his right lung, and was pelted with rocks. He was airlifted to a small hospital where X-rays showed that his chest was half-filled with blood. He underwent an emergency transfusion to prevent him from bleeding to death.

HEAD LOCK

Danielle Morgan, an 18-year-old student from the University of Derby, England, had to be cut free by fire crews after getting her head trapped inside a wire clotheshorse. After she fell off her roommate's bed, the clotheshorse landed on top of her and her head went right through the frame.

EMBARRASSING DAD Every morning for 170 days of the Utah school year, Dale Price wore a different fancy-dress costume to wave his 16-year-old son off on the school bus from their home in American Fork. Rain Price had been embarrassed when Dale had waved goodbye one day, so Dale decided to prolong the agony. He dressed as such characters as Batgirl, the Little Mermaid, Princess Leia, Elvis Presley, Little Red Riding Hood and Wonder Woman. On another occasion, Dale dragged a porcelain toilet onto the porch and sat on it reading a paper.

SCOTCH SCULPTURE University of North Florida art student Cameron Nunez made a sculpture of a group of rock music fans entirely from Scotch tape. He went through 24 rolls of tape and used himself as one of the casting models, wrapping a layer of tape sticky-side up around his head and arms before rewrapping over that, sticky-side down, to create a mold that was then removed with surgical scissors.

PREVIOUS MEETING Married couple Suzanne and Alistair Cotton from Coventry, England, met and fell in love before they discovered that they both suffered from the same rare heart condition. It turned out that 20 years earlier, in 1974, they had been in the same ward at the same hospital, where they had undergone the same operation, performed by the same surgeon, on the same day.

CHRISTMAS GLOOM Convicted of assault in 2010, Daniel Martz of Livingston, Montana, was sentenced to spend the next five Christmases in jail to stop him getting into trouble during the holidays.

DORITO TRIBUTE Following his death on September 20, 2011, Arch West, the man who invented Doritos, was buried along with some of his beloved snack chips. Friends and relatives attending the service at a Dallas, Texas, cemetery tossed Doritos around the burial box containing his ashes as a tribute.

TRIPLE BLAST Sgt. Horace Weigart, a U.S. soldier during the Mexican–American War (1846–48), was hit by three cannonballs during the siege of Fort Texas. The first wounded him, the second killed him and the third later blew apart his grave site.

DUNG WATCH In 2010, a Swiss watchmaking company produced a one-of-a-kind $11,000 wristwatch with a body made from a coprolite—a fossilized piece of dinosaur dung dating back 100 million years. The watch's band is made from the skin of an American black cane toad.

LITE-BRITE MURAL Over the course of 365 days, Rob Surette of North Andover, Massachusetts, used 504,000 Lite-Brite toy pegs to create a huge mural measuring 10 x 20 ft (3 x 6 m) and weighing about 1,750 lb (795 kg).

HAIR CAT

Veterinarians operating on a pet cat in Huntingdon, England, were shocked to discover what they thought was a tumor was actually a giant hairball—5 in (13 cm) long, and the largest they had ever seen. Gemma the cat had swallowed so much hair she could no longer eat, and the furry ball in her stomach would almost certainly have led to death had vets not intervened.

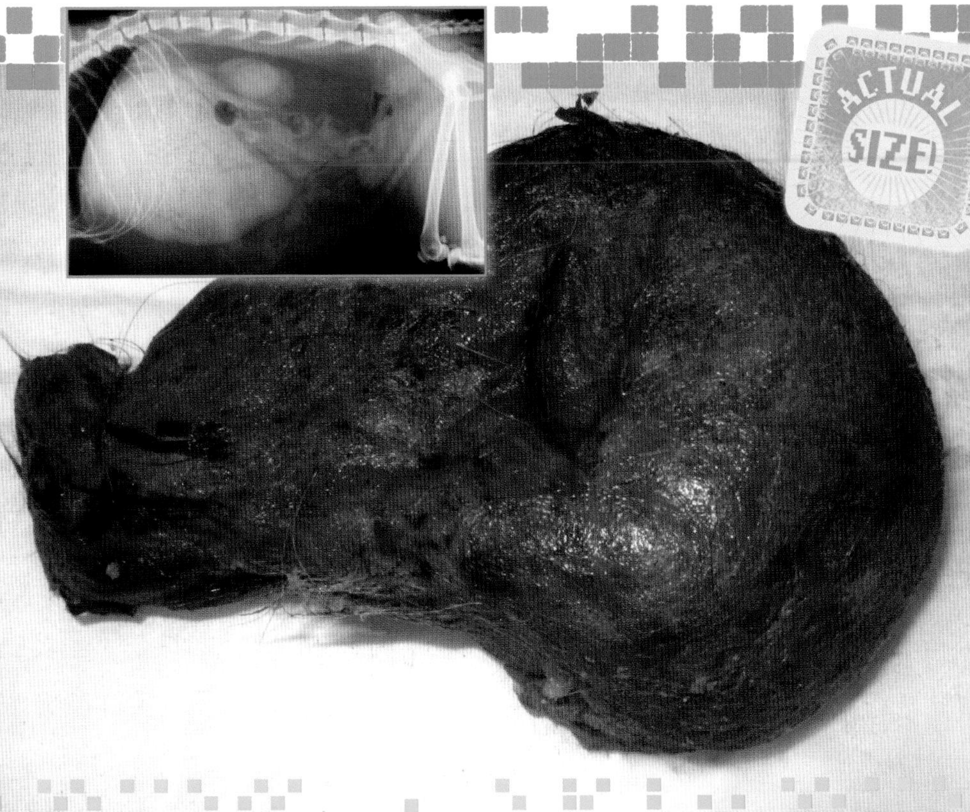

ACTUAL SIZE!

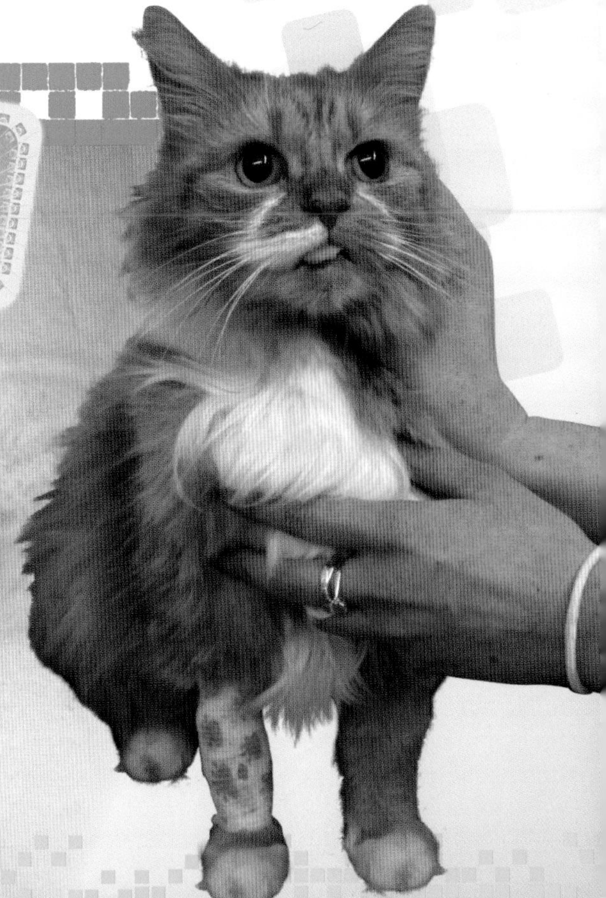

Scary Ride

An ultra-light plane hangs 33 ft (10 m) above ground from a Ferris wheel after crashing into it at a fair near Taree, Australia. The pilot and his passenger were trapped in the plane for nearly three hours, but they eventually walked away unhurt while two children who were trapped on the ride at the time also escaped injury.

NO PANTS On January 9, 2011, an estimated 3,500 commuters stripped down to their underwear and boarded subway trains across New York City for the tenth annual No Pants Subway Ride. The event has spread across the globe with tens of thousands of people taking part in 50 cities from Adelaide to Zurich. A modest band of 100 people rode the London Underground; and in Johannesburg, South Africa, 34 no-pants riders were arrested for public indecency before being released without charge.

SHARK ATTACK Kaiju Sushi and Rice Balls, a restaurant in New Smyrna Beach—the Florida town dubbed the shark attack capital of the world—offers a free shark sushi roll for anyone who has survived being bitten by a shark... and can prove it. The first customer to take advantage of the deal not only had a scar on his leg but also a YouTube video of himself on the local news in 2008 being taken away to the hospital.

NOT SO OLD In July 2010, Japanese officials went to congratulate Sogen Kato on his 111th birthday for being the oldest man in Tokyo but instead found his mummified remains lying in bed—where he had died three decades earlier.

HIDDEN LOBSTERS A shopper from Biloxi, Mississippi, was arrested for having two live lobsters in his shorts. The man was accused of trying to walk out of a grocery store without paying for food items that he had stuffed down his cargo shorts, including two bags of jumbo shrimp, a pork loin and the lobsters. Police said he had tried to escape by throwing the pork at store employees.

TREE BED A woman fell fast asleep curled up on the narrow branch of a tree 20 ft (6 m) above the streets of Lanzhou, China. Shoppers realized she was there only when one of her shoes fell off and hit someone on the head.

Ripley's Research

Saline solution is normally used to irrigate wounds in hospitals. Injected into the skin (avoiding veins) with a saline bag, a length of tubing and a thin needle, it results in the body part temporarily puffing up and deforming. The forehead is the most popular location for saline inflation, as the taut skin there makes the change more dramatic and visible. If administered incorrectly, however, the process can be dangerous, and people who have done it regularly have noticed that their skin has expanded permanently.

BAD DRIVER Gageen Preet Singh of Surrey, England, was paid up to £800 a time by driving test candidates to take the test on their behalf—yet he himself was such a bad driver that he repeatedly failed the tests. Out of eight tests he was known to have taken for clients, he failed five. To carry out the illegal impersonations, he used an array of disguises, including fake mustaches and wigs.

BURIED FINGERS Playing near Paris, France, a seven-year-old schoolboy dug up a glass jar containing several well-preserved human fingers thought to belong to a local carpenter who lost four digits in an accident more than 30 years before. At the time the carpenter's fingers could not be surgically reattached, so he put them in a jar full of alcohol and buried them near his home.

BAGELHEADS

The latest body modification craze in Japan is the "bagelhead," created by injecting a saline solution into the forehead so that it inflates alarmingly. Body inflators feel only a dull headache during the procedure, and their foreheads take about two hours to swell up. Many then prod their new lumps to create more interesting shapes, after which the inflation goes down overnight, usually leaving no unsightly scars.

YOUNG ME, NOW ME

Over 1,000 people—including superheroes—have re-created childhood pictures for an Internet project titled "Young Me/Now Me." It is the brainchild of Los Angeles-based web personality Ze Frank, who asks visitors to his site to submit a photo of their younger self along with another one as they are today in roughly the same pose, hence the lack of smiles on the faces of these superhero brothers!

SCREAMING CORPSE A 50-year-old South African man who was thought to be dead suddenly woke up after spending 21 hours in a morgue refrigerator. When the man screamed to be let out of the morgue in Libode, Eastern Cape, two mortuary attendants ran for their lives, believing he was a ghost.

HUMAN PARCEL Reluctant to pay the train fare, the parents of four-year-old May Pierstorff mailed her instead by U.S. Mail to her grandparents' home in Lewiston, Idaho. As her 48½-lb (22-kg) weight was just below the 50-lb (22.7-kg) limit, on February 19, 1914, they attached 53 cents in parcel post stamps to May's coat and she traveled the entire journey in the train's mail compartment before being delivered to her grandparents' home by the mail clerk.

VAMPIRE CONFERENCE Three hundred exorcists from all over the world traveled to Poland's Roman Catholic Jasna Góra Monastery in 2011 for a week-long congress to discuss the increase of vampirism in Europe.

ORNAMENTAL SKULL A dead man's relatives sued Czech police after officers used his skull as an ornament. The skull—wearing a police cap—was used as a bookend by officers at Volary who also took pictures of it and posted them on the Internet.

ICE RIDE Michal Kawolski of Gdansk, Poland, had to be rescued by coastguards after drifting half a mile out to sea on a sheet of ice. He had been testing the strength of the ice next to the shore, when a piece suddenly broke away and strong currents carried him out into the Baltic Sea.

HEAT HYPNOSIS In December 2010, staff at a small shoe repair shop in Bromsgrove, England, were shivering in temperatures of 8°F (–13°C) until their boss had them hypnotized into thinking they were warm. Martin Connellan always kept the door to the shop open and had tried buying jackets for his workers, but when that failed he brought in hypnotist Jim Kerwin—and after just five minutes under hypnosis some staff were complaining about how hot they were.

PASTA HAT Austrian atheist Niko Alm has won the right to be shown on his driver's license photo wearing a pasta strainer as "religious headgear." Mr. Alm, who belongs to the Church of the Flying Spaghetti Monster, said the sieve was a requirement of his religion, pastafarianism.

BONE JEWELRY

Columbine Phoenix from Somerville, Massachusetts, makes jewelry from human bones. Among her creations are an earring with a middle finger bone, a necklace from five fingertip bones and a necklace from a hand bone. She obtains the bones from universities and medical schools, and always uses hand bones because they are the only ones small enough for jewelry.

UPSIDE DOWN

Mr. Zhu rode a bicycle upside down for a quarter of a mile (400 m) in Shaoxing, China. His feet were tied tightly by two belts connected to the bike, and his head rested on the saddle.

UNUSUAL MOTIVE Jobless Richard Verone, 59, raided a bank in Gastonia, North Carolina, and demanded just $1—because he wanted to go to prison in order to receive medical treatment. After the robbery, he calmly waited inside the bank for police officers to arrive and arrest him.

A QUARTER OF YOUR BODY'S BONES ARE IN YOUR FEET.

DEADLY REVENGE A fighting cock took deadly revenge on its owner for forcing it back into the ring too soon. Birds are usually given an hour's rest before fighting another opponent, but when Singrai Soren of West Bengal, India, repeatedly tried to push the cockerel back into the ring, it attacked him and slit his throat with the metal blades attached to its legs.

STUCK IN CHIMNEY The remains of Joseph Schexnider, who went missing in 1984, were found 27 years later wedged in the chimney of the Abbeville National Bank in Abbeville, Louisiana. Schexnider, who died of dehydration after getting stuck in the chimney, may have been trying to break into the bank at the time. He had been hiding from police after skipping a court hearing over charges of possessing a stolen vehicle.

SUICIDE WATCH Don Ritchie of Sydney, Australia, lives across the street from the Gap—a rocky cliff along Sydney Harbor. So far, he has saved more than 160 people from committing suicide by convincing them not to jump from the cliff.

MISTAKEN ASHES Burglars who raided a home in Silver Springs Shores, Florida, thought they had stolen a quantity of cocaine, only later to realize they had actually discovered the cremated remains of a man and two dogs.

Light Fantastic

Rashad Alakbarov, an artist from Azerbaijan, installed this unique artwork in the Phillips de Pury gallery in London, England, in 2012. The "painting" is actually white light projected through 90 plexiglass model airplanes suspended from the ceiling. The image depicts Baku, the capital of Azerbaijan on the Caspian Sea.

HEADSHOT HERO Sergeant Paul "Headshot" Boothroyd earned his nickname after surviving a sniper's bullet to the head while serving in Helmand Province, Afghanistan, in March 2011. Just 15 minutes after being shot, he was smoking a cigarette and walking unaided to a military helicopter. Doctors say the survival rate for being shot in the head is only about one in 10,000.

BOOGER BALL

Over a period of two years, James Ford, an art student in Nottingham, England, collected his own boogers on a daily basis and molded them into a ¾-in-diameter (21-mm) ball—about the size of a Brussels sprout. He collected the boogers in an eggcup and then glued them together to create his mucus mosaic, which has been exhibited in London and Lithuania.

HOTEL FALL Four-year-old Joey Williams fell seven stories from a hotel balcony in Miami, Florida, but landed without breaking a single bone. He hit several palm trees on the way down.

ATOMIC KITCHEN A man was arrested in 2011 after attempting to split atoms in the kitchen of his home in southern Sweden. He said it was simply a hobby, but after creating a small meltdown on his stove, he was arrested for unauthorized possession of nuclear material—radium, americium and uranium.

MEDICAL MESSAGE To ensure that she does not endure a lingering death, 81-year-old grandmother Joy Tomkins from Norfolk, England, has tattooed the words "Do Not Resuscitate" across her chest. In case she collapses face down and paramedics miss the big blue letters, she has also had "P.T.O." and an arrow inked on her back.

MOHICAN GATHERING 109 staff and students gathered in a room at West Cheshire College, England, on September 16, 2011—all sporting Mohican haircuts.

WEIGHT ISSUES Believed to be one of the fattest kids in the world, Suman Khatun from West Bengal, India, weighed a staggering 201 lb (91 kg) when she was just six years old and 3 ft 5 in (1.03 m) tall—more than five times her recommended weight, and the same weight as a Great Dane. In an average week, she ate 31 lb (14 kg) of rice, 18 lb (8 kg) of potatoes, 18 lb (8 kg) of fish, and about 180 bananas, as well as assorted cream cakes and her favorite Bengali sweets.

"MALE" MOM Jackie Kelly of Blountstown, Florida, was incorrectly listed as a male on her birth certificate and has officially been a male since 1958—even though she has two children!

CUTTING EDGE A $100,000 shaving razor has gone on sale featuring white sapphire blades that last forever and have an edge less than 100 atoms wide—5,000 times thinner than the width of a hair. Designed by a Portland, Oregon, company, the razor has a handle made mainly from iridium, a metal derived almost entirely from meteorites and ten times rarer than platinum.

COMBAT GNOMES Shawn Thorsson of Petaluma, California, has created a range of Combat Garden Gnomes—regular gnomes wielding army rifles—which he sells online. The U.S. Naval Reserve officer claims he came up with the idea because he wanted a military presence in his garden.

CEMENT IMPLANTS

A fake doctor, Oneal Ron Morris, was arrested in Miami, Florida, on a charge of injecting a woman's buttocks with a mixture of cement, tire sealant and superglue to give her a more curvaceous appearance. According to detectives, Oneal (below) performed a similar procedure on herself.

SO BOOTIFUL A penguin named Bonaparte has fallen for a Wellington boot! The penguin named after the famous French emperor Napoleon has developed a romantic attachment to his keeper's black-and-white rubber boots (named in honor of the Duke of Wellington, Napoleon's adversary at the 1815 Battle of Waterloo). He even fights to keep the gumboots away from other penguins at his home in an aquarium in Germany.

STAMP STORAGE The U.S. Postal Service Stamp Fulfillment Department maintains an underground vault with nearly $500 million-worth of postage stamps in storage.

POLICE VULTURES Police chiefs in Germany hired three vultures—named Sherlock, Columbo and Miss Marple—to replace sniffer dogs in the hope that the birds' amazing eyesight, sense of smell and ability to locate dead prey would help them to find missing bodies. However, the scheme was abandoned after the disinterested vultures managed only to find a cadaver when it was placed immediately in front of their beaks.

LENTIL SPROUT A 4,000-year-old lentil seed found during a 2008 archeological excavation in Kütahya Province, Turkey, germinated and sprouted the following year.

BORDER CROSSINGS Baarle-Hertog, Belgium, and Baarle-Nassau, the Netherlands, make up a single town with twisted borders. Walking only a few streets, it is possible to cross national borders half a dozen times!

COMPLEX CHOCOLATE U.S. scientists have discovered that humans are less genetically complex than chocolate biscuits. Humans have 20–25,000 genes, but cacao, from which we make chocolate, has 35,000.

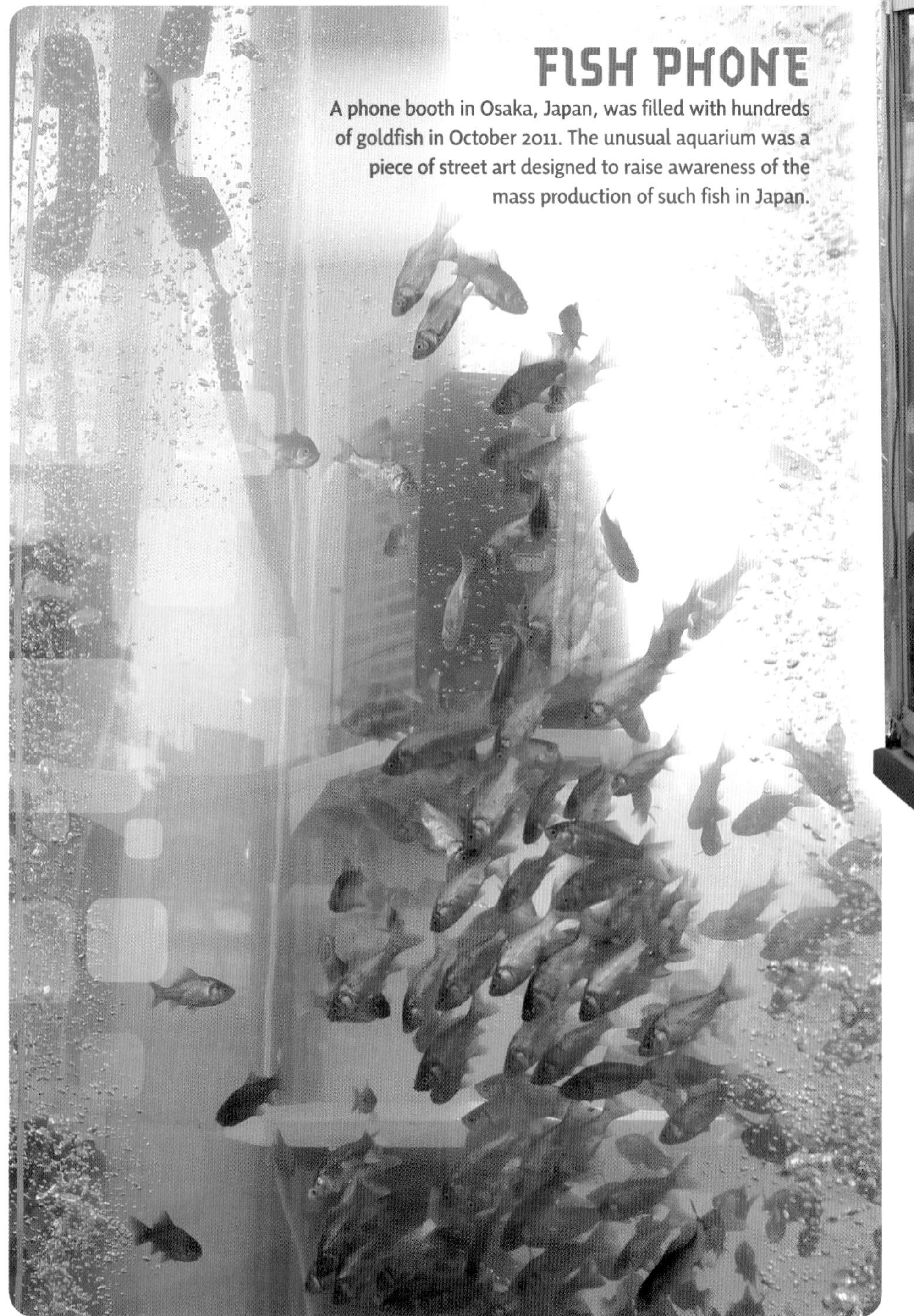

FISH PHONE

A phone booth in Osaka, Japan, was filled with hundreds of goldfish in October 2011. The unusual aquarium was a piece of street art designed to raise awareness of the mass production of such fish in Japan.

ODD PASSENGER A 59-year-old woman was arrested in Chesterton, Indiana, after being caught driving a golf cart while drunk and in the company of a large scarecrow.

EXPLODING TOILETS Two workers at a federal building in Washington, D.C., suffered cuts after a plumbing malfunction caused two toilets to explode and send tiny shards of porcelain flying through the air. The 2,500 employees in the building were warned not to use the bathrooms until the problem was fixed.

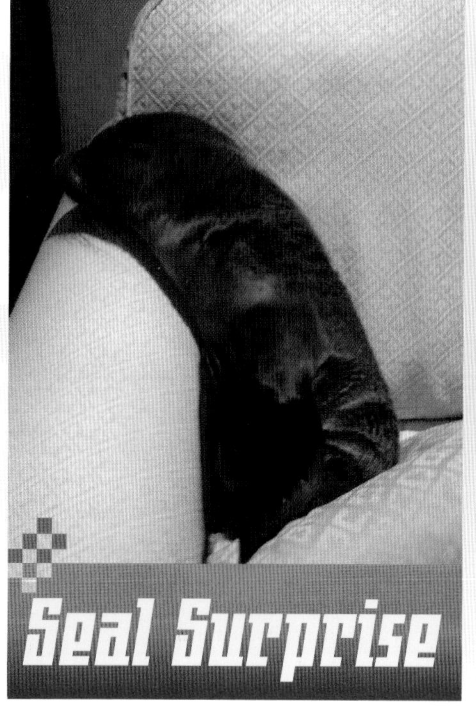

Seal Surprise

An adventurous fur seal pup gave the occupant of a house in Tauranga, New Zealand, a shock when it visited in December 2011. The seal had made its way from the nearby harbor, across a busy road and slipped through a cat flap, before making itself comfortable on the couch for the night, apparently not bothered by the resident cats and dogs. As seals can give a nasty bite, a wildlife official was deployed to recover the animal, and "Lucky," as the seal was named after his traffic-dodging abilities, was released back into the sea.

IN CUFFS A criminal suspect escaped from a police station in Buffalo, New York State, on April 26, 2011... while still wearing handcuffs. When police rearrested him, they added a new charge for stealing the handcuffs he was still wearing.

THE GRIZZLY BEAR CAN RUN AS FAST AS THE AVERAGE HORSE.

SPACE COINS Characters from Star Wars, including Darth Vader, Luke Skywalker, Princess Leia and Yoda, appear on a new set of coins that are legal tender on the South Pacific island state of Niue. Produced by the New Zealand mint, the NZ$1 and $2 coins have Queen Elizabeth II on the reverse.

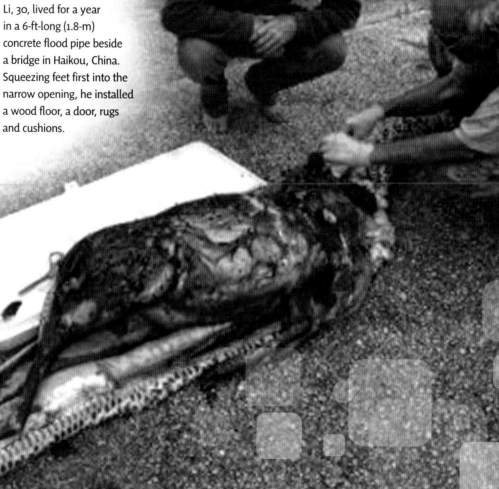

FOX'S REVENGE A hunter in Belarus was shot in the leg by a fox in January 2011. As the man attempted to club the fox to death with his rifle after shooting it, the animal's paw struck the trigger, firing the gun.

SMELLY SIREN A Japanese smoke alarm for deaf people emits such a powerful smell that those asleep wake up within 2½ minutes of the stench hitting them. Instead of a shrill wail, the device releases the chemical compound allyl isothiocyanate, which is what gives horseradish, mustard and wasabi their bite.

TWO FUNERALS Romania's fattest man, 870-lb (395-kg) Cristian Capatanescu, had postmortem liposuction so that half of him could be buried in a regular-sized coffin and the other half cremated. His family asked doctors to remove some of his bulk because they couldn't afford an extra-large reinforced coffin.

PIPE HOME Mao Li, 30, lived for a year in a 6-ft-long (1.8-m) concrete flood pipe beside a bridge in Haikou, China. Squeezing feet first into the narrow opening, he installed a wood floor, a door, rugs and cushions.

SNAKE INVADER

A giant Burmese Python captured in the Florida Everglades in October 2011 was one of the largest ever found in the state. When biologists performed an autopsy on the 15¾-ft-long (4.8-m) reptile, they discovered a recently swallowed 76-lb (34-kg) adult deer, still remarkably intact. It was the largest prey ever found inside a Florida snake. As their name suggests, Burmese Pythons are not native to Florida—the wild population, now in the tens of thousands, is thought to have grown from pet snakes that escaped in the 1990s.

MYSTERY DEATH An Irish coroner ruled that a man who burned to death in his home on December 22, 2010, died of spontaneous human combustion. The totally burned body of Michael Faherty, 76, was found lying face down near an open fire in his living room in Galway, but coroner Dr. Ciaran McLoughlin ruled that the fire was not the cause of the fatal blaze. The only damage was to the body, the ceiling immediately above and the floor directly beneath.

PERFECT SYMMETRY Richard Burton Vail of Ontario, Canada, had birth and death dates that mirrored each other as a palindrome—11-12-20 and 02-21-11.

STORED BODIES Jean Stevens of Wyalusing, Pennsylvania, kept her deceased husband's body in her home for a decade—and her twin sister's body for a year. When the authorities found out, they agreed she could keep them if she built a separate building to store them in.

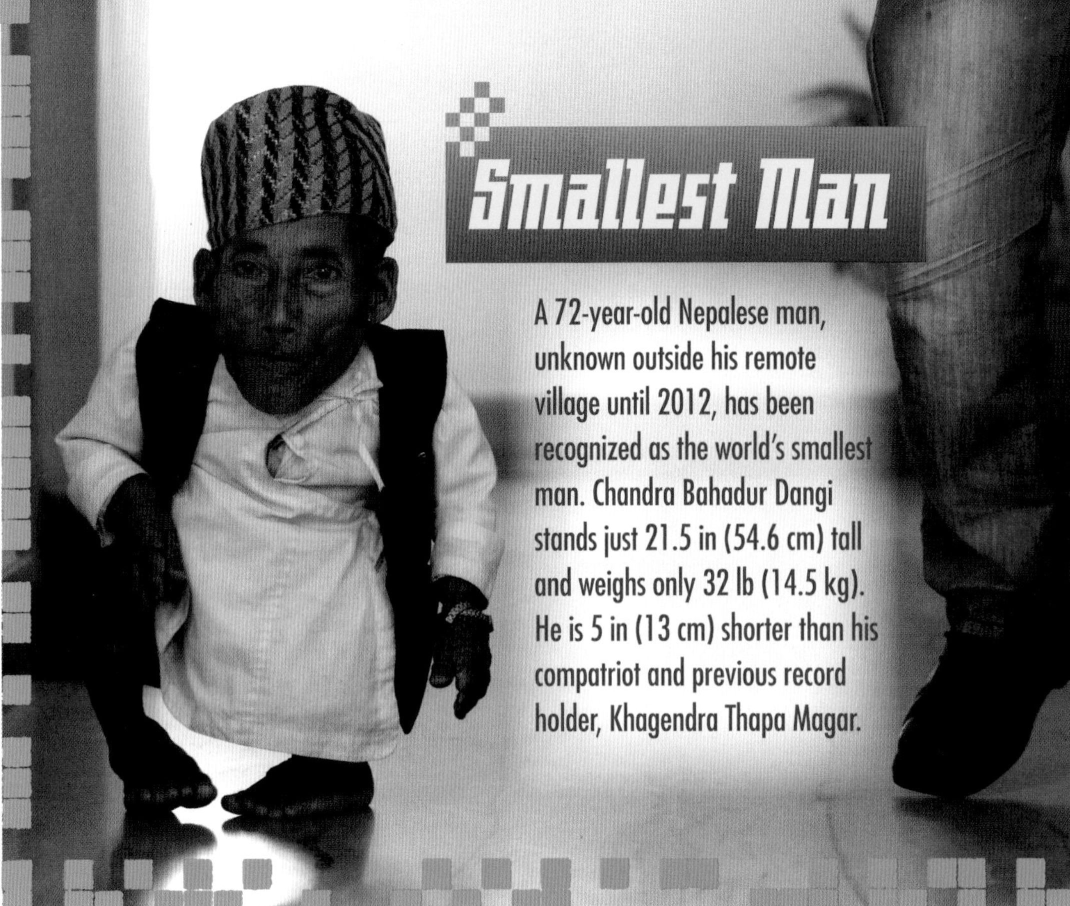

Smallest Man

A 72-year-old Nepalese man, unknown outside his remote village until 2012, has been recognized as the world's smallest man. Chandra Bahadur Dangi stands just 21.5 in (54.6 cm) tall and weighs only 32 lb (14.5 kg). He is 5 in (13 cm) shorter than his compatriot and previous record holder, Khagendra Thapa Magar.

SHELF LIFE Charles Jones Jr. lived unnoticed in the basement of the Ocean Township Library, New Jersey, for nearly two weeks in 2010.

GUMMY HEART Los Angeles candy man David Klein invented an unusual new line for Valentine's Day 2011—a 2-lb-8-oz (1.1-kg), throbbing, anatomically correct gummy heart that oozed candy blood in 11 places. He also marketed an edible bleeding nose and a gummy severed foot with a gangrenous toe.

EXPENSIVE CRASH

The Chugoku Expressway in Shimonoseki, Japan, was the scene of one of the most expensive and exclusive car wrecks in recent years. A total of 14 sports cars, including eight Ferraris, a Lamborghini and a Mercedes worth something in the region of $1.3 million, were caught out on a drive to a supercar meeting in Hiroshima. It is thought the Ferrari owners may have been driving too close to one another when one driver lost control, leaving them little time to react before smashing into each other and careening into the road barrier.

100-MPH COUCH A two-seater brown leather couch, fitted with a motorcycle engine, clocked a top speed of 101 mph (163 km/h) at Camden Airport near Sydney, Australia, in September 2011, making it the world's fastest sofa. Designed by Paul McKinnon and driven by Glenn Suter, the superfast sofa came complete with a coffee table to help the contraption's aerodynamics.

COFFIN BED Every Friday night since 1988, Zeli Rossi of Minas Gerais, Brazil, has traded his bed for a coffin. Rossi and a friend struck a deal many years ago that whoever died first would have his coffin bought by the other. Rossi's friend bought him a coffin when he mistakenly thought Rossi had died in a 1983 car crash, so when the friend died five years later, Rossi started sleeping in the coffin to honor his memory.

BACK FROM THE DEAD A morgue in Malatya Province, Turkey, has been built with a special motion-detecting alarm system—in case "dead" bodies come back to life. If a patient, declared dead by doctors, suddenly wakes up, the movement sets off an alarm in the mortuary's refrigerators, which also have doors that can be opened from the inside.

WASHROOM STOLEN In March 2011, thieves stole a 198-lb (90-kg) gray-and-white portable washroom from ski trails near Bognor, Canada.

PARTING SHOT Alabama company Holy Smoke offers to ensure that deceased gun-lovers go out with a bang by turning their ashes into ammunition that can be fired by relatives.

TAX BILL In 2011, Martine Courtois of Bruyeres, France, received a $16 land inheritance tax bill in the name of her grandfather, Pierre Barotte, who died in 1949.

WIFE DUPED To be rid of his wife, a U.K. immigration officer secretly added her name to a list of suspected terrorists while she was in Pakistan visiting her family, meaning that she was unable to fly back to Britain for three years until his deception was uncovered. The truth came out only when he applied for promotion at work and was asked about his wife being a terrorist. He confessed to the deception and was fired for gross misconduct.

BAD CHOICE Stopped by traffic police in Great Falls, Montana, a man who had three outstanding warrants for his arrest gave officers a false name—but finished up in custody anyway because the name he gave was also that of a wanted man!

LOCKED IN BATHROOM A 69-year-old woman from Paris, France, survived being locked in the bathroom of her second-floor apartment for three weeks after the door lock broke off in her hand. She tried to summon help by banging on the wall with her shoe night and day, but neighbors ignored the noise.

CAR PLUNGE Austrian teenagers Jürgen Oster and Felix Lemann escaped serious injury when their car plunged over the side of a Swiss mountain pass and crashed 900 ft (274 m) to the valley floor with such force that the vehicle folded in half.

MOON SUIT U.S. patent 3,139,622 was issued in 1964 for an astronaut moon suit. It had a large dish on the helmet to reflect solar radiation away from the astronaut.

T PARTY Students at Georgia Tech in Atlanta have been removing the letter "T" from signs all over the campus, a prank that has cost the school over $100,000 in repairs. The tradition of stealing the "T" off Tech Tower began in the 1960s, but has spread to stadium signs and even book bins in front of the library.

DIED TWICE In January 2011, Pinnitla Varalakshmi of Andhra Pradesh, India, was declared dead twice in 24 hours. She awoke as she was being prepared for her funeral, but then died for real shortly afterward.

DOLPHIN TATTOO

Heine Braeck, from Sarpsborg in Norway, lost his right arm in an accident on a railway line when he was a teenager, 20 years ago. Now, he has decided to make an unusual feature of his amputation by enlisting the help of tattoo artist Valio Ska to paint over his shortened upper arm so that it looks like a dolphin. Heine had always thought his arm looked like a dolphin's head, which is why he chose this animal for his tattoo.

Page numbers in *italic* refer to illustrations

Acknowledgments

Page 4 (t/c) Vyacheslav Oseledko/AFP/Getty Images, (t/r) James Holmdahl, (b/l) Bigfoot Hostel, Nicaragua, (b/r) Reuters/Sukree Sukplang; 5 (t/r) Phyllis Keating, (c) Sean E. Avery, (c/l) © Hideto Nagatsuka/Solent News (r) Joshua Carter; 7 (c/r) Getty Images; 11 (t/l) Courtesy of Food For Louis, (b) Andrew Lancaster/Rex Features; 14 Richard Grange / Barcroft India; 16 Kevin Grennan; 17 (l) Drs. Patrick Wenmakers/Rex Features, (r) Imagine China; 18 Justin Quinnell; 20 Reuters/Enny Nuraheni; 21 (t) Danny Lawson/PA Archive/Press Association Images, (b) Franklin Reyes/AP/Press Association Image; 22 (t) Quirky China News/Rex Features, (b) North News; 23 good.kz/Rex Features; 26–27 (b) Rusty Haight, The Collision Safety Institute; 26 (t) Miller & Maclean; 27 (c) Rusty Haight, The Collision Safety Institute; 28 (t) Picture courtesy of Duane and Sally Arnold, (b) Magrath/Folsom/Science Photo Library; 29 Reuters/Desmond Boylan; 32–33 Courtesy of Lockheed Martin; 34 (t) Amos Chapple/Rex Features, (b) Reuters; 35 Vyacheslav Oseledko/AFP/Getty Images; 36 (t) Imagine China, (b) © Chris Hellier/Corbis; 37 Reuters/Romeo Ranoco; 38 (t) Nancy Sathre-Vogel/Family on Bikes, (b) Imagine China; 39 (t, t/l, t/r, b/l, c, b/r) Nancy Sathre-Vogel/Family on Bikes, (sp) © Anton Balazh/Fotolia.com; 40 (t) © Europics, (b) www.sell-my-photo.co.uk; 41 Fernando Bustamante/AP/Press Association Images; 44 Nigel Hewitt-Cooper; 45 (t) ChinaFotoPress/Photocome/Press Association Images, (b) Quirky China News/Rex Features; 46–47 Dominik Schwarz; 46 Karin Strandås; 47 (t/l) © Bettmann/Corbis, (t/c) Karin Strandås, (t/r) © Julie Dermansky/Corbis, (b/l) Jean-Claude Francolon/Gamma-Rapho via Getty Images, (b/r) Rex Features; 48 (t) Peter Bardsley/Fotolibra, (b) © Chris Hellier/Corbis; 49 Mister Jo; 52 Katrina Bridgeford/Rex Features; 53 (t) Barcroft Media Ltd, (l) Bay Ismoyo/AFP/Getty Images, (r) John Little/Bizarre Archive.com, (c) Andi Fitriono/Demotix; 54–55 Reuters; 54 Quirky China News/Rex Features; 55 (r) Newspix/Rex Features, (c) ABC TV, (l) Panda Photo/FLPA; 56 Time & Life Pictures/Getty Images; 57 Sunshine Serpents/Rex Features; 58 (t) KeystoneUSA-Zuma/Rex Features, (b) www.sell-my-photo.co.uk; 59 Andrew Forsyth/Solent News/Rex Features; 60 Swns.com; 61 (t) Ian Butler/Solent News/Rex Features, (b) Pisces Sportfishing Fleet/Rex Features; 62 (t) © Photoshot, (b) AP/Press Association Images; 63 wenn.com; 64 (t) Jennifer Showalter, (b) Alex Coppel/Newspix/Rex Features; 65 Steven Senne/AP/Press Association Images; 66 (t) © UPPA/Photoshot, (b) Reuters; 67 James Holmdahl; 68 Ren Netherland/Barcroft Media; 69 Caters News; 70 (l) Charlie Hamilton James/naturepl.com, (b) Scottish SPCA; 71 Laurentiu Garofeanu/Barcroft USA; 72 Mohamed Babu/Solent News/Rex Features; 73 Tim Green; 74 (t) UPPA/Photoshot, (b) © DavidSpears/ HotSpot Media; 75 (t) © Thomas Marent/ardea.com, (b) Diane Kolpin; 78–79 Nippon News; 80 (t, c) James Ambler/Barcroft USA, (b/l) Wool Warriors / Barcroft USA, (b/r) Mary Schwalm/AP/Press Association Images; 81 (t) James Ambler/Barcroft USA, (b) The Canadian Press/Press Association Images; 82 (t) Sipa Press/Rex Features, (b) Reuters/Rafael Marchante; 83 (t) Jed Jacobsohn/Getty Images, (b) Reuters/Toby Melville; 85 (t/l, t/r) Bigfoot Hostel, Nicaragua, (b) Reuters/Jonne Roriz-Agencia Estado; 86 (t, c) Sky News, (b) Nazare Qualifica, E.E.M.; 87 Brian Bielmann/Solent; 88 (t/l, t/r, b/l) Stephen Morton/Getty Images, (b/r) Richard Ellis/Getty Images; 89 AFP/Getty Images; 90–91 (dp) wenn.com; 91 Caters News; 94–95 Courtesy of Food For Louis; 96 (l, r) Quirky China News/Rex Features, (b) Ricky Nakamura; 97 Circus World Museum, Baraboo, Wisconsin; 98 Alexandra Daisy Ginsberg & James King, with the University of Cambridge IGEM team 2009; 99 (b) Yang Zhichao; 100 (t/l, t/r) © HotSpot Media, (b) Steve Meddle/Rex Features; 101 Adrianne Lewis; 104 (t/l, c) Ashley/Bizarrearchive.com, (b/r) Blair/BizarreArchive.com; 105 Courtesy of Kimberleigh Smithbower Roseblade; 106–107 Mayuko Kanazawa; 106 (b) REUTERS/David Mdzinarishvili; 107 Tolu Solanke & Kathy Hayes; 108–109 © pomah/Fotolia.com; 108 (b/l) © Anyka/Fotolia.com, (t, c, b) Quirky China News/Rex Features; 109 (t) Quirky China News/Rex Features, (t/l, b/r) © Anyka/Fotolia.com; 110 (t) Circus World Museum, Baraboo, Wisconsin, (b) William England/Getty Images; 111 (t, c) Circus World Museum, Baraboo, Wisconsin; 112 (t) Rachel Betty Case, (b/l) wenn.com, (b/r) University of Arizona Medical Center, Tucson; 113 Bronek Kaminski/Barcroft India; 114 © Paramount/Everett/Rex Features; 116 NYPL/Science Source/Science Photo Library; 117 (l) © TopFoto, (r) c.Paramount/Everett/Rex Features; 118 (t/l) Sue Ford/Science Photo Library, (b/l) Dr P. Marazzi/Science Photo Library, (r) CDC/Science Photo Library; 119 (t/l) Darlyne A. Murawski /Getty Images, (r) Clouds Hill Imaging Ltd/Science Photo Library, (c/l) Vaughan Fleming/Science Photo Library, (c/r) Vaughan Fleming/Science Photo Library, (t/l) Time & Life Pictures/Getty Images, (b/c) © Dwight Davis-Fotolia.com, (b/r) © Heinz Waldukat-Fotolia.com; 120 (t) Steve Meddle/Rex Features, (b) Adrienne Antonson; 121 (t) © Bettmann/Corbis; 122 (r) Dragstrip/Solent News/Rex Feature, (t/l) Solent News/Rex Features; 123 (b/l) Solent News/Rex Features; 126 (t) Albert Tan, (b/l, b/r) www.julienberthier.org courtesy galerie GP&N Vallois, Paris; 127 (l, c, r) http://www.stanley.sg, (b) © Photoshot/TIPS; 128 (t) © Europics, (b) Swns.com, (r) Anthony Delmundo/Polaris/eyevine; 129 (t) Quirky China News/Rex Features, (c) UPPA/Photoshot, (b) KPA/Zuma/Rex Features; 130 (t) Zilvinas Abaravicius, (b) © Europics; 131 Reuters/Sukree Sukplang; 132 (t) PA Archive/Press Association Images, (c, b) Library of Congress; 133 Getty Images; 134–135 (dp) © Ralph White/Corbis; 134 (t) Getty Images, (b) Les Wilson/Rex Features; 135 © Ralph White/Corbis; 136 (t) Swns.com, (b) Charly Molinelli/Rex Features; 137 (l) Courtesy of Joe Pires, (r) FPG/Hulton Archive/Getty Images; 140 (b) © Europics, (l, r) Quirky China News/Rex Features; 141 (c/l, t/l) Courtesy of Katalin Williams, (b/l, b/r) © Europics; 142 (t/l, t/r) Dinesh Upadhyaya, (b) © Jörg Mitter/Red Bull Content Pool; 144 (t/l, t/c, t/r) Courtesy Erik Sprague; 146 Sipa Press/Rex Features; 147 Willard Wigan Ltd; 150–151 (b) Bruce Airhead; 150 (t/l, t/r) Quirky China News/Rex Features; 151 (t, l) Barbara Lindberg/Rex Features; 152 (l) Quirky China News/Rex Features, (r) Tim Stewart News/Rex Features; 153 Imagine China; 154–159 Bradford Bohonus; 160 (l) © Photoshot, (r) Darryl Learie; 161 Quirky China News/Rex Features; 162 (t/l, t/c, t/r) © Europics, (b) Jimmy Chin/National Geographic Stock; 166 (t) AP Photo/Chris Pizzello, (b) Park Ji-Hwan/AFP/Getty Images; 166–167 Caters News; 167 (c) © Picture Alliance/Photoshot; 168 (l) Phyllis Keating, (r) © 2012 Sega Corporation; 169 (t) Rex Features, (t/l) Vincent T. Migliore, (c/l) Newspix/Rex Features, (b/l) Reuters/Nicky Loh, (b) Tima Sergeev; 170 (t) Jill Johnson, (b) Reuters/Danny Moloshok; 171 (b) SP/Rex Features; 172 Strapya/Rex Features; 173 (c) Jeffrey Bautista, (t) Brent Douglas, (b) Deney Tuazon; 174–175 (t) Reuters/Kim Kyung-Hoon, Angry Birds™© 2009–2012 Rovio Entertainment Ltd. All Rights Reserved; 175 (c/l, b/l) Courtesy of Rovio, (c/r) Mike Cooper/Electricpig.co.uk; 176 (t) Courtesy of Alassan Issa Gobitaca, (b) Courtesy of Calgary Zoo; 177 (t) Mark & Ellen Zessin/www.JennyThePug.com, (b) David Devore; 180 (l) Startraks Photo/Rex Features, (sp) © Hemeroskopion/Fotolia.com; 181 (t/l, t/r) wenn.com, (b) Rex Features; 182 (t) Sian Williams, (b) Betfair/Solent News; 183 (t) © 2009 Disney/Pixar, (sp) wenn.com; 184 (t/l) Startraks Photo/Rex Features, (t/r) © Thomas Launois/Fotolia.com, (b) Brian Rasic/Rex Features; 185 (t) Nicky J. Sims/Redferns, (c) John Storey/Time Life Pictures/Getty Images, (b) Alex Sudea/Rex Features; 186 (t/l, t/r) Tim Stewart News/Rex Features, (b) © Hideto Nagatsuka/Solent News; 187 (t/l, t/r) Tim Stewart News/Rex Features, (l) Reuters/Cheryl Ravelo, (r) Rex Features; 188 (sp) Photographer: Nathan Gallagher; 189 (t) Rob Huibers/Hollandse Hoogte/eyevine, (b/l) Maya Pixelskaya/Rex Features, (b/r) Everett Collection/Rex Features; 190–191 Courtesy of the Inflatable Crowd Company; 192 (t) Rob Matthews, (b) Dario Lopez-Mills/AP/Press Association Images; 193 (t, c) Reuters/Jon Nazca, (b/l, b/r) Photographer: M2k Photo model: pink dress: Tiffany Tezna, (b/r) Sipa Press/Rex Features; 194 (t) Scott Irvine, (b) Burns!; 195 Courtesy of Voodou, Liverpool; 198–199 Natalie Irish; 198 (b) © air/fotolia.com; 199 (t) © air/fotolia.com; 200 Andrew Lancaster/Rex Features; 201 (t) Gabriel Bouys/AFP/Getty Images, (b) Courtesy of Olek; 202–203 Janne Parviainen, www.jannepaint.com; 204 Sipa Press/Rex Features; 208 (t) Taras Lesko www.visualspicer.com, (b/l, b/c, b/r) Lee Hadwin; 209 (t, c, b) DC Image Photography; 2010 Courtesy of Priska C. Juschka Fine Art, New York; 211 (t) Kerry Howley/Rex Features, (c, b) Sean E. Avery; 214 (t) Craig Sullivan, (b) John Luther Garcia; 215 Dimitri Tsykalov/Landov/Press Association Images; 216 (t) Chris Antes, (b) PizzaExpress/Rex Features; 217 Quirky China News/Rex Features; 218 (t) Reuters/Paul Yeung, (c, b) Courtesy of The Fairmont Hotel; 219 Reuters/Kham; 220 (t) wenn.com, (b) Sinopix/Rex Features; 221 (t) Quirky China News/Rex Features, (b) Matthew Holzmann; 222 (t) Caters News, (b) Swns.com; 223 Reuters/Jerry Lampen; 224 © Picture Alliance/Photoshot; 225 (l, t/r, c/r) Gareth Fuller/PA Wire, (c) W.C.P.C. Championship, (b/r) Chris Radburn/PA Wire; 226 (t) Keisuke Yamada/Rex Features, (b) Feature China/Barcroft Media; 227 (t) Anthonioo, (b, r) Benjamin Brown, Fruit bat soup recipe: The New York Times Natural Foods Cookbook (Jean Hewitt, 1971); 230–231 Circus World Museum, Baraboo, Wisconsin; 232 (t) New Zealand Herald; 233 Courtesy of Ugly Models; 234 (l, c) Sipa Press/Rex Features, (r) Joshua Carter; 235 (t) © HotSpot Media, (b/l, b/c, b/r) Geoffrey Robinson/Rex Features; 236 AAP Image/Press Association Images; 237 John Stone/Bizarrearchive.com; 238 Ze Frank/Rex Features; 239 (t/l) Columbine Phoenix, (t/r) © Dario Sabljak/Fotolia.com, (b) wenn.com; 240 Phillips de Pury & Company; 241 (l) James R. Ford (r) © Polaris/eyevine; 242 Nippon News; 243 (t) Crown Copyright: Department of Conservation Te Papa Atawhai (11 December 2011), Photographer: Christopher Clark, (b) USA National Parks Service; 244 (t) Toshiro Kubo/AP/Press Association Images (b) Reuters/Navesh Chitrakar; 245 Swns.com

Key: t = top, b = bottom, c = center, l = left, r = right, sp = single page, dp = double page
All other photos are from Ripley Entertainment Inc. Every attempt has been made to acknowledge correctly and contact copyright holders and we apologize in advance for any unintentional errors or omissions, which will be corrected in future editions.

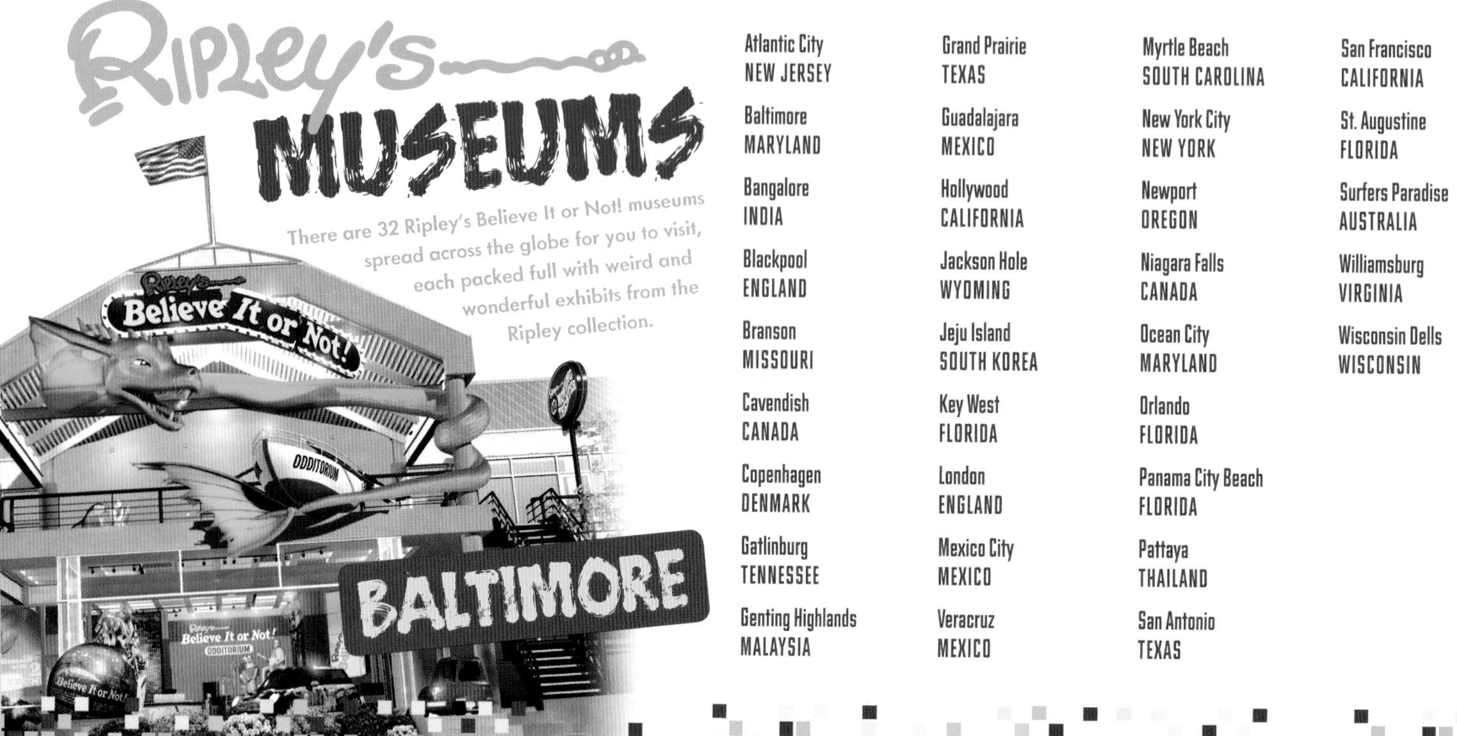

INTRODUCING...

UNBELIEVABLE STORIES FOR GUYS

This quirky new Ripley's book is filled with bizarre, very funny "Believe It or Not!" stories, trivia and lists. It's perfect for any fan of the unusual, and the ideal Father's Day gift.

unbelievable

Ripley's Believe It or Not!®

stories

for guys

ebook available

SHOUT OUTS!

A new themed collection of hilarious Ripley facts and stories

OTHER TITLES IN THIS SERIES

✸ Brrm! ✸ Yikes! ✸ Zoom! ✸ Yum! ✸ Woof! ✸ Burp! ✸ Game!

All featuring original cartoons drawn by Ripley's own cartoonist, John Graziano.

Twists

All you ever wanted to know about these exciting subjects mixed with jaw-dropping stories and pictures from the world of Ripley's Believe It or Not! Fascinating facts and fun—don't miss them!

A stunning children's reference series with a unique Ripley twist!

ebooks available

OTHER TITLES IN THIS SERIES

- Dinosaurs
- Oceans
- Wild Animals
- Space
- Human Body
- Sports
- Mighty Machines

OTHER TITLES IN THIS SERIES

- A Scaly Tale
- Running Wild
- Sub-zero Survival
- The Lost Island
- The Dragon's Triangle
- Wings of Fear
- Shock Horror

ebooks available

Join the RBI, a group of young agents with special gifts, on a series of adventures as they travel the world investigating unbelievable tales in a bid to discern fact from fiction.

ANNUALS

With ALL-NEW stories and pictures in every edition of this bestselling series, our books entertain, shock and amaze!

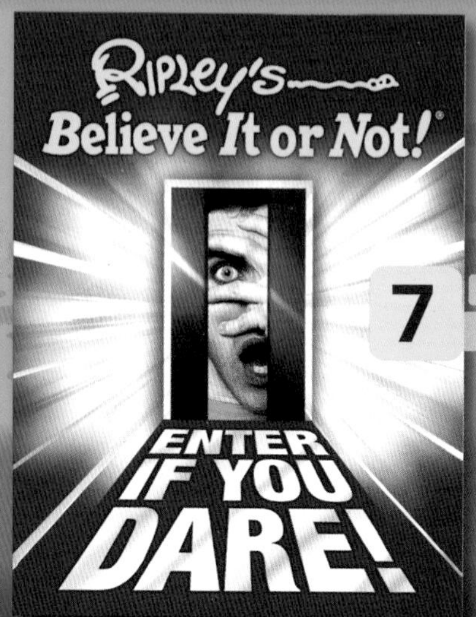

Amazing extraordinary images

To see all of our books go to www.ripleybooks.com